CW01072789

© Brill Academic Publishers International ... 2006

All rights reserved

ISBN 978-90-04-17909-7

Full text of the journal published in ...

Cover illustration: ...

© HAGUE ACADEMY OF INTERNATIONAL LAW, 2009

All rights reserved

ISBN 978-90-04-17909-7

Full text of the lecture published in August 2009 in the *Recueil des cours*, Vol. 336 (2008).

Cover illustration: Marian Maguire, *Milford Sound*, 2002. Paper-graphica Gallery (Christchurch, New Zealand).

# HAGUE ACADEMY OF INTERNATIONAL LAW

*A collection of law lectures
in pocketbook form*

AIL-POCKET

2009
MARTINUS NIJHOFF PUBLISHERS
Leiden/Boston

*Lis Pendens*
in International Litigation

# *Lis Pendens*
# in International Litigation

CAMPBELL McLACHLAN

# TABLE OF CONTENTS

# CHAPTER I *

# INTRODUCTION

## A. Of the Conflict of Litigation

When the Curatorium of the Hague Academy issued the invitation to deliver these lectures in 2003, five recent cases, all rendered in very different contexts, had served to reignite a long-smouldering controversy over the proper approach of the courts to international parallel proceedings arising out of the same dispute. In *Gasser* v. *MISAT*[1], the European Court had decided that the court first seised had priority over the court designated in a choice of forum clause. In *Fomento* v.

---

* The author would like to thank his friends Lawrence Collins (now Lord Collins of Mapesbury), Sir Kenneth and Lady Jocelyn Keith, James Crawford, Patrick Kinsch, Peter Schlosser, Peter Trooboff, Horatia Muir Watt, Gary Born, Linda Silberman, David Williams, Audley Sheppard, Nicole Roughan, Pippa Rogerson, Richard Fentiman, Alex Layton, Stephen Burbank, Catherine Kessedjian, Laurence Boisson de Chazournes, Andreas Bucher, Vaughan Lowe, Klaus Reichert, Paul Myburgh and John Fellas for their encouragement, assistance and helpful comments as he prepared these lectures. He owes a considerable intellectual debt to the late Peter Nygh and to his fellow members of the International Law Association Committee on International Civil & Commercial Litigation. The writer is also indebted to Yves Daudet and to Mara Croese of the Academy; to Herbert Smith, the Law Faculty of the University of Cambridge and the Lauterpacht Research Centre for International Law for supporting the early research work on these lectures; to Marian Maguire of Papergraphica for graciously giving permission for the publication of her lithograph *Milford Sound*; to Diane Hadley (Victoria) and Mary-Rose Russell (Auckland), librarians; and to Jack Wass for his tireless and expert research assistance. Any errors are the sole responsibility of the author.

[1] *Erich Gasser GmbH* v. *MISAT Srl*, Case C-116/02, [2003] *ECR* I-14693.

*Colon*[2], the Swiss Federal Tribunal had decided that a
Swiss arbitral tribunal should cede priority to a Panamanian court to determine whether an arbitration
agreement covering the dispute had been waived. In
*CME* v. *Czech Republic*[3] the Svea Court of Appeals
had decided that the doctrine of *lis pendens* did not
apply to preclude the pursuit of two investment treaty
arbitrations by an investment company and its shareholder. In *MOX Plant*[4], the International Tribunal for
the Law of the Sea had decided that there was no
impediment to the simultaneous pursuit of related
claims between the same States in different international fora. Finally, in *Thomas* v. *Baptiste*[5], the Privy
Council had decided that the execution of a prisoner in
Trinidad must await a pending appeal to the Inter-
American Court of Human Rights.

The central question which these lectures set out to
address is what rules or principles properly govern the
cases where exercises of adjudicatory authority in different jurisdictions over aspects of the same, or closely
related, disputes run into conflict with each other. This
controversy has long remained unresolved. As long ago
as 1925, the Permanent Court of International Justice
had commented :

> "It is a much disputed question in the teachings
> of legal authorities and in the jurisprudence of the
> principal countries whether the doctrine of *litispen-*

---

[2] *Fomento de Construcciones y Contratas SA* v. *Colon Container Terminal SA*, BGE 127 III 279 (2001, Swiss Fed. S. Ct.)
(English trans. (2001) 19 *ASA Bull.* 555).

[3] *CME Czech Republic BV (The Netherlands)* v. *Czech
Republic* (2003) 42 *ILM* 919 (Svea Court of Appeals).

[4] *MOX Plant Case (Ireland* v. *United Kingdom)*
(ITLOS Provisional Measures Order, 3 December 2001),
(2002) 126 *ILR* 334.

[5] *Thomas* v. *Baptiste*, [2000] 2 AC 1 (PC (Trinidad and
Tobago)).

*dance*, the object of which is to prevent the possibility of conflicting judgments, can be invoked in international relations . . ."[6]

It might reasonably have been thought that, in the intervening 80 years, this controversy would have been quelled. But in fact few problems of international litigation seem more capable of generating ongoing legal dispute than the incidence of parallel proceedings and the appropriate solutions to it.

Indeed, in contemporary affairs, many of the great *causes célèbres* have spawned litigation in multiple fora. The techniques applied by the courts to control excessive duplication of litigation have often proved as controversial as the conduct itself. Thus, for example, the deployment of anti-suit injunctions to restrain the pursuit of foreign litigation has sparked serious international tension, even as between Common Law countries which each recognize the remedy. Their use within Europe was described by courts in Civil Law countries as an infringement of the sovereignty of other nations[7]. But, when the European Court moved in *Turner* v. *Grovit*[8] to outlaw the practice, the Court was accused by Common lawyers of living in a "utopia"[9] in which the beneficial power of courts to prevent abusive

---

[6] Case concerning *Certain German Interests in Polish Upper Silesia*, (1925) *PCIJ Rep., Ser. A, No. 6*, 20. For an indication of the nature of the debate at that time see Donnedieu de Vabres "L'action publique et l'action civile dans les rapports de droit pénal international", (1929) 26 *Recueil des cours* 207, 261-276 and the early discussion in the Sixth Commission at the Venice Session of the Institut de droit international in 1896 *Annuaire Abrégé* (1928) 874-878, which was followed by a two paragraph resolution: *ibid.*, 494.

[7] *Re the Enforcement of an English Anti-suit Injunction*, [1997] I L. Pr. 320 (Oberlandesgericht Düsseldorf).

[8] Case C-159/02, [2004] *ECR* I-3565.

[9] Briggs, "Anti-suit Injunctions and Utopian Ideals", (2004) 120 *LQR* 529.

and oppressive foreign proceedings had been unjustly removed[10].

The controversy as to the appropriate way to deal with international parallel proceedings is not, however, simply a matter of different perspectives across the Common Law/Civil Law divide as to the appropriate response[11]. As will be seen, this distinction does not withstand historical analysis. It was in any event the court of a Civilian country[12] which first sought to test the application of the *lis pendens* rule in the Brussels Convention, where the parties had made an exclusive choice of forum[13]. As these lectures were being delivered, the question whether an anti-suit injunction could be used to restrain parallel proceedings in breach of an arbitration agreement was pending before the European Court. The Court's subsequent decision[14] provoked widespread dissent across Europe, and its effect may be reversed by subsequent regulation. So, too, the decision of the Swiss Federal Supreme Court in *Fomento* has subsequently been reversed by legislation[15].

Nor is the controversy as to parallel proceedings confined to private law disputes. Following the Privy Council's decision in *Thomas* v. *Baptiste*[16], a dissent-

---

[10] Collins, "Preface" to Collins *et al.* (eds.), *Dicey, Morris & Collins on the Conflict of Laws* (14th ed., 2006) *("Dicey")* xv.

[11] *Pace* the comments of Lord Goff of Chieveley in *Airbus Industrie GIE* v. *Patel*, [1999] 1 AC 119, 133 (HL).

[12] The Landesgericht Feldkirch, Austria.

[13] *Supra* footnote 1.

[14] *West Tankers Inc.* v. *Ras Riunione Adriatica di Sicurta SpA (The Front Comor)*, Case C-185/07 : Judgment of the House of Lords making the reference, [2007] UKHL 4, [2007] 1 Lloyd's Rep. 391, noted Bollée, [2007] *Revue de l'arbitrage* 223, Fentiman, [2007] *CLJ* 493 ; Opinion of Kokott AG, 4 September 2008 ; Judgment of ECJ *sub nom. Allianz SpA* v. *West Tankers Inc.*, 10 February 2009.

[15] Swiss Private International Law, Alinéa 1 *bis* Art. 186 (Bucher, [2007] II No. 5, *La semaine judiciaire* 153).

[16] *Supra* footnote 5.

ing law lord in a subsequent appeal accused the majority of applying "a philosopher's stone undetected by generations of judges"[17]. The United States Supreme Court has refused to give effect to orders and judgments of the International Court of Justice as to the right to consular assistance affecting prisoners on Death Row in the United States in a series of parallel cases[18], which have been described as "unprecedented"[19]. When the European Court finally held in the *MOX Plant* saga that Ireland was in breach of its obligations under European law in bringing an arbitration claim against the United Kingdom for pollution caused by the operation of a nuclear reprocessing plant, Professor Koskenniemi commented that the decision:

> "shows the ECJ imagining the European Union as a sovereign whose laws override any other legal structure. To appeal to international law against the United Kingdom, Ireland was violating the sovereignty of European law, like Soviet dissidents once upon a time, appealing to the 1966 UN Covenant on Civil and Political Rights, broke against the hermetic absolutism of the Soviet order."[20]

So, far from resolved, the problems posed by parallel litigation seem if anything to be gaining in

---

[17] *Lewis* v. *Attorney-General of Jamaica*, [2001] 2 AC 50, 88 (PC (Jamaica)), per Lord Hoffmann (dissenting).

[18] *Breard* v. *Greene*, 523 US 371, 118 S. Ct. 1352 (1998); *Medellin* v. *Dretke*, 544 US 660, 125 S. Ct. 2088 (2005) *(Medellin I)*; *Sanchez-Llamas* v. *Oregon*, 548 US 331, 126 S. Ct. 2669 (2006); *Medellin* v. *Texas*, 128 S. Ct. 1346 (2008) *(Medellin II)*.

[19] *Sanchez-Llamas, ibid.*, 386 per Breyer J.

[20] Koskenniemi, "International Law: Between Fragmentation and Constitutionalism" (unpublished lecture, Canberra, 27 November 2006) available at www.helsinki. fi/eci/Publications/Talks_Papers_MK.htm, para. 3.

frequency, urgency and complexity — matched only by the level of dissent over the appropriate solution. In part, this may be a simple function of the rise in the incidence of international litigation[21]. "The business of litigation", commented the Supreme Court of Canada, "like commerce itself, has become increasingly international."[22] The resulting exposure of opportunities for forum shopping has in turn driven increased attention to the legal means of controlling it[23].

But the current landscape of international litigation is not simply populated by national courts. The proliferation of international courts and tribunals — for inter-State disputes but also for mixed disputes involving States and private parties — has opened many more complex opportunities for forum shopping. As one recent commentator put it:

> "Forum shoppers of the future will be less concerned with the remedial possibilities in proceedings before the domestic courts of different states, but will instead seek advantage from the absence of hierarchy and coordination among the various types of international tribunals and from the often strained relationships between such tribunals and municipal courts."[24]

In its application to the concurrent jurisdiction of international courts and tribunals, therefore, the present topic has gained renewed urgency as an aspect of the concerns about the fragmentation of Public

---

[21] McLachlan, "International Litigation and the Reworking of the Conflict of Laws", (2004) 120 *LQR* 580.

[22] *Amchem Products Inc.* v. *British Columbia (Worker's Compensation Board)*, [1993] 1 SCR 897, (1993) 102 DLR (4th) 96, [25] per Sopinka J.

[23] Bell, *Forum Shopping and Venue in Transnational Litigation* (2003).

[24] Douglas, "The Hybrid Foundations of Investment Treaty Arbitration", (2003) 74 *BYIL* 151, 236.

International Law into "erratic parts and elements
which are differently structured so that one can hardly
speak of a homogeneous nature of international law"[25].
Yet, despite the rising visibility of this novel dimension
of the problem[26], it has to date (as will be seen in
Chapter IV) proved stubbornly resistant to solution.
The International Law Commission, which studied
solutions to the fragmentation of substantive law[27],
eschewed a consideration of institutional fragmentation, treating conflicts of jurisdiction between international courts as a matter for the courts themselves[28].

Is this field, then, an example of what Tennyson
once described as:

" . . . the lawless science of our law,
That codeless myriad of precedent,
That wilderness of single instances ?"[29]

It is surely the task of the scholar to seek order in
apparent confusion, and thus to provide a framework
for analysis of problems of great practical as well as
theoretical importance.

Problems of parallel proceedings have received

---

[25] ILC, "Risks Ensuing from Fragmentation of Inter-
national Law", (Hafner) *Official Records of the General
Assembly, Fifty-fifth Session, Supp. No. 10*, Annex, UN doc.
A/55/10, 144.

[26] "The Proliferation of International Tribunals:
Piecing together the Puzzle", Special Symposium Issue
(1999) 31 (4) *NYUJILP* 679.

[27] International Law Commission, "Fragmentation of
International Law: Difficulties Arising from the Diversifi-
cation and Expansion of International Law, Report of the
Study Group of the International Law Commission", (Kosken-
niemi, C) UN doc. A/CN.4/L.682, 13 April 2006 (Report);
UN doc. A/CN.4/L.702, 18 July 2006 (Conclusions).

[28] *Ibid.* (Report), [13].

[29] Alfred Lord Tennyson, "Aylmer's Field" (first published 1864), in *The Collected Poems of Alfred Lord
Tennyson* (Wordsworth, 1994) 581.

increasing attention in scholarly colloquia[30]. There have
also been a series of international law reform proposals,
which will be discussed in Chapter V. The International
Civil and Commercial Litigation Committee of the
International Law Association completed in 2000 its
Leuven/London Principles on Declining and Referring
Jurisdiction in International Civil and Commercial Litigation[31]. The Institut de droit international concluded a
resolution on the matter in 2003[32]. The American
Law Institute has evaluated the role of *lis pendens* in no
less than three of its recent projects: the Foreign Judg-
ments Act[33]; the UNIDROIT/ALI Principles of
Transnational Civil Procedure[34]; and the Intellectual
Property Principles[35]. In 2006, the International Commercial Arbitration Committee of the International

---

[30] See notably Fawcett (ed.), *Declining Jurisdiction in
Private International Law: Reports to the XIVth Congress of
the International Academy of Comparative Law, Athens,
August 1994* (1995); Karrer (ed.), *Arbitral Tribunals or State
Courts: Who Must Defer to Whom? ASA Swiss Arbitration
Association, IBA International Bar Association Conference in
Zurich of January 28, 2000* (ASA Special Series No. 15,
2001); Cremades and Lew (eds.), *Parallel State and Arbitral
Procedures in International Arbitration* (2005).

[31] Resolution No. 1/2000 (2000) 69 *ILA Rep. Conf.* 13-
18; Committee Report (McLachlan, Rapporteur), 137-166.

[32] (2003) 70-II *Annuaire* 252; Report of the Second
Commission, "Principles for Determining When the Use of
the Doctrine of *Forum non Conveniens* and Anti-suit
Injunctions Is Appropriate" (Collins and Droz, Rapporteurs) (2002-2003), 70-I *Annuaire* 14.

[33] ALI, *Recognition and Enforcement of Foreign Judgments: Proposed Federal Statute*, s. 11 (adopted 2005,
Lowenfeld and Silberman, Reporters).

[34] Available at www.unidroit.org/english/principles/
civilprocedure/ali-unidroitprinciples-e.pdf.

[35] ALI, "Intellectual Property: Principles Governing
Jurisdiction, Choice of Law, and Judgments in Transna-
tional Disputes" (Dreyfuss, Ginsburg and Dessemontet,
Reporters) (2007).

Law Association presented its report on *"Lis Pendens and Arbitration"* [36].

In all of these projects, *lis pendens* has continued to receive separate treatment, despite the fact that, at least in Common Law countries, "the existence of simultaneous proceedings is no more than a factor relevant to the determination of the appropriate forum" [37]. Thus, for example, in the American Law Institute's Proposed Federal Statute on Recognition and Enforcement of Foreign Judgments, it receives it own separate rule, although the Statute does not otherwise contain rules relating to the exercise of original jurisdiction by United States courts. One noted commentator asks "why is the ALI proposing provisions concerning *lis pendens* stays in legislation on recognizing foreign judgment[s]?" [38]

What, then, is the objective of rules for the control of international parallel proceedings? Four reasons have commonly been identified: *(a)* as a pre-emptive corollary of the *res judicata* effect of foreign judgments; *(b)* to promote judicial efficiency; *(c)* as a means of declining or fine-tuning otherwise excessive exercises of original jurisdiction; and *(d)* to promote comity between courts. It is a central theme of these lectures to submit that, useful though these rationales may be, they have tended to obscure the independent function of litispendence rules. It is necessary for this purpose to add a fifth reason, namely *(e)* to promote the Rule of Law by providing due process for the fair trial of the dispute. The concepts of comity and of the application of the Rule of Law in the adjudication of international disputes will be explored later in this chapter. For present purposes, however, it is necessary

---

[36] Committee Report (Sheppard, Rapporteur) (2006) 72 *ILA Rep. Conf.* 146.

[37] *Dicey, supra* footnote 10, [12-036].

[38] Born and Rutledge, *International Civil Litigation in United States Courts* (4th ed., 2007) 539.

to say a little more about each of the three most commonly advanced rationales, and, in the process, to
demonstrate why they do not sufficiently explain what
is really at issue in parallel proceedings cases.

*Corollary of* res judicata. There is, as will be seen,
a close link between the concept of *res judicata* and
that of *lis pendens*. If a court is to render a judgment
which will determine the issue as between the parties
so as to preclude further litigation, the doctrine of *lis
pendens* anticipates the result which will ultimately
obtain from application of the rule of *res judicata*. If
the judgment of a foreign court is capable of recognition and enforcement in this way, then, so it may be
said, similar pre-emptive effect should be given to the
pending foreign court proceedings which may result in
such a judgment. This is precisely the connection
which the Permanent Court was making in the citation
at the beginning of this chapter. It is a point which the
European Court has repeatedly emphasized in its judgments on the *lis pendens* rule in the Brussels I
Regulation, in stating that it is designed:

> "to preclude, in so far as is possible and from the
> outset, the possibility of a situation arising such as
> that referred to in Article 27 (3), that is to say the
> non-recognition of a judgment on account of its
> irreconcilability with a judgment given in a dispute
> between the same parties in the state in which
> recognition is sought" [39].

Indeed, many States see *lis pendens* as a problem
related to the recognition and enforcement of foreign

---

[39] *Gubisch Maschinenfabrik KG* v. *Giulio Palumbo*
Case 144/86, [1987] ECR 4861, [8], discussing Article 27,
Council Regulation (EC) No. 44/2001 of 22 December 2001 on Jurisdiction and the Recognition and Enforcement of Judgments in Civil and Commercial Matters
(16 January 2001), OJ L 12, 1 ("the Brussels I Regulation").

judgments[40]. This is expressly reflected in the structure of *lis pendens* rules in domestic legislation requiring the court to stay its proceedings only if there is a reasonable recognition prognosis — that the proceedings in the foreign court are likely to result in a judgment which will be enforceable locally[41].

*Judicial efficiency*. The doctrine may secondly be seen as a matter of judicial efficiency, preventing the evils of "injustice, delay [and] increased expense" (in the words of the Preamble to the Institut Resolution)[42], and promoting the essentially public purposes of "the harmonious administration of justice" (the Preamble to the Brussels I Regulation)[43].

*Declining original jurisdiction*. Thirdly, it is possible to see the doctrine of *lis pendens* as a sub-set of the rules relating to *declining* jurisdiction — rules which operate as a limitation on the jurisdiction which the court seised would otherwise enjoy[44]. This posits that both courts have jurisdiction over the cause, but that one declines to exercise that jurisdiction in view of the pending proceedings elsewhere. Thus, Professor Arthur von Mehren, in his General Course at this Academy, classified the doctrine of *lis pendens* as part of the "fine tuning" by courts of their exercise of adjudicatory authority[45].

Each of these rationales has considerable power in explaining what courts are doing when they consider

[40] Fawcett, "General Report" in Fawcett (ed.), *supra* footnote 30, 28.

[41] See the examples cited *infra* at footnotes 135 and 229.

[42] *Supra* footnote 32, Preamble [4].

[43] *Supra* footnote 39.

[44] The suggestive phrase is that adopted by Fawcett, *supra* footnote 30, and also used in Resolution 1/2000 of the ILA Committee on International Civil & Commercial Litigation, *supra* footnote 31.

[45] von Mehren, "Theory and Practice of Adjudicatory Authority in Private International Law: A Comparative

the effect of foreign pending proceedings on those
before them, and why they should give such consideration. If there were no prospect of the ultimate outcome
of a foreign court process having any effect locally,
then the value of giving such process anticipatory
effect through the doctrine of *lis pendens* would be
much more doubtful.

Further, the *consequence* of a decision to stay an
action in favour of foreign process is that the court
declines to exercise a jurisdiction which it otherwise
enjoys. The idea of declining jurisdiction has proved a
potent one, since it presents a neutral, functional way
of analysing the rules adopted in different countries
for the staying of an action in favour of a foreign
court.

These classifications of the topic also offer the com-
fort of the familiar. It is commonplace to divide the
essential concerns of Private International Law into
three: the jurisdiction of courts, choice of law, and the
enforcement of foreign judgments. A conception of *lis
pendens* as connected to both jurisdiction and enforcement apparently serves to reinforce, rather than disturb,
this tripartite division. But nevertheless this rationale
leaves out of account some vital aspects of the problem
of parallel proceedings.

The *res judicata* justification does not offer an
explanation for the many interconnections between
multiple proceedings which fall short of the strict identity of action required to recognize the preclusive effect
of a judgment. It does not deal with cases of related
litigation or *connexité*. Moreover, as will be seen, it is
quite possible to be prepared to give full *res judicata*
effect to foreign judgments once rendered, but still to

Study of the Doctrine, Policies and Practices of Common-
and Civil-Law Systems", (2002) 295 *Recueil des cours* 9,
Chap. VI, esp. 341-370.

proceed with parallel litigation in the meantime. The doctrine of *res judicata,* accepted by the International Court of Justice as a general principle of law common to civilized nations [46], serves both the public purpose of the stability of legal relations and the private right of the successful party to the enjoyment of a judgment already obtained. It achieves this through the notion of *ne bis in idem* by defining the preclusive effect of a judgment, that is what issues may not be the subject of re-litigation. These purposes cannot by definition be served by the doctrine of *lis pendens*, since it is concerned with a situation in which there is no judgment. The link with *res judicata* is therefore, at best, an attempt to avoid conflicting judgments with *res judicata* effects in the future. This is an objective which could equally be realized simply through the application of the doctrine of *res judicata* itself to the judgments of foreign courts and tribunals.

Judicial efficiency carries with it a certain utilitarian appeal. But it cannot explain, without more, why one should be concerned with the conservation of judicial resources outside the specific legal system in which the particular court is established.

Connecting *lis pendens* to the question of jurisdiction also offers an inadequate account of the factors at play, since what is involved is not merely a decision on the part of one court to decline its jurisdiction, but a

---

[46] Most recently in case concerning the *Application of the Convention on the Prevention and Punishment of the Crime of Genocide (Bosnia and Herzegovina* v. *Serbia and Montenegro)* (26 February 2007), General List No. 91, [114]-[116] ("the *Serbian Genocide* case"). For earlier references to the status of the doctrine as a general principle of law in international law see Cheng, *General Principles of Law as Applied by International Courts and Tribunals* (1953), Chap. 17. For the application of the rule in English Private International Law see Barnett, *Res Judicata, Estoppel and Foreign Judgments* (2001).

*choice* between two fora, each of which may decide to exercise, or relinquish, jurisdiction. Although it has become conventional, for example, in French doctrine to discuss the topic of jurisdiction under the heading "conflits de juridiction", this term merely balances "conflits de droit" as a convenient category for discussion of questions of jurisdiction and international civil procedure. Outside the closed order system of the Brussels I Regulation, it cannot be said that rules of jurisdiction operate in a multilateral fashion. As Holleaux put it:

> "Cette conception, en effet, a le tort d'attribuer aux règles françaises de compétence une fonction de répartition des compétences entre la France et l'étranger que ces règles n'assument nullement."[47]

Rather, to use Burbank's atmospheric phrase, the question is really one of "jurisdictional equilibration" *between* rival systems of adjudication[48].

In the result, then, this large, and growing, category of intractable international cases seems urgently to require a more satisfactory overall theory of its own. Yet its treatment in classic doctrine serves only to exacerbate the sense that no one has known quite where to place it. Dicey, writing the first edition of *The Conflict of Laws* in 1896, was in no doubt that the English court had the discretion to stay its proceedings if the same action was already pending in a foreign court and the plaintiff was proceeding vexatiously or in bad faith[49]. He headed his Note on the point "*Lis Alibi Pendens*, Staying Action." But he offered no source for

---

[47] Holleaux, "La litispendance", [1971-1973] *Travaux du Comité français de droit international privé* 203, 209.

[48] Burbank, "Jurisdictional Equilibration, the Proposed Hague Convention and Progress in National Law" (2001) 49 *AJCL* 203.

[49] Dicey, *A Digest of the Law of England with Reference to the Conflict of Laws* (1896), 355.

the Latin expression, denoting an action pending elsewhere, and placed his Note at the end of a chapter on
the effect of the English administration of a bankrupt
estate[50]. Westlake discusses the problem under the
heading *Lis pendens,* though placing it (more conven-
tionally) in a chapter on *Res judicata*[51].

The Explanatory Report on the Brussels Convention
1968[52] introduces Section 8 of the Convention, which
is headed "*Lis pendens* — related actions", without an
attempt to justify the priority principle which it contains, or to explain its derivation[53]. This may be in part
explained by the widespread existence of the doctrine
in the *internal* law of the original Member States, as
part of the codes of civil procedure. In fact, however,
as will be seen in Chapter II, the application of the
doctrine to foreign court proceedings was not part of
the established Private International Law of many Civil
Law countries, at least in the absence of a bilateral
convention. It might, therefore, have been expected to
require some greater discussion within the scheme of
the Convention.

What, then, really was the origin of the doctrine?
This question is not merely of archaeological interest.
A determination of the root of the idea might shed light
on the function which it was intended to perform, and

---

[50] In the current (14th) edition, the doctrine is discussed in a chapter on "*Forum non conveniens, Lis alibi
pendens*, anti-suit injunctions and jurisdiction agreements."

[51] Westlake *A Treatise on Private International Law*
(1st ed., 1858; 7th ed. by Bentwich, 1925) § 338.

[52] Brussels Convention on Jurisdiction and the
Recognition and Enforcement of Judgments in Civil and
Commercial Matters (signed 27 September 1968, entered
into force 1 February 1973), 1262 *UNTS* 153.

[53] Jenard Report (5 March 1979), OJ C59, Section 8;
this point is made by Schlosser, "Jurisdiction and International Judicial and Administrative Cooperation" (2000)
284 *Recueil des cours* 9, 81.

might also serve as a bridge between the sharp differences of approach which now pertain in the Civil and the Common Law systems. The widespread use of the Latin expression, in doctrine and jurisprudence, in both Civil and Common Law countries, suggests a common root in classical Roman Law. After all, the closely related doctrine of *res judicata* is extensively developed in the *Digest of Justinian*[54], and has proved the inspiration for the modern law on the recognition of the preclusive effect of judgments in Civil and Common Law countries.

But the *Digest* contains no mention of *lis pendens*. The occasional appearances of the phrase in the *Code* arise in contexts far from parallel litigation[55]. Nor does the doctrine figure in any of the well-known law dictionaries[56]. Nor may it be found mentioned in the parts of the great early modern texts which are specifically devoted to Private International Law: Huber's *De conflictu legum* (1686) or, 150 years later, in Volume 8 of Savigny's *System des Heutigen Römischen Rechts* (1849)[57]. These works were in any event principally concerned with choice of law and the enforcement of foreign judgments, and not with the exercise of adjudicatory authority. At this point, decipherment of the origins of *lis pendens* began to take on a mystery akin in the International Law context to the decipher-

---

[54] For a full discussion with references see Appendix A "Res Judicata in Roman Law" in Handley (ed.), *The Doctrine of Res Judicata: The Original Text by George Spencer Bower* (3rd ed., 1996).

[55] C 1.21 (pending litigation precludes a petition to the Emperor); C 26.2 (inheritance actions); C 27.2 (no transfers of property while an action is pending).

[56] Berger, *Encyclopaedic Dictionary of Roman Law* (1953) refers to the phrase merely in the context of petitions to the Emperor, C 1.21

[57] (Trans. W. Guthrie, 1880, reprinted 2003.)

ment of the ancient Mycenaean Greek language of Linear B ![58]

It is satisfying, therefore, to be able to record in these lectures for the Hague Academy that the doctrine may be traced to the great flowering of pre-Code Roman Law scholarship in the seventeenth-century Netherlands[59] : to Johannes Zangerus[60], to Ulrich Huber himself[61], and especially to Johannes Voet[62]. We shall revert shortly to a fuller consideration of this historical inheritance. But, at the outset, two points need to be made. First, all three scholars were writing, in accordance with the established conventions of the day, in Latin and in the form of a commentary on the classical Roman Law as contained in the *Digest*. They were propounding, therefore, what they saw as a *droit commun,* a set of general principles applicable everywhere (subject to local statutes and practice). If, on examination, the doctrine of *lis pendens* appears to be based upon the slenderest of evidence in classical Roman Law, the Dutch commentaries do not hesitate to reinterpret the ancients in order to reflect the current practice of

---

[58] Chadwick, *The Decipherment of Linear B* (2nd ed., 1967).

[59] The writer records his thanks to his friend Dr. Patrick Kinsch of Luxembourg for drawing his attention to the 1852 edition of Dalloz, *Répertoire de législation de doctrine et de jurisprudence* which, at XXIII, 101, relies in its exposition of the foundation for Article 171 of the French Code of Civil Procedure upon the authority of Voet and Zangerus.

[60] Zangerus (1557-1607), *Tractatus de Exceptionibus* (Witebergae, 1593) (original examined in the Rare Books Room of the University of Cambridge Library).

[61] Huber (1636-1694), *The Jurisprudence of My Time (Heedensdaegse Rechtsgeleertheyt)* (trans. P. Gane, Durban, 1939) 17, 12, p. 236.

[62] Johannes Voet (1647-1713), *Commentarius ad Pandectas* (1698) (trans. P. Gane, Durban, 1957), Vol. VI, Bk. XLIV, Tit. 2, pp. 557-562.

the Dutch courts. At the same time, indeed in different parts of the same works, Huber and Voet were also laying the foundations for the modern system of Private International Law[63].

Conditions had developed in seventeenth-century Holland which were peculiarly conducive to such innovation. The Treaty of Westphalia[64] (generally regarded as the first modern treaty and the earliest recognition of the idea of the modern nation State) had been signed in 1648, *inter alia* recognizing the independence of the Netherlands from Hapsburg rule. The Dutch provinces were organized as a federation:

> "But this federation affected but little the independence of the individual provinces in which there existed an intense jealousy of their local rights. This condition coupled with the fact that a growing commerce with foreign nations caused them to look upon the Conflict of Laws as arising between separate political sovereignties."[65]

Thus, the chapters of the Commentaries of Huber[66] and Voet[67] which deal with the Conflict of Laws develop a set of new principles to deal with the new reality of separate jurisdictions with different legal systems. These were not, indeed could not have been, based upon the unitary imperial assumptions of Roman Law. They saw the foundation for the application of

---

[63] Lorenzen, "Huber's De Conflictu Legum", in Wigmore, *Celebration Legal Essays* (1919) 199.

[64] Treaty of Peace between Spain and the Netherlands (signed 30 January 1648), 1 *CTS* 1; Treaty of Peace between Sweden and the Empire (signed 14 October 1648), 1 *CTS* 119; Treaty of Peace between France and the Empire (signed 14 October 1648), 1 *CTS* 271.

[65] Lorenzen, *supra* footnote 63, 201.

[66] "De Conflictu Legum", Tome III, Tit. III, Pt. 2, Bk. 1, translation appended to Lorenzen, *ibid.*.

[67] *Supra* footnote 62, "Statutes", Bk. 1, Tit. 4, App.

foreign law and of foreign judgments as being *comity,* justified by the convenience and the necessities of commerce[68]. These works, along with those of Savigny[69] and Story[70] which are derived from them[71], form the foundation for the modern system of choice of law.

Modern jurists have likewise seen the basis for the doctrine of *lis alibi pendens* as comity. F. A. Mann took this view[72]. But so have many judges. Thus, Lord Goff resorted to what "comity requires" in stating his general rule on the jurisdictional link for injunctions to restrain foreign proceedings[73]. So, too, did Judge Wilkey in the US Court of Appeals in articulating the approach which US courts ought to take to foreign parallel litigation in his seminal decision in the *Laker* affair in the 1980s[74]. Similar thinking may also be seen at work in the Public International Law context. Thus, the UNCLOS Tribunal in *MOX Plant*, when it ordered a stay of proceedings pending a decision by the

---

[68] Huber, *supra* footnote 63, [2]; Voet, *supra* footnote 62, Bk. I, Tit. 4, App., s. 12.

[69] Savigny, *System des Heutigen Römischen Rechts* (1849), Vol. 8.

[70] Story, *Commentaries on the Conflict of Laws* (1857).

[71] Lorenzen, *supra* footnote 63, 199 comments that Huber's work

> "has had a greater influence upon the development of the Conflict of Laws in England and the United States than any other work. No other foreign work has been so frequently cited. Story himself relied upon Huber more than upon any of the other foreign jurists."

[72] Mann, *Foreign Affairs in English Courts* (1986) 143, and see also Slaughter's claim of the emergence of "judicial comity" in "A Global Community of Courts" (2003) 44 *Harv. Int'l LJ* 191, 205-210.

[73] *Airbus Industrie GIE* v. *Patel*, *supra* footnote 11, 138.

[74] *Laker Airways Ltd.* v. *Sabena, Belgian World Airlines* 731 F. 2d 909 (DC Cir., 1984).

European Court of Justice, justified its decision by reference to "considerations of mutual respect and comity which should prevail between judicial institutions" [75].

But the striking difference between the conflict of laws and that of conflict of litigation, or *lis pendens*, is this. Huber, Voet and those the jurists that followed them in the formation of the modern Conflict of Laws used the concept of comity as a springboard from which they proceeded to develop a highly organized and sophisticated set of choice of law rules. In this sense, "comity" did not remain a vague desideratum — an invitation to replace law with its antithesis in mere courtesy and discretion. On the contrary, it supplied the basis for the elaboration of a detailed set of positive rules, grounded in practical reality.

By contrast, however, the early Dutch fathers of the Conflict of Laws did not, despite considering *lis pendens* as a matter of general law in conjunction with *res judicata,* and considering that the doctrine of *res judicata* could apply to foreign as much as to local judgments [76] proceed to consider the application of *lis pendens* to the problem of the conflict of litigation internationally. Perhaps the litigation of seventeenth-century Holland had yet to produce cases of parallel foreign litigation, or at least produce them with sufficient regularity to catch the attention of the jurists. As will be shortly seen, cases of this kind did not begin to tax the English courts until the nineteenth century. In any event, the application of the doctrine of *lis pendens* in the form in which Huber and Voet recognized it would have required a much stronger form of comity than

---

[75] *MOX Plant Case (Ireland* v. *United Kingdom)* (24 June 2003), Provisional Order No. 3, 126 *ILR* 310, 42 *ILM* 1187 (UNCLOS, Annex VII, Tribunal, Mensah P, Crawford, Fortier, Hafner, Watts) [28].

[76] Huber *supra* footnote 63, [6]; Voet *supra* footnote 62, [17].

they had otherwise accepted for the effects of foreign legal systems. It was not merely a matter of courts giving effect to foreign law and foreign judgments. Rather, it would have required the court to cede the power of adjudication to a foreign court.

It is submitted that this omission has left a topic of central importance substantially underdeveloped in Private International Law. The conflict of litigation is not to be reduced to a mere qualification upon the law of jurisdiction or an anticipatory application of the law on the enforcement of foreign judgments. Rather, it is a separate branch of Private International Law in itself, and one which, as the many modern cases to be discussed will show, has become of pressing practical importance[77].

If this fundamental point of departure is accepted, it has this practical consequence. It is no longer necessary, as indeed it never was possible, to solve all problems of parallel proceedings by application of a single rule or principle. As will be seen, the simple "first-to-file" rule which now dominates the European landscape applies of necessity to a narrow range of cases where complete identity of action is established. Even in that context it has proved incapable of controlling forum shopping. The modern litigation landscape is characterized by many different kinds of potential conflicts of adjudicatory authority unknown to our forebears. Nor must one await — a vain hope in this field — the emergence of a single multilateral solution, still less a hierarchy of courts.

Thus, we must begin the task of working out more detailed sets of rules and processes for the resolution of

---

[77] Compare the development in French Private International Law of the concept of conflict of procedures: Niboyet-Hoegy, "Les conflits de procédures" [1995-1998], *Travaux du Comité français de droit international privé* 71, and Moissinac Massénat, *Les conflits de procédures et de décisions en droit international privé* (2007).

conflicts of adjudication, which may differ depending upon the nature of the issue and the relationship between the respective courts or tribunals. These lectures can do no more than to begin this process by examining the problem in its different modern applications in Private International Law, in International Arbitration and in Public International Law. Such a comparison is both possible and necessary. It was Hersch Lauterpacht himself who took as the text for his *Private Law Sources and Analogies of International Law* the proposition of Holland:

> "The Law of Nations is but private law 'writ large'. It is an application to political communities of those legal ideas which were originally applied to relations of individuals."[78]

An examination across the varied terrain of Public and Private International Law of the problems of parallel litigation may also reveal more about two general questions less often asked in this context. In the first place, *why* might litigants wish to pursue proceedings in more than one forum at the same time? The answer to that question may in turn assist in resolving: *how*, in what circumstances, with what techniques and for what purpose should the law seek to control such a phenomenon? Finding the answers to those questions requires a form of case-study analysis which is rooted in the dynamics of international litigation. But its larger purpose is to examine whether common principles can be discerned from the disparate treatment of the issue.

Accordingly, the syllabus of these lectures will con-

---

[78] Lauterpacht, *Private Law Sources and Analogies of International Law (with special reference to international arbitration)* (1927), citing Holland, *Studies in International Law* (1898), 152.

sist of an examination of the problems of parallel proceedings across these areas:

*(a)* Chapter II *(lecture 2)* will examine conflicts between national courts across borders — problems of Private International Law;

*(b)* Chapter III *(lecture 3)* will look at aspects of the problem in the relations between arbitral tribunals, and between such tribunals and national courts — both in commercial arbitration and in mixed investment arbitration between States and foreign investors;

*(c)* Chapter IV *(lecture 4)* will address conflicts between tribunals adjudicating disputes on the plane of Public International Law; and between such tribunals and national courts;

*(d)* Chapter V *(lecture 5)* will revert to the major theme, and examine the implications of the study for a broader understanding of the *system* of international litigation, considering for that purpose the recent proposals for reform.

However, at the outset it is necessary to explore, in a little more detail, three fundamental aspects of the problem already stated, since they form an essential predicate for what is to come. In the first place, this chapter will address the phenomenon of litispendence, asking why it is that parties choose to litigate in more than one forum. The approach will be functional — taking as its starting-point an examination of what litigants actually do, rather than the *a priori* categories into which the particular solutions of the legal instruments *du jour* may impose. Then, it will search for the roots of the law's response to parallel proceedings. Finding the answer to this question is of no mere antiquarian interest, since the foundations of the doctrine may indicate whether it can be said to be a "general principle of law recognized by civilized nations". Then, in Section D, the range of potential techniques available to deal with parallel litigation will be examined. Finally, it will be possible in Section E to sketch in outline what might in fact form a principled basis for a modern approach to the conflict of litigation.

## B. *The Litispendence Phenomenon*

Five fundamental points about the phenomenon of litispendence need to be made at the outset.

### 1. *Forum shopping in parallel litigation*

Section 9 of the Brussels I Regulation (which contains the current version of the rule giving priority to the court first seised used to such potent effect in *Gasser*) is headed "*Lis pendens* — related actions"[79]. There is a tendency, at least in European conflicts literature, to discuss the concept of litispendence as if it were synonymous with a legal doctrine, notably the particular "first seised" solution adopted by the Regulation itself. In fact, the term denotes only the notion of a dispute, a *lis,* already pending before another court or tribunal. That is a factual phenomenon, not a legal solution to it.

The narrow conception of the doctrine is closely linked to the test for the *res judicata* effect of judgments. It requires strict identity of parties, subject-matter and cause of action. But, from a functional perspective, such categories in any event do not capture the complete universe of parallel proceedings. A case may arise in two courts at once from the same event or relationship, but different relief may be sought in each. Different substantive law may be applied to each. Further, the same event may give rise to claims by or against a number of different parties, so that there are

---

[79] *Supra* footnote 43.

related claims which each turn to some extent upon the same findings of fact or law. Each of these situations involves a problem of parallel proceedings, and the law must find its response to each. So it is first necessary to examine why it is that parties may choose to litigate the same or similar issues in different fora at the same time.

This aspect of "forum shopping" is part of a wider party-driven revolution in the Conflict of Laws. Forum shopping is as alive and well within Europe, even under the yoke of the European Court's interpretation of the Brussels I Regulation, as it is beyond. Yet, most discussions of forum shopping contemplate the choice of one forum over another. As Lord Simon of Glaisdale famously put it:

> " 'Forum shopping' is a dirty word; but it is only a pejorative way of saying that, if you offer a plaintiff a choice of jurisdictions, he will naturally choose the one in which he thinks his case can be most favourably presented: this should be a matter neither for surprise nor indignation."[80]

How, then, is the apparently irrational step of commencing two parallel actions to be explained? Litigation is, after all, frequently expensive and time-consuming, yet there are many reported examples of attempts to bring double actions on the same or similar claims. Hitherto, in the analysis of forum shopping, the incidence of the second litigation has often been seen as incidental to the remedy under consideration. Yet many of the cases which have been considered in Common Law countries as cases of appropriate forum (*forum non conveniens*), as well as all cases of anti-suit injunctions, are also cases of parallel litigation. The

---

[80] *The Atlantic Star*, [1974] AC 436, 471 (HL) per Lord Simon of Glaisdale.

very purpose of the anti-suit injunction is to quell
vexatious litigation in another forum. This suggests that
a specific focus on why parties start double litigation
may itself yield valuable insights into the appropriate
legal solutions.

Two different types of conduct may be observed,
which have quite different implications for the design
of legal solutions:

The first scenario is that the parallel litigation arises
as part of a preliminary contest for jurisdiction between
plaintiff and defendant — each party commencing
action in his preferred forum. Thus, in *Gasser*[81], the
true defendant used the device of an action for a negative declaration to seize the court in his home jurisdiction before the plaintiff had commenced action in the
contractually-chosen forum. In *Turner* v. *Grovit*[82] the
defendant sought to turn the tables on successful litigation brought by the plaintiff in England by bringing
spoiling litigation in Spain. These cases may not necessarily be about ongoing parallel litigation. On the
contrary, they may instead be a tactical skirmish
between plaintiff and defendant to determine the forum
for the litigation, or even to determine whether there is
to be ongoing litigation at all.

But, in a second scenario, the plaintiff himself may
have good reasons for pursuing parallel litigation in
more than one country. A very common example of
this is in transnational fraud litigation, where the
widespread nature of the fraud and its perpetrators, and
the dissipation of its fruits, may mandate multi-juris-
dictional litigation. However, cases of this kind may
not strictly be seen as parallel litigation. In the typical
fraud case, the claim on the merits is centralized in one

---

[81] *Supra* footnote 1.
[82] *Supra* footnote 8.

jurisdiction. The other litigation is then satellite to it: seeking disclosure or provisional measures to locate and preserve assets prior to judgment. There may also be cases where particular defendants have to be sued where they can be found, in order to ensure that the resulting judgment will be enforceable against them and their assets. Claims which seek to determine property rights *in rem*, good against all the world, may well have to be litigated in the courts of the *situs* of the property, even if such claims are very closely linked.

Despite the fact that the incidence of parallel litigation in public international law has a much more recent lineage, there are already some rich examples of multiple litigation commenced by the same plaintiff in interest. Thus, in *MOX Plant*, Ireland's claim against the United Kingdom was commenced first in the International Tribunal for the Law of the Sea in an application for provisional measures[83]. Ireland then pursued its substantive claim before an arbitral tribunal under the UN Convention on the Law of the Sea[84]. It also brought separate arbitral proceedings under the 1992 Convention for the Protection of the Marine Environment of the North East Atlantic ("OSPAR Convention") in order to seek information from the United Kingdom concerning the operation of the Mox Plant[85]. The plaintiff's multiple litigation may be seen as a search for a forum in which it might receive the

---

[83] *Supra* footnote 4.

[84] *MOX Plant Case (Ireland* v. *United Kingdom)* (UNCLOS, Annex VII, Arbitral Tribunal, Order No. 3 of 24 June 2003) (2003) 42 *ILM* 1187, 126 *ILR* 310, discussed *infra*, Chapter IV, Section B 1 *(b)*.

[85] *MOX Plant Case*: *Dispute Concerning Access to Information under Article 9 of the OSPAR Convention (Ireland* v. *United Kingdom)* (Permanent Court of Arbitration, Final Award of 2 July 2003), 42 *ILM* 1118, 126 *ILR* 334.

most favourable outcome. In a context where the establishment of jurisdiction may be quite uncertain, and where there are no clear rules requiring priority as between tribunals, a determined plaintiff state has every incentive to try its luck in multiple fora.

The same may be said of the determined investor in investment treaty arbitration. Thus, the dispute between the American investor Ron Lauder and the Czech Republic over the licensing of the TV Nova television channel formed the subject of two parallel treaty arbitrations. The first was brought under the US-Czech bilateral investment treaty by Mr. Lauder as the ultimate shareholder in interest[86]. The second was brought under the Dutch-Czech BIT by the Dutch holding company, which was the corporate vehicle for the investment[87]. Success in either claim would have sufficed. It was a high risk strategy, but it ultimately worked in favour of the claimants. Neither tribunal ceded jurisdiction to the other. One decided almost entirely against Mr. Lauder's interests, but the other decided the matter in his favour, granting a massive damages award against the Czech Republic.

## 2. Horizontality

In all of these examples, the key feature upon which the pursuit of parallel litigation is premised is the horizontality of the systems of adjudication — the absence

---

[86] *Lauder* v. *Czech Republic* (Award) 9 *ICSID Rep.* 62 (UNCITRAL, 2001, Briner C, Cutler and Klein), discussed *infra*, Chapter III, Section C 5.

[87] *CME Czech Republic BV (The Netherlands)* v. *Czech Republic* (Partial Award), 9 *ICSID Rep.* 121 (UNCITRAL, 2001, Kühn C, Schwebel and Hándl) *(CME I)*; (Final Award), 9 *ICSID* 264 (UNCITRAL, 2003, Kühn C, Schwebel and Brownlie) *(CME II)*; Svea Court of Appeals, Sweden (2003), 42 *ILM* 919.

of hierarchy between the respective courts which might require one court to cede jurisdiction to the other. The struggles for ascendancy between courts within a national legal system, which characterized the emergence of modern judicial systems, form no part of international litigation.

This point is a commonplace in Private International Law. Indeed, the very structure of the subject is predicated upon the equality of national courts and legal systems. This is so even within federations, and nascent federations, such as the European Union. Thus, the European Court of Justice conceives its very function in this field to be the enforcement of horizontality between national courts of Member States — its principle of mutual respect — rather than the imposition of uniform rules of civil procedure.

Horizontality has long been a defining feature of the international legal system generally, predicated as it is upon the sovereign equality of States. It has also proved the watch-word of the new style of public international litigation, which is characterized by a proliferation of international courts and tribunals. This much exercised the former President of the International Court of Justice, Judge Guillaume, who told the UN General Assembly in 2000 that such proliferation:

> "leads to cases of overlapping jurisdiction, opening the way for applicant States to seek out those courts which they believe, rightly or wrongly, to be more amenable to their arguments. This forum shopping, as it is usually called, may indeed stimulate the judicial imagination, but it can also generate unwanted confusion. Above all, it can distort the operation of justice, which, in my view, should not be made subject to the law of the marketplace." [88]

---

[88] Guillaume, "Address to the UNGA" (26 October 2000) 3, available at www.icj-cij.org.

Judge Guillaume saw the solution to this problem in the creation of a vertical international judicial system, with the International Court of Justice, as the judicial organ of the United Nations, at the apex of Mount Olympus. But, of course, States have not proceeded in this way.

On the contrary, in the great flowering of international law, especially in the 1990s after the end of the Cold War, States specifically chose to create a myriad of new judicial institutions, each with a separate sphere of competence.

Sometimes, these were conceived as the judicial organs of major new multilateral institutions. Thus, when the World Trade Organization was finally created by the Marrakesh Agreements of 1994, the old diplomatic model of resolving trade disputes was decisively rejected in favour of a unique judicial model, complete with an Appellate Body[89]. Similarly, the United Nations Convention on the Law of the Sea 1982 creates its own International Tribunal for the Law of the Sea, amongst a range of specific dispute resolution mechanisms[90].

In other cases, there would have been no real choice but to create a new institution, since the parties included non-State actors or the focus was regional. This is true of the International Criminal Court, where the defendants are individuals. But it is also true of the rights of individual complaint to international and regional human rights bodies, and of provision for

---

[89] Dispute Settlement Understanding, 1869 *UNTS* 401, Annex 2 to Marrakesh Agreement establishing the World Trade Organization (signed 15 April 1994, entered into force 1 January 1995), 1867 *UNTS* 3.

[90] Statute of the International Tribunal for the Law of the Sea: United Nations Convention on the Law of the Sea (signed 10 December 1982, entered into force 16 November 1994), 1833 *UNTS* 3, Annex VI.

arbitration under the auspices of the International Centre for the Settlement of Investment Disputes (ICSID)[91].

In these contexts, to borrow Lord Simon's words, it should be "neither a matter for surprise nor for indignation" that aspects of the same dispute should be litigated before different fora[92]. First, it is inherent in the very concept of an international legal system that the fact that a dispute has already been determined before a national court will not be determinative of a claim at the international level. Were it otherwise, the protections accepted by States as binding upon each other on the international plane would be of no effect. The international claim, even if it involves the same subject-matter, will be a different claim. Thus, it may be a misnomer to regard many such cases as cases of parallel litigation — they are in truth closely related litigation at the different levels of national and international law.

Further, States may have consciously decided that a choice of fora is desirable. Thus, in the Energy Charter Treaty[93], and in many modern BITs[94], claimants are given a cafeteria-style menu of different dispute-resolution options, including both national court adjudication within the host State and international arbitration under various different institutions or rules. In this context, too, States have found simple verticality to be neither possible nor desirable in international

---

[91] Convention on the Settlement of Investment Disputes between States and Nationals of Other States (signed 18 March 1965, entered into force 14 October 1966), 575 *UNTS* 159, see *infra*, Chapter III, Section C.

[92] *The Atlantic Star*, *supra* footnote 80, 471.

[93] Art. 26, Energy Charter Treaty (signed 17 December 1994, entered into force 16 April 1998), 2080 *UNTS* 100.

[94] McLachlan, Shore and Weiniger, *International Investment Arbitration*: *Substantive Principles* (2007), Chap. 3.

litigation, preferring instead to craft their own suite of
remedies.

## 3. *Overlapping jurisdiction-conferring rules*

The available choice of complementary fora in
investment cases is but one example of a much more
pervasive feature of international litigation generally:
that of overlapping jurisdictional competence.

Thus, in *Private International Law*, the rules of
original judicial jurisdiction, irrespective of whether
they are the product of unilateral development or international agreement, often have the effect that more
than one court will simultaneously have jurisdiction
over the same case. Indeed, this situation is endemic in
private international litigation, such that the choice
between equally available jurisdictions may be said to
be characteristic of it. This will frequently be the case,
for example, where the domicile of the defendant provides general jurisdiction and the place of the harmful
event constituting a tort or delict has occurred elsewhere, conferring special jurisdiction on the courts of
that place. This suggests that the question of parallel
proceedings is frequently not resolved by addressing
which court has jurisdiction. Rather, it is often necessary to consider which court should decline to exercise
a jurisdiction which it undoubtedly has.

The incidence of overlapping jurisdiction in *Public
International Law* is much less frequent. As between
national courts and international tribunals, the very
structure of classical Public International Law served
to keep the two regimes apart. In particular, the basic
rule of diplomatic protection required the national to
exhaust local remedies in the host State before his
home State could espouse his claim at the international
level. A related theme may be seen at work in the
principle of complementarity in the Rome Statute of

the International Criminal Court[95]. Here there is no requirement of prior exhaustion. On the contrary, the Statute respects the fundamental principle of criminal law that an alleged offender may only be tried once for the same offence[96]. The ICC will only have jurisdiction to the extent that the national court has been unable or unwilling to prosecute. Its jurisdiction is complementary to that of the national criminal courts.

The lower incidence of overlapping jurisdiction between public international tribunals reflects the limited choices available for international adjudication prior to the great expansion of the last decade. The primary model for international adjudication was for centuries that of *ad hoc* inter-State arbitration. By definition, this had to be the product of a specific *compromis* agreed between the contesting States after the dispute itself had arisen, in which the mode of dispute resolution would be agreed. Only with the advent of standing consent to either arbitration or litigation might States be able to shop for the most favourable forum. Even then, for many decades, the only material forum which enjoyed some measure of standing jurisdiction (however partial) was the Permanent Court of International Justice, now the International Court of Justice.

In modern times, however, this once-sparse landscape has been populated by a host of new venues for disputes at the international level, coupled with rights of direct invocation of jurisdiction by the plaintiff as a result of standing consent granted by the respondent state. This has also led to a much greater incidence of conflict between courts. Perhaps the most notorious example in recent times has been the long-running dispute on the rights of condemned foreign prisoners

---

[95] Art. 17, Rome Statute of the International Criminal Court (signed 1 July 1998, entered into force 1 July 2002) 2187 *UNTS* 3.

[96] *Ibid.*, Art. 20, *"Ne bis in idem"*.

on Death Row in the United States to consular assistance[97]. The jurisdiction of the International Court has been serially invoked by home States, invoking the submission of the United States to the Court's jurisdiction under the Consular Convention. The Court has granted provisional measures restraining the execution of the prisoners pending a decision on the merits, only to find its judgments held unenforceable by US courts.

But the conflicts between courts at the national and international level are not always played out with life or death consequences. Even in the field of mixed investor-State arbitration, the wide array of possible venues has provoked conflict. The result is to transform the problems of parallel proceedings from an ordinary game of chess to the three-dimensional variety, in which a central question is which of two courts or tribunals, each applied to, should decide to accept or decline jurisdiction.

## 4. Kompetenz-Kompetenz: *who determines jurisdiction?*

A central problem in many parallel proceedings cases — in any of the three areas of international law which will be examined — is the need to decide which of two tribunals seised of the matter is to determine the preliminary question of whether to assume jurisdiction. The modern law of international commercial arbitration recognizes the competence of the arbitral tribunal to decide upon its own jurisdiction once it is seised of the case[98]. This autonomous competence is known by its German name: *Kompetenz-Kompetenz*. Further, Article II of the New York Convention on the Recognition and Enforcement of Foreign Arbitral

[97] *Infra*, Chapter IV, Section C 2 *(a)*.
[98] For example, Art. 16, UNCITRAL Model Law on International Commercial Arbitration, UN doc. A/40/17, Annex I and A/61/17, Annex I.

Awards 1958 ("the New York Convention")[99] contains a clear rule of priority as between competing parallel court and arbitral proceedings. It requires the court to stay its proceedings where the party to an arbitration agreement so applies in respect of any matter which under the agreement is to be referred to arbitration, unless the arbitration agreement is null and void, inoperative or incapable of being performed.

However, embedded in that clear rule of priority is a set of potentially difficult questions about the scope of the arbitration agreement and its validity. Who is to decide those questions? A very strong version of arbitral autonomy, so-called negative *Kompetenz-Kompetenz*, would claim that the court should always defer to the arbitral tribunal's determination of its own competence. Thus, only after an award has been rendered could the tribunal's decision on its jurisdiction could be the subject of an application to a national court on the ground of invalidity of the agreement or excess of jurisdiction[100]. But the arbitration agreement also produces its effects on national court litigation. Article II itself contemplates that the validity of the agreement may have to be tested on a motion for a stay before a national court. If the agreement is invalid or its scope does not cover the dispute before the court, it can produce no effect on the court's jurisdiction.

Thus, despite the clear rule of priority as to substance contained in Article II, there is still a procedural question of great practical importance as to priority in the determination of jurisdiction. As will be seen in Chapter III, different arbitral rules and laws have answered that question in different ways.

---

[99] Convention on the Recognition and Enforcement of Foreign Arbitral Awards 1958 (New York Convention) (signed 10 June 1958, entered into force 7 June 1959), 330 *UNTS* 38.

[100] *Ibid.*, Art. V (1) *(a)* and *(c)*.

In other types of international litigation, as we have seen, there is no *a priori* agreement on which of two courts is to decide the case. Each has, within its own governing legal system, competent jurisdiction, and the question is whether one should stay or decline to exercise such jurisdiction in favour of the other. Many of the cases on *lis pendens* are therefore not simply concerned with the question of the forum in which the merits of the dispute are ultimately to be litigated. Rather, they are about which forum is to decide the preliminary question of priority of jurisdiction.

## C. *Intellectual Origins of the Idea of* Lis Pendens

Having sketched some of the basic dynamics of international litigation which provoke parallel proceedings, it is now possible to address the law's response. As will be seen in Section D, there are in fact a range of techniques in use in the law today. But two models nevertheless have dominated thought about the problem. The first is the Civil Law rule requiring strict deference to a prior pending suit, now codified within Europe as Article 27 of the Brussels I Regulation. The second, by contrast, is the Common Law's discretionary approach — either to decline jurisdiction on appropriate forum grounds or to control vexatious and oppressive proceedings by means of an anti-suit injunction.

Chapter II will demonstrate that neither model is in fact as universally held, or as deeply entrenched, as a solution to parallel international litigation as may commonly be thought. But, given the way in which the concepts have held such a deep paradigmatic grip upon the imagination of jurists[101], it is important to consider

---

[101] Michaels, "Two Paradigms of Jurisdiction", (2005-2006) 27 *Mich. JIL* 1003; Gardella and Radicati di Brozolo, "Civil Law, Common Law and Market Integration: The EC Approach to Conflicts of Jurisdiction", (2003) 51 *AJCL* 611.

their origins. These are rooted, not in *international* civil procedure, but rather in *internal* civil procedure. Indeed, the roots go very deep, and tell their own story about the ways in which different images of litigation within Law's great empires have marked our subject.

## 1. Civil Law: in the image of Roman Law?

Modern studies of the doctrine of *lis pendens* in Private International Law often start with the observation that the rule of deference to the court first seised of the same matter is widely entrenched in the *internal* civil procedure codes of Europe. In each case, the attributes of the rule bear a very close relationship to the elements for the *res judicata* effect of a judgment, requiring the same parties, the same subject-matter and the same cause. Pålsson concludes that the relationship is so close that *lis pendens* is merely the essential precursor to *res judicata*:

> "Summing up, the rule of *lis pendens* is a natural and rational complement to the rule of *res judicata,* more particularly to the negative side of the rule *(ne bis in idem).* As little as an issue decided by a judgment enjoying the force of *res judicata* can be reexamined in a subsequent action, as little should it be possible to reexamine it while it is being tried in a suit which is capable of resulting in such a judgment. The relation between the two institutes may also be expressed by saying that where the *lis pendens* effect ceases, the *res judicata* effect commences." [102]

If, then, there is an insoluble link between *lis pendens* and *res judicata,* one would expect to find the origins of both legal concepts at the same source. *Res*

---

[102] Pålsson, "The Institute of *Lis Pendens* in International Civil Procedure", (1970) *Scan. Stud. L.* 59, 68.

*judicata* is well established as a "general principle of
law recognized by civilized nations"[103]. The maxim *res
judicata pro veritate accipitur* is one of the fundamental principles of Roman Law collected in the *Digest of
Justinian*[104].

By contrast, however, *lis pendens* does not appear to
have been treated as a separate concept by classical
Roman jurists themselves, as recorded in the *Digest*.
This may have been because of the highly centralized,
imperial character of Roman Law. As a matter of procedure, in any event, Roman litigation knew a much more
far-reaching concept of consolidation: the *litis contestatio*. This operated as a limitation on all other personal
claims for the same right from the point proceedings
were instituted, and continuing after judgment, so that
the entire liability of the defendant was concentrated in
the consummation of the single lawsuit[105].

Writing at the close of the sixteenth century in the
Netherlands, and drawing upon other Renaissance legal
scholarship, Johannes Zangerus, identified *lis pendens*
as one of a number of pleas of exception which a
defendant could raise in a lawsuit[106]. But his treatment
of the topic is, to modern eyes, cast in a formal procedural tradition, only slowly emerging from the
Middle Ages.

---

[103] *Chorzów Factory* case (1927) *PCIJ Rep. Ser. A,
No. 9*, 27 per Judge Anzilotti; *South West Africa* case, *ICJ
Rep. 1966* 4, 240-241; Cheng, *supra* footnote 46, Chap 17.
[104] *Digest*, L, 17, 207, Ulpian, Scott (ed.), *The Civil Law*
(1973), Vol. XI, 318; Handley, *supra* footnote 54, [455]-[465].
[105] Wenger, *Institutes of the Roman Law of Civil
Procedure* (trans. Fisk, 1940) 177-183.
[106] Zangerus, *Tractatus de Exceptionibus* (1593) Chap. 11
"Exceptio litis pendentis", 197-200. The references in Voet
appear to be to the subsequent edition of 1675, Chap. 13, 213-
218 (copy inspected in the Rare Books Room of the University of Cambridge Library). The writer is indebted to
James McNamara for preparing a translation of the original.

It was left to Johannes Voet, writing at the close of the seventeenth century, to translate these concepts into the modern rule of *lis pendens*. Voet was a remarkable jurist. Born in Utrecht, and for 30 years Professor of Law at Leiden, he continued the long Civilian tradition of producing his scholarship in the form of a Commentary on the *Digest*. The reality was, however, that Voet did rather more than this. First, he reorganized the law on the subject-matters dealt with in the *Digest* in a systematic and methodical manner. Second, he synthesized the ancient Roman Law with the actual practice of the Dutch courts of his day. Voet's contribution to the early modern development of Private International Law also spread far beyond his native Holland, and traces of his ideas are found in Anglo-American law, especially by way of the influence of the Scots lawyers, who, in the eighteenth century, commonly studied at Leiden [107]. His *Commentary on the Pandects* [108] remains an authoritative text on Roman-Dutch Law today.

Critically for present purposes, Voet took the writings of Johannes Zangerus of a century earlier and developed the doctrine of *lis pendens* as part of his consideration of *res judicata*. Indeed, he opines:

> "*Exception of* lis pendens *also requires the same persons, thing and cause.* The exception that a suit is already pending is quite akin to the exception of *res judicata,* inasmuch as, when a suit is pending before another judge, this exception is granted just so often as, and in all those cases in which after a suit has been ended there is room for the exception of *res judicata* in terms of what has already been

---

[107] Anton, "The Introduction into English Practice of Continental Theories on the Conflict of Laws" (1956) 5 *ICLQ* 534, 536; Nadelman, *Conflict of Laws: International and Interstate: Selected Essays* (1972), 4.

[108] Voet, *supra* footnote 62, 552-562.

said. Thus the suit must already have started to
be mooted before another judge between the same
persons, about the same matter and on the same
cause . . ." [109]

This is all constructed on the basis of what seems to be
the slenderest reed of authority within the *Digest,*
namely the dictum of Marcellus that: "[w]herever
issue is joined, the case should also be terminated
there" [110].

But it is clear from the contemporary authorities
which Voet also cites that the raising of such a plea, as
a preliminary objection to jurisdiction, had been a
common practice in the Dutch courts at least from the
previous century [111]. In this way, the principle of *litis
contestatio* developed within the highly centralized
judicial system of imperial Rome was developed to
deal with the realities of applying Roman Law
within the decentralized system of the Dutch provinces. In turn it was applied within the other nascent
post-Westphalian States of continental Europe. From
there, it was introduced into the nineteenth-century
codes, becoming the basis, for example, of Article 171
(now Article 100) of the French Code of Civil Procedure [112].

---

[109] *Ibid.*, 560.

[110] *Digest*, V, 1, 30: Scott, *supra* footnote 104, Vol III,
148.

[111] *Supra* footnote 62, 562, fns. 2-5. Huber (1636-1694)
also refers to this: *supra* footnote 61, 17,12, p. 236, but links
it with *litis contestatio,* stating:

"When *litis contestatio* has been effected, the
defendant, who is summoned before a different Judge,
has the exception *litis pendentis,* by which he avers
that he is not obliged to plead to this new claim, since
an action in the same manner is pending before another
tribunal."

[112] *Supra* footnote 59.

None of this development was driven by international considerations. On the contrary, the doctrine evolved as a means of dealing with the administration of justice within States where the court system was decentralized, but the applicable law was the same. As will be seen in Chapter II, the expansion of the doctrine into the international arena was not to come until much later.

## 2. *Common Law*: *the legacy of Equity's struggle for supremacy in England*

By contrast, the techniques developed within English law to deal with parallel proceedings bear the hallmarks of a very different history. It is a history of the struggle for supremacy of particular courts within a system of adjudication which had no *a priori* hierarchy. Thus, in England, the anti-suit injunction precedes by several centuries the development of a discretion to stay proceedings in the light of another pending action[113].

It is bound up with the struggle of the Court of Chancery (a court which had originally developed in Mediaeval times as an appeal to the discretion of the King's Chancellor) to entertain a claim for equitable relief even where the Common Law courts were already seised of the dispute[114]. Indeed, the use of an injunction to restrain a litigant from continuing the prosecution of his claim in the Common Law courts whilst the matter was before the Court of Chancery could be said to be the classic application of injunctive relief.

---

[113] McClean, "Jurisdiction and Judicial Discretion", (1969) 18 *ICLQ* 931.

[114] Raack, "A History of Injunctions in England before 1700" (1985-1986) 61 *Ind. LJ* 539.

The final recognition of the power of Chancery to issue such injunctions, achieved by Royal Decree of James I in 1616, was decisive. It preserved a system of equity that benefited litigants by providing a degree of protection from the rigidities of the Common Law. "But", concludes one scholar of this early period, "if Chancery and common law were to coexist, this power would have to be used with restraint." [115]

Thus it was perhaps natural that when, in the nineteenth century, the English Courts first began to encounter problems of *lis alibi pendens* — parallel proceedings in courts outside England — they would resort first to the same remedy which had been used for centuries to control litigants proceeding in the Common Law courts. The central question was seen to be whether there was "vexatious harassing" or whether the respondent was proceeding abroad in a manner which was contrary to equity and good conscience [116]. The earliest fully argued and reported case in which an anti-suit injunction was granted to restrain foreign proceedings was *Bushby* v. *Munday,* decided in 1821 [117]. In that case, Leach V-C decided that an injunction should be issued to restrain proceedings in Scotland, since the two proceedings were on precisely the same question, and the English court was a more convenient jurisdiction for determining the issue.

The extension of the power to grant anti-suit injunctions to restrain foreign proceedings appears to have followed the expansion of British imperial power — from Scotland and Ireland, to the colonies and thence

---

[115] *Ibid.*, 583.
[116] *Carron Iron Co.* v. *Maclaren*, (1855) 5 HL Cas 415, 436-437 per Lord Cranworth LC; Kerr, *Injunctions in Equity* (1867) 134, cited in *Masri* v. *Consolidated Contractors Int'l Co. SAL*, [2008] EWCA Civ. 625, [39] per Lawrence Collins LJ.
[117] (1821) 5 Madd. 297, 56 ER 908.

beyond. Hoffmann J summarized the position as follows:

> "Until the last century, the English Court of Chancery regularly granted anti-suit injunctions against proceedings in the English courts of common law. Such injunctions (called 'common injunctions') were the technique by which equity asserted itself over the common law. They were granted when according to rules of equity it was 'unconscionable' for a party to rely upon his common law rights. As between the courts of Chancery and common law, no questions of comity were involved. Equity applied its own system of rules and used the common law injunction to enforce it (Lord *Diplock*'s description of unconscionable conduct in *Laker* at p 81 is based on the principles on which the old Court of Chancery would have granted common injunctions). In the early nineteenth century, when the English courts began to issue injunctions to restrain proceedings in foreign courts, it was natural to think that an anti-suit injunction could be granted on the same grounds as a court of equity would restrain proceedings in an English common law court (particularly when the proceedings were in another British jurisdiction: see Lord *Portalington* v. *Soulby* (1834) 3 Myl & K 104; 40 ER 40). Since the injunction was a discretionary remedy, the English court would take comity into account in deciding whether the injunction should be granted in respect of foreign proceedings: *Carron Iron Co* v. *Maclaren* (1855) 5 HL Cas 416; 10 ER 961. But in principle, 'unconscionable' simply meant contrary to the rules of English equity." [118]

It is, therefore, not a little ironic that, at the very

---

[118] *Barclays Bank plc* v. *Homan*, [1992] BCC 757, 762 (CA).

moment that the anti-suit injunction began to be applied internationally, its original use at home was declared redundant by statutory reform. By the Supreme Court of Judicature Act 1873, the courts of Equity and the Common Law were fused into a single High Court of Justice. This Court was to exercise full jurisdiction to apply both Law and Equity to the causes brought before it "so that, as far as possible, all matters so in controversy between the said parties respectively may be completely and finally determined, *and all multiplicity of legal proceedings concerning any of such matters avoided*"[119].

By contrast to the ready expansion of anti-suit injunctions, the courts were reluctant to accept, until much later in the nineteenth century, the proposition that they ought to stay an English action in the light of pending proceedings abroad[120]. This was accepted in cases where the same plaintiff was proceeding in two courts at once[121], as in the 1882 case of *McHenry* v. *Lewis*[122]. But the jurisdiction to stay in favour of a foreign action was a power "which one ought to exercise with extreme caution"[123] as differences in the processes and remedies of the foreign court might justify the continuation of both actions. A century was to pass before the adoption of the doctrine of *forum non conveniens* into English law provided a ready means to stay litigation in favour of a foreign court[124].

---

[119] Supreme Court of Judicature Act 1873, s. 24 (7) (emphasis added). Substantially the same language is now found in the Supreme Court Act 1981, s. 49 (2).

[120] McClean, *supra* footnote 113, 939-942.

[121] A principle recognized in domestic cases by Sir Robert Phillimore in *Walsh* v. *Bishop of Lincoln*, (1874) LR 4 A & E 242 (Arches Court).

[122] (1883) LR 22 Ch. D. 397, 400.

[123] *Ibid.*, 406 per Cotton LJ.

[124] The decisive turning-point in English law was *MacShannon* v. *Rockware Glass Ltd.*, [1978] AC 795, 812 (HL), in which Lord Diplock observed:

A very different position applied north of the border in Scotland — which (despite the Treaty of Union with England in 1707) was, and remains, a separate jurisdiction, applying a Civil Law system. The Scots had, at least since 1610, begun to develop a doctrine *forum non competens,* a predecessor to *forum non conveniens*[125]. Early Scottish Conflict of Laws was strongly influenced by the Dutch writers of the seventeenth century, since most Scottish lawyers and judges were at that stage educated in the great Dutch law schools. But this doctrine was a Scottish innovation — driven in particular by a desire on the part of the Scottish judges to curb the perceived excesses of jurisdiction based upon the arrest of goods in Scotland.

It was the Scottish judges, therefore, who had to address first the question of international application of the doctrine of *lis pendens* (a doctrine with which, by education, they would have been well familiar) and its relationship with the more general discretion to decline jurisdiction on grounds of *forum non conveniens.* This the Court of Session did, after full argument in 1842 in the case of *Hawkins* v. *Wedderburn*[126]. The Court decided that the strict rule of *lis pendens* could not be mechanically applied in international cases. The judgment of the foreign court might not be enforceable in Scotland, and might in any event proceed on different

---

"If the distinction between this re-statement of the English law and the Scottish doctrine of forum non conveniens might on examination prove to be a fine one, I cannot think that it is any worse for that."

[125] *Vernour* v. *Elvies* (1610) 1 Dict. of Dec. 326. The best account is in Nuyts, *L'exception de* forum non conveniens (2003), Chaps. 1-3. See also Brand and Jablonski, *Forum Non Conveniens*: *History, Global Practice, and Future under the Hague Convention on Choice of Court Agreements* (2007) 7-9.

[126] IV Dunlop 924.

grounds and under different procedure. But, their Lordships went on:

> "[T]hough the original and strict rule of *lis alibi pendens* may not so apply, nevertheless there seems to be no doubt, that in cases of *lis alibi pendens*, even in a foreign court, it is competent for the Court in this country to consider the effect of that circumstance, and if it be such as in reason and equity to require the dismissal, or the sisting [staying], or modification of the action raised here, to give it such effect."[127]

At this decisive turning-point, therefore Scots law — the first legal system to consider the point — rejected a strict *lis pendens* rule for international cases, but instead incorporated the existence of parallel foreign proceedings as a factor within a more general discretion to decline jurisdiction.

If the English approach to foreign parallel proceedings was to remain for a century an aspect of the assertion of centralized justice in a growing empire — in which control rather than deference was the key tool — the motivation for the exercise of such control was not imperialism for its own sake, but rather the just and fair resolution of disputes. Embedded in this was also a conception of the function of litigation as being the equitable resolution of an entire dispute arising from the same transaction or occurrence, rather than merely a particular claim between plaintiff and defendant. This conception may be seen in liberal rules for the joinder of parties and claims, and in a wide panoply of rules to prevent abusive re-litigation, beyond *res judicata* to estoppel and abuse of process[128]. Baumgartner summarizes the position:

---

[127] *Ibid.*, 939.
[128] See generally Handley, *supra* footnote 54.

"For civil lawyers should not forget that, in the common law world, the search for the just and fair resolution of every single case (*Einzelfallgerechtig-keit* in German) has a long tradition in equity procedure, which developed in response to the rigid procedure in the common law courts, and which, often manned by clergy, operated on reason and morality rather than on legal technicalities." [129]

This brief foray into legal history may help to explain something of the current psychology underlying two of the world's major legal families in addressing conflicts between courts. As will be seen in subsequent chapters, this difference has left its imprint on many aspects of the way in which courts tackle the *lis pendens* problem: in private international litigation, arbitration, and even in public international litigation.

But it cannot be said any longer, if it ever could, that the *res judicata* parallel and the anti-suit injunction comprise the universe of techniques found in legislation and treaties, and utilized by the courts to deal with modern polycentric disputes. Accordingly, the next section of this first chapter will map the broad categories of techniques which are available today.

## D. *Legal Techniques for the Control of Competing Jurisdictions*

It has already been suggested that the concept of *lis pendens* does not denote a single solution to the problem of parallel proceedings. On the contrary, comparative analysis shows a range of potential solutions. The purpose of this fourth section of Chapter I is to introduce those techniques as the contents of a legal tool-box which might be used to resolve problems of

---

[129] Baumgartner, "Related Actions", (1998) 3 *Zeitschrift für Zivilprozeß International* 203, 218.

litispendence in the difference contexts in which they arise. Five sets of techniques may be identified.

## 1. *Tolerance of parallel proceedings and* res judicata

The first option is not to deal with litispendence at all. Rather, a court could simply tolerate the pendency of parallel proceedings, and leave any questions of conflicting judgments to be dealt with at the enforcement of judgments stage, by application of the rules of *res judicata.* For Judge Wilkey in *Laker Airways* this was the preferable route in most cases. He held that:

> "the fundamental corollary to concurrent jurisdiction must ordinarily be respected: parallel proceedings on the same *in personam* claim should ordinarily be allowed to proceed simultaneously, at least until a judgment is reached in one which can be pled as *res judicata* in the other" [130].

## 2. *Rules of priority*

The second, and most obvious, set of techniques is simple rules of priority as between two concurrent proceedings. The two most well-known examples of such a rule have already been mentioned. They are those found in the New York Convention and in the Brussels I Regulation. To these should be added an example from Public International Law (Article 23 of the Dispute Settlement Understanding of the WTO), and a typical example from Private International Law outside the framework of treaty arrangements (Article 9 of the Swiss Private International Law Act).

*New York Convention.* Article II (3) of the New York Convention [131] lays down a general rule of prior-

---

[130] *Laker Airways Ltd.* v. *Sabena, Belgian World Airlines, supra* footnote 74, 926-927.

[131] *Supra* footnote 99.

ity as between judicial proceedings arbitral proceedings, namely:

> "The court of a Contracting State, when seized of an action in a matter in respect of which the parties have made an agreement within the meaning of this article, shall, at the request of one of the parties, refer the parties to arbitration, unless it finds that the said agreement is null and void, inoperative or incapable of being performed."

*Brussels I Regulation.* Article 27 of the Brussels I Regulation [132] provides a general rule of priority as between judicial proceedings in European Union Member States, as follows:

> "Where proceedings involving the same cause of action and between the same parties are brought in the courts of different Member States, any court other than the court first seised shall of its own motion stay its proceedings until such time as the jurisdiction of the court first seised is established."

Embedded in that test are the twin requirements of same cause of action and same parties, or in the French text, "le même objet et la même cause". As will be seen, the absolute obligation to stay the proceedings where the requirements of Article 27 are met has led in turn to some very careful judicial consideration of the meaning of that phrase. For present purposes, it is sufficient to note that serves to align the requirements for *lis pendens* with those of *res judicata* on the recognition of judgments.

*World Trade Organization Dispute Settlement Understanding.* A rule of priority may not necessarily lead to a requirement of deference to another tribunal. On the contrary, it may lead to a claim of priority for

---

[132] *Supra* footnote 43.

the chosen tribunal itself. Thus, the Member States of
the WTO agreed to a strong rule of priority in relation
to trade disputes when they provided, in Article 23 of
the DSU:

> "*Strengthening of the Multilateral System*
>
> 1. When members seek the redress of a violation
> of obligations . . . under the covered agreements . . .
> they shall have recourse to, and abide by, the rules
> and procedures of this Understanding.
>
> 2. In such cases, Members shall:
>
> *(a)* not make a determination to the effect that a vio-
> lation has occurred . . . except through recourse to
> dispute settlement in accordance with the rules
> and procedures of this Understanding . . ."[133]

Now of course this Rule does not directly address
the possibility of other parallel proceedings determining the same trade dispute under other international
instruments (such as a regional trade agreement). As
will be seen in Chapter IV[134], the Appellate Body has
proceeded cautiously in relation to this question, which
has not yet arisen squarely for decision. But it
undoubtedly expresses a strong policy in favour of the
exclusivity of the DSU.

*Swiss Private International Law Act.* Finally, it is
possible for a rule of priority, which does contemplate
that the tribunal may decline jurisdiction in favour of
another court, to be conditioned expressly upon the
likely enforceability of any resulting foreign judgment
within the forum. Given the very close link between *lis
pendens* and *res judicata* it is perhaps unsurprising
that, where States have provided for litispendence out-

---

[133] *Supra* footnote 89.
[134] *Mexico — Tax Measures on Soft Drinks and Other
Beverages* (6 March 2006), WT/DS308/AB/R (WTO
Appellate Body) DSR 2006: 1, 3, [53]-[54]. Chapter IV,
Section A 3 *(b)*.

side a treaty framework, such a condition has often
been included. A typical modern example is Article 9
of the Swiss Private International Law Act, which provides:

*"Art. 9*

*VIII. Litispendance*

[1] Lorsqu'une action ayant le même objet est
déjà pendante entre les mêmes parties à l'étranger,
le tribunal suisse suspend la cause s'il est à prévoir
que la juridiction étrangère rendra, dans un délai
convenable, une décision pouvant être reconnue en
Suisse.

[2] Pour déterminer quand une action a été intro-
duite en Suisse, la date du premier acte nécessaire
pour introduire l'instance est décisive. La citation en
conciliation suffit.

[3] Le tribunal suisse se dessaisit dès qu'une décision étrangère pouvant être reconnue en Suisse lui
est présentée." [135]

## 3. *Consolidation of related proceedings*

A third technique which may be employed in dealing with closely related proceedings is that of consolidation, so as to enable claims concerned with substantially the same underlying facts, but perhaps involving
different parties, to be litigated once in a single forum.
Article 6 of the Brussels I Regulation reflects a strong
policy within Europe towards consolidation of claims
against a number of defendants:

"provided the claims are so closely connected that it
is expedient to hear and determine them together to

---

[135] Loi fedérale sur le droit international privé (18 December 1987), *RS* 291.

avoid the risk of irreconcilable judgments resulting from separate proceedings"[136].

In arbitration, by contrast, the possibilities for consolidation of related proceedings are very limited. The usual starting point is that: "Each tribunal remains sovereign and may retain . . . a different solution for resolving the same problem."[137] A rare example of specific provision for consolidation is found in the North American Free Trade Agreement (NAFTA)[138] where the provision for arbitration is founded upon the treaty itself, and thus it was possible for the States parties to provide for consolidation. Article 1126 (2) of NAFTA contemplates the establishment of a special Consolidation Tribunal which may, if it:

"is satisfied that claims have been submitted to arbitration under Article 1120 [the general submission to arbitration clause under NAFTA] that have a question of law or fact in common, the Tribunal may, in the interests of fair and efficient resolution of the claims, and after hearing the disputing parties, by order:

*(a)* assume jurisdiction over, and hear and determine together, all or part of the claims; or

*(b)* assume jurisdiction over, and hear and determine one or more of the claims, the determination of which it believes would assist in the resolution of the others."

In one case under this provision[139], the Consoli-

---

[136] *Supra* footnote 43.

[137] *AES Corp.* v. *Argentine Republic* (Jurisdiction), ICSID Case No. ARB/02/17 (ICSID, 2005, Dupuy P, Böckstiegel and Janiero) [30].

[138] North American Free Trade Agreement (adopted 17 December 1992, entered into force 1 January 1994), 107 Stat. 2057; *CTS* 1994, No. 2, (1993) 32 *ILM* 289.

[139] *Canfor Corp.* v. *United States of America, Tembec et al.* v. *United States of America, Terminal Forest Products*

dation Tribunal found the overriding object and purpose of the procedure to be that of "procedural economy"[140]. The Tribunal identified three factors which would bear on that question: time; costs; and the avoidance of conflicting decisions[141]. It observed:

> "The desirability of avoiding conflicting results is not limited to cases where the parties are the same. Cases with different parties may present the same legal issues arising out of the same event or related to the same measure. Conflicting results then may take place if the findings with respect to those issues differ in two or more cases."[142]

## 4. *Party autonomy, election and waiver*

(a) *Stays of proceedings in support of choice of forum clauses.* A fourth set of techniques to deal with parallel claims flows from the large measure of autonomy granted to the parties in international disputes to choose the forum in which they wish to litigate. In contractual matters, this is done by an agreement in writing to choose an arbitral or judicial forum. As the Supreme Court of Canada has recently stressed, both arbitration agreements and choice of forum clauses serve one of the main purposes of Private International Law, because they "foster certainty and foreseeability in international commercial relations"[143]. The New York Convention enshrines international agreement on

---

*Ltd.* v. *United States of America* (Consolidation) (NAFTA, 2005, van den Berg P, de Mestral and Robinson).

[140] *Ibid.*, [73]; accord: Alvarez, "Arbitration under the North American Free Trade Agreement", (2000) 16 *Arb. Int'l* 393, 414.

[141] *Ibid.*, [126].

[142] *Ibid.*, [133].

[143] *GreCon Dimter Inc.* v. *J. R. Normand Inc.*, [2005] 2 SCR 401, 255 DLR (4th) 257, [22].

the requirement to stay litigation in support of an arbitration agreement. The new Hague Convention on Choice of Court Agreements 2005 will, when it enters into force, embody a complementary principle in the case of choice of court agreements [144].

An exclusive choice of forum clause carries with it a right to stay parallel litigation brought in breach of the clause. However, such clauses are not self-executing. The freedom of action which is the essence of party autonomy also entails responsibility. The party wishing to take the benefit of such a clause in the face of litigation which would otherwise overlap with the matters subjected to arbitration or litigation in another forum by virtue of the clause must apply for a stay. Otherwise, the benefit of the clause may be waived by submission [145]. As will be seen in Chapter III, the very fact that such an application must be made raises itself a question of parallel proceedings. Who is to decide on the validity and extent of the clause — the court which is deciding whether to relinquish jurisdiction, or the arbitral tribunal which is deciding whether to accept it?

(b) Electa una via/*Fork in the road*. But the principle of party autonomy need not simply support exclusive choices of forum. It also lies behind techniques of election between a number of equally available fora agreed between the parties. This is frequently the solution adopted in investment treaties providing for mixed arbitration between foreign investor and host State. Thus, for example, the Energy Charter Treaty permits the investor to choose between host State courts; previous contractually agreed methods of dispute resolution;

---

[144] Art. 6, available at www.hcch.net, discussed *infra*, Chapter V, Section A 3.

[145] New York Convention, *supra* footnote 99, Art. II (1) and the Brussels I Regulation, *supra* footnote 43, Art. 24.

or arbitration under ICSID; the ICSID Additional Facility; *ad hoc* under UNCITRAL Rules; or the Arbitration Institute of the Stockholm Chamber of Commerce [146]. The resulting cafeteria-style approach to choice of forum thus confers jurisdiction on a range of potential fora.

In some cases, investment treaties do not deal expressly with what the consequences may be should elements of the same dispute have been submitted to another forum (whether one of those provided under the treaty, or otherwise). But in other cases, the treaty expressly provides that, by submitting its dispute to one of the nominated fora, the investor makes an election. Thus, for example, Article 8 (3) of the Chile model BIT provides:

> "Once the investor has submitted the dispute to the competent tribunal of the Contracting Party in whose territory the investment was made or to international arbitration, that election shall be final." [147]

The Energy Charter Treaty permits Member States to choose to make an investor's prior election of a domestic remedy preclusive of the submission to international arbitration. This is done by the rather curious mechanism of scheduling a list of States parties who "do not give such unconditional consent" to the submission of the dispute to international arbitration "where the Investor has previously submitted the dispute" to local courts or to any contractually agreed dispute resolution [148]. Such clauses have become known as "fork-in-

---

[146] Energy Charter Treaty (signed 17 December 1994, entered into force 16 April 1998), 2080 *UNTS* 100, Art. 26.

[147] Chile Model BIT reprinted in UNCTAD, *International Investment Instruments: A Compendium* (1996), Vol. III, 143, 147.

[148] Energy Charter Treaty, *supra* footnote 146, Art. 26 (3) *(b)* (i). There are 24 States which have made this election (listed in Annex ID).

the-road', or *electa una via,* provisions, since they require the investor to make an irrevocable election of one dispute resolution route. Following such an election, he cannot then subsequently change his mind and pursue litigation in another of the listed fora.

The other field in which this technique is commonly found is that of human rights[149]. The prototype provision is that found in the European Convention, which precludes the Court from dealing with any individual application that "has already been submitted to another procedure of international investigation or settlement and contains no relevant new information"[150].

(c) *Waiver.* An alternative to irrevocable election at the time of commencement of the first set of proceedings is simply to provide that the claimant must waive alternative dispute resolution options at the time of commencement of the proceedings in question. That solution was adopted in NAFTA, Article 1121 (1) *(b)* of which provides:

> *"Article 1121 : Conditions Precedent*
> *to Submission of a Claim to Arbitration*
>
> 1. A disputing investor may submit a claim . . . to arbitration only if:
>
> . . .
>
> *(b)* the investor and . . . the enterprise, waive their right to initiate or continue before any administrative tribunal or court under the law of any Party, or other dispute settlement procedures, any proceedings with respect to the measure of

---

[149] See Shany, *The Competing Jurisdictions of International Courts and Tribunals* (2003) 213-217.

[150] Art. 35 (2) *(b)*, European Convention for the Protection of Human Rights and Fundamental Freedoms (signed 4 November 1950, entered into force 3 September 1953), 213 *UNTS* 221, as amended by Protocol No. 11 (signed 11 May 1994, entered into force 1 November 1998), *ETS* No. 155.

the disputing Party that is alleged to be a breach
. . . except for proceedings for injunctive,
declaratory or other extraordinary relief, not
involving the payment of damages." [151]

This provision defines the necessary parallelism not by
reference to the dispute (which, as will be seen, is a
highly problematic legal concept in this context).
Rather, the test focuses factually on the state measure
itself which is alleged to give rise to the claim.

## 5. Discretions to decline jurisdiction or control parallel litigation

A fifth set of techniques for dealing with parallel
litigation is to confer upon court the discretion to
decline jurisdiction in favour of the courts of another
State where related litigation is already pending. This
technique may be seen in both Common Law and
Civil Law countries.

(a) *The doctrine of* forum non conveniens. In Common Law countries, following the adoption from
Scotland of doctrine of *forum non conveniens, lis pendens* has been seen simply as one factor which might
lead the Court to decline to exercise its jurisdiction in
favour of a foreign court [152]. The doctrine provides a
general power in the English court to stay its proceedings if England is an inappropriate forum where there
is another court of competent jurisdiction which is
clearly more appropriate for the trial of the action and
it is not unjust to deprive the claimant of the right to
trial in England. It is difficult in historical terms to see
this doctrine as an essential part of the architecture of
Private International Law in the Common Law. On the

---

[151] *Supra* footnote 138.
[152] Collins *et al., supra* footnote 10, [12-035]-[12-037]; Bell, *Forum Shopping and Venue in Transnational Litigation* (2003), Chap. 4.

contrary, as was shown in Section C above, restraint of foreign proceedings has a much older lineage than the self-denying ordinance of *forum non conveniens,* which was a late import from Scots law, not fully consummated in English law until 1986[153].

The inclusion of *lis pendens* within this more general discretion allows the court to consider the impact of the pending foreign litigation on the dispute between the parties. If it has been commenced for purely tactical reasons, and is at an early stage, then it may have little significance on the court's overall consideration of appropriate forum. If, on the other hand, it is well advanced and likely to have a considerable effect on the parties, then it may well be an important factor. If the same claimant has commenced both sets of proceedings, he will usually be put to his election[154].

The ability of the English courts to utilize the *forum non conveniens* discretion in favour of the courts of non-Brussels I Regulation countries has now been severely circumscribed by the decision of the European Court in *Owusu* v. *Jackson*[155]. But, in the intervening two decades, it has been adopted in various degrees in many other Commonwealth countries[156].

In the United States, the doctrine of *forum non conveniens* has a much older lineage in the exercise of fed-

---

[153] *Supra* Section C 2. Reception of the Scots doctrine in England was rejected by the House of Lords in *The Atlantic Star*, *supra* footnote 80, received a cautious reception four years later in *MacShannon* v. *Rockware Glass Ltd.*, *supra* footnote 124, and full adoption in the current leading authority, *Spiliada Maritime Corp.* v. *Cansulex Ltd.*, [1987] AC 460 (HL).

[154] *Australian Commercial Research and Development Ltd.* v. *ANZ McCaughan Merchant Bank Ltd.*, [1989] 3 All ER 65 (Ch).

[155] Case C-281/02 [2005] *ECR* I-1383, discussed *infra*, Chapter II, Section B 3 *(b)*.

[156] *Infra*, Chapter II, Section C 1.

eral admiralty jurisdiction[157]. It has formed a part of the approach to jurisdiction generally since the decisions of the US Supreme Court in *Gulf Oil Corp.* v. *Gilbert*[158] and *Piper Aircraft Corp.* v. *Reyno*[159]. The application of this doctrine (in the particular form which it has taken in the United States) provides, in most cases, the framework within which American courts consider parallel litigation[160].

(b) *Related proceedings.* In international commercial litigation, it is more unusual to find express provision for the stay of related, as opposed to identical cases. But the Brussels I Regulation, developing a provision which was included in the original Brussels Convention 1968, contains just such a discretion[161]. Article 28 provides:

> "1. Where related actions are pending in the courts of different Member States, any court other than the court first seised may stay its proceedings.
>
> 2. Where these actions are pending at first instance, any court other than the court first seised may also, on the application of one of the parties, decline jurisdiction if the court first seised has jurisdiction over the actions in question and its law permits the consolidation thereof.
>
> 3. For the purposes of this Article, actions are deemed to be related where they are so closely connected that it is expedient to hear and determine them together to avoid the risk of irreconcilable judgments resulting from separate proceedings."

Article 28's overriding concern with the degree of connection between claims necessary to justify consoli-

---

[157] Brand and Jablonski, *supra* footnote 125, Chap. 3.
[158] 330 US 501, 67 S. Ct. 839 (1947).
[159] 454 US 235, 102 S. Ct. 252 (1981).
[160] von Mehren, *supra* footnote 45, 347.
[161] Magnus/Mankowski/Fentiman, *Brussels I Regulation* (2007), Art. 28.

dation is evident from both the test in Article 28 (2)
and the definition of related actions in Article 28 (3).
This has been further reinforced by the addition of the
same test for related actions into the text of Article 6
(1) of the Regulation, codifying the decision of the
European Court to this effect in *Kalfelis* v. *Schröder*[162].
In a refreshingly liberal decision, the European Court
has also confirmed that the concept of the risk of irreconcilable judgments in Article 28 is to be construed
flexibly, as being "to improve coordination of the exercise of judicial functions within the Community and
to avoid conflicting and contradictory decisions, even
where the separate enforcement of each of them is not
precluded"[163]. Thus, its provisions may operate simply
where common issues of fact arise and would be
decided in the two proceedings. It is not limited to
issues which the court would be required to decide in
order to render judgment[164].

(c) *The anti-suit injunction.* The final possible technique is to restrain the parties from pursuing parallel
litigation in another court or tribunal by issuing an
anti-suit injunction. As has been seen, this form of
order was the classical remedy exercised by the Court
of Equity in asserting its right to protect its process
from parallel litigation in the Common Law courts. It
has now found wide application by Common Law
courts in transnational cases in order to prevent vexatious and oppressive forum shopping by litigants,

---

[162] *Kalfelis* v. *Bankhaus Schröder Münchmeyer Hengst
& Co.*, Case C-189/87, [1988] *ECR* 5565; and see
Magnus/Mankowski/Muir Watt, *Brussels I Regulation*
(2007), Art. 6, notes 4-7. Art. 22 of the Brussels Convention (the predecessor to Art. 28) did not specify the degree
of connection between claims required for the operation of
Art. 6 (1).

[163] *The Tatry*, Case C-406/92, [1994] *ECR* I-5439, [54].

[164] *Sarrio SA* v. *Kuwait Investment Authority*, [1999]
AC 32 (HL).

which may amount to an abuse of the process[165]. The remedy has also surfaced in arbitration — in orders issued by national courts, sometimes to protect a choice of arbitration, and other times to repress such a choice. There is even precedent for an arbitral tribunal itself issuing an order directing the parties not to pursue parallel litigation in national courts[166].

## E. *The Rule of Law and the Function of Adjudication in International Cases*

Underlying the discussion thus far, however, is a major question which has not been squarely addressed: namely on what basis should we be concerned about international parallel proceedings at all? After all, courts and tribunals operate within specific legal systems which confer upon them their jurisdictional competence. Should they not have, as has indeed been held not infrequently, an "unflagging obligation" to exercise that the jurisdiction thus conferred? Why should they be concerned with the activities of other courts, which are operating within their own constraints, and over which they can have no direct control? The answer to this question could in turn supply important clues to the nature of the adjudicatory process within and across legal systems.

Traditional legal theory as to the nature of the obligation to obey adjudicatory authority, whether derived from Thomas Hobbes or John Locke, may well explain much about the structure of particular systems of jurisdiction[167]. Indeed the development of the Common

---

[165] *Infra*, Chapter II, Section D; for a comprehensive survey of the English authorities, see Raphael, *The Anti-suit Injunction* (2008).

[166] *Infra*, Chapter III, Section B 3.

[167] Cappalli, "Locke as the Key: A Unifed and Coherent Theory of *In Personam* Jurisdiction", (1992-1993) 43 *Case West. Res. LR* 97.

Law approach to jurisdiction may appropriately be
described as a move from power to fairness as the basis
for adjudicatory authority, terms which sit well along
the jurisprudential spectrum of these explanations of
the nature of the relationship between ruler and subject [168]. But legal theory has, traditionally at least, had
little to say about the mediation of relationships
between rival systems of adjudicatory authority, each
of which may have a claim upon the person or dispute [169].

In *Public International Law*, it is possible to take as
a point of departure the proposition that, however disparate may be the jurisdictions of particular courts and
tribunals, they all ultimately owe their origin to a
single legal system. They are creatures of treaty. Treaties
only gain legal force by virtue of the existence of a
general legal system, since they would be "mere pieces
of paper devoid of all legal effect" [170] unless they were
in turn "governed by international law" [171]. The work of
the International Law Commission's Study Group on
the Fragmentation of International Law has demonstrated that even the most detailed self-contained
regimes existing in international law today rely for
their effective operation upon the existence of general
international law [172]. In turn, the ultimate unity of
Public International Law, however diverse may be its

---

[168] Nygh, "The Common Law Approach", in McLachlan
and Nygh, *Transnational Tort Litigation: Jurisdictional
Principles* (1996) 21.

[169] von Mehren, *supra* footnote 45, 33-6; Michaels,
*supra* footnote 101, 1033.

[170] To borrow the language of Lord Diplock in the context of transnational contracts in *Amin Rasheed Shipping
Corp.* v. *Kuwait Insurance Co.*, [1984] AC 50, 65 (HL).

[171] Vienna Convention on the Law of Treaties (signed
2 May 1969, entered into force 23 May 1969), 1155 *UNTS*
331, Art. 2 (1) *(a)*.

[172] *Supra* footnote 27, [191]-[194].

judicial institutions and their procedures, makes it possible at least to consider the emergence of a common law of international adjudication in shared judicial procedures and remedies [173].

*Arbitration* might be thought to represent the most fragmented and atomized form of international dispute resolution — the jurisdiction of each arbitral tribunal limited by its *compromis* or arbitration agreement. Indeed, the Supreme Court of Canada has recently held, in *Dell Computer Corp.* v. *Union des consommateurs* that:

> "Arbitration is part of no state's judicial system . . . The arbitrator has no allegiance or connection to any single country . . . In short, arbitration is a creature that owes its existence to the will of the parties alone." [174]

Yet the field of international commercial arbitration (beginning with its own master treaty, the New York Convention) has found an increasing degree of convergence around common procedural principles, especially through the promulgation of model laws and rules which have in turn driven the reform of national laws and the rules of arbitral institutions. It is probably no longer an exaggeration to say that international commercial arbitration has become its own legal system, albeit one which ultimately depends for enforcement upon the co-operation of national courts. Gaillard in his lectures to the Academy has recently described this as an *"ordre juridique arbitral"* [175]. The recent magisterial treatise by Born

---

[173] Brown, *A Common Law of International Adjudication* (2007).

[174] [2007] 2 SCR 801, (2007) 284 DLR (4th) 577, [51].

[175] Gaillard, *Aspects philosophiques du droit de l'arbitrage international* (2007) [133].

"rests on the premise that the treatments of international commercial arbitration in different national legal systems are not diverse, unrelated phenomena, *but rather form a common corpus of international arbitration law which has a global application*"[176].

This conception of a *system* of international arbitration has now also received judicial recognition at the highest level. The French Cour de cassation held in *PT Putrabali Adyamulia* v. *Est Epices* that:

"an international arbitral award — which is not anchored to any national legal order — is an international judicial decision whose validity must be ascertained with regard to the rules applicable in the country where its recognition and enforcement is sought"[177].

In each of Public International Law and International Arbitration, therefore, it may be possible to analyse the interaction between exercises of adjudicatory authority within the structure of a larger system, however diverse the operation of individual tribunals within that system may be.

What, then, of *Private International Law*, which, after all, is the dominant context in which international parallel proceedings continue to arise? Does the proliferation of national legal systems, each with their own sources of adjudicatory authority, inevitably condemn private international litigation to fragmentation and parochialism? Certainly, the failure at The Hague in 2001 of the most recent efforts to conclude a global judgments convention bears sober witness to the difficulty of reaching multilateral agreement on the proper limits of the exercise of adjudicatory authority[178]. To

---

[176] Born, *International Commercial Arbitration* (2009) 4.
[177] 29 June 2007 (2008) 24 *Arb. Int.* 293, 295 (noted Pinsolle, (2008) 24 *Arb. Int.* 277).
[178] *Infra*, Chapter V, Section A 2.

what extent may we, in the absence of such multilateral agreement, properly speak of a "system" of private international litigation? The question is an important one, since in turn affects the extent to which a court or tribunal may or must take account of proceedings before another court.

In order to answer this question, it is necessary to return for a moment to consider the basic reasons for the emergence of rules of the conflict of laws, for it is that branch of legal science itself which in fact provides the most considered account of the interaction between legal systems. For Huber, writing at the outset of the emergence of the post-Westphalian State, the answer was to be found in *comity*. He stated his three fundamental maxims as:

> "(1) The laws of each state have force within the limits of that government and bind all subject to it, but not beyond (*Digest* 2, 1, 20).
> (2) All persons within the limits of a government, whether they live there permanently or temporarily, are deemed to be subjects thereof (*Digest*, 48, 22, 7 § 10 i.f.)
> (3) Sovereigns will so act by way of comity that rights acquired within the limits of a government retain their force everywhere so far as they do not cause prejudice to the power or rights of such government or of its subjects."[179]

Dicey scorned this account, writing in the first edition of his *Conflict of Laws* in 1896, that the need for a system of Private International Law

> "does not arise from the desire of the sovereign of England or any other sovereign to show courtesy to other states. It flows from the impossibility of

---

[179] Huber, "De Conflictu Legum", *supra* footnote 63, [2].

otherwise determining whole classes of cases without gross inconvenience and injustice to litigants, whether natives or foreigners." [180]

But the traditional contempt shown by the leading English text-book writers toward the notion of comity as a basis for Private International Law is significantly at odds with the persistent affection which judges have shown for the doctrine in explaining the rationale for their decisions [181]. It may in any event be doubted whether the conception of comity which Huber had in mind was really as much to do with courtesy between sovereigns as has often been suggested. Although couched in terms of political independence, and thus underpinned by a nascent Public International Law idea of sovereign jurisdictions, comity was to be applied by the courts through the means of a detailed set of legal rules of the *droit commun*. Indeed, he proceeds immediately to explain that:

"nothing could be more inconvenient to commerce and to international usage than that transactions valid by the law of one place should be rendered of no effect elsewhere on account of a difference in the law. And that is the reason for the third maxim . . ." [182]

Story, defending Huber's doctrine, adds:

"The true foundation on which the administration of international law must rest is, that the rules which are to govern are those which arise from mutual interest and utility, from a sense of the inconveniences which would result from a contrary

---

[180] *Supra* footnote 49, 10.
[181] Collins, "Comity in Modern Private International Law", in Fawcett (ed.), *Reform and Development of Private International Law* (2002) 89, and the cases there cited.
[182] Huber, *supra* footnote 49, [2 (3)].

doctrine, and from a sort of moral necessity to do justice, in order that justice may be done to us in return." [183]

Stated in the plainer language of today, the Supreme Court of Canada has opined that "the twin objectives sought by private international law in general [are] order and fairness" [184]. The author has elsewhere suggested that the fundamental concerns of a modern system of Private International Law are three-fold:

"*(a)* to provide functional responses to the modern international commercial context in which cross-border problems arise;

*(b)* to provide effective and fair remedies in civil disputes when those disputes cross national borders; and,

*(c)* to resolve the otherwise irreconcilable conflicts between national legal systems in order to do substantial justice between the parties" [185].

Such a formulation sees the two paramount factors being, as Lord Hope of Craighead put it, "the private interests of any of the parties or the ends of justice in

---

[183] Story, *supra* footnote 70, [37]. Watson, *Joseph Story and the Comity of Errors* (1992), argues (with erudition, spirit and wit) that Story misread Huber by treating comity as a matter of discretion rather than obligation. Cogent though this criticism may be of the subsequent uses of the doctrine in US courts, it is, in the present writer's view, a misplaced criticism of Story's own work. Story used Huber in the elaboration of a series of binding Common Law rules of choice of law. The cited passage simply seeks to explain why we must have such rules, not to suggest that they are optional matters of discretion.

[184] *Holt Cargo Systems Inc.* v. *ABC Containerline NV* [2001] 3 SCR 907, [71] citing its earlier judgment in *Morguard Investments Ltd.* v. *De Savoye*, [1990] 3 SCR 1077, (1990) 76 DLR (4th) 256.

[185] McLachlan, "International Litigation and the Reworking of the Conflict of Laws", *supra* footnote 21.

the case which is before the court" [186]. If this serves to emphasize the *private* function of rules of Private International Law, it is equally important to keep in mind its *public international* function. As La Forest J put it:

> "The truth is that a system of law built on what a particular court considers to be the expectations of the parties or what it thinks is fair, without engaging in further probing about what it means by this, does not bear the hallmarks of a rational system of law. Indeed in the present context it wholly obscures the nature of the problem. In dealing with legal issues having an impact in more than one legal jurisdiction, we are not really engaged in that kind of interest balancing. We are engaged in a structural problem . . .
>
> On the international plane, the relevant underlying reality is the territorial limits of law under the international legal order. The underlying postulate of public international law is that generally each state has jurisdiction to make and apply law within its territorial limit. Absent a breach of some overriding norm, other states as a matter of 'comity' will ordinarily respect such actions and are hesitant to interfere with what another state chooses to do within those limits. Moreover, to accommodate the movement of people, wealth and skills across state lines, a byproduct of modern civilization, they will in great measure recognize the determination of legal issues in other states. And to promote the same values, they will open their national forums for the resolution of specific legal disputes arising in other jurisdictions consistent with the interests and internal values of the forum state. These are the

---

[186] *Lubbe* v. *Cape plc*, [2000] 2 Lloyd's Rep. 383, 397 (HL).

realities that must be reflected and accommodated in private international law." [187]

Of course the reception of foreign law ultimately depends upon the consent of the receiving State, as Huber well recognized. But such consent supplies the limits of, not the justification for, the application of foreign law. Private International Law generally teaches us that the conception of justice thus applied must transcend the solutions of particular national legal systems, for only in this way can the application of foreign law be justified. The established techniques of choice of law presume the *functional* equivalence of the two potentially applicable legal systems, even if the substantive solutions found in each law are very different. Choice of law rules determine which of the respective systems of law must be applied to what is, after all, a single legal relationship or dispute.

It is submitted that this conception of the nature and purpose of the Conflict of Laws is potentially equally applicable to the conflict of litigation. In this context, the arguments advanced in French doctrine for the extension of litispendence to international cases as a matter of the *droit commun* (and not by way of international convention) are instructive. It was the argument the refusal of the courts to recognize a foreign proceeding was promoting forum shopping; favouring the unscrupulous litigant; and that such a limitation promoted disorder and frustrated the judicial process which finally provoked a change in the doctrine. In turn, following a landmark decision of the Cour de cassation in 1974, these ideas led to a change in the law [188].

---

[187] *Tolofson* v. *Jensen* [1994] 3 SCR 1022, 120 DLR (4th) 289, 302-303.

[188] Holleaux, *supra* footnote 47; *Soc. Miniera di Fragne c. C$^{ie}$ européenne d'équipement industriel* (Cass. civ., 26 November 1974, *Rev. crit.* 1975.491, note D.

It was said that, if French law could find sufficient functional equivalence with foreign legal systems to enable it to recognize and enforce their judgments, it ought to be able to recognize their process. The German courts, which began to recognize litispendence in international cases as early as the turn of the twentieth century [189], have referred to it as "für das internationale Recht gültiger Rechtsgrundsatz" (a principle of law valid in international law) [190].

So the justifications for the extension of the doctrine of litispendence internationally are really the same as those which it has been seen apply to Private International Law more generally. From the point of view of the litigants, the dispute is not of its nature confined to a particular legal system. A failure to take account of foreign proceedings relating to the same dispute could cause gross injustice to the private interests of the litigants, as well as failing to give effect as a matter of the international legal order to the judicial acts of foreign courts within their own territories.

The conception of justice which is required in response must therefore transcend particular national legal systems, but need not necessarily require the existence of a supra-national legal system. Rather, it may be justified by reference to a cosmopolitan conception of what the Rule of Law requires from the function of the process of adjudication in international cases. In a recent essay, the legal philosopher Waldron argues that modern positivist theories of the Rule of Law have systematically underplayed the significance of courts for

---

Holleaux, *Clunet*, 1975.108, note A. Ponsard, Ancel and Lequette, *Les grands arrêts de la jurisprudence française de droit international privé* (4th ed., 2001) 519, 524-525.

[189] Pålsson, *supra* footnote 102, 68-69; RG, 26 January 1892, *JW*, 1892, 124, *Clunet*, 1893, 905; RG, 23 June 1893, *JW*, 1893, 350; RG, 13 April 1901, *RGZ* 49, 340, 344.

[190] BGH 2 October 1957, *NJW*, 1958, 103.

the Rule of Law — in marked contrast to the way in which the concept is commonly used in popular and political discourse[191]. He submits, in particular, that the *structure* and *procedures* of courts are key indicators of the operation of the Rule of Law. "They capture a deep and important sense associated foundationally with the idea of a legal system, that law is a mode of governing people that treats them with respect."[192]

Now, in modern times, a number of these elements of what the Rule of Law requires, by common consent, of the adjudicatory process have found codification in the human right to a fair trial[193]. It has been illuminatingly argued that this right applies as much to a court's decision on matters of jurisdiction, as to other aspects of the litigation process[194]. Seen in this light, in the case of international parallel proceedings, the right to a fair trial as an aspect of the Rule of Law, requires the court to consider the impact of proceedings pending in other jurisdiction in order to ensure the just treatment of the litigants before it.

The Privy Council decided exactly this, when it decided that the Trinidad courts must await the out-

---

[191] Waldron, "The Concept and the Rule of Law", NYU Public Law & Legal Theory Research Paper Series Working Paper No. 08-50 (2008).

[192] *Ibid.*, 24.

[193] European Convention for the Protection of Human Rights and Fundamental Freedoms *supra* footnote 150, Art. 6 (1); American Convention on Human Rights (signed 22 November 1969, entered into force 18 July 1978), 1144 *UNTS* 123, Art. 8 (1).

[194] Schlosser, "Jurisdiction in International Litigation: The Issue of Human Rights in Relation to National Law and the Brussels Convention", [1991] *Rivista di diritto internazionale* 5; Nuyts, "The Enforcement of Jurisdiction Agreements further to *Gasser* and the Community Principle of Abuse of Right", in Vareilles-Sommières (ed.), *Forum Shopping in the European Judicial Area* (2007) 55.

come of pending application to the Inter-American
Court of Human Rights before proceeding with the
execution of a condemned prisoner in *Thomas* v.
*Baptiste*[195]. In doing so, it construed and applied a provision of the Trinidad Constitution which guaranteed
the human right to the "due process of law". The
Judicial Committee rejected the notion that this expression was confined to internal processes of Trinidadian
law. Rather, it held:

> " 'due process of law' is a compendious expression
> in which the word 'law' does not refer to any par-
> ticular law and is not a synonym for common law
> or statute. Rather it invokes the concept of the rule
> of law itself and the universally accepted standards of
> justice observed by civilised nations which observe
> the rule of law." [196]

Thus far the account of the interaction between
national court systems finds its justification in the classic foundations of the conflict of laws. One might ask
whether the process of globalization — the pervasive
phenomenon of our times — has wrought changes in
the landscape which require a fresh account of the
nature of judicial interactions. Lord Mustill asks:

> "Does the concept of a legal discipline entitled
> 'the conflict of laws' have any meaning, now that
> in cyberspace national boundaries are almost irrele-
> vant?" [197]

Certainly, globalization has proved a spur to the
massive continued growth in resort to international
commercial arbitration, as an internationalized form of

---

[195] [2000] 2 AC 1, 22 (PC (Trinidad and Tobago)).
[196] *Ibid.*
[197] Mustill, "What Are Judges For?" (23rd F. A. Mann
Lecture, 1999 (unpublished)).

dispute resolution, delocalized, so far as possible, from national control. Further, the emergence of many types of hybrid arbitral and international tribunals has served to blur conventional boundaries separating national and international law; private international disputes from public international disputes. Thus, for example, the development of investment treaty arbitration, involving the invocation of a direct claim of a foreign private party against a sovereign State before an international arbitral tribunal, represents a new paradigm for the settlement of investment disputes. As the discussion in Chapter III will show, a constant feature of such cases has been the close interaction — often contentious — between litigation before the national courts of the host State in such cases and resort to international arbitration.

Moreover, the individual now figures as a complainant before international human rights tribunals, and as a defendant before international criminal tribunals. These are both arenas which were traditionally the province of national courts alone, and in which may be expected to drive much closer inter-penetration between national and international systems of adjudication — a phenomenon explored in more detail in Chapter IV.

In these circumstances, it is no doubt tempting — as Dean Jessup so famously did in his 1956 Storrs Lectures on Jurisprudence on the topic "transnational law" [198] — to herald the emergence of a new field of "transnational litigation, presided over by a "global community of courts" [199]. Yet Anne-Marie Slaughter, a proponent of this idea, herself acknowledges its partial achievement and its limitations. Her examples are principally drawn from Common Law jurisprudence.

---

[198] Jessup, *Transnational Law* (1956).
[199] Slaughter, *supra* footnote 72.

A number of the American cases which she cites in
support of a new approach may be read, as she acknowledges[200], as much as a hegemonic American
power play as evidence of a new spirit of "ongoing interaction".

There is a real danger, too, that fuzzing the edges
between different forms of adjudication in the desire
to create a general category of transnational litigation
may actually distract from the important task of considering where the differences between courts really
matter. For example, as will be seen in Chapter III, the
early experience of investment treaty tribunals with
interactions with host State courts supports the importance of a careful delineation of the province of each
court's power and responsibility. For the reasons which
La Forest J so well explained in the passage just cited
from *Tolofson*[201], globalization, so far from weakening,
actually reinforces the need to respect, and give effect
to, the distinct province of other legal systems.

But it is undoubtedly true that the huge rise in the
incidence of litigation across borders has driven a
much deeper level of interaction between courts and
tribunals than can be fully accommodated within a
Huberian paradigm of separate national jurisdictions
and mutual recognition. This need not result in unilateral assertions of extraterritorial control in the absence
of multilateral agreement. Instead, practice in many
aspects of international civil procedure supports the
emergence of international judicial co-operation[202]. As
Millett LJ put it, the respect which two courts ought to
show for the territorial integrity of each other's jurisdiction, "should not inhibit a court in one jurisdiction

---

[200] *Ibid.*, 207-208.
[201] *Supra* footnote 187.
[202] For a very full study see Schlosser, *supra* footnote 53.

from rendering whatever assistance it properly can to a court in another" [203].

Of course, in many cases, such co-operation has been the product of international agreement by treaty. But this is not so in every case. Some of the most prominent examples of trans-border co-operation between courts in recent years were initiated by the judges themselves in the course of actual pending litigation. The agreements reached between courts in the integrated management of transnational insolvencies following the collapse of worldwide groups of companies — most notably the *Maxwell* and *BCCI* cases — provide a notable example of ground-breaking co-operation of this kind [204]. It is notable that the extensions of the doctrine of *lis pendens* to international cases have in many countries — from both the Civil and Common Law traditions — been achieved as a result of *judicial* initiative for co-operation in the interests of the international administration of justice, rather than by statute or treaty.

Surveying the development of rules on foreign *lis pendens* and connected foreign cases in 2002, Walter argues that:

> "there is a trend from confrontation to coordination . . . This development is only logical, in a day and age where politics, business life and culture are subject to globalization. However, this development is to be welcomed regardless of these factors, since it will contribute to a better administration of justice in general." [205]

---

[203] *Crédit Suisse Fides Trust SA* v. *Cuoghi*, [1998] QB 818, 827 (CA).

[204] Schlosser, *supra* footnote 53, 262-276, discussed further *infra*, Chapter V, Section B 3.

[205] Walter, "*Lis Alibi Pendens* and *Forum Non Conveniens*; From Confrontation via Co-ordination to Collaboration", (2002) 4 *European Journal of Law Reform* 69, 85.

The evidence for such a claim in the positive law and the practice of courts and tribunals will have to be considered in the ensuing chapters. In truth, as in so many other fields of international relations, different conclusions can be drawn by courts from the imperatives of globalization. Only once the nature and consequences of each approach taken currently in the law have been examined, will it be possible to assess, in Chapter V, the strength of the claim of a trend towards coordination.

In conclusion, then, the following five short propositions may be put forward on the basis of the analysis so far, which may serve as a platform for what is to come:

(1) The long-standing controversy over the extent to which the doctrine of *lis pendens* applies internationally has taken on renewed urgency and complexity today — in part simply because the process of globalization has driven much more frequent and closer interactions between courts; but in part also because a host of new international courts and tribunals have been created.

(2) Existing rationales for the rule (anticipatory *res judicata*; judicial efficiency; and declining or "finetuning" jurisdiction), while explaining some aspects, do not on examination get at the heart of why internationally parallel proceedings ought to be controlled. This cannot be reduced to a question which is related either simply to the assumption of jurisdiction or to the enforcement of judgments. Rather, it is concerned with the interaction between systems of adjudication.

(3) The doctrine of *lis pendens* had its origins not as a doctrine of Private International Law, but rather as a doctrine of internal law. It was the product of the emergence in the early post-Westphalian State, of the need to articulate the relationships between courts in a

decentralized system of justice. Likewise, the classic remedy of the Common Law, the anti-suit injunction, was also developed to deal with internal allocations of competence between courts, and not international conflicts.

(4) What is urgently needed, therefore, running alongside the conflict of laws, is a new science of the conflict of litigation. This would disaggregate the many different situations in which conflicts between courts and tribunals may arise, and examine the appropriate solutions for each:

*(a)* Such a study must be grounded in a factual assessment of the actual context in which cross-border litigation arise — the context which can result in multiple proceedings — appreciating the horizontal pattern of overlapping exercises of adjudicatory authority which is characteristic of modern litigation.

*(b)* The techniques which the law has adopted to date to deal with parallel proceedings sit on a spectrum from simply tolerating (or ignoring) any legal process outside the forum; to unilateralism, with its potential to engender conflict between adjudicatory systems; to rules of priority and deference to other pending proceedings (whether mandatory or discretionary); to consolidation, coordination and co-operation.

(5) In Public International Law and in International Arbitration, it may be possible to find a basis for rules of interaction in the existence of a wider legal system, which conditions the exercises of authority by specific tribunals, and provides, or could provide, a basis for their interaction. In Private International Law, which is, by definition, concerned with the interactions between different legal systems, the basis for rules of interaction must be found elsewhere. The same reasons

in principle for the existence of the rules of the conflict of laws may be found to support *lis pendens* rules to deal with the conflict of litigation:

(a) a private law aspect: the requirement to consider the interests of the litigants in terms of an international, and not a parochial concept of the Rule of Law in order to do substantial justice between the parties; and,

(b) a public law aspect: the requirement to respect the international relationships between the relevant systems of adjudication, and the modes of interaction between them.

While these considerations form the essential predicate for resolving conflicts of litigation, the closer interactions between courts arising as a result of globalization have also generated new forms of judicial co-operation in the management of parallel litigation arising out of the same, or closely related, disputes.

It is to an assessment of the law as it actually applies to the conflict of litigation that these lectures must now turn, beginning with the interactions between national courts in Private International Litigation.

# CHAPTER II

# PRIVATE INTERNATIONAL LITIGATION

## A. Deference, Indifference or Control?

### 1. A world of two hemispheres?

Delivering the judgment of the House of Lords in *Airbus Industrie GIE* v. *Patel*[206], Lord Goff of Chieveley began his analysis of the underlying principles on the resolution of clashes between jurisdictions with the following account of the different approaches to the problem taken by the Civil Law and Common Law systems:

> "Two different approaches to the problem have emerged in the world today, one associated with the civil law jurisdictions of continental Europe, and the other with the common law world. Each is the fruit of a distinctive legal history, and also reflects to some extent cultural differences . . . On the continent of Europe, in the early days of the European Community, the essential need was seen to be to avoid any such clash between member states of the same community . . . This system achieves its purpose, but at a price. The price is rigidity, and rigidity can be productive of injustice . . .
>
> In the common law world, the situation is precisely the opposite. There is, so to speak, a jungle of separate, broadly based, jurisdictions all over the world . . . The basic principle is that each jurisdiction is independent. There is therefore, as I have said, no embargo on concurrent proceedings in the same matter in more than one jurisdiction. There are

---

[206] [1999] 1 AC 119 (HL).

simply these two weapons, a stay (or dismissal) of proceedings and an anti-suit injunction." [207]

Of all the modes of dispute resolution under consideration in these lectures, Private International Litigation provides the richest source of experience on parallel litigation. States sit in sovereign equality to each other in international law. One of the consequences is that national courts relate to each other horizontally. No one national legal system takes priority over any other system. National rules of civil jurisdiction routinely overlap, providing many opportunities for the same, or related, litigation to be pursued concurrently in several courts. Thus, the modern law of litispendence has in many respects taken its inspiration from Private International Law. Yet the dichotomy which Lord Goff describes between modern Civilian and Common Law solutions to clashes between jurisdictions is not as firmly rooted in separate legal histories of Private International Law as he suggests. On the contrary, analysis of the development of the rules in this field shows divergent choices being made within Civil and Common Law systems as to the proper approach to be taken to parallel foreign litigation.

The general rule found within the internal procedure of Civil Law countries, which mandates deference to the court first seised, was extended in many States to the international situation only very recently. It runs against the grain of a deeply held view within the Civilian tradition that jurisdiction is to be defined strictly. It follows from this that a court which properly has jurisdiction must not decline to exercise it. Otherwise it may perpetrate a denial of justice [208]. In

---

[207] *Ibid.*, 132-133.

[208] Gaudemet-Tallon, "France", in Fawcett (ed.), *Declining Jurisdiction in Private International Law* (1995) 175, 175-179.

fact, a number of Civil Law systems preferred precisely the opposite approach of ceding no deference to foreign pending proceedings at all.

Paradoxically, therefore, the modern European Civil Law "court first seised" rule carries with it a running mate which grants the Court discretion to defer to a foreign court in cases of *related* proceedings. As Baumgartner has shown, this provision has been unjustifiably neglected in Continental international civil procedure, despite having had an express mandate under the European Judgments scheme since its inception in 1968 [209]. Is this simply the "deep civilian discomfort with judicial discretion"? [210] If so, why was such an element inserted so prominently into the scheme of the European Judgments scheme?

Nor can it be said that the twin discretionary remedies of *forum non conveniens* and anti-suit injunctions necessarily represent a deep-rooted or comprehensive scheme for resolving conflicts between jurisdictions within the Common Law legal tradition. The doctrine of *forum non conveniens* was, after all, consciously borrowed from Scots law (a Civil Law system) as recently as 1978 [211]. It was engrafted on to a jurisdictional scheme which had traditionally seen little need to defer to foreign litigation, at least where the defendant was present and could be served with process within the jurisdiction [212]. The guiding principle had been that "[t]he right of access to the King's Court must not be lightly refused" [213].

---

[209] Baumgartner, "Related Actions", (1998) 3 *Zeitschrift für Zivilprozeß International* 203.

[210] *Ibid.*, 209.

[211] *MacShannon* v. *Rockware Glass Ltd.*, [1978] AC 795, 812 (HL) per Lord Diplock.

[212] McClean, "Jurisdiction and Judicial Discretion" (1969) 18 *ICLQ* 931.

[213] *St. Pierre* v. *South American Stores (Gath and Chaves) Ltd.*, [1936] 1 KB 382, 398 (CA) per Scott LJ.

As has been seen, the use of anti-suit injunctions to prevent parallel litigation had its origin in purely internal power struggles between the English courts of law and equity. Its application to cross-border proceedings began within the British Isles (in proceedings involving Scotland and Ireland) and in the control of colonial courts. Whatever might have been the justification for the use of such a remedy in these imperial contexts, the same rationale does not necessarily hold good vis-à-vis foreign litigation.

In any event, the premise that it is possible to marry both principles as part of a general discretionary scheme for resolving conflicts of jurisdiction seems doubtful. After all, each discretion points in precisely the opposite direction: the stay in favour of deference to foreign proceedings; and the anti-suit injunction in favour of the assertion of control over those proceedings.

In order, therefore, to explore the treatment of parallel proceedings in Private International Litigation, it is proposed first to examine the alternative approaches which developed in both Civil Law and Common Law countries to the question whether there ought to be a distinct rule requiring deference to pending foreign litigation. Against this background it will be possible to re-evaluate the strict solution now found in the Brussels I Regulation; and to contrast this solution with the discretionary tools developed in both Common and Civil Law jurisdictions to decline jurisdiction in cases of parallel litigation.

## 2. *Two contrasting approaches in Civil Law systems*

The rules currently found in the Brussels I Regulation on *Lis Pendens* and Related Actions[214],

---

[214] Arts. 27 and 28, Council Regulation (EC) No. 44/2001 of 22 December 2000 on Jurisdiction and the

earlier versions of which were included in the first
text of the Brussels Convention 1968[215], bear a notable
resemblance to domestic rules on parallel proceedings
found in the civil procedure codes of the original
Member States. As Schlosser comments:

> "Both elements of viewing parallel proceed-
> ings in civil law countries have a very long tradi-
> tion. Parallel proceedings in two countries are
> approached under the very same criteria as the legal
> rules adopted for the treatment of parallel proceedings
> within the jurisdiction . . . This may explain why in
> the official report of the experts who had drafted the
> Brussels Convention, not even an attempt has been
> made to justify the priority principle."[216]

It is certainly correct, as was seen in Chapter I[217],
that the rules on *lis pendens* were well established in
the *internal* law of the original Member States. But
closer examination suggests that their reception into
*international* civil procedure was by no means assured.

Thus, the New French Code of Civil Procedure
provides, as a matter of French internal law, in
Article 100, that:

> "Si le même litige est pendant devant deux juri-
> dictions de même degré également compétentes

---

Recognition and Enforcement of Judgments in Civil and
Commercial Matters (16 January 2001), OJ L 12, 1 ("Brussels I Regulation").

[215] Arts. 21 and 22, Brussels Convention on Jurisdiction
and the Recognition and Enforcement of Judgments in
Civil and Commercial Matters (signed 27 September 1968,
entered into force 1 February 1973), 1262 *UNTS* 153
("Brussels Convention").

[216] Schlosser, "Jurisdiction and International Judicial
and Administrative Cooperation", (2000) 284 *Recueil des
cours* 13, 81 (internal footnotes omitted); the reference to
the Official Report is to Jenard, OJ C59 (5 March 1979)
Section 8.

[217] Chapter I, Section C 1.

pour en connaître, la juridiction saisie en second
lieu doit se dessaisir."

Following that strict rule of litispendence, it adds
a discretionary provision for connected cases in
Article 101. The rule requiring a mandatory stay in
cases of domestic *lis pendens* was found in the first
Code of Civil Procedure[218]. But, for a century and a
half, and despite the remonstrations of some prominent
scholars to the contrary[219], the rule was not accepted
by the courts as applicable to foreign proceedings,
except in the case of express treaty provision[220].

It was not until 1974 that the Cour de cassation
accepted in *Soc. Miniera di Fragne c. C$^{ie}$ européenne
d'équipement industriel*[221] that the doctrine was
equally applicable to other international cases. The
case arose on a conflict of pending proceedings in
France and Italy that arose just before the entry into
force of the Brussels Convention in both States[222].

---

[218] Art. 171 (1806), and see Dalloz, *Répertoire
méthodique et alphabétique de législation de doctrine et
de jurisprudence* (Vol. XXIII, 1852) 101-108.

[219] Fœlix, *Traité de droit international privé* (1843)
227-232.

[220] Gaudemet-Tallon "La litispendance internationale
dans la jurisprudence française", in *Mélanges dédiés à
Dominique Holleaux* (1990) 121, 122; note A. Ponsard in
Ancel and Lequette, *Les grands arrêts de la jurisprudence
française de droit international privé* (4th ed., 2001) 504,
[7]; Moissinac Massénat, *Les conflits de procédures et de
décisions en droit international privé* (2007) [65]. An
example of express treaty provision for *lis pendens* is
Article 4, Convention between Belgium and France relative
to the Enforcement of Judgments (signed 8 July 1899),
187 *CTS* 378, 379.

[221] Cass. Civ., 26 November 1974, *Rev. crit.*, 1975.491
note D. Holleaux, *Clunet*, 1975.108; Ponsard, *ibid.*

[222] The Brussels Convention entered into force for the
original six contracting States on 1 February 1973. The
case concerned proceedings instituted before the courts in
Milan and Paris respectively in March and May, 1972.

Although there was an older bilateral treaty in force between France and Italy, its rule of *lis pendens* had been held applicable only as ground for refusal of enforcement, and not at the stage of assumption of jurisdiction. The Court therefore had to decide, as a matter of principle, whether the doctrine of *lis pendens* should be applied in international cases. Reversing its earlier case-law to the contrary [223], the Court bowed to a sustained academic campaign led by Holleaux [224], and extended the doctrine to international cases "en vertu du droit commun français" [225].

The Court's judgment does not elaborate on the arguments on either side of this debate. But, as reviewed in the doctrine, the arguments which had been ranged against the extension of *lis pendens* to international cases bear the ring of some recurrent themes [226]. First, it was said that French plaintiffs had a right to invoke the jurisdiction of the French courts, which could not be undermined by a decision to decline jurisdiction. A second set of objections were said to arise from the sovereign independence of national judicial orders on the international plane. It was said that a doctrine of *lis pendens* would not operate effectively across borders in the absence of a Court of Appeal to enforce the rule on the court second seised, where that court was in a foreign country.

The case in favour of the extension of the doctrine was seen to depend not simply on the interests of the French judicial order itself. Rather, the very pendency

---

[223] *Soc. Anciens établissements Valla et Richard*, Ch. Civ., 1 December 1969, *Rev. crit.*, 1972.84, note H. J. Lucas, *Clunet*, 1970.707, note A. Huet.

[224] Holleaux "La litispendance" [1971-1973] *Trav. Com. fr. DIP* 203 ; and see the comment to this effect by Gaudemet-Tallon, *supra* footnote 208.

[225] *Supra* footnote 221, 520.

[226] Summarized in Ancel and Lequette, *supra* footnote 220, 525-527.

of two lawsuits for the same cause was said to be "un
gaspillage préjudiciable à l'intérêt d'économie procé-
durale"[227]. Worse, the absence of such a doctrine promoted forum shopping by the more powerful or
unscrupulous litigant, so as to secure a perceived litigation advantage in his chosen forum[228]. Thus, the
extension of the rule already found in domestic procedure was seen as the best means of avoiding disorder within international civil procedure. However, in
extending the doctrine to the international sphere, the
Cour de cassation added two significant additional
elements. First, the French judge would have to make a
prognosis that the judgment of the foreign court would
be capable of recognition in France[229]. Second, the
power to stay the French proceedings in favour of a
foreign action already pending would always be discretionary[230].

Article 101 of the New Code of Civil Procedure also
confers a liberal discretion on the judge to stay an
action before him in cases of related litigation whenever it is in the interests of justice to do so:

> "S'il existe entre des affaires portées devant deux
> juridictions distinctes un lien tel qu'il soit de l'in-
> térêt d'une bonne justice de les faire instruire et
> juger ensemble, il peut être demandé à l'une de ces
> juridictions de se dessaisir et de renvoyer en l'état la
> connaissance de l'affaire à l'autre juridiction."[231]

But this discretion for *connexité* found no secure place
in French international civil procedure (outside the
context of the European Judgments Regime) until

---

227 Holleaux *supra* footnote 224.
228 Ancel and Lequette, *supra* footnote 220, 524.
229 Gaudemet-Tallon, *supra* footnote 208, 181.
230 Huet, "Compétence des tribunaux français à l'égard
des litiges internationaux" (Juris-Classeur 2004), *Fasc.*
581-543, [36].
231 www.legifrance.gouv.fr.

1999[232]. Von Mehren concludes: "So far, the French courts have shown little inclination to extend Article 101 by analogy to international litigation and stay French proceedings where connexity exists."[233] Other Civil Law domestic civil procedure codes also contain a rule permitting the court to stay proceedings in view of a pending related action. Such States have typically been reluctant to extend such discretion to foreign proceedings[234].

But some European States held even more fundamental objections to the application of the doctrine of *lis pendens* to international cases. Thus, until 31 August 1995, Article 3 of the Italian Civil Procedure Code 1940 provided expressly:

> "La giurisdizione italiana non è esclusa della pendenza davanti a un giudice straniero della medesima causa o di altra con questa connessa . . ."

This may be translated as:

> "The competence of the Italian courts is not excluded by the fact that the same case or a connected claim is pending elsewhere . . ."[235]

---

[232] Cass. Civ., 22 June 1999, *Bull. civ.*, 1999, I no. 208, *Rev. crit.*, 2000.42 note G. Cuniberti, but see previously Cass. Civ., 20 October 1987, *Bull. civ.*, I no. 275, 198.

[233] von Mehren, "Theory and Practice of Adjudicatory Authority in Private International Law: A Comparative Study of the Doctrine, Policies and Practices of Common- and Civil-Law Systems", (2002) 295 *Recueil des cours* 9, 345.

[234] Baumgartner, *supra* footnote 209, 207. The recent study commissioned by the European Commission, Nuyts, "Study on Residual Jurisdiction", General Report (3 September 2007) found no examples of States within the European Union, other than France, having adopted a rule on related proceedings in international cases: [100].

[235] Unofficial translation in G. Walter, "*Lis Alibi Pendens* and *Forum non Conveniens*: From Confrontation via Co-ordination to Collaboration", (2002) 4 *European Journal of Law Reform* 69.

The rule was reinforced by a provision which precluded the enforcement of a foreign judgment where an
action had been instituted before the Italian courts[236].
As Walter comments, the Italian Code was thus "stead-
fast on a collision course"[237] with other legal systems.
It was only with the 1995 International Private Law
Act that Italy adopted a rule providing for the issue of
a stay of proceedings in the light of a prior foreign *lis
pendens*, where the resulting judgment would be
enforceable in Italy[238].

These awesome relics of the past are not disinterred
here with merely ghoulish interest. They demonstrate
that the extension of the doctrine of *lis pendens* to the
international situation was intimately bound up with a
larger question of the question to which one national
order was prepared to recognize and give legal effect to
judicial process in other systems in the interests of a
larger purpose.

The link which was typically made was with the
recognition of foreign judgments. For instance, the
current Swiss Private International Law Act requires
a stay of process in favour of a foreign court only
where that court's judgment would be recognized in
the forum:

"*Art. 9*

*VIII. Litispendance*

[1] Lorsqu'une action ayant le même objet est
déjà pendante entre les mêmes parties à l'étranger,
le tribunal suisse suspend la cause s'il est à prévoir

---

[236] Art. 797 (1).
[237] Walter, *supra* footnote 205, 69, and see also
Trocker, "Italy", in Fawcett, *supra* footnote 208, 279,
[238] Legge sulla riforma del sistema italiano di diritto internazionale privato [LDIP], 1995 *Gazz. Uff.* 2,
Art. 7.

que la juridiction étrangère rendra, dans un délai
convenable, une décision pouvant être reconnue en
Suisse." [239]

With a commendably Swiss focus on efficiency, this
provision adds the requirement that the court must be
satisfied that the foreign court will render its decision
within a reasonable time. But in other respects it
simply extends a classic conception of *lis pendens* to
foreign actions.

The point here is that such a European consensus
has emerged from a relatively recent past in which
there was a decidedly diverse range of responses to *foreign* pending litigation within national legal systems.
It was by no means regarded as inevitable that the
existence of a domestic rule of priority mandated a
cosmopolitan approach internationally.

Despite this, the framers of the Brussels Convention
did not feel the need to justify the inclusion of these
rules in their treaty text. Strictly, the *lis pendens* rules
in the Brussels Convention may only have been
required by reason of the double nature of the
Convention — providing both primary rules of jurisdiction and full faith and credit for the resulting judgments. But the adoption of such rules within the treaty
system of a nascent federation appears to have embold-
ened courts to embrace the notion of an international
system for the allocation of decisional competence in
non-Convention cases as well. This is so even when the
foreign court might be asserting jurisdiction on a different ground (subject only to control over the enforceability of the subsequent judgment). Further, although
in some States the results of this *bouleversement* is
now reflected in legislation, the driver for change came
largely from doctrine, and, as in the French case, was

---

[239] Loi fedérale sur le droit international privé (18 December 1987), *RS* 291.

adopted as a pure exercise in judicial innovation. The driving ideas were the need to control forum shopping by the parties, judicial efficiency, and the avoidance of multiple or inconsistent judgments. Implicit in the adoption of such principles was the notion that, messy though it may be, there was discernable beyond individual national legal systems, a notion of an *international* civil procedure.

## 3. Two contrasting approaches in a Common Law system

Evidence of a similar debate — still unresolved — may also be seen in the competing lines of case-law on the doctrine of *lis pendens* in the Common Law jurisdictions of the United States [240]. Here, the origins of both lines of thought lie in Supreme Court decisions about the application of the doctrine *within* the United States. The difference in approach stems from the different relationships between courts in a federation. Subsequent courts have, however, sought to adapt the reasoning developed in this domestic jurisprudence to the international context, and so it is first necessary to understand the competing considerations at play in the domestic cases.

In *Landis* v. *North American Co.* [241], the Supreme Court was concerned with a series of lawsuits (originally 47 in number) pending in different federal district courts. The cases involved different plaintiffs. But at issue was the same question: the Constitutional validity of an Act of Congress which sought to regulate public utility holding companies in the electricity industry. The issue had been raised by way of defence in sepa-

---

[240] Born and Rutledge *International Civil Litigation in United States Courts* (4th ed., 2007) 522-540.

[241] 299 US 248, 57 S. Ct. 163 (1936).

rate proceedings, the *Electric Bond and Share* case, brought by the US Securities and Exchange Commission against other corporate defendants in US District Court for the Southern District of New York. The District Judge in the *North American Co.* case had formed the view that that case should be stayed pending determination of *Electric Bond and Share*, provided the latter was diligently prosecuted, together with any appeal to the Supreme Court thereon. The Court of Appeals was unable to come to a clear decision on whether that approach was correct. The Supreme Court therefore granted *certiorari* in order to determine whether the District Judge had power to grant the order which he had made.

Cardozo J delivered the opinion of the Court. The Court rejected the proposition that there had to be complete identity of parties and issue before the court had power to intervene. It held:

> "[T]he power to stay proceedings is incidental to the power inherent in every court to control the disposition of the causes on its docket with economy of time and effort for itself, for counsel, and for litigants."[242]

The Supreme Court saw the matter rather differently when it was seised with the question whether a federal court ought to stay its proceedings in favour of a State court. *Colorado River* v. *United States*[243] was concerned with a battle over a different public resource: water.

The State of Colorado had sought to control the allocation of water rights. The United States had participated in various State court proceedings in relation

---

[242] *Ibid.*, 254.
[243] *Colorado River Water Conservation District* v. *United States* 424 US 800, 96 S. Ct. 1236 (1976).

to water rights in Colorado held by it both in its own right, and on behalf of various Indian tribes. It then brought a federal suit on the same question, naming some 1,000 defendants, being all those persons who might be affected by its water rights claims.

The question was whether it could be compelled to litigate its federal law claims in State court — a step which an Act of Congress clearly permitted. Brennan J, delivering the majority opinion of the Court[244], considered that:

> "there are principles ... which govern in situations involving the contemporaneous exercise of concurrent jurisdictions, either by federal courts or by state and federal courts. These principles rest on considerations of '[w]ise administration, giving regard to conservation of judicial resources and comprehensive disposition of litigation' ... Generally, as between state and federal courts, the rule is that 'the pendency of an action in the state court is no bar to proceedings in the same matter in Federal court having jurisdiction ...' ... As between federal district courts, however, though no precise rule has evolved, the general principle is to avoid duplicative litigation ... This difference in general approach between state-federal concurrent jurisdiction and wholly federal concurrent jurisdiction stems from *the virtually unflagging obligation of the federal courts to exercise the jurisdiction given them* ... Only the clearest of justifications will warrant dismissal."[245]

In the case before it, however, despite this strict test,

---

[244] *Ibid.*, Stewart, Blackmun and Stevens JJ dissenting as to the Court's application of its ruling to the facts of the case.
[245] *Ibid.*, 817-819 (references omitted, emphasis added).

the Supreme Court held that dismissal of the federal complaint was justified. There was a legislative policy of Congress, in seeking to promote the consolidation of water claims involving the United States Government. Further, the United States Government had participated in the State court proceedings, and the federal court proceedings were, by contrast, not at all advanced. The Supreme Court more recently reaffirmed the principles which it had set down in *Colorado River* in *Quackenbush* v. *Allstate Insurance Co.* [246]

What impact have these two different principles for the regulation of parallel proceedings internally within the federation had on the treatment by United States courts of parallel foreign proceedings?

*Colorado River* provided the inspiration for one of the most erudite expositions of a principle *in favour* of tolerating parallel proceedings outside the Union — the opinion of Judge Wilkey in the judgment of the US Court of Appeals in the course of the notorious *Laker Airways* litigation saga: *Laker Airways Ltd.* v. *Sabena, Belgian World Airlines* [247]. Laker Airways had operated a cut-price trans-Atlantic airline in the late 1970s. When the business failed in 1981, Laker accused the established airlines on the route of having operated a cartel, and of having decided to drive Laker out of business by means of predatory pricing. Laker brought suit in the United States court alleging violation of US anti-trust laws. One of the responses of the airlines was to apply in the English courts for a negative declaration

---

[246] 517 US 706, 116 S. Ct. 1712 (1996).

[247] 731 F. 2d 909 (DC Cir., 1984); see Collins, "Provisional and Protective Measures in International Litigation", (1992) 234 *Recueil des cours* 13, 138-149; Vollmer, "US Federal Court Use of the Antisuit Injunction to Control International Forum Selection", in Goldsmith (ed.), *International Dispute Resolution: The Regulation of Forum Selection* (1997) 237, 241-244.

and an anti-suit injunction restraining pursuit of the US action [248].

The question for the US Court of Appeals was whether it should retaliate by granting its own anti-anti-suit injunction to ensure the continuance of the American proceedings. Despite the hostile posture of the case, which was no merely incidental parallelism, Wilkey J, giving the majority opinion of the Court of Appeals, held that the ordinary starting-point should be the continuation of *both* actions. Finding that both the United States and the United Kingdom had a valid basis on which to exercise prescriptive jurisdiction, the learned judge continued:

> "However, the fundamental corollary to concurrent jurisdiction must ordinarily be respected: parallel proceedings on the same in personam claim should ordinarily be allowed to proceed simultaneously, at least until a judgment is reached in one which can be pled as res judicata in the other." [249]

Taking *Colorado River* as inspiration [250], Judge Wilkey drew a distinction between the different policies which might inform the court's discretion in an *intra-court* matter, as contrasted with an *inter-court* one. Despite this strong preference for non-intervention, the Court found that intervention in the instant case was justified since the sole purpose of the English proceedings was to seek to frustrate the action in the

---

[248] The rival English proceedings for an anti-suit injunction are reported as *British Airways Board* v. *Laker Airways Ltd. sub nom Laker Airways Ltd.* v. *Secretary of State for Trade and Industry*; *British Caledonian Airways Ltd.* v. *Laker Airways Ltd.*, [1985] AC 58 (HL); reversing [1984] QB 142 (CA).

[249] *Supra* footnote 247, 926-927.

[250] *Ibid.*, fn. 49.

American court. What could have been an irreconcilable trans-Atlantic collision between courts was narrowly averted when the House of Lords finally decided that, since Laker only had a cause of action under US law, and could not prosecute his claim in England, the anti-suit injunction ought not to be maintained[251].

The idea that parallel litigation should normally be allowed to continue has also been adopted by lower courts as a rationale for refusing to grant a stay of US proceedings in favour of concurrent litigation abroad. Thus, in *Ingersoll Milling Machine Co.* v. *Granger*[252], a US District Court had to consider proceedings for a negative declaration and injunctive relief brought by Ingersoll in an attempt to restrain a labour claim already brought by Mr. Granger in the Belgian courts. Mr. Granger sought a stay of the US action. The District Court refused to grant a stay of its own proceedings. But equally it did not enjoin the Belgian case. Only once Mr. Granger's claim had resulted in a Belgian judgment at first instance in his favour, did the District Court grant a stay of the US action pending the outcome of appeals in Belgium.

The Court of Appeals held that in principle there was no objection to parallel litigation, approving *Laker* and applying *Colorado River.* However, those cases emphasized that the courts retained discretion to stay or dismiss an action. Here, there was good reason to stay the action pending the final disposal of any appeals in Belgium:

"[C]onsiderations of judicial economy, especially the need to avoid piecemeal litigation, strongly favoured staying the district court proceedings ... Avoiding such duplication of effort and the possi-

---

[251] See *infra*, Section D 3 *(a)*.
[252] 833 F. 2d 680 (7th Cir., 1987).

bility of piecemeal litigation is hardly an abuse of
discretion." [253]

The factors which weighed particularly strongly with
the court were the fact that the District Court had only
granted a stay *after* the claim in Belgium had already
resulted in a judgment, and then only pending the final
disposition of any appeals.

By contrast, other US courts have drawn support for
the dismissal of actions before them in favour of pending
foreign proceedings from the *Landis* line of authority
within the Union. Thus, in *Continental Time Corp.* v.
*Swiss Credit Bank* [254], the Court was called upon to consider pending proceedings in Switzerland upon a letter of
credit. Continental, whose interest in the letter of credit
only revived upon its reassignment of a partial interest,
then sought to bring proceedings upon it against Swiss
Credit in the United States. The Court dismissed the
action against it. Citing *Landis* it held that it had "inherent power to dismiss or stay this action in favour of the
Swiss litigation presenting the same claims and
issues" [255]. Lasker J set forth the following list of factors
to be weighed in making the dismissal decision:

> "The relevant factors in determining whether
> to grant a stay or a dismissal because of litigation
> pending in another forum include the adequacy of
> relief available in the alternative forum, the promo-
> tion of judicial efficiency, the identity of the parties
> and the issues in the two actions, the likelihood of
> prompt resolution in the alternative forum, the con-
> venience of parties, counsel and witnesses, the pos-
> sibility of prejudice to any party, and the temporal
> sequence of filing for each action." [256]

---

[253] *Ibid.*, 685-686.
[254] 543 F. Supp. 408 (SDNY, 1982).
[255] *Ibid.*, 410.
[256] *Ibid.*

The two contrasting lines of cases which have just been considered form only a part of the range of American approaches to the problems posed by parallel proceedings[257]. In fact, such cases are rarely identified as raising a specific issue of *lis alibi pendens*. Parallel proceedings issues are more often discussed in the context of the exercise of the general discretion to stay or dismiss proceedings on grounds of *forum non conveniens* and the power to grant an anti-suit injunction — the ego and the alter ego remedies of Common Law private international litigation, which will receive further attention in Sections C and D below. Indeed, Lasker J's set of factors overlaps considerably with the factors commonly identified in *forum non conveniens* cases.

But the American cases on litispendence serve here to make a broader point about the choices to be made in this field of the law. Just as in the case of the experience in Continental Europe, the approach to international cases has been fashioned by the judges by analogy from the principles of internal civil procedure. It is unsurprising that judges, who, after all, draw their own authority from their own legal system, should look first for inspiration to their own rules of civil procedure. But, as will be seen, there may be serious difficulties in such a translation, since the internal rules as not necessarily equipped to deal adequately with the different range of factors at play in internationally parallel proceedings.

Within the polity of the United States, there is a certain logic about adopting a different set of rules to deal

---

[257] There is in general no rule of *lis pendens* as between proceedings pending in the courts of different states within the Union: von Mehren, *supra* footnote 233, 346-348. For a full study of the treatment of parallel litigation by courts in the United States see George, "Parallel Litigation", (1999) 51 *Baylor LR* 769.

with parallel litigation arising within the federal court system to that which applies as between federal and state courts. The first is undoubtedly an *intra-court* situation — just as would be the case in the case of an internal application of Article 100 of the French Civil Procedure Code. The law applicable in both courts will be the same. Both courts are part of the same system of judicial administration, and subject to appellate review within that system. The same is not true of proceedings running conterminously in federal and state court. The law applied will likely be different. Each court forms part of a different judicial hierarchy, and is subject to different avenues of appeal, to which the ultimate oversight of the US Supreme Court should not blind us.

But the logic of this distinction carries less weight when applied to the international context. In particular, *Colorado River*'s insistence on "the virtually unflagging obligation of the federal courts to exercise the jurisdiction given them", which makes considerable sense when a line must be drawn between federal and state competence, may be positively misleading in an international setting. Cases of international parallel litigation normally arise, as Judge Wilkey found in *Laker,* when *both* courts properly have international jurisdiction to determine the claim before them. If each court merely invoked an "unflagging obligation" to determine the case before it, then neither would address the hardship to litigants, or the failure of judicial economy caused by concurrent litigation. Yet, as will be seen in subsequent lectures [258], this idea had continued to resurface in the reasoning of tribunals in a range of contexts, as if it represented a reason in itself to decline to grant relief.

In truth, as was the case in the European cases, a judicial choice has to be made at the point at which any

---

[258] For example *infra*, Chapter IV, Section A 3 *(b)*.

doctrine of litispendence is applied to the international situation, as to the approach which is to be adopted. It is possible to do nothing about international parallel proceedings, at least until they have matured into a judgment — as the former Italian code would have had it, and as an application of *Colorado River* suggests. The result is that what may under a simple "first in time" rule become a race to commence proceedings turns instead into a race to judgment. Unless the court is prepared to look beyond its own national legal system, it will find neither a parallel claim, nor a reason to defer. In the light of that policy choice, it is now possible to examine in more detail the operation of each of the three major methods of dealing with parallel proceedings in Private International Law today: a strict *lis pendens* rule, requiring that the court stay in favour of another court first seised, but only if complete identity of claim is present; discretions to decline jurisdiction in favour or parallel or related proceedings; and anti-suit injunctions.

## B. *Strict* Lis Pendens: *Pursuing the* Res Judicata *Parallel*

### 1. *Translation of an internal into an international rule*

It has already been seen that the strict doctrine of *lis pendens* initially developed within internal civil procedure and was intimately linked to the rules on the recognition of the preclusive effect of judgments, or *res judicata*. Its progress as a rule of international civil procedure in Civil Law countries was halting. Despite that, however, it has now achieved widespread application to international cases, both as a *conventional* rule, where there is a treaty in force between the respective states, and as a *common law* rule of general application. Thus, a 2007 study prepared by Professor Nuyts for the European Commission on the basis of national reports found that 19 Member States of the Union accepted such a rule as part of their law applicable in non-Convention cases[259], while only 6 States had no such rule[260]. This research is particularly significant in that it extends to all of the new Member States, and not simply to those States which have already had prolonged experience with the operation of such a rule in the treaty context of the Brussels Convention and Regulation.

The link recognized in the Civil Law between *lis pendens* and *res judicata* at least since the Dutch jurists of the seventeenth century serves to focus attention on a strict identity of action between the two parallel proceedings. In the case of both *lis pendens* and *res judicata,* this is established by examination of three elements:

*(a)* the *parties (personae)*;
*(b)* the *cause* or subject-matter in dispute (the *causa petendi*); and,
*(c)* the *object* of the proceedings — what is decided, and what relief is granted in the action (the *petitum*).

Elements *(b)* and *(c)* may be separated analytically, but in practical terms they will normally fall to be con-

---

[259] Nuyts, *supra* footnote 234, [99]. Those States are: Austria, Belgium, Cyprus, England and Wales, Scotland, Estonia, France, Germany, Greece, Hungary, Ireland, Italy, Latvia, Lithuania, Luxembourg, Malta, Slovenia, Spain, Sweden, Bulgaria, Czech Republic and Slovakia. See also: Swiss Institute of Comparative Law, "Legal Opinion on Certain Effects of the Brussels and Lugano Conventions in the Relationship to Non-Contracting States" (15 March 2002) 102-113.

[260] Romania, Denmark, Finland, Netherlands, Poland and Portugal.

sidered together, as they are both concerned with a determination of the subject-matter of the action.

It is unsurprising that the rules for *res judicata* require a precise determination of the requisite degree of identity of action between the prior proceedings, which have matured into a judgment, and the subsequent action. Otherwise it would be indefensible to prevent a plaintiff from pursuing his claim. In the context of *lis pendens,* as has been seen in Chapter I, the rationale for strict rules of identity must rather be found in the prevention of abuse caused by duplication of the task of adjudication.

However, whereas the rule of *res judicata* adds to these the requirement of the first judgment to be delivered, the strict rule of *lis pendens* substitutes for this the requirement that the court be first *seised.* This is succinctly put in what has become the paradigm example of a strict rule of precedence: that adopted in the Brussels Convention, now Regulation. In the French text of Article 27 of the Brussels I Regulation the three requirements of identity are given as:

> "Lorsque des demandes ayant *le même objet* et *la même cause* sont formées entre *les mêmes parties* devant des juridictions d'Etats membres différents, la juridiction saisie en second lieu sursoit d'office à statuer jusqu'à ce que la compétence du tribunal premier saisi soit établie." [261]

A strict rule of *prior tempore* of its nature places a premium on time — the time at which the first court is seised of the proceedings. The requirement of seisin, which was the subject of much contention under the earlier language of the Brussels Convention, is now

---

[261] Emphasis added. The English text does not distinguish between elements *(b)* and *(c)*, rendering both simply as "the same cause of action".

defined autonomously in Article 30 of the Regulation
as the time at which the document is lodged with the
court or, if service is required before lodging, the time
when it is received by the authority responsible for service (provided in each case that the plaintiff proceeds
to serve or lodge as the case may be).

But a determination of litispendence cannot proceed
completely on the same footing as that of *res judicata*,
since it involves a prediction, based upon the claims
asserted by the plaintiff, of the nature of the action.
That much has been made explicit by the jurisprudence
of the European Court, interpreting the Brussels
Convention/Regulation. Thus, the second element has
been described as "the facts and rule of law relied on
as the basis of the action"[262]. These are to be determined by reference to the plaintiff's claims alone, no
account being taken of any defences to the action[263].
The third element, the object, has also been described
by the European Court prospectively as "the end the
action has in view"[264].

These elements, while prospective, are nevertheless
based upon the known quantity of the plaintiff's plead-
ings in the action. But a final element, which reinforces
the link with *res judicata*, is the enforceability of any
judgment to be given by the court first seised. Within
the closed system of the Brussels I Regulation, this
need not be made a specific requirement of the *lis pendens* rule. The court second seised merely stays its proceedings in order to enable the court first seised to
determine its jurisdiction under the rules of primary
jurisdiction laid down elsewhere in Chapter II of the
Regulation. If that court finds that it does not have
jurisdiction, then the stay has no further operation. If,

---

[262] *The Tatry Case*, C-406/92, [1994] *ECR* I-5439, [38].
[263] *Gantner Electronic GmbH* v. *Basch Exploitatie
Maatschappij BV*, Case C-111/01 [2003] *ECR* I-4207, [26].
[264] *The Tatry*, *supra* footnote 262, [40].

on the other hand, the court first seised does find that it has jurisdiction, then any other court must decline jurisdiction [265]. The resulting judgment of the first court will then become enforceable throughout the Member States under Chapter III of the Regulation.

Outside these provisions, the general law of many States recognizing a rule of priority requires the court second seised to make a prediction as to the likely enforceability in that State of the first court's judgment. This is the solution adopted in Article 9 of the Swiss Private International Law Act [266]. It is also followed in a number of EU countries in their application of the doctrine to non-Member States' courts [267]. There is a further critical difference between the approach taken in the Brussels I Regulation and that applied in the Civil Law outside the Convention. The Regulation's rule is mandatory. The court second seised "shall of its own motion stay the proceedings", and then "shall decline jurisdiction in favour of that court". By contrast, the common law rule of general application outside the Brussels system normally supplies the judge with *discretion* to decline jurisdiction where the conditions for litispendence are made out, rather than a requirement to do so [268].

It is now necessary to dissect the anatomy of the two key elements for identity of action — persons and subject-matter. This is important for at least two reasons of central relevance to the theme of these lectures. First, the application of a procedural rule of

---

[265] Art. 27 (3).
[266] *Supra*, Chapter I, Section D 2.
[267] Nuyts, *supra* footnote 234, [100], lists these as: Austria, Belgium, Cyprus, Estonia, France, Italy, Slovenia, Spain, Sweden.
[268] Nuyts, *ibid.*, [101], states that this is the position in all EU member States save for Germany, Greece and Slovenia.

*lis pendens* to the conflict of litigation across international borders exposes to view a problem which is endemic in the conflict of laws. That is: how is the court to find a basis for comparison between causes of action founded upon different national legal systems so as to apply the rule? The answer to this question could have important implications for the science of conflict of litigation not just in Private International Law, but also in the other types of disputes reviewed in this study.

Second, to what extent does the rule of priority for the court first seised actually address the underlying mischief of forum shopping to which litispendence rules should be directed? Two difficult issues in particular have arisen:

*(a)* to what extent does the rule as to parties extend to persons who are not identical to the parties to the action in the forum, but whose interests are closely linked?; and,

*(b)* to what extent does a strict *prior tempore* rule simply encourage forum shopping by inciting a litigant to issue proceedings first in his chosen forum? This risk may be particularly acute where a prospective defendant, having notice of a claim, may himself issue proceedings in his chosen forum. Such proceedings will typically be for a negative declaration — i.e. a claim in which the defendant seeks a declaration that he is *not* liable to the plaintiff.

European law has preferred a fragmented approach to the determination of same parties and moved only cautiously to extend the scope of its rule on parties. As will be seen in Section C, the effect of this strict approach is tempered by the availability of a discretionary stay for related claims. But its approach to negative declarations has exposed a potential for abuse at the heart of the European jurisdiction and judgments regime. Further, the survival in Europe of the principle of *lis pendens* as a rule of general law, capable of deference to courts in third States, depends upon the extent to which the Brussels I Regulation is seen as a closed system, or instead has an *effet réflexe*[269]. In order to make an assessment of each of these issues, it will be necessary first to explore what is meant by identity of action a little further.

## 2. *The search for identity of action*

### (a) *Same parties*

The leading cases on identity of parties in the European Court are *The Tatry*[270] and *Drouot Assurances SA* v. *Consolidated Metallurgical Industries*[271]. Both cases arose out of the alleged liability of Dutch shipowners for damage to cargo shipped from Europe's busiest port, lying just a few kilometres from The Hague at Rotterdam, and the ready use in the Rotterdam courts of the negative declaration.

The *Tatry* was a ship carrying a cargo of soya bean oil from Brazil to Rotterdam. Three groups of cargo owners (some with registered offices in London, some in Germany) alleged that the cargo had become contaminated by diesel or other hydrocarbons. The shipowners brought proceedings in Rotterdam under the Brussels Convention against all three groups of cargo owners for a declaration that they were not liable for the alleged contamination. They then sought to limit their liability in respect of the whole cargo under the International Convention Relating to the Limitation

---

[269] Droz, *Compétence judiciaire et effets des jugements dans le Marché Commun*, (1972) [165], [329].

[270] *Supra* footnote 262.

[271] Case C-351/96, [1998] *ECR* I-3075.

of the Liability of Owners of Sea-Going Ships[272].
Group 3 of the cargo owners responded with a writ in
the Admiralty Court in England seeking to have the
*Tatry* and the *Maciej Rataj* arrested ("Folio 2006").
When a guarantee was provided, arrest of the *Tatry* was
averted and the action continued. These proceedings
were repeated by Group 2 ("Folio 2007"), but no suit
was filed in England by Group 1. All three groups
brought actions in the Netherlands as a precautionary
measure.

The shipowners asked the Admiralty Court to
decline jurisdiction in favour of the Netherlands court
on the basis of Article 21 of the Convention[273] (in the
case of Folio 2006) or on the basis of Article 22[274] (in
the case of both actions). The Court refused to decline
jurisdiction because, as regards Folio 2006, the proceedings in the Netherlands did not have the same
cause of action (because a declaration was sought, not
damages) and that, as regards Folio 2007, Group 2
"was not a party to the proceedings commenced in the
Netherlands"[275] (at least until after the English suit was
begun). On appeal, the Court of Appeal referred the
construction of Articles 21 and 22 of the Convention to
the European Court of Justice. The Court held:

> "An a proper construction of Article 21 of the
> Convention, where two actions involve the same
> cause of action and some but not all of the parties to
> the second action are the same as the parties to the
> action commenced earlier in another Contracting
> State, the second court seised to decline jurisdiction

---

[272] International Convention Relating to the Limitation
of the Liability of Owners of Sea-Going Ships (signed
10 October 1957, entered into force 31 May 1968), 1412
*UNTS* 80.

[273] Now Art. 27 of the Brussels I Regulation.

[274] Now Art. 28 of the Brussels I Regulation.

[275] *The Tatry*, *supra* footnote 262, [16].

only to the extent to which the parties to the proceedings before it are also parties to the action previously commenced; it does not prevent the proceedings from continuing between the other parties." [276]

The construction of the rule thus adopted required a
strict "matching of pairs" between the litigants in each
action. The *lis* between identical litigants would be
governed by the *prior tempore* rule, even if the earlier
litigation took the form of an application for a negative
declaration. But claims arising out of the same event,
and involving in substance the same claim would not
be covered, if there were no strict identity of parties. As
Professor Pierre Mayer put it in his lectures to the Academy, this was a "solution malencontreuse, qui encourage la création artificielle de situations de litispendance
et qui consacre le choix de la partie qui, n'étant pas le
demandeur naturel, a pris son adversaire de vitesse" [277].

The Court found salvation from the potential for a
multiplicity of actions in the provisions of Article 22
on related actions. But, where the first action had been
commenced by a claim for a negative declaration, this
would serve only to consolidate proceedings in a jurisdiction which had been seised pre-emptively by one of
the defendants.

In any event, *The Tatry* did not resolve the application of Article 21 in cases of persons who were related,
but not identical, to the litigants. This question arose in
*Drouot Assurances SA* v. *Consolidated Metallurgical
Industries ("CMI")* a reference from the French Cour
de cassation [278]. CMI had arranged with a Mr. Velghe to

---

[276] *Ibid., dispositif,* [2].
[277] Mayer, "Le phénomène de la coordination des
ordres juridiques", (2007) 327 *Recueil des cours* 13, 293,
footnote 471.
[278] *Drouot Assurances SA* v. *Consolidated Metallurgical Industries, supra* footnote 271.

ship cargo of ferrochromium on the *Sequana* from
Rotterdam to France. When the ship foundered, Drouot
(the insurer of the vessel's hull) had it refloated and
CMI's cargo was salvaged. Drouot then commenced
proceedings in France against CMI, Protea (the insurer
of the cargo) and GIE Reunion (Protea's agent) for
contribution to the general average[279]. CMI and Protea
raised an objection of *lis alibi pendens* on the basis of
an action they had commenced against Mr. Velghe and
Mr. Walbrecq (the original owner of the ship) in
Rotterdam for a declaration that they were not obliged
to contribute to the general average. The Court rejected
the claim of *lis pendens* because Drouot was not a
party to the French action and Velghe and Walbrecq
were not parties to the French action. On appeal, the
Cour d'appel upheld the claim of *lis pendens*, because
Drouot was only absent from the Dutch proceedings
because of a procedural rule preventing insurers
becoming parties and that Drouot was, in fact, present
"through the intermediary of the insured"[280]. The Court
of Justice was then asked to consider the question
whether the parties to the two actions were the same.

The Court rejected the proposition that this could
depend upon the particularities of national procedural
rules[281]. Rather, the question was to be resolved by
asking objectively whether the interests of the insured
and insurer in the action were *indissociable*. This could
certainly be true where the insurer exercised its right of
subrogation to sue in the name of the insured, since in
such a case "a judgment delivered against one of them
would have the force of res judicata as against the
other"[282]. But the same could not be said of the case

---

[279]  *Ibid.*, [7].
[280]  *Ibid.*, [11].
[281]  *Ibid.*, [24].
[282]  *Ibid.*, [19].

before it, since the insurer denied liability for the anything other than the hull of the vessel.

This test of *indissociable* interests has been recently
considered by the English Court of Appeal in relation
to the assignor and assignee of a legal claim in *Kolden
Holdings Ltd.* v. *Rodette Commerce Ltd.* [283] The case
concerned a number of Russian companies incorporated in Cyprus. In 2004, three of these investment
companies entered into agreements to sell their share-
holdings in a Russian cement company to Rodette and
Taplow (the appellants). All the agreements contained a
clause submitting the dispute to the non-exclusive
jurisdiction of the English courts. It was alleged that
the appellants failed to fulfil their obligations to transfer the shares to another company, JV. In 2006, the
three investment companies issued proceedings in
England seeking a declaration that the appellants had
failed to fulfil their obligation, rectification and damages for breach of contract. A month later, the same
three companies (and three other claimants) sought
damages against the appellants for "conspiracy aiming
at fraud" [284] in Cyprus. As a result of a deed of assign-
ment the three companies were substituted in the
English action by Kolden.

In February 2007, the appellants instituted proceedings in Cyprus against the three companies and
Kolden, claiming, *inter alia,* for a declaration of non-
liability under the agreements, "the mirror image of
that sought" by the three companies in England [285].
Was Kolden to be treated as the same party, so that the
English action would continue to have priority under
Article 27? Aikens J concluded that when the Cyprus
proceedings were begun "the English court was the

---

[283] *Kolden Holdings Ltd.* v. *Rodette Commerce Ltd.*,
[2008] 1 Lloyd's Rep. 434 (CA).
[284] *Ibid.*, [22].
[285] *Ibid.*, [28].

court 'first seised' of the 'same cause of action' (the
contract cause of action) between 'the same parties'"
under Article 27 of the Regulations[286]. Lawrence
Collins LJ dismissed the appeal. Having summarized
the effect of *The Tatry* and *Drouot,* he proceeded to
analyse the position of an assignor and assignee. He
held that in English law *res judicata* would bind the
assignee as a person in "privity of interest" with the
assignor[287]. He then considered whether their interests
were "identical" and "indissociable"[288] for the purpose
of the Brussels I Regulation test. He found that they
were, reasoning:

> "In my judgment the interests are identical,
> because in relation to each of the SPAs there is only
> one right, and there are successive owners of that
> one right. It follows that the interests of assignor
> and assignee are indissociable in the sense of indi-
> visible. It does not matter that an assignment only
> passes the benefit and not the burden of a contract,
> nor that the assignor remains primarily liable to the
> obligor for the non-performance of its outstanding
> contractual obligations. The interest of the assignor
> and assignee in relation to the claim being advanced
> against the appellants is identical."[289]

This is consistent with the English Court of
Appeal's earlier decision that a wholly-owned
subsidiary could be treated as the same person as their
parent[290].

---

[286] *Ibid.*, [35].

[287] *Ibid.*, [88].

[288] Noting that the term was only used in English law
where used to translate the French word in judgments of
the ECJ, the ECHR and in acts of the European institutions: *ibid.*, [90].

[289] *Ibid.*, [91].

[290] *Berkeley Administration Inc.* v. *McClelland*, [1995]
I L. Pr. 201 (CA). By contrast, the licensee of a trade-mark

## (b) *Same subject-matter and same cause*

In confronting the scope *ratione materiae* of the strict doctrine of *lis pendens*, two questions are of central importance, especially in transnational cases. The first is the degree of identity between actions which can be achieved when the source of the legal obligation on which each is based is different. The second is the identity of a claim for a negative declaration with the primary claim for relief.

As has already been seen, the European Court has insisted on an autonomous interpretation of "cause" and "object" for the purpose of the Brussels I Regulation, defined respectively as "the facts and rule of law relied on as the basis of the action" [291]; and "the end the action has in view" [292]. The Supreme Court of Canada has also undertaken a valuable analysis of the identity of actions in *Rocois Construction Inc.* v. *Québec Ready Mix Inc.* [293], applying a Civil Law rule of *lis pendens* in the Quebec Code of Civil Procedure. Although the case involved an intra-Canadian federation problem of litispendence, its reasoning is nevertheless of more general interest for the present study.

Rocois brought an action against the respondents for unfair trade practices in the Superior Court of Quebec. The respondents sought to have the action dismissed on the grounds of *lis pendens* in Article 165 of the Quebec Code of Civil Procedure because an action was pending in the Federal Court for unfair trade practices between the same parties. The jurisdiction of the

---

was held not be capable of being treated as a same person as the licensor for the purpose of this rule: *Mecklermedia Corp.* v. *D. C. Congress GmbH*, [1998] Ch 40.

[291] *The Tatry, supra* footnote 262, [38]

[292] *Ibid.*, [40].

[293] *Rocois Construction Inc.* v. *Quebec Ready Mix Inc. and Others*, [1990] 2 SCR 400; Goldstein, "Canada (Quebec)", in Fawcett, *supra* footnote 208, 145, 159-161.

Superior Court was founded on the general law, while
the Federal Court's jurisdiction was based on the federal Combines Investigation Act. The Superior Court
refused to dismiss the action but the Supreme Court
found that there was *lis pendens*. In addition to there
being identity of parties, the Supreme Court found that
there was identity of object because, although the
grounds and precise monetary claims differed, both
actions were essentially seeking the same thing.

Recognizing that the existence of two rules of law
almost inevitably gives rise to two causes of action, the
Supreme Court saw the question as one of *characterization*:

"First, it is clear that a body of facts cannot in
itself constitute a cause of action. It is the legal
characterization given to it which makes it, in certain cases, a source of obligations. A fact taken by
itself apart from any notion of legal obligations has
no meaning in itself and cannot be a cause; it only
becomes a legal fact when it is characterized in
accordance with some rule of law. The same body
of facts may well be characterized in a number
of ways and give rise to completely separate
causes. For example, the same act may be characterized as murder in one case and as civil fault in
another . . .

It is equally clear that a rule of law removed from
the factual situation cannot be a cause of action in
itself. The rule of law gives rise to a cause of action
when it is applied to a given factual situation; it is
by the intellectual exercise of characterization, of
the linking of the fact and the law, that the cause is
revealed. It would certainly be an error to view a
cause as a rule of law regardless of its application to
the facts considered. Accordingly, the existence of
two applicable rules of law as the basis of the plain-

tiff's rights does not lead directly to the conclusion that two causes exist."[294]

It then explained that characterization required a two-stage analysis:

*(a)* Whether the two causes were based on the same legal *principle*, since

> "[t]wo statutory provisions based on different legal principles cannot give rise to identical causes since the fact regarded as the source of liability will necessarily be different; the legal characterization of the factual situation will similarly be different"[295]

and,

*(b)* Whether on application they would result in the same *effects* on the parties' rights and obligations:

> "If with respect to a given set of facts the effect produced by applying the provision relied on in the second action corresponds to the effect produced by applying the provision relied on in the first, it should be concluded that there is an identity of causes."[296]

Applying this process to the instant case, the Court held that the two causes were the same, such that the rule of *lis pendens* applied.

This analysis is potentially of great utility for international *lis pendens*. It provides a means of comparing causes of action across legal boundaries on the basis of characterization, identification of principle and effect which may well provide guidance in wider contexts. Of course, this is only so if the court approaches the process of characterization in a suitably internationalist

---

[294] *Ibid.*, 455.
[295] *Ibid.*, 456.
[296] *Ibid.*, 457.

spirit, taking into account the impossibility of precise identity of action as between different legal systems. This is a familiar consideration in all systems of the conflict of laws.

It is therefore not a little ironic that the reaction in Quebec to the test propounded by the Supreme Court was that it would operate too narrowly in international cases, since "[i]n most of the cases, the basic principles of the applicable rules will be different and, if not, then the results will be, since this is precisely the reason somebody is shopping for a forum"[297]. Concerns of this kind led the Quebec legislature to introduce a new specific rule for international litispendence, which required identity of parties, *facts*, and object, and abandoned mention of *cause*[298].

It is submitted that these concerns were misplaced. As the Supreme Court pointed out, facts alone have no legal significance unless, by virtue of a rule of law, they give rise to a cause of action. The finding of a point of comparison between causes of action in different legal systems does depend, as the Court thought, on identifying the commonality of principle behind the respective rules. Of course, if this merely meant that the outcome would be the same, because the elements of the rule, and the result which it produces are identical in each system then the Supreme Court's test would be too narrow, and the rule would fail to prevent forum shopping for a different result. It would be a mistake to read the Court's judgment, delivered with a domestic situation in mind, too literally when applied to international cases. But an examination of principle invites comparison at a level which rises above particular differences in rule or outcome, and looks instead at fundamental legal categories and object. This is of the

---

[297] Goldstein, *supra* footnote 293, 161.
[298] Civil Code of Quebec, Art. 3137.

essence of the conflict of litigation process, as it is of the conflict of laws.

## 3. *Assessment of effects*

A strict *prior tempore* rule, based upon the application of the three-fold test of identity developed for judgments in the doctrine of *res judicata*, delivers a clear but narrow response to problems of parallel proceedings. The rule addresses the central concern of litispendence — that, where there is identity, the parties' single dispute should only be litigated and determined by one court. The notion of giving priority to the court first seised operates as a "tie-break rule" in such cases [299].

Where the action in the first court is already far advanced before institution of the second proceedings, the *prior tempore* rule has a logic of its own in the avoidance of the waste of judicial resources, and the possibility of prejudice to the conduct of the first proceedings which may be caused by the late institution of subsequent proceedings. But in other contexts, a strict *prior tempore* rule is something of a "forum shopper's charter" [300], since it encourages both parties to a dispute to be the first to issue proceedings in their forum of choice. This often favours the plaintiff [301]. But it may also encourage the defendant to issue first, claiming that he is not liable to the plaintiff, in order to garner the advantage of his chosen forum. In either case, the

---

[299] *Dresser UK Ltd.* v. *Falcongate Freight Management Ltd.*, [1992] QB 502, 514 (CA).

[300] Magnus/Mankowski/Fentiman, *Brussels I Regulation* (2007), Arts. 27-30, note [17].

[301] Kessedjian in Goldsmith (ed.), *International Dispute Regulation: The Regulation of Forum Selection* (1997) 273; Fawcett, "General Report", in Fawcett (ed.), *supra* footnote 208, 1, 35.

rule encourages litigation, and discourages pre-action settlement[302].

These considerations are of little moment when applied *within* a municipal legal system, since both the substantive law and the procedure applicable in both courts will be the same. In particular, there will be common rules of venue, and the strict rule of *lis pendens* will apply equally to all courts. But none of these factors necessarily apply in an *international* context. On the contrary, it may well be that it is the very differences between the applicable law and procedures of the two courts which prompts the parties to shop for their preferred forum in the first place. Moreover, it is not at all possible to make the same basic assumption of reciprocal application of the rule in an international context. On the contrary, both the rules of primary jurisdiction and the nature and extent of any rule of litispendence may completely differ from one jurisdiction to the next[303]. Thus, while there may be considerable logic in recognizing the principle of international litispendence, the solution of a simple transposition of a *prior tempore* rule derived from internal law produces a number of unwelcome effects when applied in international cases.

All parallel proceedings rules only operate on the basis that *both* courts properly have original jurisdiction according to their own law. But there is nothing inherently superior in the first court's claim to jurisdiction. Outside a double convention providing uniform rules of original jurisdiction, the first court's assumption of jurisdiction may well be made on a basis which

---

[302] Magnus/Mankowski/Fentiman, *supra* footnote 300, note [17].

[303] Lagarde "Le principe de proximité dans le droit international privé contemporain", (1986) 196 *Recueil des cours* 9, 155; Moissinac Massénat, *supra* footnote 220, [13], [234].

has no real and substantial connection with the cause of action. Extreme cases of this kind are likely to result in the judgment being unenforceable in the second state — a factor which would, in countries adopting the recognition prognosis rule, result in the *lis pendens* rule being inapplicable. But the rule still represents a "somewhat crude solution"[304] since it permits no evaluation of the conduct of the parties or the ends of justice in the trial of the particular case.

Now, within the European jurisdiction and judgments system, one must at least assume that each court will apply the same rules of original jurisdiction. These rules, in their operation between the courts of the Member States *inter se,* are not of their nature exorbitant. The priority rule in the Brussels I Regulation does not require the court second seised to decline jurisdiction unless the first court has determined that it has jurisdiction according to these rules. But these common conditions have not in the least prevented the type of forum shopping described above. On the contrary, the mandatory stay required by Article 27 of the Regulation positively incites the issue of proceedings, when coupled with two other elements founded in the internal civil procedure of Member States, whose effect is magnified and not mitigated by the effect of the Regulation itself.

The first arises from the availability in the legal systems of many European countries of the action for a negative declaration. The problem here arises not so much from the nature of the declaratory action itself, as from its jurisdictional effect in international cases. Such an action may be used as a device to claim jurisdiction in the preferred forum of the prospective defendant.

The second problem is delay, coupled with the

---

[304] Collins *et al.* (eds.), *Dicey, Morris & Collins on the Conflict of Laws* (14th ed., 2006) *("Dicey")* [12-045].

absence in a number of legal systems of an ability to
secure an early determination of jurisdiction, prior to
the courts' determination of the merits of the action.
These factors combine in what has become known as a
"torpedo" — the institution of an action in an over-
crowded court, where there is no prospect of an early
determination of the question of jurisdiction. In such a
situation, even a contractual choice of exclusive jurisdiction may not provide protection, if there is no
prospect of securing early enforcement of such a
clause. A rule of litispendence which makes no provision or exception for this problem encourages abuse. It
is necessary to explore each of these problems in a
little more detail in the light of the experience of
the European jurisprudence.

(a) *The negative declaration*

The leading decision of the European Court on the
effect of negative declarations under (now) Article 27
is *Gubisch Maschinenfabrik KG* v. *Giulio Palumbo*[305].
Mr. Palumbo, an Italian resident, brought proceedings
against Gubisch, a German company, in the Tribunale
di Roma seeking a declaration that a contract for the
purchase of a machine was inoperative on a number of
grounds. Gubisch claimed that the Italian court lacked
jurisdiction as a German court (the Flensburg Land-
gericht) was already seised with the suit which
Gubisch had filed to enforce the contract. The Italian
court refused to decline jurisdiction, and on appeal the
Cour de cassation referred to the European Court the
following question: whether Article 21 of the Brussels
Convention (the predecessor of Article 27) covered the
situation where one party sought in one Contracting
State to have a contract declared inoperative or dis-

---

[305] *Gubisch Maschinenfabrik KG* v. *Palumbo*, Case C-
144/86, [1987] *ECR* 4861.

charged and the other party sought in another Contracting State to have the contract enforced. The European Court decided that it did. It held that Article 21 of the Convention had to be construed autonomously and that the two actions had the same subject-matter, since "[t]he question whether the contract is binding therefore lies at the heart of the two actions"[306].

The actual result in *Gubisch* was benign, as it operated to give the German substantive action, which had been started first, priority over the second spoiling action started by the Italian defendant in Rome. But it was not long before defendants began to explore the possibility of launching a so-called "Italian torpedo" in order to pre-empt litigation in the forum which would otherwise be chosen by the plaintiff. This form of application sought to take advantage of the very considerable delays occasioned by the backlog of litigation in Italian courts. In the context of international disputes, the existence of general delays was exacerbated by the fact that a determination of jurisdiction was generally joined to the merits. In this way, determination of the plaintiff's primary claim could be effectively buried.

Commercial parties sought to take refuge from this risk by including in their contracts exclusive jurisdiction clauses. In this way, they hoped to take advantage of the priority accorded in the Convention to party autonomy in choice of forum[307]. But this left unanswered a seemingly technical question of great practical importance. Did Article 17 (now Article 23) take priority over Article 21 (now Article 27), so as to permit a Court, which was second seised, but endowed with jurisdiction by virtue of an exclusive jurisdiction clause, to declare its own jurisdiction and proceed, despite the pendency of a prior action for a negative

---

[306] *Ibid.*, [16].
[307] Art. 17, now Art. 23, Brussels I Regulation.

declaration in a court which had yet to determine its own jurisdiction?

Given that this point was one on which strong views in favour had been entertained in England[308], it was a nice irony that it was through the frustrations of an Austrian court that the European Court was invested with the responsibility to decide the issue in *Erich Gasser GmbH* v. *MISAT Srl*[309]. Gasser, a company incorporated in Austria, sold children's clothes to MISAT, an Italian company, for several years. On 19 April 2000 MISAT applied to the Tribunale di Roma for a ruling that the contract between them had been terminated and seeking damages. On 4 December 2000, Gasser brought an action before the Landesgericht Feldkirch to obtain payment of outstanding invoices. Although under Article 21 the Tribunale was first seised, Gasser claimed that the Landesgericht had jurisdiction not only because Austria was the place of performance but because Gasser's invoices had always included a choice of court clause in the Landesgericht's favour to which MISAT had never objected.

The reference to the European Court therefore squarely raised the question of the relationship between litispendence and an exclusive jurisdiction clause, in circumstances in which there was little prospect of an early jurisdictional decision by the Italian court. The European Court found decisively in favour of the priority of the court first seised, irrespective of either the exclusive jurisdiction clause or the prospect of delay. The Court held that:

> "the court second seised is never in a better position than the court first seised to determine whether the latter has jurisdiction. That jurisdiction is deter-

---

[308] *Continental Bank NA* v. *Aeakos Compania Naviera SA*, [1994] 2 All ER 540 (CA).
[309] Case C-116/02, [2003] *ECR* I-14693.

mined directly by the rules of the Brussels Convention, which are common to both courts and may be interpreted and applied with the same authority by each of them" [310].

This rule still applied in cases where one of the parties sought to rely on an exclusive jurisdiction clause [311].

Nor was the Court impressed by the arguments of delay:

> "[A]n interpretation of Article 21 of the Brussels Convention whereby the application of that article should be set aside where the court first seised belongs to a Member State in whose courts there are, in general, excessive delays in dealing with cases would be manifestly contrary both to the letter and spirit and to the aim of the Convention … [I]t must be borne in mind that the Brussels Convention is necessarily based on the trust …" [312].

It is doubtful whether the emphasis which the European Court continues to place on mutual trust as the paramount value in these cases is really justified. There is an underlying problem of the abuse of the system by litigants which is not addressed by such reasoning. In any event, all Member States of the Union are also parties to the European Convention on Human Rights. Article 6 of the Convention protects the right to a fair trial "within a reasonable time". The European Court of Human Rights has frequently found the courts of some Member States, including Italy, to be in breach of this right by virtue of their excessive delays. As Richard Fentiman has pointed out [313], this provision is potentially applicable to the rules of the European

---

[310] *Ibid.*, [48].
[311] *Ibid.*, [49].
[312] *Ibid.*, [70], [72].
[313] Magnus/Mankowski/Fentiman, *supra* footnote 300, notes [32]-[47].

order themselves, if they have the same effect. In any
event, the European Court considered the position only
where the court first seised was generally known for
excessive delays[314]. A court second seised may well
be able, indeed, required, to apply Article 6 ECHR
directly if, in a particular case, there was a showing of
excessive delay[315].

But, at the more general level of the design of rules
for the conflict of litigations, is there a solution to this
problem? There are three possible options, (which are
not necessarily mutually exclusive). One answer may
be to treat actions for negative declarations differently
from a jurisdictional perspective than other actions.
Whether or not, as Tesauro AG opined in *The Tatry,*
negative declarations are "generally allowed under the
various national procedural laws"[316], it does not necessarily follow that, at least in an international context,
that they are "entirely legitimate in every respect"[317].
German law has one of the most expansive provisions
for declaratory actions[318]. But the German courts have
long held the view as a matter of internal civil procedure that the institution of such an action does not
establish litispendence as against a subsequent coercive
action[319]. In 1996, the Bundesgerichtshof suggested
that such a rule should also apply internationally so
that a subsequent coercive action brought outside the
EU might displace an earlier declaratory action brought
in Germany[320]. In England, actions for negative declara-

---

[314] *Erich Gasser GmbH* v. *MISAT Srl, supra* footnote 309, [56]-[57].
[315] Hess/Pfeiffer/Schlosser, *The Brussels I-Regulation
(EC) No. 44/2001)* (2008), [433]-[440].
[316] *Supra* footnote 262, [23] (Opinion of Tesauro AG).
[317] *Ibid.*
[318] German Code of Civil Procedure, s. 256.
[319] von Mehren, *supra* footnote 233, 353-362.
[320] BGH, 11 December 1996, 134 BGHZ 201, 209-
211, von Mehren, *ibid.*, 359, Gebauer, *"Lis Pendens,* Nega-

tions are scrutinized carefully. If brought as a mere device to seek to secure a forum advantage, such an action is likely to be seen as an abuse of process and is unlikely to avail the applicant in a determination of forum[321].

This option has the advantage that it strikes directly at the form of action which has proved so amenable to abuse in an international situation. But an application of the rule which automatically ceded jurisdiction whenever the action was declaratory could itself wreak injustice where the plaintiff in such a case had a genuine commercial or other reason for seeking a declaration. Sifting out such cases from cases of abuse would require the court to make an evaluation of the motivation for the litigant's conduct. This is inherent in any exception based upon *abus de droit*. But the acceptance of an exception in cases of abuse of rights would not of itself determine which of the two courts seised should make such a determination.

A second possibility would be the reversal of the specific result in *Gasser*, by according the court second seised priority to decide upon jurisdiction where it is the court designated by an exclusive jurisdiction clause (in Brussels Regulation terms — to make Article 27 subject to Article 23). Of course, it is normally for the court whose jurisdiction is challenged to decide the issue, and Article 27 in theory goes no further than to permit that court to make such a determination first.

---

tive Declaratory-Judgment Actions and the First-in-Time Principle", in Gottshalk (ed.), *Conflict of Laws in a Globalized World* (2007) 89. Lower courts in Germany have followed the same approach even in cases under Article 27 (contrary to *Gasser*) holding that negative declaratory actions will not be taken into account on grounds of bad faith: LG Düsseldorf, 19 December 2002, *InstGE* 3.

[321] *Dicey, supra* footnote 304, [12-039]-[12-041]; Bell, "Negative Declarations in Transnational Litigation", (1995) 111 *LQR* 674.

The argument in favour of an exception for the court designated by an exclusive jurisdiction clause is two-fold. In the first place, since such a designation is *exclusive*, by definition it ousts the jurisdiction which other courts would otherwise enjoy. In the second place, the inclusion of a jurisdiction clause is an expression of party autonomy — the combined will of *both* parties, and not merely the result of a choice of forum by one of the parties alone.

Of course, it may be objected that this assumes that the clause is valid, and that it covers the dispute in question. But these are questions, too, which the court designated by the clause is in most cases in the best position to address. As we shall shortly see in Chapter III, these questions have been much addressed in the context of arbitration agreements, where it will be argued that the negative aspect of the *Kompetenz-Kompetenz* principle mandates that the arbitral tribunal should normally have priority in determining its own jurisdiction.

The recent conclusion of the Hague Convention on Choice of Court Agreements 2005[322] strengthens the case for the priority of the chosen court. Articles 5 (1) and (2) provide:

> "1. The court or courts of a Contracting State designated in an exclusive choice of court agreement shall have jurisdiction to decide a dispute to which the agreement applies, unless the agreement is null and void under the law of that State.
> 2. A court that has jurisdiction under paragraph 1 shall not decline to exercise jurisdiction on the ground that the dispute should be decided in a court of another State."

Article 5 (2) is specifically designed to eliminate the

---

[322] See www.hcch.net.

possibility of a plea of *lis pendens* as well as of *forum non conveniens* before the parties' chosen court in cases of exclusive jurisdiction agreements, giving priority to the parties' common choice of forum [323]. The Convention achieves this result by tolerating some risk of parallel proceedings. Thus, Article 6 requires a court not chosen to suspend or dismiss proceedings to which an exclusive jurisdiction clause applies. But that Article is subject to six exceptions, including the nullity of the agreement. It is inherent in the structure of Article 6 that the court not chosen is to make the determination as to whether there is an exclusive choice of court agreement, and, if there is, whether one of the exceptions applies [324] (although the option to suspend rather than to dismiss proceedings would permit that court to defer to the chosen court, if there is a pending motion to dismiss in the chosen court as well). Furthermore, the chosen court may proceed to hear the action irrespective of the decision of another court under Article 6. Thus, the Hague Convention achieves a priority for jurisdiction agreements, without completely eliminating the possibility of parallel proceedings [325].

The conclusion of this Convention may have particular implications for the Brussels I Regulation rule. The European Union signed the Hague Convention, in an exercise of Community competence on behalf of all the Member States, on 1 April 2009. When the Convention is ratified and enters into force, it will not automatically supplant the rules of the Brussels I Regulation as they are applied between the Member States

---

[323] Hartley and Dougachi, "Convention of 30 June 2005 on Choice of Court Agreements Explanatory Report" (2007) [133].

[324] *Ibid.*, [144].

[325] Accord: Brand and Herrup, *The 2005 Hague Convention on Choice of Court Agreements Commentary and Documents* (2008) 88-89.

*inter se*[326]. But nevertheless, the existence of a different rule in relations with third States could well give rise to unacceptable inconsistencies in approach. There is in any event considerable concern within the European Union at the potential of the current law for the abusive flouting of jurisdiction clauses[327]. An influential report commissioned by the European Commission recommends an intermediate solution. It submits that there should be an exception to Article 27 in cases of exclusive jurisdiction clauses, so as to permit the chosen court to continue to hear the case, even if there had been a prior reference to another court[328]. But it does not recommend priority in the determination of the question of jurisdiction in favour of the court designated by the jurisdiction clause. The authors consider that it would be going too far to require any other court always to defer to the court so designated to determine jurisdiction, particularly where there might be an issue over the validity of the jurisdiction clause[329]. If this recommendation is accepted, the outcome under the Brussels I Regulation will be similar to the solution adopted in the Hague Choice of Court Convention.

(b) *The reflexive effect of a convention*

There remains one question which is still undecided as to the scope of the doctrine of *lis pendens* in Europe. That is the question whether a court within the European Union, which has jurisdiction under the Brussels I Regulation over a defendant on the basis of

---

[326] Art. 26 (6).

[327] Hess/Pfeiffer/Schlosser, *supra* footnote 315, [369]-[375], citing in particular the attempt at forum shopping by the debtor on a corporate loan in *J. P. Morgan Europe Ltd.* v. *Primacom AG*, [2005] 2 Lloyd's Rep. 665 (QB); L. G. Mainz, 13 September 2005, WM 2005, 2319.

[328] *Ibid.*, [437]. The question is currently out for public consultation: COM (2009) 175 (21 April 2009), 5-6.

[329] *Ibid.*, [438].

his domicile, may properly decline to exercise that jurisdiction on the ground that the same proceedings are already pending in a court outside the Union.

In *Owusu* v. *Jackson*[330], the Court decided that the Convention did not permit the Court of a Member State to decline jurisdiction on the grounds of the general discretion of *forum non conveniens* in favour of the courts of a non-Contracting State. Owusu, a British national, rented a holiday villa in Jamaica from Mr. Jackson. Both were domiciled in the United Kingdom. Mammee Bay Club Ltd., the owner of the beach, allowed free access to it and on 10 October 1997, Owusu dived in and struck his head against a sub-merged sand bank, rendering him a tetraplegic. He claimed in the United Kingdom for breach of contract against Mr. Jackson, arguing that the contract contained an implied term that the beach would be reasonably safe or free from hidden dangers. Several tort claims were brought against Mammee and others. The defendants asked the English Court to decline jurisdiction on the basis of *forum non conveniens*. Owusu relied on Article 2 of the Convention, which provides that "persons domiciled in a Contracting State shall, whatever their nationality, be sued in the courts of that State", arguing that this removed the English Court's power to stay its proceedings in favour of Jamaica.

The trial Judge held in Owusu's favour. The Court of Appeal referred to the Court of Justice the question whether it was consistent with Article 2 for a Contracting State

"to exercise a discretionary power, available under its national law, to decline to hear proceedings . . . in favour of the courts of a non-Contracting State:
*(a)* if the jurisdiction of no other Contracting State . . .

---

[330] *Owusu* v. *Jackson*, Case C-281/02, [2005] *ECR* I-1383.

is in issue; *(b)* if the proceedings have no connecting factors to any other Contracting State"[331].

If the answer to either question were "yes", the Court
of Appeal sought guidance on whether it would be consistent in all circumstances or only in some, and if so
which. The point of this second part of the reference was
specifically to obtain guidance on the position which
would apply in cases of identical or related proceedings.

The European Court concluded that derogations
from Article 2 could only be permitted when they were
expressly provided for in the Convention. It held that
Article 2 "of the Brussels Convention is mandatory in
nature and . . . according to its terms, there can be no
derogation from the principle it lays down except in the
cases expressly provided for by the Convention"[332].
The *forum non conveniens* principle undermined this
legal certainty and the legal protection of persons
established in the Community[333]. Derogation in such
circumstances was not permitted. In so doing, the
Court necessarily rejected the position that the
Convention only applied in cases as between the courts
of Member States, and accepted that Article 2, as a rule
of original jurisdiction, applied generally for the benefit of the persons domiciled in Contracting States[334].

*Owusu* was not a case in which other proceedings
were already pending in the foreign court (although the
practical result of the Court's decision could well have
been to create two actions determining liability on
the same facts in two separate courts). The Court
studiously declined to answer the second question
in the reference, holding that the question was hypo-

---

[331] *Ibid.*, [22].

[332] *Ibid.*, [37], followed in *Opinion 1/03* [2006] *ECR*
I-1145, [145]-[146].

[333] *Ibid.*, [41], [45].

[334] For the case to the contrary see Collins, "*Forum Non Conveniens* and the Brussels Convention", (1990) 106 *LQR* 535.

thetical, and there was therefore no need to answer it[335]. Article 27 on its terms appears only to contemplate proceedings pending in another Member State. But a reading of the Regulation which precluded any application of the doctrine of litispendence in relation to the courts of a non-Convention State would consign European international civil procedure to incurable insularity: no deference to a foreign court save where there is a express treaty rule providing for it.

Is there any answer to this conundrum? The answer given by Georges Droz (the eminent French scholar of Private International Law and former Secretary-General of the Hague Conference on Private International Law) was that, in situations where the Convention's rules would otherwise require deference to a court of exclusive jurisdiction, but the court referred to was in a non-Convention State, it was open to the court to give the Convention an *"effet réflexe"*[336]. This was particularly so where there was another treaty in force providing for litispendence. But Droz considered that the same result should apply where states admitted litispendence as a principle of their general law:

> "Mais même en dehors de tout Traité, on ne voit pas pourquoi on empêcherait les Etats dont le droit commun admet la litispendance de la respecter et de parvenir ainsi, dans les relations internationales générales, à cette bonne administration de la justice que la Convention de Bruxelles cherche à réaliser dans le cadre de la Communauté."[337]

Returning to the issue some two decades later, Droz remained of the same view[338]. The editors of *Dicey* conclude that:

---

[335] *Supra* footnote 330, [48]-[52].
[336] Droz, *supra* footnote 269.
[337] *Ibid.*, [329].
[338] *Rev. crit.*, 1990.1.

"there can be no sensible justification for insisting that a [Regulation State] court is required to blind itself to the fact that there is a *lis alibi pendens* in a non-Regulation State, especially when the judgment of a court in a non-Regulation State may well be entitled to recognition . . ." [339].

In the light of recent developments in the European Constitutional sphere, it is perhaps unsurprising that it has recently fallen to the High Court in *Ireland* to rule on this point in *Goshawk Dedicated and Others* v. *Life Receivables Ireland Ltd.* [340] Life Receivables was an Irish company, while Goshawk and Cavell (the plaintiffs) were English companies. In June 2005, Life Receivables purchased a partnership interest in a Delaware limited liability partnership. Alleging it was induced into the purchase by misrepresentation, Life Receivables instituted proceedings in Georgia against the plaintiffs. The plaintiffs then began mirror proceedings claiming the opposite relief in Ireland. Life Receivables argued that, notwithstanding Article 2 (which applied as Life Receivables was domiciled in Ireland) the Court retained a discretion to stay proceedings on the basis of *lis alibi pendens*.

Clarke J concluded, however, that the Court was restrained from staying the Irish proceedings by Article 2. He accepted that *Owusu* did not expressly decide the point. But he dismissed the doctrine of "reflexive effect". It was, he thought, an argument which worked by analogy only. But the analogy could not apply, since the "non Member State will not be bound by the terms of the Regulation in its consideration of whether it has jurisdiction" [341]. The consequence was that the Irish proceedings must continue

---

[339] *Dicey*, *supra* footnote 304, [12-044].
[340] [2008] IEHC 90.
[341] *Ibid.*, [6.11]-[6.13].

despite the prior American action, since he had no jurisdiction to stay the action. The decision was appealed to the Supreme Court of Ireland, which, on 30 January 2009 decided to refer it to the European Court of Justice [342].

It is no doubt true that the *lis pendens* rule, like the other rules according exclusive jurisdiction to a single court, cannot be applied strictly to non-Convention States [343]. But the argument as to the reciprocity inherent in a double convention, providing for both jurisdiction and the mutual enforcement of judgments, is only half the story. It leaves out of account the underlying reasons why a court other than that specified should decline jurisdiction — whether because another court has been chosen by the parties (a case where the European Court has already accepted the enforceability of a clause choosing a non-Convention court [344]); or because another court has exclusive jurisdiction *ratione materiae*, as, for example, where the dispute concerns title to foreign land [345]; *or* because the same litigation is already pending in another court. These reasons hold good as much where courts in Member States are considering the position vis-à-vis third States as they do *intra* Community.

Professor Nuyts reached the conclusion in his 2007 study for the European Commission of the options for the exercise of "residual jurisdiction" by Member States vis-à-vis third States that:

> "The best approach would thus probably consist to provide [*sic*] a general reference to national law for declining jurisdiction in favour of non-EU courts, irrespective of the ground of jurisdiction. But

---

[342] [2009] IESC 7, [2009] *IL Pr.* 435.

[343] Nuyts, *supra* footnote 234, [183].

[344] *Coreck Maritime GmbH* v. *Handelsveem BV*, Case C-387/98, [2000] *ECR* I-9337, [19].

[345] Droz, *supra* footnote 338.

such rule should be accompanied by the principle that jurisdiction can be declined under national law only when the court of another EU State has exclusive jurisdiction, has been seized of a parallel proceedings, or has been appointed by the parties."[346]

This result — applying the categories of exception to Article 2 recognized by the Regulation vis-à-vis third States, but leaving the precise definition of the scope of the exception to national law — is one which could sensibly be reached by determining the spatial application of the Regulation as a matter of construction of its object and purpose as a whole, even in cases where the defendant is domiciled in a Member State[347]. It is to be hoped that this is the conclusion reached by the European Court, since otherwise the application of the Regulation's rules is likely to precipitate widespread abuse to the detriment of both Europeans and non-Europeans, neither of whom will be protected against duplicate proceedings. Further, and particularly in the case of the heads of exclusive jurisdiction, it would lead to unjustified incursions upon the legitimate territorial domain of states outside the Union.

At this stage in the analysis, then, it may be observed that the idea that a court ought to defer to a court which is already hearing the same case, at least where the judgment of that court is likely to be recognized in the forum, is now an established principle in Civil Law legal systems. However, the question whether such a general principle will be accepted as applicable outside the *lex specialis* of a treaty remains unanswered by the European Court. The majority of

---

[346] Nuyts, *supra* footnote 234, [185].

[347] Accord *Dicey*, *supra* footnote 304, [12-022]; Hare "Forum Non Conveniens in Europe: Game Over or Time for Reflexion ?", [2006] *JBL* 157, 174-175.

Continental European countries have adopted a liberal rule of recognition in their general law, applying *lis pendens* to foreign court proceedings on a discretionary basis. This has disposed many writers to consider that such a rule should still be applicable, even within the framework of the Brussels I Regulation.

Application of the strict rule shows that the test for the comparability of proceedings depends upon identifying similarities in the *principle* which the legal rule in each system is designed to serve, and the *effect* which the application of the rule will have. A strict rule of *lis pendens* will not, however, control forum shopping, unless it is capable of dealing with the pursuit of claims by related parties; and the pursuit of reverse litigation, the claim for a negative declaration, as a means of pre-empting the choice of forum.

This chapter will now therefore turn to examine to what extent these problems can be addressed by means of judicial discretions to decline jurisdiction.

## C. *Jurisdiction-declining Discretions*

The Common Law may have been slow to embrace the notion that it could decline to exercise jurisdiction on the ground that another court was a more appropriate forum for the resolution of the matter. But, at least in the last quarter century[348], English law has adopted the Scottish doctrine of *forum non conveniens* (appropriate forum) with the fervour of the convert. Indeed, as Lord Goff observed in the passage with which this chapter opened, the doctrine is, along with the anti-suit injunction, now seen as one of the Common Law's two weapons to deal with clashes of jurisdiction between courts. Thus, for the Common lawyer, the situation of

---

[348] Since *MacShannon* v. *Rockware Glass Ltd.*, *supra* footnote 211.

litispendence is simply regarded as a factor within a larger question of identifying the appropriate forum for the resolution of the dispute[349]. This is a question which frequently arises when there is no litigation already pending in the foreign forum at all. Indeed, as has been seen, in its origins in Scotland, the doctrine was primarily concerned with curbing the excesses of jurisdiction, rather than with parallel proceedings.

The study of deference to foreign litigation in the Common Law is therefore a matter of assessing the weight given to this factor in the context of the exercise of a wider discretion. Two different situations may be identified:

*(a)* the pursuit of parallel litigation by the same plaintiff in two jurisdictions — which is seen as a question of election; and,

*(b)* the treatment of parallel litigation when it is part of a forum contest between plaintiff and defendant — where the court will engage in a wider assessment of where the dispute as a whole can be best resolved.

*1. Litispendence within the* forum non conveniens *enquiry*

  (a) *Double litigation by the same plaintiff*

The English courts for long vacillated on the extent to which they were prepared to intervene where the plaintiff had already commenced a foreign action on the same cause, and then sought to litigate the same cause in England[350]. But it is now clear that the plain-

---

[349] *Dicey, supra* footnote 304, [12-036]; Bell, *Forum Shopping and Venue in Transnational Litigation* (2003) [3.96]-[3.113].
[350] Early cases in which it was thought that either a stay should be granted or the plaintiff should be put to his

tiff will be put to his election in such a case. This is not
a matter of meeting some higher test of vexation[351]; or
of determining *in abstracto* the appropriate forum.

In *Australian Commercial Research and Development Ltd.* v. *ANZ McCaughan Merchant Bank Ltd.*[352]
the plaintiff, a Queensland company, entered into an
agreement with the defendant and five brokers for the
placement of shares in the plaintiff. The defendant and
brokers were based in London but were part of an
Australian banking group carrying on business in
Australia. When a dispute arose, the plaintiff issued
proceedings in England against the defendant only, to
which the defendant replied with a counterclaim. In the
meantime the plaintiff issued proceedings against the
defendant and the broker in Queensland. The plaintiff
then applied in England for a stay of the counterclaim,
offering to stay its English claim to allow the whole
dispute to be litigated in Queensland. Sir Nicholas
Browne-Wilkinson V-C ruled that the plaintiff in such
circumstances had to elect which claim to pursue and
which to have dismissed (not merely stayed). It was a
question of election, and not of *forum non conve-*

---

election include: *The Mali Ivo*, (1869) LR 2 A. & E. 356
(Admiralty action in England and prior proceedings in
the Austrian consular court in Constantinople); and
*The Christiansborg*, (1885) LR 10 PD 141 (collision
action in the Netherlands, subsequent action in England
stayed).
[351] As Lord Denning MR apparently thought in *Ionian
Bank Ltd.* v. *Couvreur*, [1969] 2 All ER 651 (CA), applying *McHenry* v. *Lewis*, (1882) 22 Ch. D. 397 and *Peruvian
Guano* v. *Bockwoldt*, (1883) LR 23 Ch. D. 225 (both cases
in which the English proceedings had in fact been commenced first). The early cases are analysed in McClean,
*supra* footnote 212, 940-943, and Bell, *supra* footnote 349,
[3.71]-[3.77].
[352] *Australian Commercial Research and Development
Ltd.* v. *ANZ McCaughan Merchant Bank Ltd.*, [1989] 3 All
ER 65 (Ch.).

*niens*[353]. In the circumstances it was appropriate for the Court to give the plaintiff leave to discontinue the English action and stay the counterclaim.

In this situation, the Court may, if necessary, reinforce the election by granting an injunction to restrain the plaintiff from pursuit of his litigation abroad, if to do so would be oppressive[354].

### (b) *A forum contest between plaintiff and defendant*

But the technique of election cannot operate where two opposing parties have started rival proceedings in two countries. This was the situation in one of the landmark cases in the formation of the modern English doctrine of *forum non conveniens*. Right up to 1983, the English courts had insisted as orthodox that the disadvantages involved in a situation of litispendence "by themselves, have never hitherto been considered sufficient to justify a stay"[355]. The doctrine of *lis pendens*, it was said, "is no part of the law of England"[356].

Then, in 1984, an appeal was brought on to the House of Lords in a case called *The Abidin Daver*[357]. The case concerned a collision in the Bosphorus between ships owned by the Cuban plaintiffs and the Turkish defendants. In April 1982 the defendants began suit in the Turkish courts claiming damages. In June the plaintiffs brought an action *in rem* against the defendants in the Admiralty Court in England, to

---

[353] *Ibid.*, 70.

[354] *McHenry* v. *Lewis*, *supra* footnote 351, and *Peruvian Guano Co.* v. *Bockwoldt*, *supra* footnote 351, approved by the Privy Council in *SNI Aerospatiale* v. *Lee Kui Jak*, [1987] AC 871, 893 (PC (Brunei)).

[355] *The Tillie Lykes*, [1977] 1 Lloyd's Rep 124, 126 (QB) per Brandon J, approved by the Court of Appeal in *The Abidin Daver*, [1983] 1 WLR 884.

[356] *Ibid.*, 128.

[357] *The Abidin Daver*, [1984] AC 398 (HL).

which the defendants responded by requesting a stay of the English action. At first instance this was granted on the basis that justice could be done in Turkey at substantially less expense and inconvenience and that it would not deprive the plaintiffs of a legitimate advantage. The Court of Appeal reversed this decision. But the House of Lords reinstated the stay, holding that the additional inconvenience and expense resulting from the plaintiff instituting a mirror action could only be justified if the would-be plaintiff could establish that staying the English proceedings would deprive him of some personal or juridical advantage and thereby cause injustice.

Lord Diplock specifically considered

"the extent to which the existence of *lis alibi pendens* ought to influence a judge in exercising his discretion whether or not to impose a stay upon an action which it is sought to bring in England on the same subject matter by a person who is already a defendant in the foreign action"[358].

He held:

"[T]he essential change in the attitude of the English courts to pending or prospective litigation in foreign jurisdictions that has been achieved step-by-step during the last 10 years as a result of the successive decisions of this House in *The Atlantic Star* [1974] AC 436; *MacShannon* [1978] AC 795 and *Amin Rasheed* [1984] AC 50, is that judicial chauvinism has been replaced by judicial comity to an extent which I think the time is now ripe to acknowledge frankly is, in the field of law with which this appeal is concerned, indistinguishable from the Scottish legal doctrine of forum non conveniens.

---

[358] *Ibid.*, 409.

Where a suit about a particular subject matter between a plaintiff and a defendant is already pending in a foreign court which is a natural and appropriate forum for the resolution of the dispute between them, and the defendant in the foreign suit seeks to institute as plaintiff an action in England about the same matter to which the person who is plaintiff in the foreign suit is made defendant, then the additional inconvenience and expense which must result from allowing two sets of legal proceedings to be pursued concurrently in two different countries where the same facts will be in issue and the testimony of the same witnesses required, can only be justified if the would-be plaintiff can establish objectively by cogent evidence that there is some personal or judicial advantage that would be available to him only in the English action that is of such importance that it would cause injustice to him to deprive him of it." [359]

Lord Diplock's test would have established a strong presumption in favour of the foreign court first seised. But it was rapidly to face reinterpretation by the House of Lords, under the leadership in this field of Lord Goff, as the House sought to lay down general principles of the modern doctrine of *forum non conveniens*. The leading modern case on the general doctrine, *Spiliada Maritime Corporation* v. *Cansulex Ltd.* [360], was decided by the House of Lords three years later. It did not involve litigation already pending in another jurisdiction. But the existence of *related* litigation already pending in England nevertheless did prove to be decisive in the appropriate forum equation. In that case, Liberian shipowners chartered their vessel to an Indian

---

[359] *Ibid.*, 411-412.
[360] *Spiliada Maritime Corporation* v. *Cansulex Ltd.* [1987] AC 460 (HL).

company for the transport of sulphur from Vancouver to India. The shipowners alleged that Cansulex, the Canadian sulphur producer, loaded wet sulphur on board and this caused significant damage to the hold. Leave was obtained by the shipowners to serve a writ on Cansulex outside the jurisdiction on the basis that the action was in respect of a contract governed by English law (pursuant to the bills of lading). Simultaneous with Cansulex's application before Staughton J to set aside the leave, the same judge heard a very similar action concerning similar allegations against Cansulex in relation to another ship, the *Cambridgeshire*. The *Cambridgeshire* action involved 15 counsel, each "equipped with 75 files; . . . the then estimate for the length of the trial was six months" [361].

Staughton J refused to set aside the proceedings, concluding that the availability of witnesses, the potential multiplicity of proceedings and the accumulated experience of counsel and solicitors from involvement in the *Cambridgeshire* action (described as the crucial "*Cambridgeshire* factor") [362] favoured continuation of the claim in England. The House of Lords agreed. Lord Goff restated the basic principle of the doctrine of *forum non conveniens* in the following terms:

> "[A] stay will only be granted on the ground of forum non conveniens where the court is satisfied that there is some other available forum, having competent jurisdiction, which is the appropriate forum for the trial of the action, i.e. in which the case may be tried more suitably for the interests of all the parties and the ends of justice." [363]

The following year, the House was specifically

---

[361] *Ibid.*, 467.
[362] *Ibid.*, 485.
[363] *Ibid.*, 476.

asked to consider the relevance within the *Spiliada* test of the existence of concurrent identical proceedings in another jurisdiction. The case concerned concurrent divorce proceedings brought by the Count and Countess de Dampierre in France and England respectively[364]. The United Kingdom Parliament had specifically legislated to provide that the English courts could grant a stay in a case where divorce proceedings were already pending in a foreign court[365]. The question for the House was how such discretion was to be exercised. Lord Goff considered that the statutory test was on all fours with the doctrine of *forum non conveniens,* and he therefore stated the test in terms equally applicable to the Common Law as to the statute. In his view, what was required was an assessment of the purpose for which the foreign proceedings had been instituted and the stage which they had reached:

> "[T]he existence of such proceedings may, depending on the circumstances, be relevant to the inquiry. Sometimes they may be of no relevance at all, for example, if one party has commenced the proceedings for the purpose of demonstrating the existence of a competing jurisdiction, or the proceedings have not passed beyond the stage of the

---

[364] *de Dampierre* v. *de Dampierre*, [1988] AC 92 (HL).

[365] Schedule 1, para. 9, of the Domicile and Matrimonial Proceedings Act 1973 provides that English divorce proceedings may be stayed if it appears to the court

"(1) . . . *(b)* that the balance of fairness (including convenience) as between the parties to the marriage is such that it is appropriate for the proceedings in [another jurisdiction] to be disposed of before further steps are taken in the proceedings [in England] . . .

(2) In considering the balance of fairness and convenience . . . the court shall have regard to all factors appearing to be relevant, including the convenience of witnesses and any delay."

initiating process. But if, for example, genuine proceedings have been started and have not merely
been started but have developed to the stage where
they have had some impact upon the dispute
between the parties, especially if such impact is
likely to have a continuing effect, then this may be a
relevant factor to be taken into account when considering whether the foreign jurisdiction provides
the appropriate forum for the resolution of the dispute between the parties." [366]

The result, then, of this restatement of the place of
litispendence within the doctrine of *forum non conveniens* is that pending foreign litigation will be only one
factor within the court's assessment of the appropriate
forum. The mere fact that such litigation has been commenced will not necessarily be decisive:

*(a)* if, as may be the case of an action for a negative
declaration, the foreign litigation has transparently
been commenced purely for tactical purposes, in
order to try to shift the forum in accordance with
the defendant's preferences, it is likely to be
accorded relatively little weight [367];
*(b)* if, on the other hand, the litigation is far advanced,
and likely to determine the whole dispute, it will
be granted greater weight in the determination of
appropriate forum — just as the pendency of
related litigation in the forum may be an important
factor in the same determination, as was the case in
*The Spiliada* itself.

Even the High Court of Australia, which alone
amongst Anglo-Commonwealth jurisdictions has
declined to adopt the modern doctrine of *forum non*

---

[366] *de Dampierre* v. *de Dampierre, supra* footnote 364,
108.
[367] *Dicey, supra* footnote 304, [12-039].

*conveniens* [368], has nevertheless recognized the importance of foreign parallel proceedings in determining whether Australian proceedings ought to be stayed as vexatious and oppressive. "It is", thought the High Court in a case which also involved parallel divorce proceedings, "prima facie vexatious and oppressive, in the strict sense of those terms, to commence a second or subsequent action in the courts of this country if an action is already pending with respect to the matter in issue." [369] The practical problems which arose where the same controversy was litigated in different countries meant that such a principle was equally applicable to international cases as to domestic ones.

## 2. *Declining jurisdiction in favour of related proceedings*

Beyond cases of identity of action, the Common Law principle of *forum non conveniens* has also, as *Spiliada* and subsequent cases show, been deployed to ensure that, so far as possible, closely related claims are litigated together so that the whole dispute might be resolved [370].

But it should not be thought that the exercise of discretion to decline jurisdiction in favour of the courts of another country is the exclusive preserve of the Common Law. On the contrary, as has been seen, the civil procedure codes of many Civil Law countries also include a provision permitting the court to stay its proceedings in favour of a court exercising jurisdiction over related proceedings. Yet, despite the move towards extending *lis pendens* to foreign litigation, there has

---

[368] *Voth* v. *Manildra Flour Mills Pty Ltd.* (1990) 171 CLR 538.

[369] *Henry* v. *Henry*, (1995-1996) 185 CLR 571, 591.

[370] See for example *McConnell Dowell Constructors Ltd* v. *Lloyd's Syndicate 396*, [1988] 2 NZLR 257 (CA).

been no similar movement towards the translation of the related proceedings discretion across borders in national civil procedure codes. Indeed, Baumgartner observes that "the courts of many civil law countries appear to remain hostile to the notion of applying these rules to transnational cases"[371].

In, France, for example, despite the views of many eminent scholars in favour of international *connexité*, the courts have until recently opposed it, on the grounds that there is little risk of irreconcilable judgments, since the French court can always refuse enforcement of a foreign contrary judgment[372]. This reasoning only holds good up to a point, since the resistance of the French court to recognition or enforcement at home cannot protect the French litigant from the effects of two contrary judgments abroad.

At all events, in framing the Brussels Convention, in line with earlier bilateral precedents, the Member States included a provision for a discretionary stay in favour of a related action. The provision is now found in a broader revised form in Article 28 of the Brussels I Regulation. The discretion is extended to any court other than the first seised. Paragraph 3 reinforces the perceived necessary link between related actions and enforcement by adding the following definition of related actions:

> "For the purposes of this Article, actions are deemed to be related where they are so closely connected that it is expedient to hear and determine them together to avoid the risk of irreconcilable judgments resulting from separate proceedings."

Yet despite, or perhaps because of, the width of the

---

[371] Baumgartner, *supra* footnote 209, 207.

[372] Huet, *Compétence des tribunaux français à l'égard des litiges internationaux* (2004) [41]-[43].

discretion granted by this Article, there is relatively
little reported jurisprudence on its application. The
European Court had emphasized in *The Tatry* that the
objective of Article 22 of the Brussels Convention (the
predecessor to Article 28) is to improve co-ordination
of the exercise of judicial functions within the
Community and to avoid conflicting and contradictory
decisions, thus facilitating the proper administration of
justice in the Community [373]. On this basis the court
rejected the argument that the phrase "irreconcilable
judgments" should be interpreted so as to confine it to
cases where the decisions would have mutually exclusive legal consequences.

The House of Lords in England applied this broad
view in *Sarrio S.A.* v. *Kuwait Investment Authority* [374].
which concerned competing proceedings in Spain and
England. The parties had negotiated the sale and purchase of the plaintiff Spanish company's paper business. In February 1993 the plaintiff commenced proceedings in Spain claiming that the defendant and
others were liable for amounts unpaid under a put
option in connection with the sale of the business.
Subsequently, the plaintiff also commenced proceedings against the defendant for misrepresentation that, it
alleged, induced the plaintiff into the sale. The point at
issue was whether these constituted "related proceedings" for the purposes of Article 22 of the Brussels
Convention, in which case deference to the Spanish
court may be appropriate as the court first seised.
Mance J held that the risk of irreconcilable judgments
required the English proceedings be stayed. After the
Court of Appeal reversed this decision the House of
Lords reinstated the stay. It was not appropriate to dis-

---

[373] *The Tatry*, *supra* footnote 262, [31], [51], [54].
[374] *Sarrio SA* v. *Kuwait Investment Authority*, [1999] 1
AC 32 (HL).

tinguish between primary issues necessary to establish a cause of action and incidental issues. Rather, the Court should adopt a "broad commonsense approach", bearing in mind the objectives of the Article[375].

## D. The Rise and Fall of the Anti-suit Injunction

### 1. Commonwealth use of anti-suit injunctions to control foreign parallel litigation

The final technique which has been used in Private International litigation to deal with parallel litigation is the anti-suit injunction — an order directed to one of the parties directing it not to pursue litigation in a foreign court. It has been seen that this remedy, which owes its origins to the historic battle between the Courts of Equity and of the Common Law in England, is considerably older, at least in English practice, than *forum non conveniens*. The remedy is inherently controversial, since it contemplates interference, even if only indirectly, with the process of a foreign court. Its very subject-matter is parallel proceedings. Yet the central concern which lies behind this remedy is not the control of foreign courts, but rather the control of litigants who are acting in bad faith by pursuing vexatious and oppressive litigation. The remedy is therefore rather deeply attached to the central function of Equity — namely to ensure that the strict letter of the law is not allowed to subvert good conscience.

In its application to international cases in Victorian times, the anti-suit injunction was used primarily in cases where an English judgment had already been rendered, thus supporting the *res judicata* effect of English judgments[376]. Only secondarily was it seen as

---

[375] *Ibid.*, 41.
[376] See for example *Booth* v. *Leycester*, (1837) 1 Keen 579, 48 ER 430.

dealing with pre-judgment parallel proceedings, where an assessment had to be made as to whether the foreign action was less well suited to further the ends of justice than an English one. As it was put in the leading text, *Kerr on Injunctions*:

> "Even though no decree has been obtained in this country, yet if a suit instituted abroad does not appear so well calculated to answer the ends of justice as the suit here, the Court will restrain the foreign action, imposing, however, terms which it considers reasonable for protecting the party whom it enjoins." [377]

Where the remedy is sought in the context of parallel *pending* proceedings, this assessment necessitates a two-step determination of the most appropriate forum for the trial of the action, and whether the defendant's pursuit of the foreign action can be seen as oppressive. The way in which this may work out in practice is well illustrated by the leading decision of the Privy Council on appeal from Brunei.

*Société Nationale Industrielle Aerospatiale* v. *Lee Kui Jak* [378] concerned a helicopter crash in Brunei. The widow and estate of the deceased commenced proceedings, *inter alia*, in both Brunei and Texas against Aerospatiale, the French manufacturer of the helicopter. In the Texas proceedings jurisdiction was established on the basis that Aerospatiale was regarded as "doing business" there. An application by Aerospatiale to the Texas court for dismissal of the action on the grounds of *forum non conveniens* was declined. Aerospatiale therefore brought an application to High

---

[377] Kerr, *Injunctions in Equity* (1st ed., 1867) 156, (6th ed., 1927) 599; this point is made by Lawrence Collins LJ in *Masri* v. *Consolidated Contractors International Co. SAL*, [2008] EWCA Civ. 625, [2008] 1 CLC 887, [84].

[378] *Supra* footnote 354.

Court in Brunei for an anti-suit injunction restraining
the Texas proceedings. The High Court declined the
application. The Court of Appeal upheld the refusal to
grant the anti-suit injunction on the basis that the work
done by the plaintiffs' Texas attorneys had rendered
Texas the natural and appropriate forum.

The Privy Council reversed the Court of Appeal. It
found that it was not sufficient merely to determine
which of the two fora was the more appropriate,
approaching the matter as the reverse side of a stay
application[379]. Vexatious or oppressive conduct
amounting to injustice on the part of the foreign plaintiff had to be found. In this case, this requirement was
satisfied not simply because the plaintiff was proceeding in a forum which had no material connection with
the claim or the defendant. Rather, if the proceedings
continued in Texas, Aerospatiale would suffer injustice
in the difficulties which it would encounter in bringing
a contribution claim against the owners of the helicopter, Bristow Malaysia.

Lord Goff restated the basic test as follows:

> "From an early stage, certain basic principles
> emerged which are now beyond dispute. First, the
> jurisdiction is to be exercised when the 'ends of jus-
> tice' require it . . . Second, where the court decides
> to grant an injunction restraining proceedings in a
> foreign court, its order is directed not against the
> foreign court but against the parties so proceeding
> or threatening to proceed. . . . Third, it follows that
> an injunction will only be issued restraining a party
> who is amenable to the jurisdiction of the court,
> against whom an injunction will be an effective
> remedy . . . Fourth, it has been emphasised on many

---

[379] As had for a time been thought: *Castanho* v. *Brown
& Root (UK) Ltd.*, [1981] AC 557, 575 (HL); *British Airways Board* v. *Laker Airways Ltd.*, *supra* footnote 248, 80.

occasions that, since such an order indirectly affects the foreign court, the jurisdiction is one which must be exercised with caution . . .

In the opinion of their Lordships, in a case such as the present where a remedy for a particular wrong is available both in the English (or, as here, the Brunei) court and in a foreign court, the English or Brunei court will, generally speaking, only restrain the plaintiff from pursuing proceedings in the foreign court if such pursuit would be vexatious or oppressive. . . . So the court will not grant an injunction if, by doing so, it will deprive the plaintiff of advantages in the foreign forum of which it would be unjust to deprive him. Fortunately, however, as the present case shows, that problem can often be overcome by appropriate undertakings given by the defendant, or by granting an injunction upon appropriate terms." [380]

Returning, therefore, to the image of litigation which animates each legal system's remedies in this field, the factor which was decisive for the Privy Council was the need to consolidate the entire dispute (and not merely the claim as between the litigants currently before the court in either country) in Brunei. This was not merely because it was the natural forum, being the place where the accident had occurred. It was also because, if the claim against Aerospatiale did turn out to be well-founded, it would need to be able to join a third party, Bristow Malaysia, to the action. That was something which the evidence showed it would be unable to compel in Texas, but which was open to it in Brunei.

The anti-suit injunction has also been applied to the control of trans-national parallel litigation in other

---

[380] *Supra* footnote 354, 892, 896.

Commonwealth countries[381], with notable judgments by the Supreme Court of Canada and the High Court of Australia.

In *Workers' Compensation Board* v. *Amchem Products Inc.*[382] the plaintiff, who had paid out compensation to workers who had suffered injury from asbestos, sought to recover damages from the US manufacturers by means of its subrogated interest. Most of the workers were from British Columbia, while the defendant companies had no connection with the province. The Board sued the companies in Texas, alleging tortious behaviour in the manufacture and marketing of asbestos, and the Texas court found it had jurisdiction and rejected the availability of a plea of *forum non conveniens*. The Supreme Court of British Columbia, meanwhile, granted an anti-suit injunction to halt the Texas actions, which was upheld on appeal. The Texas court responded with an anti-anti-suit injunction.

The Supreme Court of Canada, asked to rule on the principles upon which a court should exercise its discretion to grant an anti-suit injunction, concluded that there was sufficient evidence to support the Texas claim to jurisdiction, and therefore an anti-suit injunction was not appropriate. It considered the relationship between the notion of comity and the grant of anti-suit injunctions, holding:

"In a world where comity was universally respected and the courts of countries which are the potential fora for litigation applied consistent prin-

---

[381] For a comparative assessment see Briggs, "Anti-suit Injunctions in a Complex World", in Rose (ed.), *Lex Mercatoria*: *Essays on International Commercial Law in Honour of Francis Reynolds* (2000) 219; Raphael, *The Anti-suit Injunction* (2008).
[382] [1993] 1 SCR 897, (1993) 102 DLR (4th) 96.

ciples with respect to the stay of proceedings, anti-
suit injunctions would not be necessary. A court
which qualified as the appropriate forum for the
action would not find it necessary to enjoin similar
proceedings in a foreign jurisdiction because it
could count on the foreign court staying those proceedings . . .

While the above scenario is one we should strive
to attain, it has not yet been achieved. Courts of
other jurisdictions do occasionally accept jurisdiction over cases that do not satisfy the basic requirements of the forum non conveniens test. Comity is
not universally respected. In some cases a serious
injustice will be occasioned as a result of the failure
of a foreign court to decline jurisdiction. It is only
in such circumstances that a court should entertain
an application for an anti-suit injunction." [383]

The Court therefore set itself the task of reconciling
the dictates of the principle of comity with the reality
of inconsistent national approaches to determinations
of forum:

"The result of the application of these principles
is that when a foreign court assumes jurisdiction on
a basis that generally conforms to our rule of private
international law relating to the forum non conveniens, that decision will be respected and a
Canadian court will not purport to make the decision for the foreign court. The policy of our courts
with respect to comity demands no less. If, however,
a foreign court assumes jurisdiction on a basis that
is inconsistent with our rules of private international
law and an injustice results to a litigant or 'would-
be' litigant in our courts, then the assumption of
jurisdiction is inequitable and the party invoking the

---

[383] *Ibid.*, [29]-[30].

foreign jurisdiction can be restrained. The foreign court, not having, itself, observed the rules of comity, cannot expect its decision to be respected on the basis of comity." [384]

The significance of this decision for the present study is in the emphasis placed by the Supreme Court of Canada on the concept of comity in assessing whether the foreign courts' assumption of jurisdiction was legitimate. It did not matter for this purpose whether or not the foreign court applied the same rules, so long as the result was consistent. Only if it were not would the court intervene by way of an injunction.

*CSR Ltd.* v. *Cigna Insurance Australia Ltd.* [385] also involved claims relating to asbestos, and a jurisdiction battle involving courts in the United States. An Australian company and its subsidiary instituted proceedings against their insurers and the parent of the Australian lead insurer in the United States District Court, District of New Jersey. They sought declarations that they were entitled to indemnities in respect of asbestos claims made against the Australian company. The company had been sued in Australia and the United States for selling asbestos fibre to New Jersey companies. A number of the insurers (including the lead insurer) commenced proceedings in New South Wales seeking a declaration that they were not liable to indemnify the Australian company or its subsidiary and requesting an anti-suit injunction to restrain the United States proceedings. The Australian company and its subsidiary sought a stay of the Australian proceedings. The Supreme Court granted the injunction and refused the stay.

The High Court of Australia decided that the

---

[384] *Ibid.*, [61].
[385] *CSR Ltd.* v. *Cigna Insurance Australia Ltd.,* (1996-1997) 189 CLR 345.

Supreme Court had erred in holding that there was no
serious question to be tried as to whether the United
States proceedings were vexatious or oppressive.
Furthermore, the High Court ruled that the New South
Wales proceedings should be stayed as they *were*
oppressive and no more than an attempt to thwart the
United States proceedings. In an important passage, the
High Court specifically considered the approach which
ought to be taken when there were proceedings pend-
ing both in Australia and abroad:

> "It was held by this Court in *Henry* v. *Henry* that,
> where proceedings are pending both in an
> Australian court and in a court of another country, it
> is necessary for the Australian court to have regard
> to the existence of the foreign proceedings in deter-
> mining whether to stay its own proceedings on
> forum non conveniens grounds . . .
>
> The situation involved in the present case is not
> precisely the same as that considered in *Henry* v.
> *Henry*. In that case, the parties were identical and
> the same subject matter, namely, the parties' marital
> relationship, was involved in both proceedings.
> There is not the same correspondence of subject
> matter in this case . . .
>
> In cases such as the present, where different
> issues are involved in the local and foreign proceed-
> ings, albeit that the different proceedings arise out
> of the same sub-stratum of fact, the question is not
> whether the Australian court is a clearly inappro-
> priate forum for the litigation of the issues involved
> in the Australian proceedings. Rather, the question
> must be whether, having regard to the contro-
> versy as a whole, the Australian proceedings are
> vexatious or oppressive in the *Voth* sense of
> those terms, namely, that they are 'productive of
> serious and unjustified trouble and harassment' or

'seriously and unfairly burdensome, prejudicial or damaging'." [386]

Applying that test to the case before it, the High Court concluded:

> "The facts indicate that the respondents' dominant purpose in instituting the NSW proceedings was to prevent the appellants from pursuing remedies available in the US proceedings but not in the NSW proceedings. It follows that the NSW proceedings are oppressive, in the *Voth* sense, and should be stayed. The appropriate course is for them to be stayed pending the outcome of the US proceedings with liberty to the parties to apply on seven days notice if circumstances so require." [387]

The High Court's test, then, for parallel related proceedings was one which required an assessment of the requisite degree of injustice *"having regard to the controversy as a whole"* [388].

## 2. *A division of principle in the United States*

In the United States, there has been no authoritative determination by the Supreme Court of the standard applicable to the grant of anti-suit injunctions to restrain foreign parallel litigation [389]. In the absence of such direction, the circuits of the United States courts have divided on the question. Some circuits (notably the 5th, 7th and 9th) take a "lax" approach, finding that

---

[386] *Ibid.*, 399-401 (citations omitted).
[387] *Ibid.*, 402.
[388] *Ibid.* (emphasis added).
[389] For discussion see Vollmer, *supra* footnote 247, 237; Born and Rutledge, *supra* footnote 240, 540-560; Treviño de Coale, "Stay, Dismiss, Enjoin, or Abstain?: A Survey of Foreign Parallel Litigation in the Federal Courts of the United States", (1999) 17 *BU Int'l LJ* 79.

the very pendency of parallel litigation can provide a ground for the grant of an injunction. Others (notably the District of Columbia, 1st, 2nd, 3rd and 6th circuits) take a strict approach, following the seminal reasoning of Judge Wilkey in *Laker Airways,* and do not regard parallel litigation as offensive *per se.* For these courts, some much greater interference with the court's own process is required to justify the grant of an anti-suit injunction. An example of each approach will demonstrate contrasting principles which the courts have considered. Both cases concerned disputes over the distribution of American products in Asia.

*Kaepa, Inc.* v. *Achilles Corporation*[390] is a 5th Circuit decision exemplifying the "lax" or interventionist approach. It involved an agreement under which Achilles, a Japanese company, distributed in Japan shoes produced by Kaepa, an American manufacturer. The contract expressly provided that it was governed by Texas law; that it would be enforceable in Texas and that Achilles submitted to the jurisdiction of the Texas courts. After difficulties arose, Kaepa commenced proceedings alleging both that it had been induced into the agreement by fraud and misrepresentation and that Achilles had breached the contract. Achilles then brought a mirror application in Japan, alleging that it was Kaepa which had induced it to enter into the contract by fraud, and that is was Kaepa which had breached the contract. Kaepa responded by seeking an anti-suit injunction. The district court refused Achilles' motion to dismiss the substantive action on the ground of *forum non conveniens* and granted the injunction. The Court of Appeals, Fifth Circuit, ruled that the Judge had not abused his discretion in granting the injunction and it was upheld.

The Court held:

---

[390]  76 F. 3d 624 (5th Cir., 1996).

"[A] district court does not abuse its discretion by issuing an antisuit injunction when it has determined "that allowing simultaneous prosecution of the same action in a foreign forum thousands of miles away would result in 'inequitable hardship' and 'tend to frustrate and delay the speedy and efficient determination of the cause'.

... We decline, however, to require a district court to genuflect before a vague and omnipotent notion of comity every time that it must decide whether to enjoin a foreign action.

In the instant case, for example, it simply cannot be said that the grant of the antisuit injunction actually threatens relations between the United States and Japan. First, no public international issue is implicated by the case: Achilles is a private party engaged in a contractual dispute with another private party. Second, the dispute has been long and firmly ensconced within the confines of the United States judicial system: Achilles consented to jurisdiction in Texas; stipulated that Texas law and the English language would govern any dispute; appeared in an action brought in Texas; removed that action to a federal court in Texas; engaged in extensive discovery pursuant to the directives of the federal court; and only then, with the federal action moving steadily toward trial, brought identical claims in Japan. Under these circumstances, we cannot conclude that the district court's grant of an antisuit injunction in any way trampled on notions of comity.

On the contrary, the facts detailed above strongly support the conclusion that the prosecution of the Japanese action ... would result in unwarranted inconvenience, expense, and vexation." [391]

---

[391] *Ibid.*, 626-627 (citations omitted, long quotation from *In re Unterweser Reederei Gmbh*, 428 F. 2d 888, 896 (5th Cir., 1970)).

In *Kaepa* two factors were present which spoke in favour of control: first the jurisdiction clause by which Achilles had submitted to the jurisdiction of the Texas courts; and second the fact that the Texas proceedings had been commenced first, and Achilles had already entered an appearance on the merits there, and engaged in the preparation of the case for trial.

A contrasting example of the strict approach is *Gau Shan Company Limited* v. *Bankers Trust Co.*[392] This case involved a Chinese cotton distributor, Gau Shan, who agreed to purchase cotton from an American company, Julien. Gau Shan's director sought assurances from Julien's primary financer, Bankers Trust, as to its financial support for the transaction. Bankers Trust's vice president promised to "work something out". Bankers Trust then refused to advance the necessary money to Julien unless Gau Shan signed a $20 million promissory note payable to the bank. Under protest, Gau Shan did so. The note contained a clause providing that it would be governed by New York law. This money was then used to pay a separate debt owed by Julien. As a result of problems with that repayment, Gau Shan received only 24 per cent of the cotton it was owed. Bankers Trust nevertheless demanded payment of the promissory note.

Notwithstanding Bankers Trust's threat to enforce the note in Hong Kong, Gau Shan filed a suit in Tennessee for rescission of the note for fraud, also claiming common law fraud, deceit and negligence. A restraining order was issued enjoining Bankers Trust from initiating any action against Gau Shan in Hong Kong. The district court found that such an injunction did not breach international comity, holding that Gau Shan would be irreparably harmed if it were sued in

---

[392] *Gau Shan Company Limited* v. *Bankers Trust Company* 956 F. 2d 1349 (6th Cir., 1992).

Hong Kong. The 6th Circuit Court of Appeals reviewed the positions adopted by various circuits to anti-suit injunctions and concluded that the district court had abused its discretion in granting an injunction inconsistent with international comity. It held that

"the standard for granting a foreign antisuit injunction is whether the injunction is necessary to protect the forum court's jurisdiction or to prevent evasion of the forum court's important public policies" [393].

The Court's consideration of the relevance of comity to this equation is illuminating:

"The days of American hegemony over international economic affairs have long since passed. The United States cannot today impose its economic will on the rest of the world and expect meek compliance, if indeed it ever could. The modern era is one of world economic interdependence, and economic interdependence requires cooperation and comity between nations. . . . Gau Shan asks this court to disregard the principles of international comity and affirm the issuance of an antisuit injunction which effectively denies the Hong Kong court jurisdiction over a matter otherwise properly before it, and reserves to a United States court exclusive jurisdiction over a dispute involving parties from different nations. . . .

Such action conveys the message, intended or not, that the issuing court has so little confidence in the foreign court's ability to adjudicate a given dispute fairly and efficiently that it is unwilling even to allow the possibility. Foreign courts can be expected to reciprocate such disrespect. Reciprocity and cooperation can only suffer as a result. Accordingly,

---

[393] *Ibid.*, 1353.

foreign antisuit injunctions should be issued only in the most extreme cases." [394]

Save where the Court's jurisdiction was exercised *in rem*, such a situation would only arise where the "foreign court is not merely proceeding in parallel but is attempting to carve out exclusive jurisdiction over the action" [395]. That, thought the Court, had been the situation in *Laker Airways* [396], but it was not the situation in the case before it.

An example of a case where the application of the "strict" (or non-interventionist) approach may nevertheless lead to the grant of an injunction is furnished by the decision of the First Circuit Court of Appeals in *Quaak* v. *KPMG-B* [397]. The case concerned the auditing by the defendant, KPMG-B (the Belgian arm of the well-known international accountancy firm), of Lernout & Hausie, a Belgian company, whose shares had been publicly traded in the United States, and which had collapsed amidst allegations of securities fraud by investors [398]. KPMG-B refused to release auditing records and work papers on the basis that to do so would violate Belgian law. A Belgian magistrate judge rejected this excuse. Undeterred, KPMG-B began pro-

---

[394] *Ibid.*, 1354-1355.

[395] *Ibid.*, 1356.

[396] *Supra* footnote 247.

[397] *Quaak* v. *Klynveld Peat Marwick Goer-Deler Bedrijfsrevisoren*, 361 F. 3d 11 (1st Cir., 2004).

[398] An application by another investor for an anti-suit injunction to restrain Lernout & Hausie from pursuing bankruptcy proceedings in Belgium as well as in the United States was remanded by the 1st Circuit Court of Appeals to the Bankruptcy Court for further consideration: *Stoningtom Partners Inc.* v. *Lernout & Hauspie Speech Products NV*, 310 F. 3d 118 (3rd Cir., 2002). The Court of Appeals advocated co-ordination following dialogue between the courts, rather than enjoining the proceedings before the Belgian court, see *infra*, Chapter V, Section B 3.

ceedings in Belgium to enjoin any parties from pursuing discovery, to which Quaak replied with an application for an anti-suit injunction to halt the Belgian proceedings. This was granted by the district court, and the First Circuit of the Court of Appeals ultimately upheld the injunction.

The Court, recognizing that "judicial process is a fundamental cornerstone of the American way of life"[399], nevertheless took the view that international relations factors called for "a more cautious and measured approach"[400]. Such an approach required a two-stage analysis. First the court should adopt a threshold enquiry as to litispendence:

> "The gatekeeping inquiry is, of course, whether parallel suits involve the same parties and issues. Unless that condition is met, a court ordinarily should go no further and refuse the issuance of an international antisuit injunction. . . . In this analysis, considerations of international comity must be given substantial weight — and those considerations ordinarily establish a rebuttable presumption against the issuance of an order that has the effect of halting foreign judicial proceedings."[401]

Such a presumption could, however, be rebutted by consideration of a number of factors:

> "These include (but are by no means limited to) such things as: the nature of the two actions (ie, whether they are merely parallel or whether the foreign action is more properly classified as interdictory); the posture of the proceedings in the two countries; the conduct of the parties (including their good faith or lack thereof); the importance of the

---

[399] *Supra* footnote 397, 17.
[400] *Ibid.*
[401] *Ibid.*, 18.

policies at stake in the litigation; and, finally, the extent to which the foreign action has the potential to undermine the forum court's ability to reach a just and speedy result."[402]

In the case before it, the Court considered, applying this test, that the District Court had been entitled to issue an injunction. KPMG-B's application in Belgium was made simply to seek to frustrate the normal operation of discovery in US proceedings to which it was a party (and in which the Court had already affirmed its jurisdiction over it). The case was thus akin to *Laker Airways*, and the US Court was entitled to compel a party before it not to frustrate its own processes.

### 3. Contraction of the anti-suit injunction in the face of comity concerns

So battle is joined in the United States on the relevance of comity — by which the Courts appear to mean a preference for non-intervention in foreign court proceedings — in the calculus as to whether an anti-suit injunction ought to be ordered. In England, from whence the doctrine originated, the use of a remedy has been under sustained attack. This controversy has arisen from the conflict which the remedy has provoked, especially in the United States and in Europe. It has led to the development of three important limitations on its application. An anti-suit injunction will not be available:

(a) unless the substantive suit *can* be litigated in the forum. If the claim is by its nature only known to the foreign court, the English court will not intervene;

(b) unless the substantive suit *will* be litigated in the

---

[402] *Ibid.*, 19.

forum. The English court will not act as a global policeman to protect the jurisdictions of other courts from unwarranted incursions; and,

*(c)* where the litigation is pursued in another Member State of the European Union, since that would be inconsistent with the requirement of mutual trust underlying the Brussels I Regulation.

In each case, the nature of the limitation is best illustrated by the leading case which decided the point.

(a) *Conflict of laws cedes where no true litispendence*

*British Airways Board* v. *Laker Airways Ltd.*[403] is the British reverse half of the litigation in which Judge Wilkey had rendered his anti-suit injunction in the DC Court of Appeals[404]. Laker Airways, a low-cost trans-Atlantic airline operating during the 1970s and 1980s, commenced anti-trust proceedings in the District of Columbia claiming that British Airways (BA), British Caledonian Airways (BC) and others had formed a conspiracy to monopolize trans-Atlantic air transportation and that this caused Laker's collapse in 1982. BA and BC responded with an action in the Queen's Bench Division seeking a declaration that they were under no liability to Laker and requesting an anti-suit injunction. An interim injunction was granted *ex parte,* and was maintained (despite the considered view of Parker J *inter partes* that no injunction ought to be granted[405]) pending an appeal to the Court of Appeal, which held that the injunction ought to be maintained[406].

---

[403] *Supra* footnote 248, as to which see Collins, "Provisional and Protective Measures in International Litigation", (1992) 234 *Recueil des cours* 9, 138-151.

[404] *Supra* footnote 247.

[405] [1984] QB 142, 169 (QB).

[406] *Ibid.*, 202 (CA).

It was this injunction which Judge Greene of the US
District Court had in mind when he issued his own
injunction to restrain those other airlines which had
been sued as allegedly part of the conspiracy in the
United States from making their own application to the
English courts[407]. At this point, positions hardened in
what had become a serious trans-Atlantic conflict,
involving both the judiciary and the executive[408]. Judge
Greene described the English court's order as "a direct
interference with the proceedings in this Court"[409],
provoking some judicial hand-wringing on the part of
Lord Donaldson in the English Court of Appeal that
"we and all other English judges would deeply regret
any misunderstanding on the part of our brethren in the
United States of what exactly we are doing and why
we are doing it"[410].

The House of Lords ultimately reversed the Court of
Appeal, and in the process averted the trans-Atlantic
judicial crisis. It held that, because Laker's claim dis-
closed no cause of action justiciable in England, to
enjoin Laker from proceeding in the United States
would deny it a claim at all. As BA and BC were
not able to prove that they had a legal or equitable right

---

[407] *Laker Airways Ltd.* v. *Pan American Airways*, 559 F.
Supp. 1124 (DC DC, 1983), affd. *sub nom Laker Airways
Ltd.* v. *Sabena Belgian Airlines*, *supra* footnote 247.
[408] The British Government had exercised its powers
under the Protection of Trading Interests Act 1980 to determine that the measures taken in the United States threatened UK trading interests and restraining persons carrying
on business in the United Kingdom (other than US air car-
riers) from complying with US anti-trust measures in the
US courts arising out of an arrangement relating to air carriage under the relevant treaty arrangements.
[409] *Laker Airways Ltd.* v. *Pan American Airways*, *supra*
footnote 407, 1128.
[410] *British Airways Board* v. *Laker Airways*, *supra* footnote 248, 185.

not to be sued in the American action, it was not unconscionable for Laker to pursue the litigation in the United States. As Lord Diplock put it:

> "In the result your Lordships are confronted in the civil actions with a case in which there is a single forum only that is of competent jurisdiction to determine the merits of the claim; and the single forum is a foreign court. For an English court to enjoin the claimant from having access to that foreign court is, in effect, to take upon itself a one-sided jurisdiction to determine the claim upon the merits *against* the claimant but also to prevent its being decided upon the merits *in his favour.* This poses a novel problem, different in kind from that involved where there are alternative fora in which a particular civil claim can be pursued: an English court and a court of some foreign country both of which are recognised under English rules of conflict of laws as having jurisdiction to entertain proceedings against a defendant for a remedy for acts or omissions which constitute an actionable wrong under the substantive law of both England and that foreign country."[411]

## (b) *Requirement of a jurisdictional nexus*

*Airbus Industrie GIE* v. *Patel*[412] concerned a plane crash at Bangalore airport in which the courts of India, Texas and England became embroiled. On 14 February 1990, an Indian airlines flight had taken off from Bombay on a domestic flight to Bangalore. The aircraft was an Airbus A320, manufactured in Toulouse, France. There was a full complement of passengers. Almost all of them were Indian. But there were also

---

[411] *Ibid.*, 80.
[412] *Supra* footnote 206.

two British families and three Americans. During its
final approach to land in Bangalore, the aircraft struck
the ground short of the runway. Ninety-two persons
died. No-one escaped uninjured. An Indian Board of
Enquiry found that the principal cause of the accident
was pilot error. But it also found that the Bangalore airport company was at fault in failing to have adequate
safety procedures in place. In India, litigation against
the airline and the airport company resulted in a total
award for all of US\$75,000 (after costs). The English
plaintiffs (the heirs of the British citizens who had died
in the accident) then brought an action in Texas against
a number of parties who may have had some connection to the aircraft or its operation. One such party was
the manufacturer, Airbus. The English plaintiffs were
able to sue in Texas because their claim was taken on a
contingency fee. Texas did not at that stage recognize
the principle of *forum non conveniens*, and the Texas
court assumed jurisdiction over Airbus on the basis that
it was "doing business" there. Airbus applied successfully to the Indian court for an injunction to restrain the
English plaintiffs from suing it anywhere other than
India. But the injunction had no effect because the
English plaintiffs were outside India and thus not
amenable to the process of the Indian court.

Airbus therefore came to England and sought an
injunction in the home courts of the English plaintiffs
to stop them from continuing the Texas action against
it. In the Court of Appeal, Airbus succeeded [413]. But the
House of Lords thought otherwise. Lord Goff held that
an injunction was not justified in the circumstances,
notwithstanding the Indian courts' inability to grant
effective relief and the potentially oppressive nature of
the Texas proceedings. He stated the general rule as
being that:

---

[413]  [1997] 2 Lloyd's Rep. 8 (CA).

"before an anti-suit injunction can properly be granted by an English court to restrain a person from pursuing proceedings in a foreign jurisdiction in cases of the kind under consideration in the present case, comity requires that the English forum should have a sufficient interest in, or connection with, the matter in question to justify the indirect interference with the foreign court which an anti-suit injunction entails"[414].

The fact that the Indian court could not make its own order effective did not alter the equation:

"In a world which consists of independent jurisdictions, interference, even indirect interference, by the courts of one jurisdiction with the exercise of the jurisdiction of a foreign court cannot in my opinion be justified by the fact that a third jurisdiction is affected but is powerless to intervene. The basic principle is that only the courts of an interested jurisdiction can act in the matter; and if they are powerless to do so, that will not of itself be enough to justify the courts of another jurisdiction to act in their place."[415]

The House had accepted the argument of Sydney Kentridge QC that the English courts should not take it on themselves "to act as policeman of the world"[416].

### (c) *European law constraints*

*Turner* v. *Grovit* concerned an attempt in the English courts to restrain abusive litigation in Spain[417]. Mr. Turner was initially employed in England by a

---

414 *Supra* footnote 206, 138.
415 *Ibid.*, 141.
416 *Ibid.*, 121.
417 *Turner* v. *Grovit*, Case C-159/02, [2004] *ECR* I-3565.

group of companies running bureaux de change, headed by Mr. Grovit. A year after transferring to a Spanish company within the group, Turner resigned and took an action in London, arguing that he had been the victim of efforts to implicate him in illegal conduct. His claim was successful. A short time later one of the employer companies took an action in Madrid against Turner claiming damages for loss as a result of his professional conduct. On Turner's application the High Court in England granted an interlocutory injunction to restrain the Spanish proceedings, which was upheld by the Court of Appeal on the basis that they had been taken in bad faith and were an attempt to vex Turner's claims in England. The House of Lords referred to the Court of Justice the question as to whether it is consistent with the Convention for a court to issue an injunction in such circumstances[418].

The ECJ held that such an injunction constituted unjustifiable interference with the courts of the other Member State, and therefore was not consistent with the principle of mutual trust underlying the Convention[419]. This was so even where one of the parties was acting in bad faith and with a view to frustrating the proceedings[420]. The only solutions provided by the Convention were the specific mechanisms for cases of *lis alibi pendens* and related proceedings[421]. Otherwise, recourse to such injunctions was "liable to give rise to situations involving conflicts for which the Convention contains no rules"[422].

There was a certain fatalism attending the outcome of *Turner* in Common Law circles. The conventional mantra that the anti-suit injunction is directed against

---

[418]   [2001] UKHL 65, [2002] 1 WLR 107.
[419]   *Ibid.*, [27].
[420]   *Ibid.*, [31].
[421]   *Ibid.*, [30].
[422]   *Ibid.*

the party, and not the foreign court[423], had not been accepted by foreign courts whose cases are affected by such an injunction, even when those courts were in other Common Law countries[424], still less by other courts within the European Union[425]. But it would be difficult to imagine a clearer case of deliberate abuse than that presented by the facts in *Turner*. The Convention's rule on *lis pendens* could have responded to this situation, though only if the Spanish court had been prepared to accept that the companies in Mr. Grovit's Chequepoint group were *indissociable* with him and with each other. Alternatively the Spanish action could have been stayed in favour of the English related proceedings under Article 28. In the particular case, Mr. Grovit had discontinued the Spanish action in compliance with the English injunction and history does not relate whether it was subsequently resumed. But it is striking that Spain entered no appearance before the European Court (although the United Kingdom, Germany and Italy did) and the record discloses nothing about what the Spanish court itself did, or would have done in the light of the prior English action. In this context, the European Court's willingness to accept the *abus de droit*, so far from presenting a Utopian vision, seems to abdicate the judicial task in its bland acceptance of recidivism.

## E. Interim Conclusions

What lessons may be learned from a comparison of the experiences of each of the Civil Law and Common

---

[423] Repeated by Lord Hobhouse *supra* footnote 418, [23].

[424] See the comments of Judge Greene in *Laker Airways*, *supra* footnote 407, 1128.

[425] *Re the enforcement of an English anti-suit injunction*, [1997] I L. Pr. 320 (Oberlandesgericht Düsseldorf).

Law systems with the export of their internal remedies
for the control of parallel proceedings into the international arena?

The Civil Law's simple court first-seised rule has
unassailable logic *within* a single legal system — since
no other factors enter equation other than avoidance of
multiplicity of litigation. A tie-break rule is therefore
all that is required. Moreover, the deferring court can
be sure that court first seised will exercise jurisdiction,
and will apply the same *lis pendens* rule reciprocally
when the boot is on the other foot.

In international cases, the rule promotes legal certainty in cases in which both courts have a claim to
jurisdiction, and has the merit of directly addressing
the central problem of duplication of proceedings in a
manner which respects comity — by deferring to an
earlier-seised court. As Niboyet-Hoegy put it in her
spirited defence of the rule:

> "[L]a règle *prior tempore* satisfait quatre prin-
> cipes généraux du droit international privé:
> — le respect des attentes légitimes des plaideurs
> — le principe d'efficacité
> — le principe de l'harmonie internationale des
>    solutions et
> — le principe de cohérence des systèmes natio-
>    naux." [426]

The first two of her principles encapsulate the *private* aspect of private international litigation. The first
is the notion that, if a foreign judgment is likely to
become enforceable within the forum, the protection
of the reasonable expectation of the parties justifies
recognizing the foreign proceedings once instituted.

---

[426] Niboyet-Hoegy, "Les conflits de procédures",
[1995-1998] *Travaux du Comité français de droit international privé* 71, 78.

The second is the idea that proceedings, once commenced, should be completed, and not frustrated by other actions of the parties. The second two of her principles emphasize the *public* and *international* dimensions of the rule — promoting harmony and coherence between legal systems.

However, none of the ready assumptions of same law and procedure which apply in the internal operation of the rule necessarily apply to its international application. Great differences between substantive law and procedures in different legal systems motivate forum choice, even within an area with common jurisdiction rules. Indeed, within Europe, it has been the failure to resolve key procedural distortions within European civil procedure systems (such as in the Italian court system), and the inability to obtain prompt early determination of jurisdiction which has led to many of the perceived injustices in the application of the strict rule. The lesson of *Gasser* is that a strict court first seised rule can actually promote forum shopping with a race to commence proceedings, especially where the claim for a negative declaration used as forum shopping device.

The international effect of the rule may be further distorted in contexts where there are no common rules of jurisdiction. The court first seised may be in a forum with very limited contacts with the defendant or the subject-matter of the action. The court second seised must cede jurisdiction with no guarantee of reciprocity. Finally, the strict application of the rule leads to excessive formalism in the determination of identity of claims — essential for the preclusive effect of *res judicata* but not necessarily in the case of parallel proceedings.

These shortcomings suggest that the transposition *en bloc* of the internal rule of *lis pendens* into the international arena is unlikely to achieve satisfactory results. Some mechanism needs to be found to address at least cases of *abus de droit* and denial of justice; and to ensure adequate protection of party autonomy in forum selection. There are signs of a growing willingness to make enhanced provision for courts empowered under choice of court clauses. But the European Court's rulings in *Gasser* and *Turner* have insisted on a strict application of *lis pendens* in aid of the mutual trust between Member States. The development of denial of justice by reason of delay in a specific case will have to await the Regulation's revision; and *abus de droit,* despite its acceptance by the Court as a general principle of Community law, does not appear to be on any revision agenda at this stage as an exception to the court first-seised rule[427].

The Common Law's classic remedy to deal with cases of parallel litigation has been the anti-suit injunction. Here, however, the cure may be worse than the malady. Equity's desire to prevent harassment may end up producing harassment of its own; as Muir-Watt memorably put it: "harcèlement sur harcèlement ne vaut"[428]. Indeed, intensive experience with the application of the anti-suit injunction to international cases has produced some very serious conflicts between courts. The remedy offers no ready solution in the face of two courts each equally determined not to cede jurisdiction[429]. Thus, concerns about the *negative* aspect of comity — the avoidance of trespass upon the sovereign jurisdiction of foreign courts — have led in recent times to significant retrenchment in the remedy[430], emphasizing, *inter alia*, the need for the forum

---

[427] See further *infra*, Chapter V, Section A 3.

[428] Muir Watt, "Harcèlement sur harcèlement ne vaut", *Justices*, 1999.747.

[429] As in the example of the *Laker* litigation discussed *supra*, Section D 3 *(a)*.

[430] *Supra* Section D 3.

to have a sufficient connection with the claim to justify the indirect incursion upon a foreign court's jurisdiction.

A requirement of sufficient connection may well justify the exercise of international jurisdiction to grant the anti-suit injunction[431]. But it does *not* mean that remedy is suitable one to resolve international conflicts of jurisdiction. Peremptory intervention of this kind is difficult to justify, save where it is essential to protect the court or tribunal's ability to hold a fair trial; to enforce its judgments[432]; or *(pace Gasser)* to hold parties to their common choice of an exclusive forum.

The Common Law's far more recent embrace of the doctrine of *forum non conveniens* offers the considerable advantage of flexible deference to foreign proceedings. At least as applied to parallel or related proceedings, the notion of a discretionary stay is not as antithetical to Civilian notions of justice as is sometimes suggested. The exercise of discretion in cases of *related* litigation *(connexité)* is after all widely accepted in Civil Law countries as well (Art. 101 French NCPC; Art. 28 Brussels I Regulation); and the extension of the internal doctrine of *lis pendens* to international cases as part of the general law of Civil Law countries (outside treaty obligations) has generally been in the form of a discretion, rather than a binding obligation.

The principal problems with the operation of the doctrine of *forum non conveniens* in Common Law countries are not in cases of litispendence, but rather

---

[431] Accord Mann "The Doctrine of Jurisdiction in International Law", (1964) 111 *Recueil des cours* 1, reprinted in Mann, *Studies in International Law* (1973) 131-132.

[432] The principal application of the anti-suit injunction when it was first extended to international cases: *Masri* v. *Consolidated Contractors International Co. SAL, supra* footnote 377, [84].

where the plaintiff's chosen forum is overridden in
favour of a forum which has not been invoked at all.
These are, in the present author's view, really problems
of avoidance of responsibility of corporate defendants at their domicile which can lead to denial of justice[433].

But nevertheless, the exercise of a general discretion
tends to promote heavy satellite litigation about where
to litigate in many cases, which could be solved by
standing rules of jurisdiction. This may not justify the
visceral antipathy of the young Georges Droz, which
led him to observe in 1972: "Il valait mieux tuer dans
l'œuf cette source de chicane"![434] But the risk of re-
invention of the wheel case-by-case is particularly
acute in those States where the forum question has
become in effect the only controlling test for the
assumption of jurisdiction[435], rather than being seen as
a residual corrective against possible excesses of jurisdiction.

Moreover, the doctrine of *forum non conveniens*
may give too little weight to the fact of parallel litigation. Rather than deferring to the foreign court's determination of its own jurisdiction, it in instead requires

---

[433] For example *Re Union Carbide Gas Plant Disaster,*
809 F. 2d 195 (2d Cir., 1987); compare the approach of
the House of Lords in England in *Connelly* v. *RTZ Corp.
plc (No. 2)*, [1988] AC 854, and *Lubbe* v. *Cape plc (No. 2),*
[2000] 1 WLR 1545; and see Brand and Jablonski, *Forum
non Conveniens: History, Global Practice, and Future
under the Hague Convention on Choice of Court Agreements* (2007) 128-140 for an account of the reaction of
Latin American States to this application of the doctrine in
the United States.

[434] Droz, *supra* footnote 269, 129.

[435] For example United States: *International Shoe Co.*
v. *Washington*, 326 US 310 (1945); Canada: *Morguard
Investments Ltd.* v. *De Savoye*, [1990] 3 SCR 1077;
*Tolofson* v. *Jensen*, [1994] 3 SCR 1022; New Zealand:
HCR 6.28 (as added in 2009).

the court to second-guess the forum determination. The doctrine assumes that every case has a natural forum — a proposition which litigation experience suggests is often highly debatable. Since a situation of litispendence only arises where two courts are seised with the case, the doctrine does not resolve — as the strict *lis pendens* rule does — the question of which court decides whether to exercise jurisdiction, and which court's determination of appropriate forum is to take priority. The very open-textured nature of the test, and its different interpretation by courts in different countries, opens the possibility that so far from resolving conflicts between courts, the application of the doctrine may actually exacerbate them[436].

But the enduring value of the doctrine is that it enables the court *first* seised to defer to another court, where the court first seised is clearly inappropriate, or has been seised in an abuse of right. In this way, as will be seen in Chapter V[437], it may be possible to find common ground between the two approaches. For the moment, five interim conclusions may be drawn from this analysis of the doctrine of *lis pendens* in Private International Litigation:

(1) *An emerging principle of international litispendence.* The final quarter of the twentieth century saw the widespread adoption, in both Civil and Common Law countries, of legal techniques which

---

[436] For example the difference of view between family courts in Australia (applying the strict test in *Voth*, *supra* footnote 368) and New Zealand, which led to parallel litigation as to matrimonial property continuing in both jurisdictions after a forum determination in each: *In the Marriage of Gilmore*, (1993) 16 Fam. LR 285 (Aust.); compare *Gilmore* v. *Gilmore*, [1993] NZFLR 561; Garnett, "Stay of Proceedings in Australia: A 'Clearly Inappropriate' Test?", (1999) 23 *Melb. ULR* 30.

[437] Chapter V, Section B 2.

enabled courts to decline jurisdiction and defer to a foreign court already seised of the matter:

*(a)* In *Civil Law* countries, this was achieved by the extension, both by treaty and also by the courts as a principle of *droit commun,* of internal rules of litispendence.

*(b)* In *Common Law* countries, it was achieved primarily as part of the application by the courts of the doctrine of *forum non conveniens.*

In both cases, the development reflected a choice to accept that national judicial systems had to respond to a global litigation context, in which the decisions of foreign courts could be recognised and given effect. The justification for the extension was found in both

(i) the *private interest* of ensuring justice between litigants, and preventing forum shopping; and,

(ii) the *public interest* of judicial economy and comity.

But it cannot be said that the status of international litispendence as a general principle of law is yet secure. The countervailing tendency to revert to an "unflagging obligation" to exercise jurisdiction may still be seen in both European and American jurisprudence.

(2) *Determining identity of action.* Once litispendence is accepted outside the *lex specialis* of a particular national legal system, it is necessary to determine the basis upon which a comparison of causes of action is to be made. This requires a comparison of the principle which the rule relied upon in each case is intended to serve; and the effect or ends in view of each action.

(3) *Limitations of strict rule of priority.* A strict rule of priority, which always requires the court second

seised to defer to the court first seised will not control forum shopping unless:

*(a)* the Court first seised itself has some ability to assess whether it is the natural forum for the trial of the action and whether the claim before it is an abuse of right. This is particularly so in the case of reverse litigation (the claim for a negative declaration) which has been brought as a means of pre-empting choice of forum; and,

*(b)* the Court first seised determines its jurisdiction promptly and at the outset so as to avoid a denial of justice and ensure a fair trial; and,

*(c)* the Court second seised can also decline jurisdiction where the claim is in reality the same claim, but brought by a connected party. This result may be achieved either by development of the approach to privity of interest for the purpose of determining identity of parties, or through a related proceedings rule.

(4) *A principle of consolidation of related proceedings.* Both Civil and Common Law countries have also recognized that, beyond a strict rule of priority, there is also a principle favouring a discretion to consolidate related proceedings, in order, so far as possible, to resolve all aspects of the wider dispute.

(5) *A limited role for anti-suit injunctions.* Sustained experience with the use of the anti-suit injunction in transnational cases suggests that, in many cases, it is likely to aggravate conflicts between courts, rather than resolve them. For that reason, the anti-suit injunction is not an appropriate remedy to deal generally with international litispendence. It is generally preferable to allow the other court to make its own decision as to whether to decline

jurisdiction. However, the ability of a court to control in some way the conduct of the parties before it in pursuit of identical litigation abroad may be justified *(a)* where it is essential to ensure a fair trial; *(b)* to ensure the effectiveness of the court's judgment; or *(c)* to uphold the parties' joint agreement as to choice of forum. Such an agreement may take the form of either a choice of court (an issue already considered in this chapter) or an arbitration agreement. It is to the significance of the exercise of party autonomy in arbitration that we must now turn.

CHAPTER III

INTERNATIONAL ARBITRATION

A. *The Place of Parallel Proceedings
in International Arbitration*

1. *The use of party autonomy as an escape from
multiple fora*

The New York Convention on the Recognition and
Enforcement of Foreign Arbitral Awards celebrated its
60th birthday in 2008[438]. It has become the most
widely accepted multilateral treaty on commercial disputes which the world has ever known[439]. A principal
purpose of the Convention was to provide a decisive
rule of priority for international commercial arbitration
over national court litigation. Thus Article II, having
required States Parties to recognize arbitration agreements goes on to provide, in clause 3:

> "The court of a Contracting State, when seized of
> an action in a matter in respect of which the parties
> have made an agreement within the meaning of this
> article, shall, at the request of one of the parties,
> refer the parties to arbitration, unless it finds that
> the said agreement is null and void, inoperative or
> incapable of being performed."

One of the perceived advantages of arbitration over
litigation in international commercial disputes is pre-

---

[438] Signed 10 June 1958, entered into force 7 June
1959, 330 *UNTS* 38.
[439] The Convention had 144 States parties as at
30 April 2009: http://www.uncitral.org/uncitral/en/unci-
tral_texts/arbitration/NYConvention_status.html.

cisely to provide a neutral forum, outside the parochial preoccupations of national courts, within which cross-border disputes can be determined. As Lord Hoffmann recently put it, the parties to an arbitration agreement

"want those disputes decided by a tribunal which they have chosen, commonly on the grounds of such matters as its neutrality, expertise and privacy, the availability of legal services at the seat of the arbitration and the unobtrusive efficiency of its supervisory law. Particularly in the case of international contracts, they want a quick and efficient adjudication and do not want to take the risks of delay and, in too many cases, partiality, in proceedings before a national court jurisdiction." [440]

The idea that one of the objectives of an international arbitration agreement is to provide a centralized dispute resolution forum, and thereby to escape from the multiplicity and rivalry of national court proceedings, runs very deep in the history of arbitration [441]. Thus, it has been said that one reason for the popularity of arbitration in mediaeval times was the multiplicity of parallel jurisdictions:

"The most serious cases could be heard in many different courts exercising parallel jurisdiction. Undoubtedly there were certain rules which, in theory, determined the limits of competence of the various courts; but in spite of them uncertainty persisted. The feudal records that have come down to us abound in charters relating to disputes between rival jurisdictions. Despairing of knowing before

---

[440] *Premium Nafta Products Ltd.* v. *Fili Shipping Co. Ltd.*, [2008] 1 Lloyd's Rep. 254, [6] (HL).

[441] Born, *International Commercial Arbitration* (2009) 74-76.

which authority to bring their suits, litigants often agreed to set up arbitrators of their own." [442]

The need to eliminate the uncertainty and potential for inconvenience arising from the overlapping jurisdictions of national courts remains a powerful factor promoting and justifying international arbitration today [443].

It might be thought, therefore, that when parties had expressed a clear preference for arbitration over litigation in any particular dispute by entering into an arbitration agreement, the problem of parallel litigation would be avoided, consigning it to the dustbin of the history of international civil procedure as an "awesome relic of the past". As two distinguished Swiss practitioners put it, the doctrine of *lis pendens*:

> "presupposes that the two courts have equal jurisdiction. In arbitration, on the other hand, there can be no question of two equally competent bodies: the jurisdiction of an arbitral tribunal requires a valid arbitration agreement, and one of the main legal consequences of such an agreement is precisely that it evicts the jurisdiction of national courts" [444].

Further, the joint choice of an arbitral forum by the parties is often guided by a wish to choose a *neutral* forum, with no connection to the parties or the underlying subject-matter of the dispute. Thus, the existence of an arbitration agreement removes the requirement to seek, whether by the application of pre-determined rules or by the exercise of discretion, the *natural* forum

---

[442] Bloch, *Feudal Society* (1939, trans. Manyon 1961) 359.

[443] *M/S Bremen* v. *Zapata Off-Shore Co.*, 92 S. Ct. 1907, 407 US 1, 13-14 (1972).

[444] Geisinger and Lévy, "*Lis Alibi Pendens* in International Commercial Arbitration", [2003] *ICC Bull. (Special Supp.)* 53, 53.

for the resolution of the dispute, which, as has been seen, exercises an important role in private international litigation.

Indeed, despite the proliferation of symposia and studies recently devoted to this area[445], a view which is often expressed is that the techniques for the allocation of priority between competing fora, which are the subject of these lectures, should have no place in arbitration: that it is a "non-sujet par excellence"[446]. As an instinctive reaction, this may perhaps be understandable in relation to anti-suit injunctions. Fouchard concluded a recent volume on this topic with the remark: "Anti-suit injunctions are not to be encouraged in any type of litigation."[447] Others have reached equally sweeping conclusions even about the more deferential solutions of *lis pendens*. Thus, one well-known arbitrator concludes:

> "There is no place for the concept of *lis pendens* in international arbitration. It will not and cannot resolve the problem of parallel and simultaneous forums."[448]

---

[445] See, notably, the ILA Commercial Arbitration Committee, "Final Report on Lis Pendens and Arbitration" (2006) 72 *ILA Rep. Conf.* 146; Cremades and Lew, *Parallel State and Arbitral Procedures in International Arbitration* (2005); Gaillard (ed.), *Anti-suit Injunctions in International Arbitration* (2005); Hanotiau, *Complex Arbitrations: Multiparty, Multicontract, Multi-issue and Class Actions* (2005).

[446] Schweizer and Guillod, "L'exception de litispendance et l'arbitrage international", in Knoepfler (ed.), *Le juriste suisse face au droit et aux jugements étrangers: ouverture ou repli?* (1988) 71.

[447] Fouchard, "Anti-Suit Injunctions in International Arbitration: What Remedies?", in Gaillard, *supra* footnote 445, 153, 153.

[448] Lew, "Concluding Remarks", in Cremades and Lew, *supra* footnote 445, 311.

Nor has this controversy been confined to doctrinal discussion. It has also extended to jurisprudence. When the Swiss Federal Tribunal recognized the doctrine of *lis pendens* as applying so as to accord a foreign court priority in the determination of the validity and extent of an arbitration agreement conferring jurisdiction on a Swiss arbitral tribunal, the Swiss legislature intervened to reverse the result by legislation[449]. By contrast, the very recent judgment of the European Court in *The Front Comor*[450] opens up the possibility of parallel determination of arbitral jurisdiction (and, depending upon the result, parallel determinations of liability) by national courts in European States and by arbitral tribunals.

## 2. *Instances of overlapping jurisdiction*

What real and continuing relevance, then, does our topic have in the field of arbitration? Is it no more than a catalogue of the pathology of arbitration: cases in which courts have failed to respect the autonomy and priority of the arbitral process, as the New York Convention mandates? There is no doubt, as will be seen, that some of the problems of parallel proceedings in this field may be solved simply by the proper application of a rule of priority for arbitration. But other problems will persist. Many of these flow from the

---

[449] *Fomento de Construcciones y Contratas SA* v. *Colon Container Terminal SA*, BGE 127 III 279 (2001), (English trans. (2001) 19 *ASA Bull.* 555), as to which see Geisinger and Lévy, *supra* footnote 444, 53, Oetiker (2002) 18 *Arb. Int.* 137. But see now Art. 186 (1*bis*) Swiss Private International Law, as adopted and in force from 1 March 2007 (RO, 2007, 387), as to which see Bucher, "L'examen de la competence internationale par le juge suisse", 2007 II No. 5, *La semaine judiciaire* 153, 188-196, discussed *infra*, footnote 501.

[450] *Infra* footnote 456.

same basic attribute of arbitration as a form of dispute resolution chosen by the parties. The jurisdiction of the arbitral tribunal is, of its nature, limited by the extent, and validity, of the arbitration agreement. Such an agreement is not self-executing. It relies on the intervention of national courts to secure its application.

This raises at least three contexts for parallel proceedings:

(a) *Parallel proceedings as to the arbitrators' jurisdiction.* Modern arbitration law entitles the arbitral tribunal to determine its own jurisdiction. As has been seen in Chapter I, the exercise of that power is commonly known by its German title *Kompetenz-Kompetenz.* The tribunal's ability to do so is protected by another related doctrine, which protects the validity of the reference to arbitration from collateral attacks upon the validity of the underlying contract to be arbitrated. The doctrine of the separability of the arbitration agreement is now so well recognized that it is seen as "part of the very alphabet of arbitration law"[451]. It has been held to apply even where the underlying contract may be avoided for fraud or illegality[452]. But, to what extent does the *power* of the tribunal to determine its own competence also operate as an ability to *exclude* the power of a national court to do the same, especially when it is already seised of the dispute? Does the doctrine of *Kompetenz-Kompetenz* have the "negative effect" of excluding any judicial consideration of an arbitral tribunal's jurisdiction before the tribunal has itself considered the matter[453]? To what

---

[451] *Lesotho Highlands Development Authority* v. *Impregilo SpA*, [2006] 1 AC 221, [21] (HL) per Lord Steyn.

[452] *Buckeye Check Cashing, Inc.* v. *Cardegna*, 546 US 440 (2006); *Premium Nafta Products, supra* footnote 440.

[453] Park, "The Arbitrator's Jurisdiction to Determine Jurisdiction", in *International Arbitration 2006: Back to*

extent may the courts of the seat prevent an arbitration from continuing where they have determined that the arbitration agreement is null and void? What are the responsibilities of courts outside the seat when the validity of the arbitration agreement is challenged?

(b) *Parallel and related arbitral proceedings.* The jurisdiction of an arbitral tribunal will be limited to disputes actually submitted by the parties under the arbitration agreement. Thus, the arbitration may well take place within a context in which other closely related disputes are decided by other courts or tribunals. This may be so where the *subject-matter* of the dispute between the same parties falls outside the ambit of the agreement. This situation may also arise where the subject-matter is the same, but the parties are different. Arbitral tribunals typically lack the ability to consolidate closely-related proceedings without the agreement of the parties. Seen in this light, arbitration provides, of its nature, a fragmented solution for international disputes. May a tribunal stay its own proceedings in light of related actions elsewhere?

(c) *Anti-suit injunctions.* It is commonly assumed that anti-suit injunctions are an *installation sauvage* in international arbitration, imported from the crude and combative world of the Common Law[454]. In fact, the evidence from the reported cases suggests that attempts to control parallel proceedings in the arbitration context are not limited to Common Law courts. Not only have some Civil Law courts issued orders enjoining the parties from continuing with an arbitral proceeding, but also arbitral tribunals have themselves on occasion

---

*Basics*? (ICCA Congress Series No. 13, Kluwer, The Hague, 2007) 55.

[454] See for example Gaillard, "Introduction", in Gaillard, *supra* footnote 445, 1.

sought to prevent pursuit of parallel litigation[455]. Moreover, the anti-suit injunction has been used to support the arbitration agreement, where one party has issued process in a national court in breach of such a clause, a remedy now disallowed in Europe by virtue of the judgment of the European Court in *The Front Comor*[456]. In these circumstances, a general dismissal of the remedy does not seem warranted — at least without further enquiry.

Accordingly, this chapter will address each of these sets of issues in turn in the context of international commercial arbitration (Section B).

It will then be possible to turn, in Section C, to look at the particular sets of problems which arise in the hybrid field of investment treaty arbitration. The arbitration of claims brought by private investors against host States pursuant to investment treaties gives rise to some particularly difficult problems of parallel proceedings. This type of arbitration, uniquely, does not proceed from privity of contract between the parties, but rather derives from a right conferred by treaty[457]. One recent observer has commented in this context that:

> "There is as yet no established body of principles

---

[455] Lévy, "Anti-suit Injunctions Issued by Arbitrators", in Gaillard, *ibid.*, 115; Gaillard, "Anti-suit Injunctions Issued by Arbitrators", (2007) ICCA Congress Series No. 13, 235.

[456] *West Tankers Inc.* v. *Ras Riunione Adriatica di Sicurta SpA (The Front Comor)*, [2005] 2 Lloyd's Rep. 257 (QB); [2007] 1 Lloyd's Rep. 391 (HL), note Bollée [2007] *Revue de l'arbitrage* 223, Carrier (2006) 21 (9) *Int. Arb. Rep.* 18, Steinbruck (2007) 26 (Jul.) CJQ 358; Case C-185/07 *sub nom Allianz SpA* v. *West Tankers Inc*, Opinion of Kokott AG (4 September 2008); Judgment (10 February 2009).

[457] Paulsson, "Arbitration without Privity" (1995) 10 *ICSID Rev.-FILJ* 232.

to deal adequately with the new realities of vertical and horizontal clashes of adjudicative competence. At the same time, the conceivable range of remedies available to foreign investors has become remarkably broad."[458]

This is because the underlying dispute between an investor and its host State may give rise to multiple claims. If there is a contract between State and investor, that contract will create its own justiciable rights and duties, the breach of which may give rise either to litigation before host State courts or to arbitration before a tribunal to whose jurisdiction the parties have submitted. Even if there is no such contract, the underlying property rights of the investor, which form the subject-matter of the investment, may have been the subject of adjudication by the host State courts. Further, the investor may have sought vindication of its rights in the host State courts. In any one of these cases, the very nature of investment arbitration gives rise to the possibility of parallel proceedings, or of determinations in another forum which may be said to affect the issue to be determined by the investment tribunal. Moreover, it is possible that more than one investment tribunal, each constituted by a different investment treaty, may be asked to rule upon the same underlying factual dispute.

In any one of these situations, the tribunal may have to consider the impact of the proceedings in the other court or tribunal upon its own work. Should it stay its own proceedings in deference to the alternative tribunal? Should it, on the contrary, insist on the priority of its own process? Should it put the parties to their election as to which mode of adjudication they wish to choose for the resolution of their dispute?

---

[458] Douglas, "The Hybrid Foundations of Investment Treaty Arbitration", (2003) 74 *BYIL* 151, 236.

### B. International Commercial Arbitration

#### 1. Kompetenz-Kompetenz or who decides on arbitral jurisdiction

##### (a) The arbitral tribunal or the courts

Professor Park has recently wisely commented of the principle of *Kompetenz-Kompetenz*:

> "[T]his much-vexed principle possesses a chameleon-like quality that changes color according to the national and institutional background of its application. . . . To say that arbitrators may make jurisdictional decisions tells only part of the story. Every jurisdictional ruling by an arbitrator begs two further questions, one relating to timing and the other to finality. The timing question asks when judges should intervene in the arbitral process to monitor possible jurisdictional excess." [459]

Finality is a question of *res judicata*. But timing is a question of *lis pendens* — parallel proceedings between courts and arbitral tribunals on the question of arbitral jurisdiction. Modern practice supports three quite different solutions to the priority as between court and tribunal: (i) sequencing; (ii) waiver; and (iii) parallel consideration.

(i) *Sequencing*. The European Convention on International Commercial Arbitration 1961 makes detailed provision in Article VI for the relationship between courts and arbitral tribunals on issues of the validity of arbitration agreements [460]. The first situation is where the court is first seised, because the plaintiff

---

[459] Park, *supra* footnote 453, 56.
[460] European Convention on International Commercial Arbitration (signed 21 April 1961, entered into force 1 January 1964), 484 *UNTS* 364.

had brought his claim in a court; the defendant asserts that the claim is covered by an arbitration agreement; and the plaintiff then contends that the arbitration agreement is invalid. Paragraph (1) contemplates that in these circumstances the court should proceed to determine the issue of validity itself.

Where, however, the arbitration is commenced first, paragraph (3) specifically provides:

> "Where either party to an arbitration agreement has initiated arbitration proceedings before any resort is had to a court, courts of Contracting States subsequently asked to deal with the same subject-matter between the same parties or with the question whether the arbitration agreement was non-existent or null and void or had lapsed, shall stay their ruling on the arbitrator's jurisdiction until the arbitral award is made, unless they have good and substantial reasons to the contrary." [461]

(ii) *Waiver.* A second solution is to provide that reference to arbitration includes an agreement to refer first to the arbitral tribunal on any issue of jurisdiction, and to require the parties, as a condition of their choice of arbitration to waive their right to seek a prior determination of arbitral jurisdiction from a national court. This is the solution adopted in the Rules of the London Court of International Arbitration, Article 23.4 of which provides:

> "By agreeing to arbitration under these Rules, the parties shall be treated as having agreed not to apply to any state court or other judicial authority for any relief regarding the Arbitral Tribunal's jurisdiction or authority, except with the agreement in writing of all parties to the arbitration or the prior authorisa-

---

[461] *Ibid.*

tion of the Arbitral Tribunal or following the latter's award ruling on the objection to its jurisdiction or authority." [462]

(iii) *Parallel consideration.* By contrast, the UNCITRAL Model Law on International Commercial Arbitration, which has proved a hugely influential model for national legislation on arbitration around the world, prefers simply to tolerate parallel consideration. Article 8 (1) of the Model Law essentially replicates Article II of the New York Convention, by compelling a court, when a matter is covered by an arbitration agreement, to refer the matter before it to arbitration, unless it finds that the agreement is invalid. But Article 8 (2) adds:

> "Where an action referred to in paragraph (1) of this article has been brought, arbitral proceedings may nevertheless be commenced or continued, and an award may be made, while the issue is pending before the court." [463]

This provision, together with Article 16, empowers the tribunal to proceed to its own jurisdictional determination irrespective of whether the same issue is pending in a national court. But it does not determine what a national court, in a state which applies the Model Law, should do in such a situation. It could still proceed to decide first on the effect of the arbitration agreement itself; or it could refer the question to the arbitral tribunal in all cases; or it could exercise a discretion whether to decide for itself or to refer the matter to the arbitral tribunal [464].

---

[462] Available at: www.lcia.org.
[463] UN doc. A/40/17, Annex 1, as amended by UN doc. A/61/17, Annex 1.
[464] Kawharu, "Arbitral Jurisdiction", (2008) 23 *NZULR* 238, 243.

The approach taken in major arbitral jurisdictions which do not apply the Model Law reveals a spectrum of answers to this question[465]. Thus, in England, section 30 of the Arbitration Act 1996 recognizes the competence of the arbitral tribunal to decide upon its own jurisdiction, including as to whether there is a valid arbitration agreement[466]. The court may not entertain an application for determination of a jurisdictional issue unless the parties agree, or the tribunal so permits. The court must also be satisfied that the application was made without delay; that its determination of the issue is likely to produce substantial savings in costs; and that there is good reason why the issue should be decided by the court[467]. Otherwise, the party wishing to contest the arbitrator's jurisdiction should so apply to the arbitral tribunal. There is then a right to challenge the award as to jurisdiction in court, where England is the seat of the arbitration[468]. The Court should not intervene in the arbitral process except as provided by the Act[469].

Where, however, a question of the validity of the arbitration agreement is raised by a respondent to an application for a stay under Section 9 of the Act, the court has power to decide the question itself. In general it will be right for the arbitral tribunal to be the first to

---

[465] For further detail of the position as a matter of comparative arbitration law see Park, *supra* footnote 453, 68-86.

[466] Chap. 16, "Arbitration & Foreign Awards", in Collins *et al.* (eds.), *Dicey, Morris and Collins on the Conflict of Laws* (14th ed., 2006) *("Dicey")* [16-075]-[16-076]. The author bears editorial responsibility (with Collins) for Chapter 16 in the 14th edition.

[467] S. 32.

[468] S. 67.

[469] S. 1 *(c)*, *Vale do Rio Doce Navegacos SA* v. *Shanghai Bao Steel Ocean Shipping Co. Ltd.*, [2000] 2 Lloyd's Rep. 1, [51]-[52] (QB).

consider whether it has jurisdiction[470]. However, where
the issue is whether the underlying dispute is subject to
an arbitration agreement at all the court has a choice
whether to decide that issue itself, or to stay proceedings while that that issue is referred to arbitration for
the tribunal to decide under Section 30 of the Act[471].
The dominant factors are the interests of the parties
and the avoidance of unnecessary delay or expense.
The argument in favour of judicial determination is that
there may otherwise be a real danger that there will be
two hearings: the first before the arbitrator under
Section 30 and the second before the court on a challenge under Section 67. A stay under the inherent jurisdiction might be sensible in a situation where the court
cannot be sure of those matters but can see that good
sense and litigation management makes it desirable for
an arbitrator to consider the whole matter first.

By contrast, in France, the application of the negative effect of the *Kompetenz-Kompetenz* principle has
led to the adoption of a rule, applicable as much to
international as to French arbitrations, which requires
the State court to defer to the arbitral tribunal on an
issue of arbitral jurisdiction, even where the arbitral tribunal has not yet been constituted, unless the arbitration agreement is manifestly null and void[472].

---

[470] *Fiona Trust & Holding Corp.* v. *Privalov*, [2007] 2
Lloyd's Rep. 267, [34] (CA), affirmed (but not deciding
this point), *Premium Nafta Products Ltd.* v. *Fili Shipping
Co. Ltd.*, *supra* footnote 440.

[471] *Al-Naimi* v. *Islamic Press Agency Inc.*, [2000] 1
Lloyd's Rep. 522 (CA) (a domestic case), approving *Birse
Construction Ltd.* v. *St. David Ltd.*, [1999] BLR 194, 196-
197 (TCC) per Judge Humphrey Lloyd QC. See also *Azov
Shipping Co.* v. *Baltic Shipping Co. (No. 1)*, [1999] 1
Lloyd's Rep. 68 (QB); *Law Debenture Trust Corp. Plc* v.
*Elektrim Finance BV*, [2005] 2 Lloyd's Rep. 755 (Ch.).

[472] Art. 1458, NCCP; Fouchard, Gaillard, Goldman,
*International Commercial Arbitration* (ed. Gaillard and

Practice under the Model Law is not conclusive as to whether Article 8 mandates a full or a prima facie review by the court before remitting the question of arbitral jurisdiction to the tribunal itself[473]. But there are signs that the standard of prima facie review is gaining ground, even in Common Law jurisdictions. It has been recently accepted by the Supreme Court of India[474]. The Supreme Court of Canada has held that a challenge to the arbitrator's jurisdiction should in general be referred first to the arbitral tribunal. The court should only depart from this principle where the challenge is based solely on a question of law (or involves questions of fact which require only superficial consideration based on the record). Even then, the court must be satisfied that hearing the challenge itself would not lead to unnecessary delay or impair the conduct of the arbitral process[475].

The principal argument in favour of deference to the arbitral tribunal in the first instance is that it avoids parallel determinations of the same issue by court and tribunal at the same time. Since the tribunal's determination of its own jurisdiction may always be the subject of review by the national courts at the seat, the application of a prima facie review by the court at a preliminary stage does not ultimately deprive the party contesting arbitral jurisdiction of access to a court. But it does ensure that the arbitral process itself cannot be derailed by dilatory applications to court.

---

Savage, 1999) [671]-[682]; Lew, Mistelis and Kröll, *Comparative International Commercial Arbitration* [14-49]-[14-64].

[473] Kawharu, *supra* footnote 464, 254-256; Bachand, (2006) 22 *Arb. Intl* 463; Born, *supra* footnote 441, 880-894.

[474] *Shin-Etsu Chemical Co. Ltd.* v. *Aksh Optifibre Ltd.*, (2005) 7 Supreme Court Cases 234, (2006) 31 *Ybk. Comm. Arb.* 747.

[475] *Union des consommateurs* v. *Dell Computer Corp.*, 2007 SCC 34 (2007), 284 DLR (4th) 577, [84]-[87].

### (b) The courts of the seat and other courts

Where the arbitral tribunal has its seat in the same jurisdiction as that of the court to which one of the parties seeks resort, the question is simply one of the timing of the exercise of supervisory jurisdiction. Where, however, the national court is in a different State to that of the arbitral seat, more complex problems can arise. Such a court may, but for the arbitration agreement, have a perfectly valid basis for the exercise of jurisdiction, based, for example, on the domicile of the defendant, or on the occurrence there of the events giving rise to the claim. Arbitration agreements are not self-executing. They must be invoked by the party seeking a stay of the judicial proceedings [476]. The right to a stay may be lost if the party wishing to rely upon the agreement takes a step in the proceedings to answer the substantive claim, so as to waive his right to arbitration [477].

On the other hand, the arbitral tribunal has the power to rule on its own jurisdiction under the *Kompetenz-Kompetenz* principle. The court which has the supervisory power over such a determination is the court of the seat. The relative weight to be accorded to each of these courts' powers to determine their own jurisdiction is nicely illustrated by the contrasting facts of two recent *causes célèbres*: the *Julius* affair involving an arbitration in Switzerland and court proceedings in England; and the *Fomento* affair involving an arbitration in Switzerland and court proceedings in Panama. In *Julius*, the English court, which would otherwise have had jurisdiction, chose to stay its proceedings, deferring to the Swiss arbitral tribunal, and to the supervisory jurisdiction of the Swiss courts, even though it was not bound to do so. In *Fomento,* the Panamanian court determined for itself the question of

---

[476] New York Convention, *supra* footnote 438, Art. II.
[477] *Dicey, supra* footnote 466, [16-070].

whether the arbitration agreement had been waived. The Swiss Federal Tribunal held that the arbitral tribunal was bound by the doctrine of *lis pendens* to stay its own jurisdictional determination pending the final outcome of the Panamanian court's decision on the same point. The decision was subsequently reversed by legislation.

The *Julius* affair arose out of a dispute between two metal trading brothers, Amir and Rami, in relation to a trust established by Amir of which Rami was a protector[478]. The brothers signed a settlement agreement and appointed Anthony Julius (the prominent English solicitor who had represented Diana, Princess of Wales, in her divorce from Prince Charles) as arbitrator to resolve outstanding disputes. The arbitration agreement was governed by Swiss law and the seat of the arbitration was Geneva. Amir sought an injunction from the English courts to restrain Mr. Julius personally from acting as arbitrator. Amir claimed that the arbitration agreement was void or voidable for misrepresentation. Rami and Mr. Julius responded by seeking a stay of those proceedings, and Mr. Julius asserted that he would assess his own jurisdiction, subject to the Swiss courts' power of review. In the case reported as *Weissfisch* v. *Julius* Amir then sought a temporary injunction pending the outcome of the stay proceedings[479]. Amir argued that the English courts had jurisdiction, notwithstanding the fact that the seat of the arbitration was Geneva, because Amir's claim was for breach of fiduciary duty, a claim not covered by the arbitration agreement and only justiciable in England. He further argued that Mr. Julius could not rule on his own jurisdiction where there was a challenge to that

---

[478] *Weissfisch* v. *Julius*, [2006] 1 Lloyd's Rep. 716 (CA); *A* v. *B*, [2007] 1 Lloyd's Rep. 237 (QB).
[479] *Weissfisch, ibid.*

jurisdiction based on his own breach of duty. The Court of Appeal rejected Amir's application, holding that an injunction was not justified.

The Court considered that, Switzerland being the seat of the arbitration, its courts had supervisory jurisdiction over the conduct of any arbitration there [480]. Swiss law recognized that an arbitral tribunal sitting in Switzerland had competence to determine its own jurisdiction, and it also provided a right of appeal to the Swiss courts on any such decision [481]. In these circumstances, there was no warrant for the intervention of the English court to restrain Mr. Julius from acting as an arbitrator, even if the basis of the claim in England sought to attack the propriety of Mr. Julius so acting.

At the next stage in the saga, the stay application came before Colman J in the Queen's Bench Division [482]. Amir (A) contested the stay application on the basis that, because Julius (B) was domiciled in England, Article 2 of the Lugano Convention and the Brussels I Regulation required the English Court to assert jurisdiction over him. Colman J decided that the arbitration claims against Julius would be stayed and that the personal claims against Julius (involving breach of fiduciary duty, for example) would be stayed until he had rendered his final award. The judge held that the principal object of the principal claims was arbitration, a matter excluded from the scope of the Regulation and Convention, and that he was not therefore bound to assume jurisdiction under Article 2 in relation to those claims [483]. The arbitration agreement did not, of course, bind Mr. Julius directly, since he was

---

[480]  *Ibid.*, [25].
[481]  *Ibid.*, [24].
[482]  Reported as *A* v. *B*, *supra* footnote 478.
[483]  *Ibid.*, [96]-[97].

not a party to it, but rather was the arbitrator appointed under it. Therefore the court was not under a mandatory obligation to grant a stay, applying Article II (3) of the New York Convention[484]. Nevertheless, the judge considered that

> "the court retains an inherent jurisdiction to stay English proceedings in favour of arbitration in a case where there is an issue whether the parties entered into a binding agreement to arbitrate or whether the subject matter of the action was within the scope of the arbitration"[485].

In deciding whether to exercise this discretion, the judge considered that, although the essence of the claim was that the agreement was induced by fraudulent misrepresentation, the law governing that question was Swiss law, and it was the Swiss courts that had supervisory jurisdiction over it[486]. The consequence of this was that

> "anything done by any party which was contrary to this second consequence of the agreement whereby supervisory jurisdiction was vested exclusively in the Swiss courts would in substance equally amount to a breach of the agreement to arbitrate"[487].

There being no other factor which outweighed the significance of the supervisory jurisdiction of the Swiss courts, the arbitration claims would have to be stayed.

The personal claims, which alleged breach of fiduciary and professional duty, could not be decided by Mr. Julius as arbitrator. However, they were so closely related to the principal claims that there would be a

---

[484] Given effect in the United Kingdom by Arbitration Act 1996, s 9.

[485] *A* v. *B*, *supra* footnote 478, [107].

[486] *Ibid.*, [111].

[487] *Ibid.*, [112].

serious risk of conflicting decisions were the English
courts to proceed to determine them at the same time
as the arbitration continued in Switzerland[488]. In order
to avoid such a risk, the judge ordered a temporary stay
on case management grounds pending the outcome of
the Swiss proceedings.

In *Fomento*[489], the seat of the arbitration was also in
Switzerland, but the Panamanian courts had been
seised first with the dispute, and with the question of
whether the arbitration agreement applied or had been
waived. Fomento, a Spanish company, had entered into
a contract with a Panamanian company, CCT, for the
construction of a container terminal at Colon in
Panama. The contract provided for the resolution of
disputes by arbitration in Switzerland. In the course of
performance of the contract, a dispute arose between
the parties, leading to the termination of the contract
on both sides. In 1998, Fomento issued proceedings
against CCT in Panama. CCT argued that the court was
barred from hearing the claim by virtue of the arbitration agreement. The court of first instance dismissed
this challenge to its jurisdiction on the basis that it had
been raised too late.

CCT then initiated arbitration proceedings in
Switzerland. The parties had agreed that the arbitration
was to be governed by ICC Arbitration Rules, supple-
mented by the Swiss federal rules of civil procedure.
Fomento argued that the arbitral tribunal did not have
jurisdiction to hear the dispute because Fomento had
waived the arbitration agreement by issuing proceedings in Panama, and CCT had accepted this waiver by
failing to challenge the court's jurisdiction on time. In
the meantime, the Panamanian Court of Appeal had
reversed the finding of the court of first instance and

---

[488] *Ibid.*, [127].
[489] *Supra* footnote 449.

concluded that the arbitration defence had been raised in time. Referring to that decision, the arbitral tribunal concluded that it had jurisdiction to hear the matter.

However, the Supreme Court of Panama subsequently held that CCT had not raised the defence in time and ordered the continuance of judicial proceedings in Panama. Fomento challenged the arbitral tribunal's assumption of jurisdiction before the Swiss Federal Tribunal, claiming that the tribunal's acceptance of jurisdiction had breached the rules of *lis pendens*. The Federal Tribunal began its reasoning by observing that, within a specific legal order, it was contrary to public policy for two judicial decisions to contradict each other in the same action and between the same parties. The principles of *lis pendens* and *res judicata* applied to avoid such a situation[490]. By virtue of Article 9 of the Swiss Federal Private International Law[491], the rule of *lis pendens* was also capable of applying to foreign court proceedings. The question, then, was whether such a rule applied where the second seised tribunal was not a Swiss court, but an arbitral tribunal sitting in Switzerland. The Federal Tribunal considered that, since arbitral awards were enforceable in the same way as judgments, the same underlying principle of the avoidance of contradictory decisions in the same legal order should apply[492]. Given the close connection between the principles of *res judicata* and *lis pendens,* it was logical to apply the rule of priority to a court first seised of the same issue[493], provided that the foreign court's judgment was susceptible of enforcement in Switzerland[494].

Having reached this point in principle, the Federal

---

[490] *Ibid.*, [2 *(b)*].
[491] *Supra* Chapter I, Section D 2.
[492] *Fomento, supra* footnote 449, [2 *(c) (aa)*].
[493] *Ibid.*, [2 *(c) (bb)*].
[494] *Ibid.*, [2 *(c) (dd)*].

Tribunal then turned to consider whether the Arbitral
Tribunal, by reason of its particular nature, would not
have a privileged right to decide its jurisdiction[495]. This
required the Federal Tribunal to consider the scope of
the *Kompetenz-Kompetenz* principle — did it privilege
the decision of the arbitral tribunal as to its own jurisdiction over the decision of a State court, such that the
State court was compelled to cede priority to the
Arbitral Tribunal? Referring to Article II (3) of the
New York Convention, the Federal Tribunal thought
that a State court seised of a substantive claim was
entitled to examine for itself whether the arbitration
agreement was valid:

> "The State Court seized of an action on the mer-
> its . . . must rule on its own jurisdiction even if in
> order to do so it has to express a view on the valid-
> ity of an arbitration clause . . . When one of the par-
> ties relies on an arbitration agreement and the other
> argues that a subsequent agreement took place in
> favour of the State Court, it is clear from the outset
> that both courts in competition (the Arbitral Tri-
> bunal and the State Court) are equally empowered
> to deal with the issue. There is therefore no reason
> to grant a priority to the Arbitral Tribunal which has
> no legal foundation and justification. The rule of *lis
> pendens* must be upheld . . ."[496]

On the facts of the case, the Federal Tribunal considered that the Panamanian courts were actually in a
better position to decide the issue in any event, since the
question turned on whether the arbitration agreement
had been waived by unconditional appearance before
the court — a question of which had to be decided by
reference to Panamanian law[497]. Accordingly, the

---

[495] *Ibid.*, [2 *(c) (ee)*].
[496] *Ibid.*
[497] *Ibid.*

Federal Tribunal allowed the appeal and annulled the award.

Following opposition to this ruling from the arbitral community in Switzerland, Article 186 of the Swiss Code on Private International Law (which deals with the jurisdiction of arbitral tribunals) was amended to add a new paragraph, Article 186 1*bis*, which provides:

> "Il statue sur sa compétence sans égard à une action ayant le même objet déjà pendante entre les mêmes parties devant un autre tribunal étatique ou arbitral, sauf si des motifs sérieux commandent de suspendre la procédure." [498]

How may this particularly Helvetian controversy help us to understand the wider issues of the role of litispendence as between national courts and arbitration? In the first place, it may be observed that the fact that each of the court and the arbitral tribunal has competence to rule on its own competence does not answer the question of how to deal with competing concurrent determinations of competence [499]. On the facts of *Fomento,* the Panamanian courts would undoubtedly have had proper jurisdiction were it not for the arbitration clause. The subject-matter of the contract was the construction of a harbour terminal in Panama. Fomento's claim in the Panamanian courts was brought against a Panamanian party, CCT. However, if the arbitration agreement were valid and applicable (questions governed by Swiss law as the governing law of the arbitration agreement), it would oust the jurisdiction of the Panamanian court.

---

[498] Introduced by Chapter I of the Federal Law of 6 October 2006 (Arbitration. Jurisdiction), in force since 1 March 2007 (RO 2007 387, 388; FF 2006 4469, 4481), available at www.admin.ch.

[499] Bucher, *supra* footnote 449, 175.

*Fomento* represented the culmination of a clear trend in the Swiss Federal Tribunal to seek to place arbitral tribunals and national courts on an equal basis[500]. Yet the relationship is not one of two courts of equal standing and competence, requiring the "tie-break" of a *lis pendens* to determine priority. In this sense, arbitration is a separate exception, requiring a different rule of priority to that required by the *lis pendens* rule applicable to conflicts of jurisdiction as between national courts[501]. Rather, it has been convincingly argued that the negative aspect of *Kompetenz-Kompetenz* requires deference to the arbitral tribunal to determine its own jurisdiction, subject to a prima facie review by the court whose jurisdiction was first invoked, and the possibility of a full challenge to the arbitral tribunal's jurisdiction in the courts of the seat, once the tribunal has issued its own jurisdictional decision. Although Article II of the New York Convention does not of itself require such a solution, nevertheless the judgment of a foreign court which overrode a valid arbitration agreement could not be enforceable elsewhere, since that would itself be a breach of the foreign state's obligations under Article II[502].

Was, then, *Fomento,* a false turn in the development of the law? The facts of the case presented peculiarly cogent grounds for deference to the Panamanian courts. This was not a case where it was disputed that there was an arbitration agreement; or that such agreement covered the dispute. Rather, the issue was whether one of the parties had waived its right to rely

---

[500] Geisinger and Lévy, *supra* footnote 444, 56, citing *Emirats Arabes Unis* v. *Westland Helicopters* (19 April 1994) Swiss Federal Tribunal ATF 120 II 155 and *Compañia Miniera Condesa SA* v. *BRGM-Pérou SAS* (19 December 1997), Swiss Federal Tribunal ATF 124 III 83.

[501] Bucher, *supra* footnote 449, 182-183.

[502] *Condesa, supra* footnote 500, 86-87.

upon the agreement by taking a step in the Panamanian proceedings. The determination of that issue required a close examination of the facts as to the steps taken in Panama, and their legal significance — a matter which could only sensibly be judged according to Panamanian procedural law. It was not said that the Panamanian courts were likely to come to a conclusion on the point which was contrary to the New York Convention, nor that the pursuit of appeals before those courts was for dilatory purposes. In all these circumstances, then, the arbitral tribunal could well have been best advised to stay its proceedings to have the point of Panamanian law determined by the Panamanian courts[503].

It was, rather, the automatic and mandatory character of the *lis pendens* rule in Swiss Private International Law which created alarm in the aftermath of *Fomento*. If an arbitral tribunal were always required to suspend its proceedings if a court in another country were first seised with the dispute, this would encourage forum shopping. A prospective defendant would have every incentive to issue proceedings in a national court, particularly in a jurisdiction known for court delays, and thereby to delay the resolution of the dispute on the merits by arbitration, even in cases in which the arbitration agreement was clearly applicable. Of course, in a clear case, the requirement that a judgment of the foreign court be capable of recognition in Switzerland would provide a safety-valve. But this protection may not be available in all cases. In particular, there is a

---

[503] Accord ILA, *supra* footnote 445, 182 [5.9], where the Committee accepted that one situation where the arbitral tribunal might defer to the State court is "where there is prima facie evidence that the claimant in the arbitration has taken a substantive step in the foreign litigation thereby waiving its right to rely on the agreement to arbitrate".

continuing debate about whether a judgment of another court under the Lugano Convention, even if in breach of an arbitration agreement, requires enforcement[504].

Thus, the solution of the Swiss legislature to re-affirm the duty of the arbitral tribunal to determine its own competence, subject to a discretion where "motifs sérieux" justify suspension of the proceedings, seems to preserve the right balance. Plainly, for this exception to apply, there must be something more than mere overlap between the arbitration and court proceedings. Normally, both principle and practical considerations will justify continuation of the arbitral proceedings. However, exceptional circumstances may justify a departure. Bucher suggests that grounds for a suspension may include: the agreement of the parties; the implication of a third party; the difficulty of determining the scope of the arbitration agreement; and the evaluation, in the interest of the parties, of the risk of non-enforcement of the arbitral award in the state whose court was seised with the parallel dispute[505].

## 2. *Parallel and related arbitral proceedings*

In contrast to the fraught field of relations between arbitral tribunals and courts, there are relatively few recorded instances of parallel proceedings *between* arbitral tribunals in international commercial arbitration. This results from the elementary point that the parties' agreement to refer a dispute to arbitration operates, with the support of Article II of the New York Convention, to confer *exclusive* jurisdiction on the chosen tribunal. Thus, only an unusual fact pattern will produce an outright conflict of jurisdiction between arbitral tribunals. This is not so in the context of invest-

---

[504] Bucher, *supra* footnote 449, 186.
[505] *Ibid.*

ment disputes, where, as will be seen, the fundamental distinction between treaty and contract disputes may well produce overlapping disputes between the treaty tribunal and a tribunal appointed to decide a contractual dispute between the same parties[506]; and where (more problematically) investors have invoked parallel rights to arbitration in relation to the same underlying dispute under different bilateral investment treaties[507].

Cases which have produced parallel arbitration proceedings have arisen either where there is a dispute of which of two successive, but different, arbitration agreements apply; or where the clause itself confers jurisdiction on more than one arbitral tribunal. An example of each will illustrate the issues.

In *Arthur Andersen* v. *Andersen Consulting*[508], the majority of the Andersen Consulting firms brought ICC arbitration proceedings in Switzerland against the majority of the Arthur Andersen firms, relying upon the most recent arbitration agreement (not yet signed by all member firms). Subsequently, one Arthur Andersen firm brought separate *ad hoc* arbitral proceedings against one Andersen Consulting firm in Geneva, relying on an earlier arbitration agreement, which had been signed by all parties. The respondent firm in the second case refused to appoint an arbitrator, and the Geneva court declined to appoint one judicially on the ground that the arbitral tribunal in the first arbitration should decide on its own jurisdiction first. This dispute was

---

[506] *Infra*, Section C 2, and, for examples in the practice of the Iran-United States Claims Tribunal: *Reading and Bates Corp.* v. *Iran* (Interim Award of 9 June 1983), 2 *Iran-US CTR* 401; *Fluor Corp.* v. *Iran* (Interim Award of 6 August 1986) 11 *Iran-US CTR* 296.

[507] *Infra*, Section C 5.

[508] Geneva Court (30 September 1998), [1999] 9 *Rev. suisse de droit int'l et droit européen* 628; Swiss Federal Tribunal (8 December 1999), [2000] *ASA Bull.* 546, noted Geisinger and Lévy, *supra* footnote 444, 66-68.

only finally resolved when the Swiss Federal Tribunal upheld the jurisdiction of the first arbitral tribunal on appeal.

In that case, the two rival arbitrations both had their seat in Switzerland. The situation becomes more complicated when the two arbitrations proceed in different countries. In *Tema-Frugoli SpA* v. *Hubei Space Quarry Industry Co. Ltd.* [509], the Italian seller (Tema) and the Chinese buyer (Hubei) had agreed to an arbitration agreement in their sale of goods contract, which provided that, if the claim was filed by the seller, it was to be settled by arbitration at the Stockholm Arbitration Institute, whereas, if instituted by the buyer, it was to be settled by the China International Economic Trade Arbitration Commission (CIETAC). A dispute arose as to Tema's performance. Tema filed first in Stockholm seeking a declaration from the tribunal that it had complied with its contractual obligations. Hubei participated in those proceedings, which resulted in an award in Tema's favour. A few weeks later, Hubei filed its claim against Tema for non-performance at CIETAC. Tema took no part in the CIETAC proceedings, which eventually resulted in an award in favour of Hubei. Tema obtained enforcement of the Stockholm award in Rome. Hubei then sought enforcement of the CIETAC award against Tema in Milan. Tema opposed on the ground that, once the first arbitration had been commenced, the second, Chinese, arbitration was precluded — in essence a plea of *lis pendens*. The consequence, said Tema, was that the CIETAC award should not be enforced.

The Milan Court of Appeal disagreed, construing the arbitration agreement to confer valid jurisdiction on both arbitral tribunals, and holding that the inconsis-

---

[509] Milan Court of Appeal (2 July 1999), (2001) 26 *Ybk. Comm. Arb.* 807.

tency between the two awards was not a ground for refusing to enforce the second award under the New York Convention. Such an objection would have to be taken, if available, by way of review before the courts of the seat.

This result is highly unsatisfactory. The recourse of Tema to Stockholm arbitration appears to be a rare example of the use of the negative declaration as a means of forum shopping between available arbitral institutions. But nevertheless, that tribunal undoubtedly had jurisdiction, both parties participated in its hearings, which resulted in an award determining the issue. In these circumstances, the CIETAC tribunal ought to have stayed its proceedings. It is simply no answer to say that it, too, enjoyed jurisdiction. In the words of the ILA Committee on International Commercial Arbitration, considering situations of litispendence between arbitral tribunals:

> "It is argued by some commentators that the tribunal is mandated to determine the dispute referred to it by the claimant, and should proceed to do so. The Committee disagrees. *Lis pendens* is recognized in most legal systems, and has also been recognized as prima facie applicable in international arbitration. The Committee submits that the second tribunal should stay its proceedings." [510]

It may well be right that it was Tema's obligation to raise this objection at CIETAC[511], and, if necessary before the Chinese courts. But the resulting enforcement of both awards in Italy is a nonsense, since the courts could not at one and the same time give effect to

---

[510] *Supra* footnote 445, [4.48], and see the Committee's Recommendation 5 at [5.13]; accord Born, *supra* footnote 441, 2949.

[511] *Ibid.*, Recommendation 7 at [5.13].

an award declaring Tema to have met its contractual obligations, and an award declaring that it had not.

Beyond these mercifully rare cases of direct overlap, there is a much more pervasive issue in international commercial arbitration of the management of related proceedings arising out of the same dispute. Here, arbitration presents some well-recognized differences with litigation:

> "In the context of litigation, problems of potentially conflicting judgments arrived at between different parties to the same overall complex of disputes are met by provisions for joinder of parties or proceedings or for trial together, if necessary on a mandatory basis using the courts' compulsive powers ... All this is facilitated by the public nature of litigation, the public interest in the efficient administration of justice and the courts' coercive powers ... Arbitration is in contrast a consensual, private affair between the particular parties to a particular arbitration agreement. The resulting inability to enforce the solutions of joinder of parties or proceedings in arbitration, or to try connected arbitrations together other than by consent, is well-recognised — though the popularity of arbitration may indicate that this inability is not often inconvenient or that perceived advantages of arbitration, including confidentiality and privacy are seen as outweighing any inconvenience."[512]

From this starting-point, arbitration law has evolved many processes to accommodate related claims, whether between the same parties, or between different parties but arising out of the same underlying project

---

[512] *Sun Life Insurance Co. of Canada* v. *Lincoln National Life Insurance Co.*, [2005] 1 Lloyd's Rep. 606, [68] (CA) per Mance LJ.

or dispute within the same arbitration. The issues which may arise in these cases go well beyond the scope of the present lectures[513]. The fundamental restriction which runs through the jurisprudence is the requirement of the consent of all parties[514]. In the absence of consent, it is rare for there to be provision for consolidation. Even where such provision is made[515], it is even rarer for it to be exercised against the opposition of one of the parties.

### 3. *The anti-suit injunction and arbitration*

The anti-suit injunction has been employed in relation to international arbitration in three very different settings:

(a) *Issue of anti-suit injunctions by arbitrators.* In the first place, there is some practice showing the use by arbitral tribunals of their interim relief powers to restrain parties from pursuing duplicative court proceedings in breach of an arbitration agreement;

(b) *Anti-suit injunctions in aid of arbitration.* In the second place, Common Law courts have developed a widespread practice of granting anti-suit injunctions in aid of arbitration. Such injunctions seek to compel adherence to an arbitration agreement, where one of the parties, in breach of the agreement, is pursuing litigation in another court. It is this practice which has now been excluded within the European Jurisdiction and Judgments area by the European Court's decision in *The Front Comor*[516];

---

[513] But see the recent study of Hanotiau, which helpfully presents much of the material: *supra* footnote 445.

[514] Craig, Park, Paulsson, *International Chamber of Commerce Arbitration* (3rd ed., 1998) [11.06]; and see Born, *supra* footnote 441, Chap. 17.

[515] As, for example, in ICC Rules, Art. 4 (6), and Stockholm Chamber of Commerce Rules, Art. 11.

[516] *Supra* footnote 456.

(c) *Anti-arbitration injunctions.* In the third place, there has been an increasing incidence of national courts granting injunctions to seek to restrain resort to international arbitration, particularly on the application of a state corporation in the relevant country.

Despite the apparent similarity in remedy, these three very different applications of the anti-suit injunction require separate consideration.

### (a) *Issue of anti-suit injunctions by arbitrators*[517]

There are few recorded instances of an arbitral tribunal in international commercial arbitration restraining the parties before it from pursuing parallel proceedings in other fora[518]. Most of the cases where this question has arisen have involved tribunals established by international treaty, where the State party has, by virtue of its specific agreement as a matter of Public International Law, agreed to ensure the effectiveness of the tribunal's decisions. This is particularly so of the practice of the Iran-United States Claims Tribunal[519]. But there is also evidence of such an approach in ICSID investment treaty cases[520]. However, even in

---

[517] Lévy, *supra* footnote 455, 115.

[518] But see, in addition to the cases discussed *infra*, *ICC Case No. 3896* (23 December 1982) (Lalive P, Robert and Goldman) (1983) 110 *JDI* 914, Jarvin and Derains (eds.), *Collection of ICC Arbitral Awards 1974-1985* (1990) 161 and the unpublished cases discussed by Gaillard, *supra* footnote 455, 251-259.

[519] *E-Systems* v. *Iran* (Interim Award of 4 February 1983) 2 *Iran-US CTR* 51, 56 (Full Tribunal); *infra*, Chapter IV, Section B 2.

[520] *SGS Société de Surveillance SA* v. *Pakistan* (Procedural Order No. 2 of 16 October 2002), 8 *ICSID Rep.* 388, discussed *infra*, Section C 4; *MINE* v. *Guinea* (Award), 4 *ICSID Rep.* 59, 69; *CSOB* v. *Slovak Republic* ICSID Case No. ARB/97/4 (Procedural Order No. 2 of 9 September

these contexts, tribunals have adopted a cautious approach. Often, as will be seen, this is because the jurisdiction of the tribunal does not preclude the pursuit of other related litigation in national courts[521]. But it also reflects a conscious wish to limit the intervention of the tribunal in the exercise of jurisdiction by other courts and tribunals. As Laurent Lévy puts it "arbitrators should not take the risk of ordering a judge or other arbitrators how to behave. They are the arbitrators' equals and have no orders to receive."[522]

Nevertheless, there may be exceptional cases where the issue of a provisional or protective measure is necessary to protect the arbitral proceedings. Thus, the 2006 amendments to the UNICTRAL Model Law on International Commercial Arbitration add an elaborate code on interim measures[523]. One of the circumstances in which an arbitral tribunal is permitted to grant interim measures is where the tribunal orders a party to:

> "Take action that would prevent, or refrain from taking action that is likely to cause, current or imminent harm or prejudice to the arbitral process itself."[524]

This will be particularly appropriate where one of the parties starts subsequent court proceedings in a fraudulent attempt to undermine the jurisdiction of the arbitral tribunal. An illustration of this situation is pro-

---

1998; Procedural Order No. 4 of 11 January 1999; Procedural Order No. 5 of 1 March 2000); *Tokios Tokelés* v. *Ukraine*, ICSID Case No. ARB/02/18 (Procedural Order No. 1 of 1 July 2003, Procedural Order No. 3 of 18 January 2005); *Plama Consortium Ltd.* v. *Bulgaria*, ICSID Case No. ARB/03/24 (Procedural Order of 6 September 2005).

[521] *E-Systems* v. *Iran*, *supra* footnote 519.
[522] *Supra* footnote 455, 128.
[523] Arts. 17-17J (7 July 2006), UN doc. A/61/17, Annex 1.
[524] *Ibid.*, Art. 17 (2) *(b)*.

vided by *ICC Case No. 8307*[525]. This was a long-running dispute concerning the alleged fraudulent misappropriation of B's shares in B Properties by A and C by means of a settlement agreement between B Properties and E Bank. Arbitration had been commenced under an exclusive arbitration clause contained in the Shareholders' Agreement to which all parties were bound. The Agreement specified that Italian law should apply. While the dispute was being arbitrated, B instituted proceedings in the Royal Courts of Country X. A and C applied to the Sole Arbitrator for an anti-suit order halting these proceedings.

The Sole Arbitrator Tercier concluded that the parties, the claims and the subject-matter of the two sets of proceedings were essentially the same[526]. Rejecting B's objections, the Sole Arbitrator concluded that pursuit of B's claims in country X "violates the arbitration clause" that gives "the Sole Arbitrator the sole jurisdiction to decide on these questions"[527]. The court proceedings were, in the Arbitrator's view, an attempt to obtain exemplary damages that were not available under Italian law, which the parties had chosen to govern their contract.

He then turned to consider whether he had "the power to order the particular conservative measure of refraining from initiating or pursuing an action in state courts"[528]. Relying upon some earlier ICC practice[529], Tercier decided:

---

[525] ICC Case No. 8307 (Interim Award) published in Gaillard, *supra* footnote 455, 308 (2001, Sole Arbitrator Tercier).

[526] *Ibid.*, [5], [7].

[527] *Ibid.*, [8].

[528] *Ibid.*, [9].

[529] ICC Case No. 8887 (Final Award of April 1997) (2000) 11 *ICC Bull.* 91; ICC Case No. 5650 (Final Award of 1989) 16 *Ybk. Comm. Arb.* 85; ICC Case No. 3896, *supra* footnote 518.

"[T]he agreement to arbitrate implies that the parties have renounced to submit to judicial courts the disputes envisaged by the arbitral clause . . . It is not contested that an arbitrator has the power to order the parties to comply with their contractual commitments. The agreement to arbitrate being one of them, its violation must be dealt with in the same manner when it is patent that the action initiated in a state court is outside the jurisdiction of such court and is therefore abusive. This is also a guarantee of the efficiency and credibility of international arbitration."[530]

This example is significant in demonstrating that, even if rarely exercised, arbitral tribunals retain a residual power to ensure that the parties before it do not engage in abusive satellite litigation in a way which may undermine the power of the tribunal to decide the dispute referred to it[531].

To what extent may the national court at the seat of the arbitration issue a similar order in support of the arbitration? This question was centrally at issue in the recent litigation before the European Court in *The Front Comor*[532]. But in order to place that decision in context, it is necessary to say a little about the development of the anti-suit injunction in aid of arbitration in Common Law jurisprudence.

### (b) The Front Comor *and anti-suit injunctions in aid of arbitration*

The remedy of the anti-suit injunction has been utilized by the English court since at least 1911[533], to

---

[530] *Supra* footnote 525, [9]-[10] (emphasis in original).
[531] Accord Lévy, *supra* footnote 455, 128; Born, *supra* footnote 441, 2009-2011.
[532] *Supra* footnote 456.
[533] *Pena Copper Mines Ltd.* v. *Rio Tinto Co. Ltd.*, (1911) 105 LT 846 (CA). For discussion of the law prior to

restrain a defendant from bringing foreign proceedings
in breach of an arbitration agreement governed by
English law. The injunction is granted on the basis that
without it the claimant will be deprived of its contractual right to have disputes settled by arbitration in a situation in which damages are manifestly an inadequate
remedy[534]. In 1994, in *The Angelic Grace*[535], Millett
LJ said that the time had come to lay aside the ritual
incantation that this was a jurisdiction which should be
exercised only sparingly and with great caution, and
said that there was no reason for diffidence in granting
an injunction to restrain foreign proceedings brought in
breach of an arbitration agreement, on the clear and
simple ground that the defendant had promised not to
bring them. Subsequent decisions have continued in
equally robust vein to protect a reference to arbitration
in England from court proceedings[536]; and also the
exclusive power of the English court to determine an
application for annulment of an English arbitration
award[537].

In the United States, a power to order anti-suit
injunctions in the enforcement of arbitration agreements also exists, but it is exercised more sparingly.
The importance of holding the parties to their agreement as to forum is a very important factor. But it has
not been finally decided whether this factor alone
is sufficient to justify an injunction. In the leading

---

the decision of the European Court in *The Front Comor*
see *Dicey*, *supra* footnote 466, Rule 58 (2), [16-088]-
[16-093].

[534] *The Angelic Grace*, [1995] 1 Lloyd's Rep. 87 (CA).
[535] *Ibid.*, 96 per Millet LJ, cited in *Through Transport
Mutual Insurance Assn. (Eurasia) Ltd.* v. *New India Assurance Assn. Co. Ltd.*, [2005] 1 Lloyd's Rep. 67, [87]-[91]
(CA).
[536] *Starlight Shipping Co.* v. *Tai Ping Ins. Co. Ltd.
(Hubei Branch)*, [2008] 1 Lloyd's Rep. 230 (QB).
[537] *C* v. *D*, [2007] 2 Lloyd's Rep. 367.

modern case, *Paramedics Electro* v. *GE Medical Systems* [538], the Second Circuit Court of Appeals upheld an injunction restraining a party from pursuing Brazilian proceedings in breach of the arbitration agreement. But both the District Court and the Arbitral Tribunal itself had already ruled that the arbitration agreement was valid and enforceable. It covered the dispute which was the subject of the litigation in Brazil, which had been started after the reference to arbitration, and was thus "a tactic to evade arbitration" [539]. Thus the injunction could be supported on the stronger ground of the *res judicata* effect of the determinations already made as to the arbitration agreement [540]. The US Court will consider whether the desirability of enforcing the arbitration agreement may be outweighed by comity concerns, which mandate non-intervention in the foreign court's decision [541].

The recent revisions to the UNCITRAL Model Law, as has been seen, empower an arbitral tribunal to order an interim measure where the actions of one of the parties may "prejudice the arbitral process itself" [542]. Such a measure is binding and enforceable in national courts, irrespective of the country in which it was issued [543]. Moreover, a national court

"shall have the same power of issuing an interim measure in relation to arbitration proceedings, irrespective of whether their place is in the territory of

---

[538] *Paramedics Electro* v. *GE Medical Systems*, 369 F. 3d 645 (2nd Cir., 2004), note Fellas (2005) 20 (4) *Int. Arb. Rep.* 25, Tan (2006) 21 (7) *Int. Arb. Rep.* 39.

[539] *Ibid.*, 654.

[540] *Ibid.*

[541] *Infra*, Section B 3 *(c)*, discussing *KBC* v. *Pertamina*, 335 F. 3d 357 (5th Cir., 2003); 465 F. Supp. 2d 283 (SDNY 2006).

[542] *Supra* footnote 463.

[543] *Ibid.*, Art. 17H.

this State, as it has in relation to proceedings in courts. The court shall exercise such power in accordance with its own procedures in consideration of the specific features of international arbitration."[544]

Thus, where national law includes the power to issue an anti-suit injunction, this provision permits its exercise in aid of arbitration.

In Europe, however, the application of this Common Law remedy was until the decision of the European Court in *The Front Comor*[545] a controversial question. An attempt by an English court to serve anti-suit injunctive proceedings in support of an English arbitration upon German parties was met with hostility by the German court:

> "Such injunctions constitute an infringement of the jurisdiction of Germany because the German courts alone decide, in accordance with the procedural laws governing them and in accordance with existing international agreements, whether they are competent to adjudicate on a matter or whether they must respect the jurisdiction of another domestic or a foreign court (including arbitration courts)."[546]

The controversy gained force and urgency as a result of decisions of the European Court on the general regime of the Brussels I Regulation, which, it has already been seen, gives priority to the court first seised to determine its own jurisdiction and does not permit anti-suit injunctions[547]. On the other hand arbitration is excluded as a whole from the scope of the Regulation

---

[544] *Ibid.*, Art. 17J.

[545] *Supra* footnote 456.

[546] *Re the enforcement of an English anti-suit injunction*, [1997] IL Pr. 320 (Oberlandesgericht Düsseldorf).

[547] *Supra* Chapter II, Sections B 1 and D 3 *(c)*.

under Article 1 (2) *(d)* [548]. The question, as applied to anti-suit injunctions in aid of arbitration, depended primarily on *(a)* whether the anti-suit injunction proceedings were outside the scope of the Brussels I Regulation because of the provision in Article 1 (2) *(d)* that it shall not apply to "arbitration"; and *(b)* whether the claim for injunctive relief involved the same cause of action as the claim in the foreign proceedings for the purposes of what is now Article 27 of the Brussels I Regulation. Views had been divided in particular on whether the arbitration exception applied [549].

The question was referred to the European Court in *Toepfer International GmbH* v. *Cargill France SA* [550], but the case was settled before the Court had reached a decision. In *Through Transport* [551], the English Court of Appeal held that it was open to the court in which the issue whether the arbitration exception applied to consider that question, even if it was the court second seised [552]. If it concluded that the arbitration exception applied, the court was entitled to proceed. In that event, the ruling in *Turner* v. *Grovit* [553] did not affect the principle that in general an injunction would be granted to restrain breach of an arbitration agreement. The principal focus of the English proceedings was arbitration, and accordingly the English proceedings came within

---

[548] *Van Uden Maritime BV* v. *Firma Deco-Line*, Case C-391/95, [1998] *ECR* I-7091, [24].

[549] *Toepfer International GmbH* v. *Molino Boschi Srl*, [1996] 1 Lloyd's Rep. 510 (QB); *Charterers Mutual Assurance Assn Ltd.* v. *British & Foreign*, [1998] IL Pr. 838 (QB), compare *Toepfer International GmbH* v. *Cargill France*, [1997] 2 Lloyd's Rep. 98 (QB); *The Ivan Zagubanski*, [2002] 1 Lloyd's Rep. 106 (QB).

[550] [1998] 1 Lloyd's Rep. 379 (CA).

[551] *Supra* footnote 535.

[552] Relying on the case of *Marc Rich & Co. AG* v. *Soc. Italiana Impianti SpA*, C-190/89, [1991] *ECR* I-3855, [1992] 1 Lloyd's Rep. 342.

[553] Case C-159/02, [2004] 2 Lloyd's Rep. 169.

the arbitration exception. Accordingly there was nothing in the Brussels I Regulation to prevent an English court from granting an injunction. However, as a matter of discretion, the injunction was refused.

This was where matters stood until a maritime collision in Italy, by a vessel carrying goods under a charter-party with an English arbitration clause, provoked the *cause célèbre* of *The Front Comor*[554]. The facts were as follows. *The Front Comor*, a vessel owned by West Tankers and chartered to Erg Petroli SpA, collided with a jetty owned by Erg. The charter-party provided for arbitration of disputes in London. While Erg began arbitration to recover the losses not covered by their insurers, the insurers exercised their statutory right of subrogation under Italian law to commence proceedings against West Tankers in Italy for the insured losses. West Tankers responded with proceedings in England, seeking a declaration that, as the dispute being litigated in Italy arose out of the charter-party, the insurers inherited the obligation to refer it to arbitration. West Tankers sought an injunction that the insurers not pursue the claim further except by way of arbitration, and in particular that they discontinue the Italian proceedings.

Colman J held that the insurers' claim was subject to the arbitration clause and that the Court had jurisdiction to grant the injunction because arbitration was excluded from the Brussels I Regulation. The House of Lords agreed that it was not inconsistent with the New York Convention to grant an injunction in such circumstances and that as a matter of discretion an English court need not refuse to restrain proceedings in another Member State[555]. But their Lordships decided to refer to the European Court of Justice the question

---

[554] *Supra* footnote 456.
[555] *Ibid.*, [8].

"Is it consistent with EC Regulation 44/2001 for a court of a Member State to make an order to restrain a person from commencing or continuing proceedings in another Member State on the ground that such proceedings are in breach of an arbitration agreement?"[556]

Their Lordships indicated a strong inclination that it was. As Lord Hoffmann put it:

"The arbitration agreement lies outside the system of allocation of court jurisdictions which the Regulation creates. There is no dispute that, under the Regulation, the Tribunale di Siracusa has jurisdiction to try the delictual claim. But the arbitration clause is an agreement not to *invoke* that jurisdiction . . . [A]n arbitration clause takes effect outside the Regulation and its enforcement is not subject to its terms."[557]

He then emphasized the principles of party autonomy and *Kompetenz-Kompetenz* underpinning the operation of arbitration as a method of resolving international disputes:

"People engaged in commerce choose arbitration in order to be outside the procedures of *any* national court. They frequently prefer the privacy, informality and absence of any prolongation of the dispute by appeal which arbitration offers. Nor is it only a matter of procedure. The choice of arbitration may affect the substantive rights of the parties . . . The principle of autonomy of the parties should allow them these choices.[558]

---

[556] *Ibid.*, [25].
[557] *Ibid.*, [16] (emphasis in original), citing with approval Schlosser "Anti-suit injunctions zur Unterstützung von internationalen Schiedsverfahren", (2006) *RIW* 486-492.
[558] *Ibid.*, [19] (emphasis in original).

. . . In proceedings falling within the Regulation it is right, as the Court of Justice said in *Gasser* and *Turner* v. *Grovit*, that courts of Member States should trust each other to apply the Regulation. But in cases concerning arbitration, falling outside the Regulation, it is in my opinion equally necessary that Member States should trust the arbitrators (under the doctrine of *Kompetenz-Kompetenz*) or the court exercising supervisory jurisdiction to decide whether the arbitration clause is binding and then to enforce that decision by orders which require the parties to arbitrate and not litigate." [559]

These arguments were of no avail in the European Court, which, in a cursory judgment of just six pages, approached the matter from the opposite point of view. It held that the first question was whether the delictual proceedings before the Italian Court came within the scope of the Convention. Since they did, the effect of the arbitration agreement, including its validity, were an incidental question, which also came within the scope of the Convention [560]. Accordingly, it was the Italian court which had the exclusive power under the Convention to rule on the effect of the arbitration agreement for its jurisdiction. The issue of an anti-suit injunction by another court "necessarily amounts to stripping that court of the power to rule on its own jurisdiction" [561]. The structure of the Convention contemplated that each court ruled for itself on its own jurisdiction. It was incompatible with the system of mutual trust created by the Convention for another court to obstruct such a determination [562].

---

[559] *Ibid.*, [22].
[560] *Supra* footnote 456, [26], see also Opinion of Kokott AG, *supra* footnote 456, [33].
[561] *Ibid.*, [28].
[562] *Ibid.*, [29]-[30].

The judgment has the effect, as Kokott AG recognized[563], that there could be parallel determinations, by the arbitral tribunal and by a national court in another European country, on the validity and scope of the arbitration agreement, and its effect on the pending court proceedings. That could, in turn, lead to inconsistent decisions. The Advocate General saw the solution to this problem as not being in the issue of anti-suit injunctions, but rather in the amendment of the Brussels I Regulation so as to bring arbitration within its scheme[564].

The Court's judgment was no surprise to those following the trend of ECJ jurisprudence on both the priority of choice of forum clauses and on the compatibility of anti-suit injunctions with the Convention[565]. But, for all that, it has stirred a heated debate in the legal community. It has been seen as a broadside attack on the priority to be accorded to arbitration within the European Union. Even Civil lawyers, despite the traditional hostility of the Civil Law tradition to the anti-suit injunction, have seen the merits of the remedy when applied in the enforcement of an arbitration agreement, and expressed concern at the ECJ's approach[566].

Yet the issue is not as straight-forward as is suggested by either the European Court or its opponents. In the first case, the facts hardly present a text-book case of parallel proceedings, despite the short statement of Colman J that there is "complete overlap"[567]. Unusually, Erg was both charterer of *The Front Comor*,

---

[563] *Supra* footnote 456, [70]-[72].

[564] *Ibid.*, [73].

[565] *Supra*, Chapter II, Sections B 3 *(a)* and D 3 *(c)*.

[566] Schlosser, *supra* footnote 557; Bollée, *supra* footnote 456; Kessedjian, at http://conflictoflaws.net/2009/kessedjian-on-west-tankers.

[567] *Supra* footnote 456, [6].

and owner of the jetty in Syracuse. It was the losses arising from the damage to the jetty which formed the subject-matter of the claim. The arbitration agreement was concluded in relation to a standard-form Asba-tankvoy tanker voyage charter-party[568]. This contains, in clause 19, a general exclusion of liability on the part of the vessel, master and owner for any defaults of the master or other servants of the owner in the navigation of the vessel. The purpose of this sweeping clause is to allocate risk as between owner and charterer in a vessel chartered for the carriage of goods[569]. In any event, such an exclusion arises only by way of the owner's defence, and not the primary claim. If the jetty owner had been a third party, the arbitration agreement could have had no conceivable application to its claim for damage in tort. The overlap between the two cases therefore seems to have been invited by Erg's strategy of claiming under the charter-party in the arbitration in England, which was in turn bound to invite a defence and counter-claim by West Tankers to the effect that it was protected by the contractual exclusion of liability. Were it not for this approach, the application of the arbitration agreement to the Syracuse proceedings would have been much more difficult. This point is independent of the question of the effect of the arbitration agreement in the charter-party upon Erg's insurers who pursued their claim in Syracuse on a subrogated basis.

The Syracuse proceedings cannot therefore be criticized on the conventional ground that they were an "Italian torpedo" designed to pre-empt a valid choice of forum by negative declaratory proceedings in a court which was unlikely to prorogate its jurisdiction on a

---

[568] Asbatankvoy Charterparty, available at http://asbatankvoy.ning.com.

[569] See also Hague Rules, Art. IV, rule 2 *(a)*; Girvin, *Carriage of Goods by Sea* (2007) [28.06].

speedy basis à la *Gasser* v. *MISAT*[570]. There were solid grounds for proceeding in Italy, since it was the location of the events giving rise to the tort claim. Insurers could well have taken the view that Erg's claim for the uninsured losses by arbitration under the charter-party was misconceived, precisely because it invited a defence based upon the exclusion clause.

In any event, it may be asked what effect the Syracuse proceedings were likely to have upon the London arbitration. Since the arbitration was commenced some three years before the Italian claim, and was, by the time of the application for the anti-suit injunction, already far advanced, it was likely to reach an award well before any determination by the Italian court. Such an award would be enforceable in any State Party to the New York Convention. A court-ordered anti-suit injunction may well have seemed warranted in order to reach the insurers, who were not directly parties to the arbitration. The arbitral tribunal, after all, had the power, if necessary, to order provisional measures to restrain the parties from the pursuit of litigation which interfered with its process. The court's injunction was in any event unenforceable outside the United Kingdom under the Brussels I Regulation, by virtue of the arbitration exclusion in Article 1 (2) *(d)*[571]. All things considered, then, *The Front Comor* is hardly a text-book case of a party flouting an arbitration agreement. At the least, there were substantial questions of the application of the agreement to the Syracuse proceedings.

However, for all that, the effect of the decision of the European Court will apply to a much wider range of cases, including where there is a clear breach of an

---

[570] *Erich Gasser GmbH* v. *MISAT Sri*, Case C-116/02 [2003] *ECR* I-14693.

[571] CA Paris (15 June 2006), [2007] *Rev. Arb.* 87, note Bollée.

arbitration agreement. The decision betrays little analysis of the relationship between arbitral and judicial proceedings, beyond a single-minded determination to exclude all possibility of anti-suit injunctions granted by national courts in aid of arbitration within the European judgments area. Perhaps the most telling aspect of the Court's brief reasoning is its characterization of the issue as being one relating to

> "the attainment of the objectives of unification of the rules of conflict of jurisdiction in civil and commercial matters and the free movement of decisions in those matters"[572].

This is to leave out of account the central question of who, as between the *arbitral tribunal* and the national court, is to decide on the application of the arbitration agreement to the dispute in hand, and how that decision is to be given effect. As Schlosser has pointed out, in the context of arbitration the anti-suit injunction merely performs the role of ordering specific performance of the parties' agreement to arbitrate their dispute[573]. In this way, it achieves the same result as a judgment declaring such an agreement valid and enforceable as between the parties. The fact that Article II of the New York Convention *requires* the national court seised in breach of such an agreement to stay its proceedings does not mean that the Convention excludes other relief in other courts aimed at the same objective. It may be that the objection to the anti-suit injunction relates not so much to its purpose, as to the quasi-penal consequences which attach to a breach of the order.

The decision of the Court can in no way affect the power of the arbitral tribunal to determine its own jurisdiction under the principle of *Kompetenz-Kompetenz*. Thus, the outcome in *Gasser* — pursuant to which

---

[572] *Supra* footnote 456, [24].
[573] *Supra* footnote 557.

the court enjoying jurisdiction under a jurisdiction clause must cede priority to another court first seised under the *lis pendens* rule — will not apply to an arbitral tribunal. There is no risk of a *Fomento*-style application of the strict first-in-time rule. Nor, given the current scope of the arbitration exclusion in the Brussels I Regulation, can there be any objection to declaratory proceedings as to the validity of the arbitration agreement in the courts of the seat. The consequence, therefore, of the Court's ruling will be that duplicative proceedings will not be avoided. This leaves open the risk that the arbitral tribunal and the court come to conflicting decisions as to the applicability of the arbitration agreement. Worse, the court may not determine the effect of the arbitration agreement upon its proceedings in a prompt preliminary hearing at all. In that event, the race to issue proceedings will merely be replaced by a race to judgment or award.

The solution proposed in the Heidelberg Report[574], reviewing the operation of the Brussels I Regulation, is to add a new Article 27A, which would provide:

> "A court of a Member State shall stay the proceedings once the defendant contests the jurisdiction of the court with respect to existence and scope of an arbitration agreement if a court of the Member State that is designated as place of arbitration in the arbitration agreement is seized for declaratory relief in respect of the existence, the validity and/or the scope of that arbitration agreement."[575]

---

[574] Hess/Pfeiffer/Schlosser, *The Brussels I-Regulation 44/2001* (2008) ("The Heidelberg Report"), apparently supported in the Commission's Green Paper COM (2009) 175 (21 April 2009), 8-9.

[575] *Ibid.*, [133]. The Report proposes adding a new recital which would provide:

> "The place of arbitration shall depend upon the agreement of the parties or be determined by the arbi-

This proposal would have the merit of reinforcing
the principal supervisory role of the courts of the seat
of the arbitration. This principle, as has been seen in
the *Julius* case[576], makes much sound sense, but only
on the basis that the court should defer first to the arbitral tribunal's own decision as to jurisdiction, and then
secondarily to the review role of the courts of the seat.
Where, under Common Law practice, the court of the
seat grants an injunction, it is doing so as a protective
measure to support the arbitration. This is a very different matter to fully fledged litigation as to the validity and scope of the arbitration agreement, where, as
has been seen, the court should normally defer to the
arbitral tribunal to determine its own jurisdiction in the
first instance, provided the arbitration agreement is
prima facie valid and enforceable.

The proposed new Article 27A, understandable
though its objective may be, risks encouraging a new
species of satellite litigation in the courts of the seat,
which cuts across the priority which ought to be
accorded to the arbitral tribunal itself. None of this
seems calculated to address the central issue of the best
way to handle determination of issues of validity and
scope of an arbitration agreement as between the
national court which would otherwise have jurisdiction
and the arbitral tribunal. In addressing that question,
the most significant impediments to a coherent
approach are the absence of a consistent adherence to a
prima facie review test in deferring in the first instance
to the arbitral tribunal; and (even more importantly)

---

tral tribunal. Otherwise, the court of the Capital of the
designated Member State shall be competent. Lacking
such a designation the court shall be competent that
would have general jurisdiction over the dispute under
the Regulation if there was no arbitration agreement":
[135].

[576] *Supra* footnote 478.

the failure to ensure that national courts have in place procedures to decide upon jurisdictional challenges at the outset of proceedings. The failure of the Heidelberg Study to address this latter point, which is at the heart of a number of the difficult parallel proceedings cases, is regrettable. It is no answer to say that the Convention does not address the internal civil procedural rules of Member States, since the effect of *Turner* v. *Grovit* and *The Front Comor* is that it does just this where the domestic procedure is perceived to have a deleterious effect on the operation of the Convention. Where the jurisdiction of the arbitral tribunal is established by the tribunal then, subject to any challenge to such a decision in the courts of the seat, there ought to be no objection to the courts of the seat granting provisional and protective measures to support the arbitral tribunal by holding the parties to their choice of forum.

Thus far, the discussion has been devoted to the use of anti-suit injunctions either by arbitrators, or in support of the arbitral process. It is now necessary to consider the reverse situation — where a court issues an injunction in an attempt to restrain the parties from pursuit of arbitration.

### (c) *Anti-arbitration injunctions*

A quartet of cases, which were all decided within the space of a few months around the turn of the millennium, served to focus great attention on the use of the anti-suit injunction by national courts not to compel arbitration, but rather to restrain resort to it. These cases, *Himpurna* v. *Indonesia*[577], *Salini* v.

---

[577] *Himpurna California Energy Ltd.* v. *Republic of Indonesia*, (2000) 25 *Ybk. Comm. Arb.* 109 (Interim Award of 26 September 1999); 186 (Final Award of 16 October 1999) (UNCITRAL, Paulsson P, de Fina and Priyatna), note Cornell and Handley, (2000) 15 (9) *Int. Arb. Rep.* 39.

*Ethiopia*[578], *HUBCO* v. *Pakistan WAPDA*[579], and *KBC* v. *Pertamina*[580] all involved claims by foreign investors against State-owned corporations in developing countries under concession contracts for natural resource developments. In each case, provision had been made for resort to international arbitration in the event of a dispute — either *ad hoc* under UNCITRAL Rules, or under the auspices of the ICC. In the first two of these cases, *Himpurna* and *Salini,* the arbitration agreement nominated the host State as the seat of the arbitration. In *HUBCO* and *KBC,* the chosen seat was in a neutral third State (England and Switzerland respectively). In the first three cases, after commencement of the arbitration but before any award, the State-owned respondent sought, and was granted, an injunction from its home courts restraining resort to arbitration. In *KBC,* the injunction was sought to restrain actions for the enforcement of the award. The course of proceedings in each of these cases merits careful study.

---

[578] *Salini Construttori SpA* v. *Federal Democratic Republic of Ethiopia, Addis Ababa Water and Sewerage Authority,* ICC Arbitration No. 10623/AER/ACS (Partial Award of 7 December 2001) (ICC, Gaillard C, Bernadini and Bunni) in Gaillard, *supra* footnote 445, 227, note Bachand, (2005) 20 (3) *Int. Arb. Rep.* 47, reply Mohtashami, (2005) 20 (5) *Int. Arb. Rep.* 44.

[579] *Hub Power Company Limited (HUBCO)* v. *Pakistan Water & Power Development Authority (WAPDA)* (Pakistan Sup. Ct.) (20 June 2000), 16 *Arb. Int.* 439 (Muhammad Bashir Jehangiri J), noted Majeed, (2000) 16 *Arb. Int.* 431 and Cornell and Handley, *supra* footnote 577.

[580] *Karaha Bodas Company, LLC ("KBC")* v. *Perusahaan Pertambangan Minyak Dan Gas Bumi Negara ("Pertamina")* (Preliminary Award of 30 September 1999) (UNICTRAL, Derains C, Bernadini and El-Kosheri) (2001) 16 No. 3 *Mealey's Int. Arb. Rep.* C-17; (Final Award of 18 December 2000), (2001) 16 No. 3 *Mealey's Int. Arb. Rep.* C-2; 335 F. 3d 357 (5th Cir., 2003); 465 F. Supp. 2d 283 (SDNY 2006).

*Himpurna* v. *Indonesia*[581] featured attempts by the Republic of Indonesia to thwart claims by foreign-owned energy investment companies for damages arising out of the 1997 Asian financial crisis. An arbitral tribunal had awarded Himpurna California Energy and Patuha Power Ltd. $572 million in damages from PLN, the Indonesian State-owned electricity corporation, for a failure to observe an obligation to purchase electricity from them. When PLN failed to satisfy the award, Himpurna and Patuha revived arbitral proceedings under UNCITRAL Rules against Indonesia itself, claiming that a letter from its Minister of Finance had pledged to ensure PLN's performance. The seat of the arbitration was Jakarta. Before the hearings began, two suits were filed on the same day in the Central District Court of Jakarta: Indonesia sought annulment of the substantive awards, while Pertamina (a State-owned Indonesian company) sought an injunction suspending the pending arbitration.

On 22 July 1999, the District Court granted the injunction, ordering suspension of the arbitral proceedings, breach of which would incur a fine of $1 million per day. The Arbitral Tribunal then decided to hold its hearings at the Permanent Court of Arbitration in The Hague[582]. Although Indonesia professed an intention to appeal against this injunction[583], it (as opposed to Pertamina) then sought a matching injunction from the District Court of The Hague, on the grounds that it would be in breach of the Indonesian court injunction by appearing in the arbitration, and thus exposed to the penalty imposed by the Indonesian court. This application was refused by the Dutch Court on 21 September 1999 on the ground that Indonesia was entitled to pur-

---

[581] *Supra* footnote 577.

[582] Procedural Order of 7 September 1999 reproduced in the Interim Award, *supra* footnote 577, [73].

[583] *Ibid.*, [42].

sue an appeal from the Indonesian injunction, which would have suspended its enforcement, but had not done so[584].

On the same day, the Indonesian Arbitrator, H. Priyatna Abdurrasyid, who had travelled to the Netherlands for the scheduled arbitration hearing, was met at Amsterdam Schipol airport by Indonesian officials and invited to return to Jakarta and not to participate in the deliberations of the arbitral tribunal[585]. According to a statement filed by Professor van den Berg, who met Professor Priyatna at Schipol airport immediately prior to his return to Jakarta, Priyatna had been handed a letter from an Indonesian Government minister asking him not to take part in the arbitration[586].

In these circumstances, the Arbitral Tribunal proceeded to deliver an Interim Award on 26 September 1999, the terms of which had been agreed by all three members of the Tribunal, but which could only be signed by two of them. This was followed by a final award of the Tribunal, rendered by the two remaining members only. In its Interim Award, the Tribunal considered that: "This case does not, in the Arbitral Tribunal's view, require general pronouncements on the relative allocation of authority between courts and arbitrators."[587] The central issue was simply whether the Jakarta court injunction provided Indonesia with a valid excuse for non-participation in the arbitration hearing[588]. The Tribunal found that

---

[584] *Indonesia* v. *Himpurna California Energy Ltd.*, Kort Geding, 1999, No. 281 (2000) 25 *Ybk. Comm. Arb.* 469, [10]-[11].

[585] See *Himpurna, supra* footnote 577 (Interim Award), [95]-[102] for details of Abdurrasyid's failure to appear, and (Final Award) [4]-[67] for the Tribunal's discussion of whether this denied it jurisdiction.

[586] *Ibid.* (Interim Award), [97].

[587] *Ibid.*, [105].

[588] *Ibid.*, [107].

"Indonesia had the power to overcome or avoid the impediment which it now invokes to excuse its default. The Arbitral Tribunal also deems Pertamina's initiatives not to be independent of the Republic of Indonesia's will."[589]

This led it to the conclusion that the injunction "is the consequence of the refusal of the Republic of Indonesia to submit to an arbitration to which it has previously consented"[590].

The Tribunal further held that the decision of the Jakarta Court was imputable to Indonesia as a matter of international law, and could not therefore be relied upon by Indonesia as a valid excuse for non-performance of its agreement to arbitrate[591]. The Tribunal reasoned that a State could not rely upon its internal legislation as a basis for disavowing an agreement to arbitrate[592]. A court judgment was as attributable to the State as legislation[593]. Finally, the agreement of the State with an alien to have recourse to international arbitration removed the contract from the jurisdiction of municipal law[594]. The Tribunal concluded:

"[I]t is a denial of justice for the courts of a State to prevent a foreign party from pursuing its remedies before a forum to the authority of which the state consented, and on the availability of which

---

[589] *Ibid.*, [109].
[590] *Ibid.*, [148].
[591] *Ibid.*, [169]-[183].
[592] *Ibid.*, [169]-[171], citing *Benteler KE* v. *Belgium*, (1985) 8 ECC 101.
[593] *Ibid.*, citing Jiménez de Aréchaga, "International Law in the Past Third of a Century" (1978) 159 *Recueil des cours* 9, 278, and *Iran* v. *USA*, Award A27 of 5 June 1998, (1999) 24a *Ybk. Comm. Arb.* 512.
[594] *Ibid.*, [179] citing Garcia Amador, *Responsibility of the States for Injuries Caused in Its Territory to the Person or Property of Aliens* (1959).

the foreigner relied in making investments explicitly envisaged by that state." [595]

In its Final Award, the Tribunal decided that, despite Professor Priyatna's withdrawal, the other two members of the Tribunal were still empowered to render a decision. On the merits, the letter provided by the Ministry of Finance in connection with the project did amount to a binding legal undertaking, ensuring the performance of PLN. Accordingly, Himpurna was entitled to an award against Indonesia in the amount of the award against PLN.

*Salini* v. *Ethiopia* [596] involved a contract awarded to Salini Costruttori SpA, an Italian company, by the Addis Ababa Water and Sewerage Authority (AAWSA), an entity of the Ethiopian State, to construct a raw water sewerage reservoir and transmission main. When a dispute arose, Salini commenced ICC arbitration. The contract was governed by Ethiopian substantive law and nominated Addis Ababa as the seat of the arbitration. In accordance with the agreed Terms of Reference, the arbitrators decided to hold at least the first hearing in Paris, without prejudice to the fact that the seat of the arbitration was Addis Ababa. AAWSA then challenged all three arbitrators before the ICC Court of Arbitration, claiming that the Tribunal had failed to perform its function; had "failed to act 'fairly and impartially'"[597]; and had abused its discretion to hold meetings at locations other than the seat. AAWSA alleged that the Tribunal "had "improperly" and "abusively" had regard to its own convenience and to the convenience of the Claimant"[598]. The Arbitral Tribunal responded that it had merely acted in accordance with

---

[595] *Ibid.*, [184].
[596] *Supra* footnote 578.
[597] *Ibid.*, [68].
[598] *Ibid.*, [69].

the Terms of Reference, and that it was not motivated by bias. The ICC Court rejected AAWSA's challenge to the arbitrators[599].

AAWSA then filed an appeal from the ICC Court's decision with the Addis Ababa Court of Appeal. Finding that it had jurisdiction, the Court of Appeal issued a temporary injunction to suspend the arbitration proceedings pending determination of the appeal. AAWSA then refused to participate further in the arbitration. It also applied to the Federal Court of First Instance in Ethiopia for a judgment that the Tribunal lacked jurisdiction. The arbitration agreement included a clause in the general contractual provisions providing for ICC arbitration if no other method was specified, but another clause, part of the special contractual conditions, stipulated that arbitration was to be governed by the arbitration rules in the Ethiopian Civil Code. The First Instance Court issued a similar injunction to that issued by the Court of Appeal pending determination of that application.

The ICC Arbitral Tribunal ultimately concluded that it was not restrained by the injunctions and, having jurisdiction under the ICC arbitration clause, proceeded to issue a partial award. It reasoned that, in agreeing to ICC Rules, AAWSA had agreed that any challenge to the arbitrators would be decided finally by the ICC Court[600], and that the arbitral tribunal itself had power to determine its own jurisdiction under the *Kompetenz-Kompetenz* principle[601]. Resort to the Ethiopian courts breached both aspects of this agreement, since it sought to "appeal" the decision of the ICC Court, and to halt the proceedings before the arbitral tribunal. It held:

---

[599] *Ibid.*, [74].
[600] *Ibid.*, [159], pursuant to ICC Rules, Art. 11 (3) *(c)*.
[601] *Ibid.*, [160].

"In effect, there is no difference between a state unilaterally repudiating an international arbitration agreement or changing its internal law in an attempt to free itself from such an agreement, on the one hand, and a state going before its own courts to have the arbitral proceedings suspended or terminated (whether on the basis of alleged nullity of the arbitration agreement, alleged bias on the part of the arbitral tribunal, or some other ground), on the other hand. Both amount to the state reneging on its own agreement to submit disputes to international arbitration." [602]

The tribunal had jurisdiction, since there was no inconsistency between the ICC clause and the reference to the arbitration provisions of the Ethiopian Civil Code. The latter merely provided the procedural law of the seat, which would apply to the extent that the matter was not already covered by the ICC Rules [603].

*HUBCO* v. *Pakistan* [604] concerned a contract for the construction of one of the world's largest power plants, located in Hub in the province of Balochistan, Pakistan. The Hub Power Company (Hubco) was a public listed Pakistani company, but it had received substantial foreign investment from many international sources, including the World Bank [605]. As part of the contractual arrangements, it had entered into a Power Purchase Agreement with the Pakistan Water and Power Development Authority (WAPDA). The agreement was guaranteed by the Pakistan Government. It was governed by English law, and provided for arbitration in London under ICC Rules. This agreement was amended several times with the effect of increas-

---

[602] *Ibid.*, [166].
[603] *Ibid.*, [263].
[604] *Supra* footnote 579.
[605] Majeed, *supra* footnote 579, 431-432.

ing the tariffs payable by WAPDA. Following a decision by the Pakistan Supreme Court that the full tariffs were not payable because they were the result of fraudulent collusion between WAPDA and Hubco, WAPDA ceased to pay the full tariffs due[606]. Hubco referred the dispute to ICC arbitration. WAPDA responded by claiming that the amendments were illegal, fraudulent, collusive, without consideration, *mala fide* and designed to cause wrongful loss. It was alleged (though apparently never proven) that the amendments were obtained

"in collusion with the concerned authorities of WAPDA and the high officials of the Federal Government who were in a position to exert influence on the WAPDA authorities through the payment of bribe *[sic]* and kick backs"[607].

On Hubco's application, the Sindh High Court declared that the parties were bound to go to arbitration, but on appeal the Division Bench disagreed and restrained Hubco (over whom, as a Pakistan-incorporated company, it had jurisdiction) from taking further steps in the arbitration. Hubco appealed this decision to the Supreme Court. WAPDA's argument was that issues of fraud and illegality were not arbitrable, either because they fell outside the scope of the arbitration agreement or by virtue of public policy. In a short decision with no reference to authority, a 3-2 majority concluded that they were not arbitrable[608]. The Court upheld the anti-arbitration injunction.

---

[606] It was possible for WAPDA to, in effect, rely on its on fraudulent behaviour to avoid paying the full tariffs because the Government had just changed from that of Benazir Bhutto to that of Nawaz Sharif (again), and therefore WAPDA could claim that "its" fraudulent behaviour was actually that of the deposed Government.

[607] *Supra* footnote 579, 456-457, Sh. Riaz Ahmad J (Sh Ijaz Nisar and Munir A, Sheikh JJ, concurring).

[608] *Ibid.*, 456-458.

The dissenting judges[609] emphasized that this finding breached the fundamental principle of the separability of arbitration agreements, which applied irrespective of whether fraud was alleged[610]. The governing law of the arbitration agreement being English law, the question of the validity of that agreement was to be decided according to the principles of English law[611].

In *KBC* v. *Pertamina*[612], KBC, a Cayman Islands company, had contracted with Pertamina and PLN, two Indonesian State-owned companies, to construct a geothermal power plant in Indonesia. The arbitration agreement provided for arbitration under UNICTRAL Rules in Geneva. An Arbitral Tribunal constituted under UNCITRAL Rules awarded KBC more than $260 million against PLN and Pertamina. The award debtors' challenge to the award before the Swiss Federal Tribunal failed. The United States District Court then granted KBC's motion for summary judgment to enforce the award. Pertamina then successfully applied to the Central District Court of Jakarta to annul the award and for an injunction to prevent KBC enforcing it. The District Court determined that KBC would suffer irreparable harm if the Indonesian injunction was granted and, therefore, ordered Pertamina to withdraw its application and take no more substantive steps. Pertamina did not withdraw its application and a provisional injunction was issued by the Jakarta Court, to which Pertamina's president-director responded with a statement that Pertamina would not attempt to enforce this injunction in the United States.

Two applications followed by KBC in the District

---

[609] Muhammad Bashir Jehangiri ACJ (Abdur Rehman Khan J, concurring).
[610] *Ibid.*, [31].
[611] *Ibid.*, [43].
[612] *Supra* footnote 580.

Court, claiming breach of the order to discontinue the Jakarta proceedings and requesting restatement of that order. Following the District Court's preliminary injunction to this effect, Pertamina requested the Indonesian court to suspend the proceedings, but the court maintained that it retained the authority to adjudicate; concluding that it had primary jurisdiction under the New York Convention, it annulled the Award on the grounds that it was contrary to the Convention and Indonesian arbitration law. It enjoined KBC from seeking enforcement subject to a fine of $500,000 per day. Meanwhile, KBC pursued enforcement actions in Hong Kong[613], Singapore and Canada.

The 5th Circuit Court of Appeals decided that the District Court's injunction restraining further pursuit by Pertamina of the Indonesian proceedings ought to be set aside. It reasoned:

> "By allowing concurrent enforcement and annulment actions, as well as simultaneous enforcement actions in third countries, the [New York] Convention necessarily envisions multiple proceedings that address the same substantive challenges to an arbitral award ... [A]s the Convention already provides for multiple simultaneous proceedings, it is difficult to envision how court proceedings in Indonesia could amount to an inequitable hardship."[614]

Although the Indonesian court's injunction might impose hardship on KBC, it was not enforceable in the United States; would not impede the US Court's consideration of enforcement of the Award; and did not threaten the integrity of its jurisdiction. Thus, the Court thought that principles of comity mandated forbearance here:

---

[613] Court of First Instance (20 December 2002, 22 March 2003), (2003) 28 *Ybk. Comm. Arb.* 752.

[614] *Supra* footnote 580, 367-368.

"Reaching out to enjoin proceedings abroad cuts against the Convention's grants of separate and limited roles of primary-jurisdiction courts to annul awards, and of secondary-jurisdiction courts to enforce, or refuse to enforce, awards in their own countries."[615]

The equation was struck differently in 2006, once judgments enforcing the award had been entered in both Texas and New York, with all final appeals by Pertamina in the United States exhausted. Then Pertamina commenced proceedings in the Cayman Islands alleging fraud in connection with the contract and the arbitration award. This was no longer simply a case of parallel proceedings, since final judgments had already been entered in the United States. Accordingly, the US District Court took the view that Pertamina's conduct was vexatious, and that it should be restrained by injunction entirely from pursuing its Cayman Islands action[616].

What are we to make of these *causes célèbres* of conflict between national courts and international arbitral tribunals? Are they merely examples of the pathology of arbitration, or is there a wider significance for the present study? In the first place, these four cases are not isolated instances of national court orders seeking to restrain arbitration[617]. Nor can it be said that the anti-suit injunction is a peculiarly Common Law aberration. Neither Indonesia nor Ethiopia is a Common Law country, yet their judges had no difficulty granting orders of this kind.

---

[615] *Ibid.*, 373.
[616] *Supra* footnote 580.
[617] For further examples see Gaillard, *Aspects philosophiques du droit de l'arbitrage international*, (2007) 329 *Recueil des cours* 61, II A (also published as a Pocketbook in 2007).

As Emmanuel Gaillard has illuminatingly shown in his recent lectures to the Academy[618], the response of the lawyer to the grant of such an injunction is likely to be affected by the larger conception of the place of arbitration which he or she holds. He suggests three possible models: State positivism (according to which arbitration is and always remains subject to complete state court control); a Westphalian model (a variant of the above, which emphasizes the need for each State for restrict its control to arbitrations on its territory, and to limit the reach of its powers to the territories of other States); and the notion of a separate arbitral juridical order (according to which the arbitral tribunal would not be limited by national court control, prior to the rendering of its award).

These different perspectives as to the permissible extent of judicial control of arbitration are richly illustrated by the decisions discussed above. In *HUBCO, Salini,* and *Himpurna,* the seat of the arbitration was, by the parties' agreement, located in the developing country, and the courts had little difficulty in asserting control over what they saw as local arbitrations. In *HUBCO,* the dissenting judges disagreed, taking a Westphalian approach — that there were limits to State control where (as in that case) the law applicable to the arbitration agreement was the law of a third State (English law) and not the law of Pakistan. Similarly, the US Court in *Pertamina* adopted a Westphalian approach, limiting the extent of its intervention on the basis that the Indonesian court's order, even if illegitimate, had only local application and did not impede the US Court's consideration of the enforcement of the award under the New York Convention. Only when the award debtor sought to challenge the finality of the award in a third jurisdiction, after exhausting all chal-

---

[618]  *Ibid.*

lenges in the United States, was an injunction considered justified.

Yet in each case we find a robust assertion of arbitral autonomy by the tribunal, even where the seat is in
the country of the court issuing the injunction — most
notably in the eloquent awards of the tribunal in
*Himpurna.* The exchanges between international arbitrators and national court judges appear as the modern
day equivalent of the old struggles for supremacy
between the English courts of Law and Equity, which
led to the creation of the anti-suit injunction in the first
place[619]. In one corner of the ring is the national court,
which can exercise completely effective power, but
limited to its own territory. In the other corner is the
international tribunal. Its *lex arbitri* is normally the law
of the seat of the arbitration[620], but it may nevertheless
conduct its hearings outside the territory of the national
court. The tribunal is ultimately reliant upon national
courts for enforcement of its award. But, as the Court
pointed out in *Pertamina,* the system for enforcement
under the New York Convention allows concurrent
enforcement and annulment actions, and multiple
enforcement actions in different New York Convention
States. Invalidity of the arbitration agreement under the
law of the seat, or the setting aside of the award there
may give a good ground for the refusal of enforcement
of the award in other Member States[621]. But these
grounds to refuse enforcement are permissive and not
mandatory[622]. In practice, the potential enforceability

---

[619] Discussed in Chapter I, Section C 2.
[620] *Dicey, supra* footnote 466, Rule 57 (2); Petrochilos
*Procedural Law in International Arbitration*, (2004)
[3.31]-[3.72].
[621] New York Convention, *supra* footnote 438, Art. V
(1) *(a)* and *(e).*
[622] *Svenska Petroleum Exploration AB* v. *Lithuania,*
[2005] 1 Lloyd's Rep. 515 (QB).

of an international arbitral award, even where the national court at the seat has invalidated the agreement or annulled the award, is very considerable — far in excess of the potential enforceability of any national court judgment.

Does that mean that a national court — especially the court of the seat — should never restrain an arbitral proceeding? No doubt the adherents of the theory of a separate arbitral order would consider that it should not. Even in England, where the use of the anti-suit injunction is perhaps the most developed, it has recently been held that the court should be very slow to restrain a party from continuing with an arbitration, properly brought under an arbitration agreement, whether the seat of the arbitration is in England or abroad, and even if there are related concurrent proceedings [623]. Two such situations where an injunction may nevertheless be appropriate are: *(a)* where the arbitral tribunal's determination of its jurisdiction has already been reviewed by the court of the seat, and that court has decided that the tribunal lacked jurisdiction, yet one party is still claiming the right to pursue the arbitration [624] ; and *(b)* where the essence of the challenge to the arbitral tribunal's jurisdiction is that the arbitration agreement is a forgery, and it has been agreed that the English court may determine that question [625]. Neither of these cases is a true exception to the principle stated above, since, in both cases, the essential claim was that there was no arbitration agreement

---

[623] *Elektrim SA* v. *Vivendi Universal SA (No. 2)*, [2007] 2 Lloyd's Rep. 8 (QB) (doubting *Intermet FZCO* v. *Ansol Ltd.*, [2007] EWHC 226 (Comm.), where the point was not fully argued).

[624] *Republic of Kazakhstan* v. *Istil Group Inc. (No. 2)* [2008] 1 Lloyd's Rep. 382 (QB).

[625] *Albon* v. *Naza Motor Trading Sdn Bhd*, [2008] 1 Lloyd's Rep. 1 (CA), upholding [2007] 2 Lloyd's Rep. 420.

at all, and the English court either had determined, or was entitled to determine, that point. Such cases are likely to be very rare.

The distinctive feature of the quartet of cases discussed above is that they all involved State-owned entities resorting to the courts of their own States for relief from an arbitration agreement to which they had voluntarily committed themselves. In resorting to the language of international law to justify removal of the contract from the jurisdiction of municipal law, and in finding the attempt to prevent recourse to arbitration as a denial of justice, the Tribunal in *Himpurna* consciously sought to distinguish the State concession contract from an ordinary commercial dispute. A line of earlier arbitral awards supports the broader principle that a State may not rely on illegality under its own law to justify breach of a concession contract with an alien [626]. It may be that this principle, and not a blanket prohibition on the courts of the seat controlling arbitral proceedings, provides the best explanation of the issues in the State-related anti-arbitration cases.

Applying this approach, however, *Salini* is perhaps the most difficult of the arbitral decisions on jurisdiction. After all, some real weight must be given not simply to the parties" autonomy not to choose arbitra-

------

[626] *Lena Goldfields Ltd.* v. *Soviet Union* (3 September 1930), *The Times*, reprinted in (1950) 36 *Cornell LQ* 42, discussed Veeder, "The *Lena Goldfields* Arbitration: The Historical Roots of Three Ideas", (1998) 47 *ICLQ* 747; *Revere Copper and Brass Inc.* v. *Overseas Private Investment Corp.*, (1978) 17 *ILM* 1321, 1331-1343, applying *Saudi Arabia* v. *Aramco*, (1958) 27 *ILR* 117; *Shufeldt (US* v. *Guatamala)*, 2 *RIAA* 1079 (Sir Herbert Sisnett, 1930); and *Sapphire* v. *NIOC*, (1967) 35 *ILR* 136; *Sandline* v. *Papua New Guinea*, (1999) 117 *ILR* 552 (Somers P, Kerr and Dawson). See Meron, "Repudiation of *Ultra Vires* State Contracts and the International Responsibility of States", (1957) 6 *ICLQ* 273.

tion, but also to choose the seat of the arbitration, and thus the *lex arbitri*. Where the purpose of resort to the courts of the seat is not to frustrate the whole operation of the arbitration agreement, but rather to seek recourse where the *lex arbitri* so provides (and where that is not inconsistent with the arbitration agreement), it ought not to be a cause of surprise nor indignation that the court would seek to make the exercise of its own supervisory jurisdiction effective by enjoining further pursuit of the arbitration. One such instance may be where there is a challenge to the independence of the arbitral tribunal, which has already been ruled upon by the arbitral institution [627].

## C. Investment Treaty Arbitration [628]

### 1. The particular potential for conflicts of jurisdiction in treaty arbitration

If resort to arbitration in international commercial disputes has not served wholly to exclude parallel proceedings, at least the problems arise within a multilateral framework (the New York Convention) which encapsulates a clear priority for arbitration. The position is much less straight-forward in the new and fast-growing field of investment arbitration under bilateral investment treaties. Four features of the mixed character of investment arbitration may be singled out as pro-

---

[627] Accord Mohtashami, *supra* footnote 478, 47 who makes the point (relying upon *AT&T Corp.* v. *Saudi Cable Co.*, [2000] 2 Lloyd's Rep. 127 (CA)) that a decision of the ICC Court on this issue under ICC Rules, Art. 7 (4), does not exclude national court review.

[628] For a more detailed treatment of aspects of this topic beyond the scope of these lectures by the author see: Chapter IV, "Parallel Proceedings", in McLachlan, Shore and Weiniger, *International Investment Arbitration*: *Substantive Principles* (2007).

voking both more, and more complex, possibilities of parallel litigation[629] :

(a) *Bilateralism*. The first feature is the very nature of the basis for such arbitration in bilateral treaties. The consequence of this is that every dispute comes before a tribunal which has been separately constituted to determine a dispute based upon the adjudication of rights arising from that treaty. Even where the tribunal is constituted according to ICSID Rules, it enjoys a wholly separate identity.

(b) *Non-exclusivity*. Investment arbitration was created in order to provide an alternative avenue for redress to the courts of the host State. But investment treaties rarely exclude all recourse to State courts. Much more commonly, the treaty leaves it equally open to the claimant to seek its remedy in those courts. The dividing line is especially difficult to draw in those cases where the investor has a concession contract with the State. In such cases, it may be necessary to distinguish between contract claims and treaty claims arising out of the same factual matrix[630].

(c) *Exclusion of local remedies rule*. Investment treaties typically exclude the operation of the exhaustion of local remedies rule, so that the investor is not required to complete all recourse to host State courts before instituting a claim before an international arbitral tribunal. On the contrary, it may elect to proceed directly to the international forum. Whatever may be its impact on the substantive rights of the parties, the local remedies rule has no application as a procedural

---

[629] See generally Douglas, *supra* footnote 458, 236-281.

[630] The issue which proved of particular difficulty in *Compañia de Aguas del Aconquija SA and Vivendi Universal* v. *Argentine Republic* (Decision on Annulment), 6 *ICSID Rep.* 327 (ICSID, 2002, Fortier P, Crawford and Fernández Rozas), discussed *infra*, Section C 2 *(b)*.

bar to recourse to investment arbitration, unless the host State has expressly imposed such a condition by treaty[631].

(d) *Multiple investor claims.* The extended definition of what constitutes an investment for the purpose of many bilateral investment treaties has opened up the possibility for different companies in a chain of investment each to pursue their own parallel treaty claims.[632]

## 2. *The distinction between breach of contract and breach of treaty*

The first issue which arbitral tribunals have had to confront in considering the impact of other forms of dispute resolution upon their jurisdiction has been how to distinguish the proper sphere of the treaty dispute from other disputes arising from the factual matrix of the same investment, which either have been, or are in the course of being, litigated in other fora; or are subjected by contractual submission to other forms of dispute resolution.

---

[631] Thus, Art. 26 of the Convention on the Settlement of Investment Disputes between States and Nationals of Other States (signed 18 March 1965, entered into force 14 October 1966), 575 *UNTS* 159 ("ICSID Convention") permits a State to reserve the right to require the exhaustion of local remedies as a condition of its consent to arbitration.

[632] See further McLachlan, Shore and Weiniger, *International Investment Arbitration: Substantive Principles, supra* footnote 628, Chap. 6. An example of this is *Lauder* v. *Czech Republic* (Award), 9 *ICSID Rep.* 62 (UNCITRAL, 2001, Briner C, Cutler and Klein), and *CME Czech Republic BV (The Netherlands)* v. *Czech Republic* (Partial Award), 9 *ICSID Rep.* 121 (UNCITRAL, 2001, Kühn C, Schwebel and Hándl), discussed further *infra*, Section C 5.

(a) *National law and international law remedies distinguished*

The starting-point in analysing this distinction is to recall the basic principle that rights created by treaty exist on the plane of international law. Consequently, no provision of national law may constitute a defence to such a claim[633]. The importance of this distinction was well explained by the Tribunal in *GAMI Investments Inc.* v. *Mexico*[634]. Mexico had raised an objection to the jurisdiction of the NAFTA Tribunal. It claimed that GAMI, an American minority shareholder in a Mexican company, GAM, was precluded from bringing its claim because GAM had already challenged the measure which GAMI claimed was expropriatory before the Mexican courts. In an important passage, the Tribunal rejected this submission on the basis of the separate role of international law[635]. It cited *Selwyn*, in which the Umpire had held:

> "International arbitration is not affected jurisdictionally by the fact that the same question is in the courts of one of the nations. Such international tribunal has power to act without reference thereto, and if judgment has been pronounced by such court, to disregard the same so far as it affects the indemnity to the individual . . ."[636]

This ruling was in turn based upon the venerable

---

[633] Art. 27 of the Vienna Convention on the Law of Treaties (signed 23 May 1969, entered into force 27 January 1980), 1155 *UNTS* 331, and Art. 3 of the ILC Draft Articles on Responsibilities of States for Internationally Wrongful Acts (2001), Supp. No. 10, UN doc. A/56/10, 43.

[634] *GAMI Investments Inc.* v. *United Mexican States* (Award), (2005) 44 *ILM* 545 (NAFTA/UNCITRAL, 2004, Paulsson P, Muró and Reisman).

[635] *Ibid.*, 552.

[636] *Selwyn Case (Britain* v. *Venezuela)* (Interlocutory Decision), (1903) 9 *RIAA* 380, 381 (Plumley U).

authority of *The Betsey* (1796), in which the American members of the Claims Commission established under the Jay Treaty had opined that even decisions of the British Lords Commissioners of Appeal in Prize Cases were not binding upon the international tribunal [637]. The *GAMI* Tribunal continued:

> "ultimately each jurisdiction is responsible for the application of the law under which it exercises its mandate. It was for the Mexican courts to determine whether the expropriation was legitimate under Mexican law. It is for the present Tribunal to judge whether there have been breaches of international law by any agency of the Mexican government. A fundamental postulate in applying NAFTA is that enshrined in Article 27 of the Vienna Convention on the Law of Treaties: 'A party may not invoke the provisions of its own internal law as justification for its failure to perform a treaty.' Whether such national laws have been upheld by national courts is ultimately of no moment in this regard." [638]

Whether particular conduct involves a breach of a treaty is not determined by asking whether the conduct involves a breach of contract, since a breach of contract is not *per se* a breach of the international treaty obligation [639]. It will only be where the host State acts in the exercise of its governmental or sovereign authority, rather than merely as a commercial party, that it can be liable for breach of treaty. As it was put in *Impregilo SpA* v. *Pakistan*:

> "In fact, the State or its emanation, may have behaved as an ordinary contracting party having a

---

[637] *The Betsey* (1796): J. Moore, *International Adjudications* (Modern Series, Vol. IV, 1931) 182.

[638] *GAMI*, *supra* footnote 634, 552.

[639] This is subject to the effect of umbrella clauses, discussed *infra*, Section C 4.

difference of approach, in fact or law, with the
investor. In order that the alleged breach of contract
may constitute a violation of the BIT, it must be the
result of behaviour going beyond that which an ordinary contracting party could adopt. Only the State in
the exercise of its sovereign authority ('puissance
publique'), and not as a contracting party, may
breach the obligations assumed under the BIT." [640]

The Tribunal went on to emphasize that this meant
that a treaty and a contract claim may overlap or
coincide, but that, even if they did so, they would
remain analytically distinct. This was important
because different rules, for example on issues such
as attribution, would apply to each [641].

### (b) *Effect of contractual jurisdiction clause*

If, then, a claim to breach of treaty is in principle a
claim governed exclusively by international law which
is separate and distinct to a claim of breach of national
law, what is the effect of an investor's contractual submission to the jurisdiction of the host State courts?
This question was answered decisively by the Tribunal
(as to jurisdiction) and the Annulment Committee (as
to the merits) in the *Vivendi* affair [642]. The result was a

---

[640] *Impregilo SpA* v. *Islamic Republic of Pakistan*
(Jurisdiction), ICSID Case No. ARB/03/3 (ICSID, 2005,
Guillaume P, Cremades and Landau) [260]. See also *Joy
Mining Machinery Ltd.* v. *Arab Republic of Egypt* (Juris-
diction), (2004) 19 *ICSID Rev.-FILJ* 486 (ICSID, 2004,
Orrego Vicuña P, Weeramantry and Craig).

[641] *Ibid.*, [262].

[642] *Compañía de Aguas del Aconquija SA and Compa-
gnie Générale des Eaux* v. *Argentine Republic* (Award), 5
*ICSID Rep.* 296 (ICSID, 2000, Rezek P, Buergenthal and
Trooboff) *(CGE)*; *Compañía de Aguas del Aconquija SA
and Vivendi Universal* v. *Argentine Republic* (Decision on
Annulment), 6 *ICSID Rep.* 327 (ICSID, 2002, Fortier P,
Crawford and Fernández Rozas) *(CAA and Vivendi)*.

clear affirmation that the investor was entitled to pursue his claim for breach of treaty irrespective of such a clause, since the nature and basis of the cause of action before the international tribunal was entirely different.

In that case, the claimants (a French company and its Argentine affiliate, together "CGE") had entered into a concession contract with the Argentine province of Tucumán, pursuant to which they had assumed responsibility for the operation of the provincial sewage and water system. The contract contained an exclusive jurisdiction clause (clause 16.4) in favour of the administrative courts of the Province of Tucumán. From an early stage in the performance of the contract, disputes arose between CGE and the Province. Ultimately, the Province terminated the contract, whereupon CGE brought a claim against Argentina under the French/Argentine BIT[643]. The gravamen of the claim was that Argentina had breached its treaty obligations by failing to ensure that the Province properly performed the contract. Alternatively, it claimed that the actions of the Province were attributed to Argentina as a matter of international law, and that those actions themselves constituted a breach of the treaty. Argentina submitted that the Tribunal had no jurisdiction to hear the claim in light of the contractual jurisdiction clause.

The Tribunal held that it had jurisdiction, but denied the claim on the merits. In both cases, the decisive factor was the Tribunal's view of the impact of the jurisdiction clause choosing local courts. As to jurisdiction, the Tribunal held that the claim was properly brought against Argentina itself, whether on the basis of its own

---

[643] Accord sur l'encouragement et la protection réciproques des investissements ("Agreement on the Reciprocal Promotion and Protection of Investments") (France-Argentina) (signed 3 July 1991, entered into force 3 March 1993), 1728 *UNTS* 281.

defaults, or on the basis of the attribution to it, as a matter of State responsibility, of the defaults of its Province[644]. It also held that the contractual jurisdiction clause did not deprive it of jurisdiction, since the claims were not based on the contract, but alleged a cause of action under the BIT[645]. However, the Tribunal found against CGE on the merits, holding that unless the contractual remedy had first been sought and denied there could be no breach of treaty[646].

The award was challenged by CGE by way of annulment proceedings. The Annulment Committee agreed with the Tribunal's analysis as to jurisdiction[647]. However, it annulled its decision on the merits in so far as it applied to the claims based on Argentina's responsibility for the actions of the provincial authorities[648]. The Committee's reasoning has been widely adopted and followed in subsequent awards[649]. It was as follows:

---

[644] *CGE, supra* footnote 642, 313-314.

[645] *Ibid.*, 315, applying *Lanco International Inc.* v. *Argentine Republic* (Jurisdiction), 5 *ICSID Rep.* 367 (ICSID, 1998, Cremades P, Alvarez and Baptista).

[646] *CGE, supra* footnote 642, 321.

[647] *CAA and Vivendi, supra* footnote 642, 360-362.

[648] *Ibid.*, 364-371.

[649] *CMS Gas Transmission Co.* v. *Argentine Republic* (Jurisdiction), 7 *ICSID Rep.* 492 (ICSID, 2003, Orrego Vicuña P, Lalonde and Rezek); *Azurix Corp* v. *Argentine Republic* (Jurisdiction), (2004) 43 *ILM* 262 (ICSID, 2003, Sureda P, Lauterpacht and Martens); *SGS Société de Surveillance SA* v. *Islamic Republic of Pakistan* (Jurisdiction), (2002) 8 *ICSID Rep.* 406 (Feliciano P, Faurès and Thomas); *PSEG Global Inc et al.* v. *Republic of Turkey* (Jurisdiction), ICSID Case No. ARB/02/5 (ICSID, 2004, Orrego Vicuña P, Fortier and Kaufmann-Kohler); *Enron Corp and Anor* v. *Argentine Republic* (Jurisdiction), ICSID Case No. ARB/01/3 (ICSID, 2004, Orrego Vicuña P, Gros Espiell and Tschanz); *AES Corp.* v. *Argentine Republic* (Jurisdiction), ICSID Case No. ARB/02/17 (ICSID, 2005,

(i) A State may breach a treaty without breaching a contract and vice versa, since the treaty sets an independent standard: Article 3 International Law Commission Draft Articles on State Responsibility[650];

(ii) Each claim is to be determined by its own proper law: in the case of the treaty claim — international law; in the case of the contract claim — the proper law of the contract, in this case the law of Tucumán. Different legal consequences may well flow from the application of the different applicable law[651];

(iii) In a case where the essential basis of a claim brought before an international tribunal is a breach of contract, the tribunal will give effect to any valid choice of forum clause in the contract: citing *Woodruff*[652] in which the American-Venezuelan Mixed Commission of 1903 had dismissed a claim under a contract with an exclusive jurisdiction clause in favour of the Venezuelan courts on the ground that "by the very agreement that is the fundamental basis of the claim, it was withdrawn from the jurisdiction of the Commission"[653].

(iv) "On the other hand, where 'the fundamental basis of the claim' is a treaty laying down an independent standard by which the conduct of the parties is to

---

Dupuy P, Böckstiegel and Janiero); *Impregilo SpA* v. *Islamic Republic of Pakistan* (Jurisdiction), ICSID Case No. ARB/03/3 (ICSID, 2005, Guillaume P, Cremades and Landau); *Eureko BV* v. *Republic of Poland* (Partial Award) (*Ad hoc*, 2005, Fortier P, Schwebel and Rajski); *Bayindir Insaat Turizm Ticaret Ve Sanayi AS* v. *Islamic Republic of Pakistan* (Jurisdiction), ICSID Case No. ARB/03/29 (ICSID, 2005, Kaufmann-Kohler P, Bermann and Böckstiegel).

[650] *CAA and Vivendi*, *supra* footnote 642, 365.

[651] *Ibid.*

[652] *Woodruff Case (United States* v. *Venezuela)*, (1903) 9 *RIAA* 213, 221-222 (Barge U).

[653] *Ibid.*, 223.

be judged, the existence of an exclusive jurisdiction clause in a contract between the claimant and the respondent state or one of its subdivisions cannot operate as a bar to the application of the treaty standard."[654]

## 3. Election and waiver

### (a) The fork in the road

To what extent, then, are these basic distinctions between national law and international law, and between contract claims and treaty claims, affected by an express treaty provision requiring an irrevocable election in remedies to be made? As has been seen[655], provisions of this kind, known as "fork in the road" provisions, abound in bilateral investment treaties[656].

It is submitted that, where the parties to an investment treaty agree that the choice of any particular dispute settlement option will preclude resort to any other option, the operation of the clause will be affected by the juridical nature of the claims asserted:

(i) *Different applicable law.* If the claims asserted in the host State courts or other arbitral tribunal are contractual and not treaty-based, the existence of a fork in the road clause will have no effect upon the subsequent invocation of a treaty claim before an investment tribunal, since the fundamental basis of the claim is different. The same reasoning applies to attempts on the part of the investor to obtain relief from the host state measure in the local courts, which fall short of seeking substantially the same relief as that claimed in the treaty arbitration.

---

[654] *CAA and Vivendi*, *supra* footnote 642, 367.

[655] *Supra* Chapter I, Section D 4.

[656] See Schreuer, "Travelling the BIT Route: Of Waiting Periods, Umbrella Clauses and Forks in the Road", (2004) 5 *J. World Investment and Trade* 231.

(ii) *Parallel applicable law.* On the other hand, if the claims asserted before the investment tribunal are substantially the same as those already asserted before host State courts (or another arbitral tribunal contemplated in the relevant clause), the investor will be held to his election. Thus, if a *contract* claim has already been submitted to a national court or other arbitral tribunal, then the investor will be precluded from subsequently re-litigating that dispute before an investment tribunal. Similarly, where the investor chooses to invoke in substance his *treaty* rights before a host State's administrative courts he may forfeit the right to challenge the same State measure before an investment tribunal.

Most attempts by States to invoke fork in the road provisions in bilateral investment treaties have failed because the fundamental basis of the claims asserted in the other proceedings has been found to be different. In a number of cases, tribunals have rejected the State's attempted invocation of a fork in the road clause on the grounds that there is insufficient identity either of cause of action or parties. The rationale for this was well explained in *Genin* v. *Estonia*[657], in which the respondent State had challenged ICSID jurisdiction on the grounds that, under the terms of the United States-Estonia BIT[658], such jurisdiction was precluded if the investor had previously submitted the dispute to the Estonian courts. The local bank which was the subject of the investment had taken proceedings in Estonia to seek to overturn the decision of the Bank of Estonia to

---

[657] *Genin, Eastern Credit Ltd Inc. and AS Baltoil* v. *Republic of Estonia* (Award), 6 *ICSID Rep.* 236 (ICSID, 2001, Fortier P, Heth and van den Berg).

[658] Treaty concerning the Encouragement and Reciprocal Protection of Investment (United States-Estonia) (signed 19 April 1994, entered into force 16 February 1997), *Senate Treaty Doc.* 103-138.

revoke its banking licence. The Tribunal held that this could not disqualify Genin from its ICSID claim. First, the parties to the two claims were different. In the Estonian proceedings, the local bank sued in its own name, and the outcome affected all shareholders, and other stakeholders, in the bank[659]. The ICSID proceedings were concerned with Genin's investment alone. Second, the cause of action was different. It was obvious, the Tribunal considered, that the claim for restoration of the banking licence had to be pursued in Estonia. The ICSID claim was, however, concerned only with whether the losses suffered by Genin were attributable to breaches of the Treaty[660]. Thus, it concluded that:

> "Although certain aspects of the facts that gave rise to this dispute were also at issue in the Estonian litigation, the 'investment dispute' itself was not, and the Claimants should not therefore be barred from using the ICSID arbitration mechanism."[661]

Similar reasoning has been applied by tribunals to find that such a clause was not applicable when the claim pursued locally was for breach of contract, not breach of treaty. Thus, for example, in *CMS* v. *Argentina*[662], the Tribunal observed:

> "Decisions of several ICSID tribunals have held that as contractual claims are different from treaty claims, even if there had been or there currently was a recourse to the local courts for breach of contract,

---

[659] *Genin, supra* footnote 657, 291-292.
[660] *Ibid.*, 292.
[661] *Ibid.*
[662] *CMS, supra* footnote 649, 511, applied in *Azurix Corp* v. *Argentine Republic* (Jurisdiction), (2004) 43 *ILM* 262, 280 (ICSID, 2003, Sureda P, Lauterpacht and Martins).

this would not have prevented submission of the treaty claims to arbitration."

Where, however, the claims are in fact between the same parties, have the same object and are founded upon the same cause of action, in principle a fork-in-the-road clause ought to be effective. This was recognised in *CMS*, where the Tribunal accepted that the investor could renounce recourse to arbitration by bringing his claim before the local courts[663]. Where the claim sought to be brought is founded upon contract in both tribunals, determination of sufficient identity of parties, cause of action and object should in most cases be relatively straightforward. The determination of sufficient identity of cause of action is more difficult where the claim is of a kind typically protected by investment treaty (expropriation, fair and equitable treatment and the like). It is, of course, possible to take the view that treaty claims exist only on the plane of international law, and thus that no claim brought before a municipal court could ever satisfy such a clause. To some extent, the reasoning applied in those cases which have considered the breach of treaty/breach of contract distinction would support such an analysis. The problem with it in the present context is that it would give no effective scope of operation to the fork-in-the-road clause in the context of the rights which are the principal subject of investment treaties. It is a basic principle of treaty interpretation that treaties should be interpreted, so far as possible, to give an effective meaning to their provisions[664]. The choice which such

---

[663] *CMS*, *supra* footnote 649, 511.

[664] For example, the principle of effectiveness enunciated by Fitzmaurice on the basis of the jurisprudence of the International Court of Justice; Fitzmaurice "The Law and Procedure of the International Court of Justice: Treaty Interpretation and Certain Other Treaty Points", (1951) 28

clauses offer to the investor must be construed as being between real alternatives.

Of course, it cannot be every administrative appeal from a decision of a State agency, even if brought by the investor himself, rather than the local investment company, which provokes the operation of the clause. Many such proceedings could be seen as an inevitable by-product of doing business in the relevant country. They would not be apt to seek damages from the State for its substantive default — being expropriation, failure to provide fair and equitable treatment and so on. But nor is it necessary to go as far as Schreuer and conclude that the disputes have to be identical, so that, if the dispute before the international tribunal concerns breach of the BIT "the dispute before the domestic courts or administrative tribunals would also have to concern an alleged breach of a right conferred or created by the BIT"[665]. In jurisdictions which apply a dualist approach to the reception of conventional international law[666], the rights created by the BIT will not be capable of direct vindication as such before national courts. However, as Wälde and Kolo have shown[667], such jurisdictions may well have remedies against the State which are substantively equivalent to those rights protected under the treaty. Thus, for example, there are close parallels between the protection afforded by international law against regulatory taking as expropriation, and the protection against regulatory taking under the US Constitution or the 1st Protocol of the

---

*BYIL* 1; Fitzmaurice, "The Law and Procedure of the International Court of Justice 1951-4: Treaty Interpretation and Other Treaty Points", (1957) 33 *BYIL* 203.

[665] Schreuer, *supra* footnote 656, 248.

[666] Shaw *International Law* (5th ed., 2003) 121-122.

[667] Wälde and Kolo, "Environmental Regulation, Investment Protection and 'Regulatory Taking' in International Law", (2001) 50 *ICLQ* 811.

European Convention on Human Rights[668]. In the absence of direct authority as yet, it is submitted that the fork in the road clause ought to operate should the investor choose to pursue *a claim equivalent in substance* to that created by the BIT against the host State.

### (b) *Waiver*

An alternative method to that of election at the time of institution of proceedings is to require the claimant to waive all other claims at the time when he brings his claim before an investment tribunal. This route presents an advantage for both the investor and the host State, in that the investor may choose to seek to resolve his dispute in the local courts of the host State, without prejudice to subsequent resort to an investment tribunal should the investor still consider that the treaty standards have not been met. Once treaty arbitration has been invoked, the tribunal will be able to view the host State's conduct in the round, including the treatment accorded to the investor in the State's courts or administrative tribunals. But neither the tribunal nor the host State will, at that stage, have to contend with parallel proceedings.

The main example in practice of the adoption of such a method is Article 1121 of NAFTA[669], which provides that the investor may submit a claim to arbitration only if:

> "Both the investor and an enterprise of another Party that is a juridical person that the investor owns or controls directly or indirectly, waive their right to

---

[668] *Ibid.*, 826-835.

[669] North American Free Trade Agreement (1992), 107 Stat. 2057; *CTS* 1994 No. 2; (1993) 32 *ILM* 289 (emphasis added); and see also 2004 US Model BIT, Art. 26 (2), reproduced as McLachlan, Shore and Weiniger, *supra* footnote 628, Appendix 6.

initiate or continue before any administrative tribunal or court under the domestic law of any Party
*any proceedings with respect to the measure of the
disputing Party* that is alleged to be a breach of
Subchapter A of this Chapter . . . except for proceedings for injunctive, declaratory or other extraordinary
relief, not involving the payment of damages . . ."

The test therefore focuses not on the juridical nature
of the cause of action, but rather on whether the local
proceedings were brought "with respect to the measure
of the disputing Party" that was alleged to be a breach
of treaty. Moreover, Article 1121 requires the investor
to procure a waiver both on its own behalf and on
behalf of any enterprise which it owned or controlled,
directly or indirectly — thus catching the complete
economic investment unit within its purview *ratione
personae*. Its focus is on avoiding any risk of double
recovery through awards of damages. The Article
makes a useful distinction between claims for damages
and other forms of relief, respecting the power of the
local courts to grant injunctions and the like. In *Waste
Management I*[670], the tribunal held that Article 1121
was not limited to a waiver of claims equivalent to, or
based upon, breaches of NAFTA. Rather, it extended to
any claims, whatever their legal basis, which were
derived from or concerned the same measures adopted
by the host State, which were to be the subject of the
investment arbitration claim.

---

[670] *Waste Management Inc.* v. *United Mexican States
("Waste Management I")* (Award) 5 *ICSID Rep.* 443
(NAFTA/ICSID (AF), 2000, Cremades P, Highet and
Siquecros), 457-460, Highet dissenting. The NAFTA claim
was allowed to proceed only once such an unequivocal
waiver had been provided by the investor: *Waste Mana-
gement Inc.* v. *United Mexican States (No. 2)* (Preliminary
Objections), 6 *ICSID Rep.* 538 (NAFTA/ICSID (AF), 2002,
Crawford P, Civiletti and Magallón Gómez) *(Waste
Management II (Preliminary Objections))*.

## 4. *The impact of an umbrella clause*

Thus far, the problems of litispendence in investment arbitration have proved capable of resolution mainly on the grounds of a lack of true parallelism. Since the claims open to an investor by treaty are founded upon a different cause of action to those created by contract, there is no inconsistency in the pursuit of both claims. However, the clarity of this distinction between breach of treaty (under international law) and breach of contract (under the contract's applicable law) is potentially disturbed by the inclusion in some investment treaties of an "umbrella clause", whereby the host State guarantees by treaty the specific undertakings which it has entered into by contract or otherwise with investors of the other contracting State, bringing those undertakings under the umbrella of protection of the treaty[671].

There is, of course, nothing unusual about an arbitral tribunal established under ICSID determining claims founded upon breach of a concession contract, and based primarily upon host State law. After all, the most direct route by which ICSID may receive jurisdiction is where the host State and investor have specifically agreed by contract to confer such jurisdiction upon it. Indeed, for much of the first three decades of the life of the ICSID Convention, the claims entertained by ICSID tribunals were primarily founded on such a basis. The applicable law for such claims was, pursuant to Article 42 of the Convention, and absent

---

[671] Seidl-Hohenveldern, "The Abs-Shawcross Draft Convention to Protect Private Foreign Investment: Comments on the Round-table", (1961) 10 *J. Pub. Law* 100, 104. One account of the history of such clauses is Sinclair, "The Origins of the Umbrella Clause in the International Law of Investment Protection", (2004) 20 *Arb. Int.* 411.

express provision: "the law of the Contracting State
party to the dispute (including its rules on the conflict
of laws) and such rules of international law as may be
applicable".

Thus, where the parties to an investment treaty
agree that any dispute arising between an investor and
a host State may be submitted to arbitration under the
provisions of the treaty, it is submitted that there is no
reason in principle to exclude contract claims from the
operation of the clause. In such a case, however, the
treaty provision does no more than confer jurisdiction
upon the tribunal. The cause of action has to be found
elsewhere: in the provisions of the contract itself,
interpreted in accordance with its applicable law. The
claim thus entertained would remain a contract claim
irrespective of whether it was adjudicated by a treaty
tribunal.

The issue raised by umbrella clauses is therefore a
different, and substantive, one. It is whether the inclusion of such a clause in the treaty transforms the nature
of the obligation being enforced, so that it may be said
that the tribunal is now concerned with a breach of
treaty and not a breach of contract *simpliciter*. The
underlying concept behind an umbrella clause may be
linked to the (contested) proposition in customary
international law that contracts entered into between
States and foreign investors are entitled to special protection, especially in light of the host State's municipal
law-making competence, which can subsequently
affect the parties' contractual bargain [672]. This concept
is supported by the jurisprudence of a number of international arbitral tribunals, adjudicating upon long-term
concession contracts, which have found that interna-

---

[672] See Wälde, "The 'Umbrella' (or Sanctity of Con-
tract/Pacta Sunt Servanda) Clause in Investment Arbitration: A Comment on Original Intentions and Recent
Cases", (2004) 1 (4) *TDM* 1.

tional law rules are applicable to such contracts, even where host State law is otherwise considered to be applicable to the contract[673] ; and that a State is bound as a matter of international law by its contracts with foreign parties notwithstanding the power of its legislature under municipal law to alter the contract[674]. But these propositions were always strongly contested by those, usually non-Western, States which contended that the foreign investment contract was in no different position than an ordinary municipal contract.

The idea of using investment treaties to give effect to this principle has been traced from negotiations on Iranian oil nationalization dispute to the Abs-Shawcross draft of 1959[675]. A centre-piece of the substantive provisions of that draft was Article II, which provided:

> "Each Party shall at all times ensure the observance of any undertakings which it may have given in relation to investments made by nationals of any other Party."

This provision was regarded as of fundamental importance by its drafters, who saw it as an application of the principle of *pacta sunt servanda* to agreements concluded between a State and foreigners[676]. The provision was subsequently incorporated into the OECD Draft Convention as well[677]. From there, it may be traced into the BIT-drafting practice of a number of States.

---

[673] *Lena Goldfields*, *supra* footnote 626.

[674] See *supra* footnote 626.

[675] Abs and Shawcross, "The Proposed Convention to Protect Private Foreign Investment", (1960) 9 *J. Pub. Law* 115. For the evidence in support of this historical origin see Sinclair, *supra* footnote 671.

[676] *Ibid.*, 120.

[677] OECD Draft Convention on the Protection of Foreign Property and Resolution of the Council of the OECD on the Draft Convention (1967), Art. 2.

However, the protection of contractual rights by treaty under an umbrella clause does not find universal application in modern investment treaties. On the contrary, it is notably absent from the model forms of many, in particular non-Western, States[678]. In each case, the definition of "investment" includes concession agreements, so that the other substantive protections of the treaty are extended to this class of property. But the treaties do not separately confirm the enforceability of undertakings. By contrast, the practice of Western States has been to seek to include such a protection as a distinct obligation[679]. Further, Article 10 (1) of the Energy Charter Treaty provides, in its final sentence, that:

> "Each Contracting Party shall observe any obligations it has entered into with an Investor or an Investment of an Investor of any other Contracting State."[680]

The question of the proper construction to apply to an "umbrella clause" has been considered in two awards arising on substantially similar facts: *SGS* v.

---

[678] For example China Model BIT, reprinted in UNCTAD, *International Investment Instruments: A Compendium* (1996), Vol. III, 151; Chile Model BIT, reprinted in *ibid.*, 143; Sri Lanka Model BIT, reprinted as McLachlan, Shore and Weiniger, *supra* footnote 628, Appendix 9.

[679] United Kingdom Model BIT, Art. 2, reprinted as McLachlan, Shore and Weiniger, *ibid.*, Appendix 4; United States 2004 Model BIT, Art. 24, reprinted *ibid.*, Appendix 6; French Model BIT, Art. 10, reprinted *ibid.*, Appendix 10.

[680] Pursuant to Art. 26 (3) *(c)*, States may enter a reservation to this article. The States withholding their consent to arbitration under this clause are: Australia, Canada, Hungary and Norway (Annex IA). Of those, Canada did not in the event sign the ECT, and ratification of it is still pending in Australia and Norway.

*Pakistan*[681] and *SGS* v. *Philippines*[682]. In these cases, the arbitrators came to diametrically opposed views on the key issues. This clash of views has provoked a spirited further debate in subsequent arbitral awards[683].

In *SGS* v. *Pakistan,* the Swiss company SGS provided services in Pakistan under the terms of a concession contract providing for local arbitration in Pakistan. When disputes arose between the parties, SGS sued in the Swiss courts. The Swiss courts held the contractual arbitration clause to be enforceable, and SGS then commenced arbitration of its contract claims in Pakistan. Only subsequently did it bring a claim before a treaty tribunal under the Swiss/Pakistan BIT[684]. The Treaty contained a clause (Article 11) by which:

> "Either Contracting Party shall constantly guarantee the observance of the commitments it has entered into with respect to the investments of the investors of the other Contracting Party."

---

[681] *Supra* footnote 649.

[682] *SGS Société de Surveillance SA* v. *Philippines* (Jurisdiction), 8 *ICSID Rep.* 515 (ICSID, 2004, El-Kosheri P, Crawford and Crivellaro).

[683] Decisions in essence following the *SGS* v. *Pakistan* approach include: *Salini Costruttori SpA* v. *Hashemite Kingdom of Jordan* (Jurisdiction), ICSID Case No. ARB/02/13 (ICSID, 2004, Guillaume P, Cremades and Sinclair); *Joy Mining Machinery Ltd.* v. *Arab Republic of Egypt* (Jurisdiction), *supra* footnote 640; *El Paso Energy International Co.* v. *Argentine Republic* (Jurisdiction), ICSID Case No. ARB/03/15 (ICSID, 2006, Caflisch P, Stern and Bernadini). Decisions in essence following the *SGS* v. *Philippines* approach include: *Eureko BV* v. *Republic of Poland*, *supra* footnote 649, and *Noble Ventures Inc.* v. *Romania* (Award), ICSID Case No. ARB/01/11 (ICSID, 2005, Böckstiegel P, Lever and Dupuy).

[684] Accord concernant la promotion et la protection réciproque des investissements ("Agreement concerning the Promotion and Reciprocal Protection of Investments") (Switzerland-Pakistan) (signed 11 July 1995, entered into force 6 May 1996), RO 1998 2601.

The claim made in the treaty arbitration alleged both breaches of contract, on the basis of the umbrella clause, and breaches of other independent standards enshrined in the Treaty.

The Supreme Court of Pakistan held that SGS had waived its right to commence the treaty arbitration by commencing the local arbitration, and issued an injunction restraining SGS from proceeding with the treaty arbitration[685]. The ICSID Arbitral Tribunal issued a preliminary order recommending that Pakistan refrain from pursuing an application for contempt in the Pakistan courts, and that the local arbitration be stayed, pending the Tribunal's consideration of its own jurisdiction[686]. It observed:

> "[N]ormally it would be wasteful of resources for two proceedings relating to the same or substantially the same matter to unfold separately while the jurisdiction of one tribunal awaits determination . . . At the same time, the Tribunal is concerned that Pakistan not be effectively deprived of a forum for the hearing of its own claims . . ."[687]

The Tribunal decided that it had jurisdiction to entertain the independent treaty claims. But it held that the umbrella clause did not operate so as to make the contract claims justiciable before it. The Tribunal construed the reference in the dispute settlement clause in the BIT conferring jurisdiction in relation to "disputes with respect to investments" as merely denoting the factual subject-matter of the claims, and not their legal

---

[685] *Société Générale de Surveillance SA* v. *Pakistan* (Judgment), 8 *ICSID Rep.* 352 (Supreme Court of Pakistan, Appellate Jurisdiction, 2002, Sheikh, Farooq and Dogar JJ).

[686] *SGS Société de Surveillance SA* v. *Pakistan* (Procedural Order No. 2 of 16 October 2002), *supra* footnote 520, 388.

[687] *Ibid.*, 396.

basis. Such a reference was insufficient, concluded the Tribunal, to convey an implication that the parties had intended to subject contract claims to ICSID arbitration[688]. Rather, the Tribunal maintained a strict delineation between breaches of the treaty and contract claims, and found that the arbitration clause in the contract "is a valid forum selection clause *so far as concerns the Claimant's contract claims which do not also amount to BIT claims*"[689]. Equally, the prior assertion of those claims in other fora could not preclude the investor from pursuing its treaty claims before the ICSID Tribunal[690].

The Tribunal then decided that the umbrella clause did not have the effect of elevating the contract claims to treaty claims. It reasoned that, under general international law, a violation of a contract entered into by a State with an investor of another State was not by itself a violation of international law[691]. The Tribunal was concerned that, if construed so as to extend to all commitments of the host State, such clause might be capable of infinite expansion, and render all other commitments in the treaty superfluous[692]. It would also negate the effect of the contractual submission clause. In consequence, therefore, the clause was to be interpreted merely as a commitment to enact implementing rules to give effect to the host State's contractual commitments. The Tribunal also speculated that if a host State, for example, deprived the investor of a contractually agreed right to submit his contract claim to international arbitration, that might itself constitute a breach of the clause[693]. But this did not mean that the clause

---

[688] *SGS* v. *Pakistan*, *supra* footnote 649, 441.
[689] *Ibid.*
[690] *Ibid.*, 447.
[691] *Ibid.*, 443.
[692] *Ibid.*, 443-444.
[693] *Ibid.*, 445-446.

mandated the "instant transubstantiation of contract claims into BIT claims"[694]. Accordingly, the Tribunal concluded that it had jurisdiction over the treaty claims, but not over the contract claims.

The subsequent award of a differently constituted Tribunal in *SGS* v. *Philippines*[695] was concerned with a very similar claim. Just as in the *Pakistan* case, SGS had a concession contract with the Philippines. It contained its own jurisdiction clause[696], which in this case submitted disputes to the Philippine courts. The Swiss/Philippines BIT also contained an umbrella clause[697]. The claim brought before the ICSID Tribunal also concerned allegations of both direct breach of treaty and breach of contract. The latter were alleged by SGS to be justiciable by virtue of the umbrella clause.

The Tribunal agreed with the Tribunal in *SGS* v. *Pakistan* as to the law applicable to the contractual claims. It held that the extent of the parties' contractual obligation "is still governed by the contract, and it can only be determined by reference to the terms of the contract"[698]. The validity of a contractual obligation was "a matter for determination under the applicable law, normally the law of the host State"[699]. However, the Tribunal differed fundamentally as to the consequences of that upon the jurisdiction of the ICSID Tribunal in view of the umbrella clause. The Tribunal held that such a clause could bring specific obligations of a host state vis-à-vis a particular investor within the

---

[694]  *Ibid.*, 446.
[695]  *Supra* footnote 682.
[696]  Clause 12.
[697]  Art. X (2), Accord concernant la promotion et la protection réciproque des investissements ("Agreement concerning the Promotion and Reciprocal Protection of Investments") (Switzerland-Philippines) (signed 31 March 1997, entered into force 23 April 1999), RO 2001 438.
[698]  *SGS* v. *Philippines*, *supra* footnote 682, 553.
[699]  *Ibid.*, 550.

framework of the BIT[700] ; and that the general reference in the dispute settlement clause to "disputes with respect to investments" was apt to confer jurisdiction upon the tribunal to adjudicate the contract claims[701].

However, that did not mean that the parties' express and exclusive choice of forum by contract was overridden by the Treaty clauses. The Tribunal held that:

> "The basic principle in each case is that a binding exclusive jurisdiction clause in a contract should be respected, unless overridden by another valid provision."[702]

The general provisions of the BIT did not override the contractual jurisdiction clause: "It is not to be presumed that such a general provision has the effect of overriding specific provisions of particular contracts, freely negotiated between the parties."[703] A BIT should be seen as a framework treaty "to support and supplement, not to override or replace, the actually negotiated investment arrangements made between the investor and the host State"[704]. Article 26 of the ICSID Convention did not have the effect of creating a subsequent agreement between the parties in favour of ICSID as the exclusive remedy for the simple reason that Article 26 itself was subject to contrary provision by the parties. Such contrary provision could include a contractual choice of forum nominating local host State courts[705]. Thus the Tribunal found that it

---

[700] *Ibid.*, 550-551.
[701] *Ibid.*, 554-556.
[702] *Ibid.*, 557.
[703] *Ibid.*, 557-558.
[704] *Ibid.*, 558.
[705] Citing *inter alia* Woodruff, *supra* footnote 652; *North American Dredging Co of Texas* v. *United Mexican States*, (1926) 4 *RIAA* 26; accord Schreuer, Schreuer, *The ICSID Convention: A Commentary* (2001) 363.

had jurisdiction over the contract claim, but that it was not *admissible* in light of the jurisdiction clause:

> "SGS should not be able to approbate and reprobate in respect of the same contract: if it claims under the contract, it should comply with the contract in respect of the very matter which is the foundation of its claim."[706]

The Request for Arbitration did not clearly disclose breaches of treaty, since in substance the only claim made by SGS against the Philippines was its failure to pay the alleged sum due under the contract. An unjustified refusal to pay sums payable under a contract might potentially amount to a breach of the fair and equitable treatment standard, but it would be premature so to hold in view of the fact that there was undoubtedly a dispute between the parties as to what sum was contractually due[707]. In the circumstances, the Tribunal decided to stay the case pending the outcome of the proceedings in the host State courts[708].

Neither of the *SGS* decisions has found favour with those who would wish to extend the greatest possible freedom to investors to bring their claims against host States, even if they are founded on contract, before an investment arbitral tribunal. In both cases, the result was to remit the contract claims to adjudication within

---

[706] *SGS* v. *Philippines, supra* footnote 682, 561-562. Crivellaro dissented on the ground that the treaty dispute settlement clause post-dated the contract, and signalled an intention on the part of the contracting States to extend to investors the choice between contractual methods of dispute resolution and the new treaty mechanism: Dissenting Opinion, 568.

[707] *Ibid.*, 563.

[708] Citing *MOX Plant Case (Ireland* v. *United Kingdom)* (24 June 2003), Provisional Order No. 3, 126 *ILR* 310, 42 *ILM* 1187, 1199 (UNCLOS, Annex VII, Tribunal, Mensah P, Crawford, Fortier, Hafner and Watts), discussed *infra*, Chapter IV, Section B 2.

the host State, and to exclude those claims, at least initially, from the purview of the ICSID tribunal. This was so despite the existence of broad jurisdiction and umbrella clauses in the relevant treaties. Yet the need to distinguish between the proper province of treaty arbitration and contract dispute resolution, where the parties have already chosen an exclusive forum for the latter, represents a powerful imperative, both as a matter of principle and policy.

In articulating the balance to be struck, it is submitted that the approach taken in *SGS* v. *Philippines* is to be preferred. There is no reason to give a construction to either the dispute resolution or the umbrella clauses of an investment treaty which would exclude claims in contract *per se* from the purview of an investment arbitral tribunal. After all, ICSID arbitration is specifically designed to provide an available forum where the host State has entered into direct contractual relations with a foreign investor. States are at liberty to extend the benefit of such arbitration to their respective investors. They may do so by giving their consent by treaty, with the investor giving its own consent when bringing its claim. None of this should occasion surprise or difficulty. The result, as the Tribunal in the *Philippines* case found, is simply to give the ICSID tribunal jurisdiction over a contract claim, which is subject to its governing law. Neither the formulation nor the background to umbrella clauses (in so far as it is known) indicates a contrary intention.

However, it is equally right that, if the investor wishes to enforce its contract, it must do so in accordance with its terms. Absent evidence to the contrary, these represent a joint specific exercise of party autonomy between State and investor as to the arrangements for the resolution of any disputes. The binding nature of such clauses in relation to contractual claims within their scope is not to be undermined by a general provision in a treaty extending a number of dispute resolution options to investors of two States generally.

The issue to which the award in *SGS* v. *Philippines* did not advert, however, is this: Does the umbrella clause nevertheless provide a substantive guarantee of the observance of undertakings by the host State given on the making of the investment, where the host State's own law may not? Lying behind many of the measures introduced in relation to State contracts has been a concern to protect investors from subsequent changes in host State law, especially where they may have been introduced specifically to excuse the State from liability under the concession contract in question. Of course, if the governing law of the contract chosen by the parties is international law, such changes would have no effect. Similarly, where there is no express choice of law, Article 42 of the ICSID Convention permits the tribunal to disregard provisions of host State law which infringe international law[709].

Where the parties have, however, expressly chosen host State law as the applicable law, the inclusion of an umbrella clause in the treaty does not affect that choice, or its ordinary incidents. As the Annulment Committee put it in *CMS* v. *Argentina*:

> "The effect of the umbrella clause is not to transform the obligation which is relied on into something else; the content of the obligation is unaffected, as is its proper law."[710]

But what if the provisions of the contract, construed

---

[709] Schreuer, *supra* footnote 705, 612 ff.; and McLachlan, "Investment Treaty Arbitration: The Legal Framework", [2008] ICCA Congress Series No. 15 (in press).

[710] *CMS Gas Transmission Co.* v. *Argentine Republic* ICSID Case No. ARB/01/8 (Decision on Annulment) (ICSID, 2007, Guillaume P, Elaraby and Crawford) [95 *(c)*].

in accordance with their applicable law at the date of the conclusion of the contract, have been affected by a subsequent change in the law imposed by the host State? In such a case, it is submitted that the existence of an umbrella clause provides an independent treaty standard pursuant to which the investor could require the host State to honour its original bargain irrespective of subsequent changes in its law. This construction would give the clause an independent, and additional, sphere of operation on the plane of international law. It would link the operation of the clause with the general require-ment emerging in the jurisprudence on the contract/treaty divide, requiring the breach of treaty to involve the exercise of sovereign authority but without requiring the inclusion in the contract of a stabilization clause[711].

It is submitted that it is possible for the umbrella clause to operate on both levels at once. In the case of an ordinary contract claim, it would operate in the manner decided in *SGS* v. *Philippines*, conferring juris-diction upon the treaty tribunal, but only to the extent that the parties have not by contract selected a more specific mode of dispute resolution. Where, however, there had been State interference in the contract, for example by subsequent changes in host State law which had the effect of defeating the specific undertakings which the State had given to the investor, the umbrella clause would also operate. The clause would apply in that bulwark role if, and to the extent that, the alterna-

---

[711] It is submitted that the Tribunal in *El Paso Energy*, *supra* footnote 683, [81] (followed in *Pan American Energy Int'l Co.* v. *Argentina* (Jurisdiction), ICSID Case No. ARB/03/13, and *Sempra Energy Int'l* v. *Argentina*, ICSID Case No. ARB/02/16 (ICSID, 2007, Orrego Vicuña P, Lalonde and Rico), (2008) 20 *World Trade and Arb. Mat.* 117, [310]) goes too far in apparently requiring the inclusion of such a clause as a prerequisite to the invoca-tion of an umbrella clause.

tive contractual forum could not (as a matter of applicable law), or did not, uphold the undertaking of the
state.

## 5. *Parallel treaty arbitration*

Thus far this chapter has been concerned with the
relationship between treaty arbitration and claims made
between the same parties in national courts or in commercial arbitration. In those cases, as has been seen,
there are often difficult questions of overlap in applicable law. But the rival fora are indisputably each operating within a different legal order. A different, but no
less difficult, set of issues is raised by the incidence of
parallel *treaty* arbitrations, each of which is concerned
with the same underlying factual dispute. This is a by-
product of the fragmented nature of modern investment
protection by treaty, made up, as it is, of a huge net-
work of bilateral arrangements.

It is inherent in the structure of investment treaties
that indirect investors, who hold their investments by
way of shareholding in the investment company, may
bring a claim against the host State. Equally, the investment company itself may have a claim. If each of these
potential claimants is to be treated as the national of
a different home State, each such investor may be
entitled to invoke the provisions of a different BIT
with the host State. In this situation, the consolidation
provisions now included in NAFTA and some new-
model US investment treaties [712] will be of little assistance. These provisions assume that the parallel arbitrations are brought within the same treaty regime.

This issue arose directly in the *Lauder* affair [713]. In

---

[712] *Supra*, Chapter I, Section D 3.

[713] *Lauder* v. *Czech Republic* (Award), 9 *ICSID Rep.* 62
(UNCITRAL, 2001, Briner C, Cutler and Klein); *CME
Czech Republic BV (The Netherlands)* v. *Czech Republic*

those cases, the American entrepreneur Ron Lauder brought a claim against the Czech Republic alleging expropriation of his investment in the Czech television channel, TV Nova, under the provisions of the United States/Czech BIT[714]. Mr. Lauder's investment was exercised through a Dutch investment company, CME Czech Republic BV ("CME"), over which he had control[715]. CME brought its own claim for expropriation under the provisions of the Dutch/Czech BIT[716]. In both cases, the investor elected for UNCITRAL arbitration, which was one of the options available under the dispute resolution clauses of the respective treaties. The tribunals were constituted of different arbitrators in each case. Significantly, the Czech Republic did not agree to a *de facto* consolidation of the two proceedings, instead insisting on a different arbitral tribunal to hear the CME claim[717]. The evidence presented to the two tribunals was substantially the same. The allegations made against the Republic in each case were substantially the same.

The two tribunals delivered their awards within 10 days of each other. The *Lauder* Tribunal did so on 3 September 2001 in London. It decided that, save on

---

*supra* footnote 632 *(CME I)*; (Final Award), 9 *ICSID* 264 (UNCITRAL, 2003, Kühn C, Schwebel and Brownlie) *(CME II)*; Svea Court of Appeals, Sweden, (2003) 42 *ILM* 919.

[714] Treaty concerning the Reciprocal Encouragement and Protection of Investment (United States-Czech Republic) (signed 22 October 1991, entered into force 19 December 1992) *Senate Treaty Doc.* 102-131.

[715] *Lauder*, *supra* footnote 632, 76.

[716] Agreement on Encouragement and Reciprocal Protection of Investments (Netherlands-Czech Republic) (signed 29 April 1991, entered into force 1 October 1992), 2242 *UNTS* 206, *Tractatenblad*, 1992, 146; 569/ 1992 Sb.

[717] *Lauder, supra* footnote 632, 87; *CME I*, *supra* footnote 632, 195.

one aspect, the Czech Republic had committed no
breach of treaty. Rather, the whole matter was to be
seen as a private commercial dispute between Mr.
Lauder and his Czech investment partner. "The investment treaty created no duty of due diligence on the part
of the Czech Republic to intervene in the dispute
between the two companies over the nature of their
legal relationships."[718] The *CME* Tribunal delivered its
award 10 days later in Stockholm. By a majority[719],
it decided that the Czech Republic had committed
multiple violations of the treaty, and was liable to
remedy its injury to the claimant by paying the fair
market value of the investment as it was prior to the
Republic's breach.

There were thus diametrically opposed decisions of
two tribunals hearing in substance the same dispute.
Mr. Lauder, having lost his claim in the *Lauder* arbitration, would be the substantial beneficiary of the award
of damages in *CME*. The claims thus raised important
questions about the scope of the principles of *lis pendens* (and of *res judicata*) in investment treaty arbitration. The Czech Republic presented submissions as to
the application of these principles, and as to an alleged
broader notion of abuse of process, before both tribunals, and before the Svea Court of Appeals, when it
challenged the award in Sweden. In each case, the
Republic's submissions were rejected.

In *Lauder*, the only question which arose was one of
litispendence, since this Tribunal delivered its decision
first. The Tribunal rejected the application of the doctrine of *lis pendens* holding:

> "The Arbitral Tribunal considers that the
> Respondent's recourse to the principle of *lis alibi*

---

[718] *Lauder, ibid.*, 111.
[719] One of the arbitrators, Hándl, refused to sign the
award and delivered a dissenting opinion.

*pendens* to be of no use, since all the other court and arbitration proceedings involve different parties and different causes of action . . . Therefore, no possibility exists that any other court or arbitral tribunal can render a decision similar to or inconsistent with the award which will be issued by this Arbitral Tribunal, i.e. that the Czech Republic breached or did not breach the Treaty, and is or is not liable for damages towards Mr. Lauder." [720]

For similar reasons, it rejected the argument of abuse of process, finding that: "the Arbitral Tribunal is the only forum with jurisdiction to hear Mr Lauder's claims based on the Treaty" [721]. The most the Tribunal was prepared to accept was that there should be no double recovery [722], a matter which it considered should be taken into account by the second seised arbitral tribunal in assessing any award of damages which it might decide to make.

In *CME*, the Tribunal also rejected an abuse of process argument on similar grounds. Emphasizing that the Czech Republic had not sought consolidation, it observed: "Should two different Treaties grant remedies to the respective claimants deriving from the same facts and circumstances, this does not deprive one of the claimants of jurisdiction." [723] In its Final Award, delivered in March 2003, the *CME* Tribunal also considered whether the *Lauder* award amounted to *res judicata*. It rejected this submission as well for absence of identity of parties and source of legal rights [724].

The Svea Court of Appeals also rejected the proposition that the principles of *lis pendens* and *res judicata*

---

[720] *Lauder, supra* footnote 632, 87.
[721] *Ibid.*
[722] *Ibid.*
[723] *CME I, supra* footnote 632, 195.
[724] *CME II, supra* footnote 713, 355.

applied to this case[725]. There was no identity of parties, as Mr. Lauder had a controlling interest in CME, but did not hold a majority of the share capital. Thus, to deny effect to the CME claim would be to deny a remedy to the other investors. Moreover, there was no identity of claim, as the arbitral proceedings had been brought under two different bilateral treaties, which were not identical.

The *Lauder* litigation provides the most sustained examination yet undertaken in investment arbitration jurisprudence as to the manner in which the issues of parallel treaty arbitrations are to be resolved. But the result there expressed needs to be put into context. Neither the *Lauder* nor the *CME* Tribunals, nor the Swedish Court, expressly rejected the proposition that the principles of *lis pendens* and *res judicata* might have an application in this field[726]. In part this may have been because the case was argued on the broader ground of abuse of process. However, the reasoning of the tribunals and the Court in each case essentially rejected the submission by applying elements of the formal legal test, requiring identity of parties, object and cause of action[727].

It is submitted that the doctrines may in principle be applied in investment treaty arbitration, provided that the conditions for their application are made out, since the decisions of investment treaty tribunals are all rendered within the same legal order of Public International Law[728]. The doctrine of *res judicata* has

---

[725] *CME* (Svea Court of Appeal), *supra* footnote 713, 953.

[726] For example the implicit acceptance of the doctrine of *res judicata* in *CME II, supra* footnote 713, 356.

[727] Accord *Benvenuti & Bonfant Srl* v. *People's Republic of the Congo* (Award), 1 *ICSID Rep.* 330, 340 (ICSID, 1980, Trolle P, Bystricky and Razafindralambo).

[728] See *infra*, Chapter IV, Section B 2, for a discussion of the extent to which *lis pendens* is a general principle of law applicable to international tribunals in their relations *inter se.*

been specifically upheld in the context of investment arbitration[729]. International tribunals have also accepted that they have a *discretion* to stay their proceedings, if there is another tribunal seised of the matter, and it is more appropriate in the interests of both parties and the ends of justice to defer to that tribunal. As it was put in *SPP* v. *Egypt*:

> "When the jurisdictions of two unrelated and independent tribunals extend to the same dispute, there is no rule of international law which prevents either tribunal from exercising its jurisdiction. *However, in the interest of international judicial order, either of the tribunals may, in its discretion and as a matter of comity, decide to stay the exercise of its jurisdiction pending a decision by the other tribunal.*"[730]

The Tribunal in *SPP* did in fact decide to stay the exercise of its jurisdiction pending a decision by the courts at the seat of a parallel ICC arbitration as to the scope of the ICC arbitration clause.

However, if the view taken by the tribunals on the application of the tests of identity of parties and cause of action to the context of investment arbitration prevails, the doctrines will have a very limited application, since they will be confined to concurrent arbitrations brought by the identical claimant under the same investment treaty. In these circumstances, it is neces-

---

[729] *Waste Management II (Preliminary Objections)*, *supra* footnote 670, 559-562, citing, *inter alia*, the earlier practice of the mixed claims commissions in *Compagnie Générale de l'Orénoque*, (1905) *Ralston's Report* 244, 355-357, and *In the Matter of the SS Newchwang, Claim No. 21*, (1922) 16 *AJIL* 323, 324.

[730] *Southern Pacific Properties (Middle East) Ltd. [SPP]* v. *Arab Republic of Egypt* (First Jurisdiction), 3 *ICSID Rep.* 101, 129 (ICSID, 1985, Jiménez de Aréchaga P, El Mahdi and Pietrowski) (emphasis added).

sary to examine in a little more detail the reasoning applied to the two elements of the test, which were said not to have been met in the *Lauder* case.

The principal basis adopted by each of the tribunals and the Svea Court for finding a lack of identity of *cause of action* was that each of the claims had been brought under different investment treaties[731]. The *CME* Tribunal decided that "[b]ecause the two bilateral investment treaties create rights that are not in all respects exactly the same, different claims are necessarily formulated"[732]. Even if another court or tribunal were seised of the identical dispute, opined the Tribunal, this would not deprive it of jurisdiction[733].

It is plainly right that there may be important differences between the substantive obligations created by different investment treaties. Thus, to return to the formulation in Private International Law[734], claims under two different investment treaties may involve the application of different underlying principles, even if to the same facts, and with the same end in view. But, it is submitted that the mere fact that the rules appear in different treaties should not *per se* result in the same forms of legal protection being treated as different. Although each may owe its binding force to a different legal obligation, both obligations operate upon the same plane of public international law. In the same way, a claim in tort made in a French court has its origin within French law, from which it derives its obligatory force. But this does not of itself deprive a defendant of the opportunity of raising a plea of litis-

---

[731] Applying the reasoning of ITLOS in *The MOX Plant* case (ITLOS, Provisional Measures, Order of 3 December 2001), (2002) 126 *ILR* 334, 413, discussed further *infra*, Chapter IV B 2.

[732] *CME II, supra* footnote 713, 355.

[733] Citing, *inter alia*, *SPP* v. *Egypt, supra* footnote 730.

[734] *Supra*, Chapter II, Section B 2 *(b)*.

pendence should in substance the same claim be raised before an English court, even though the basis for the legal obligation might in that case be English rather than French law. Both claims are made on a symmetrical basis[735], since they are both made before national courts.

This is not a question of the *jurisdiction* of the tribunal. Rather, as the Tribunal correctly observed in *SPP,* it is a question of whether the tribunal should stay the exercise of its jurisdiction. Whilst the Tribunal in *CME* was content to rely upon *SPP* for the proposition that it was not deprived of jurisdiction, it did not refer to this second part of the Tribunal's reasoning, which in fact formed the ratio of the decision. Thus the fact that the two tribunals were constituted under different legal arrangements was not ultimately dispositive of the question whether there was sufficient identity of claims to justify a stay.

The tribunals in the *Lauder* litigation also took a strict view of the requirement of identity of *parties*. On the fact pattern as it arose in those cases, this is perhaps unsurprising. The *Lauder* Tribunal was first seised, and applying normal principles of litispendence, one might therefore have expected the *CME* Tribunal to be the one which deferred as to process and result. However, the benefit of any damages award in *CME* would have extended to other shareholders in the company in addition to Mr. Lauder. Yet, can it really be said that the limit of a tribunal's obligations is to ensure that the same parties do not secure a double recovery? The doctrine of *res judicata* also exists in order to prevent re-litigation by a claimant who has failed in his first claim, and not merely to prevent double recovery.

---

[735] The term utilized by Douglas, *supra* footnote 458, 238.

The *CME* Tribunal specifically rejected an argument based on the economic identity of the parties. It held that the single economic entity theory had only been accepted by courts or tribunals in exceptional cases, such as in competition law. Moreover, the company group theory had not gained acceptance in international arbitration. The Tribunal held that its conclusion accorded with established international law, citing *Barcelona Traction*[736]. However, *Barcelona Traction* cannot provide a sound basis for a decision on this point in the case of a claim made in investment arbitration. The International Court of Justice rejected the economic entity theory in *Barcelona Traction* in the context of a claim to diplomatic protection made by the state of nationality of the shareholders in a company. Despite its distinguished opponents[737], this rule is still part of the customary international law of diplomatic protection, and has been recently upheld by the International Law Commission[738]. But this restriction in the customary law is one of the matters addressed by the broad definition of investment in investment treaties. This very point was made in *CMS* v. *Argentina*[739]. In that case, Argentina had contended, relying on *Barcelona Traction,* that a minority shareholder, with a different nationality to that of the investment company, could not pursue his own claim against it

---

[736] Case concerning the *Barcelona Traction, Light and Power Co. (New Application: 1962) (Belgium* v. *Spain) Second Phase* (Judgment), *ICJ Rep. 1970* 3, 48-50.

[737] Mann, "The Protection of Shareholders' Interests in the Light of the *Barcelona Traction* Case", (1973) 67 *AJIL* 259, reprinted in Mann, *Further Studies in International Law* (1990) 217.

[738] ILC (Dugard, Special Rapporteur), "Draft Articles on Diplomatic Protection with Commentaries", *Yearbook of the International Law Commission* (Vol. II, Pt. 2, 2006) 58-65, Art. 11.

[739] *CMS, supra* footnote 649, 502-506.

under a bilateral investment treaty. The Tribunal distinguished *Barcelona Traction* on the basis that it was concerned solely with diplomatic protection, which had become a "residual mechanism to be resorted to in the absence of other arrangements recognizing the direct right of action by individuals"[740]. The Tribunal went on:

> "It is precisely this kind of arrangement that has come to prevail under international law, particularly in respect of foreign investments, the paramount example being that of the 1965 [ICSID] Convention."[741]

If, then, the definition of investment preferred in the majority of investment treaties permits a minority shareholder with a different nationality from that of the investment company to have the benefit of pursuing his own direct claim against the host State, surely a consistent approach should also be taken to the definition of identity of parties for the purpose of the rules of *lis pendens* and *res judicata*. Otherwise, the investor would be able to approbate and reprobate from the same investment treaty. He would take the benefit of an extended right of direct action — looking through the investment company at the economic effect of the host state's actions directly upon his shareholding — which would not found the basis of a claim under customary international law. But he would not bear the burden of being bound by any finding arising out of a claim by the investment company itself on the same facts. In Private International Law, the test of identity of parties for the application of the doctrine of *lis pendens* has also been applied to those whose interests are indissociable or indivisible[742]. It is submitted that parallel

---

[740] *Ibid.*, 503.
[741] *Ibid.*
[742] *Supra* Chapter II, Section B 2 *(a)*.

treaty arbitration claims by company and shareholder relating to the same underlying facts should be held to meet this criterion.

## D.  Interim Conclusions

Questions of parallel proceedings in international arbitration take on a very different hue, depending upon whether the jurisdiction of the arbitral tribunal is based upon contract or treaty. Accordingly, these conclusions will take each situation separately.

*International commercial arbitration*

(1) *Priority of Party Autonomy.* Article II of the New York Convention embodies a clear rule of priority as between court proceedings and arbitration, respecting the autonomy of the parties to choose jointly the specific venue of dispute resolution. Part of the purpose of resort to international arbitration is to avoid problems caused by parallel proceedings before different national courts. The parties' choice of arbitration necessarily entails positive *Kompetenz-Kompetenz* — that the tribunal has jurisdiction to rule upon its own jurisdiction.

(2) *Parallel proceedings are endemic in international arbitration.* Despite this, it is inherent in the very nature of arbitration that problems of parallel proceedings will arise. The question of the scope and validity of an arbitration agreement is one which necessarily affects the jurisdiction of two tribunals: the arbitral tribunal which depends upon the validity of the clause for its jurisdiction; and the national court, which would otherwise enjoy jurisdiction. Article II of the New York Convention, in requiring a stay of national court proceedings unless the court finds that the arbitration agreement is null and void, inoperative or

incapable of being performed, necessarily contemplates that the court, as well as the arbitral tribunal, may rule on jurisdictional questions.

(3) *Deference to the arbitral tribunal and the courts of the seat.* Nevertheless, there will often be good reasons to accord priority to the arbitral tribunal's determination of its own jurisdiction — especially where the tribunal is already seised of the matter — applying a principle of negative *Kompetenz-Kompetenz.* Where the court applied to is not the seat of the arbitration, there will be particular reason to stay the action, and defer to the tribunal, leaving any challenge to the tribunal's own determination to the courts of the seat *(Julius).* Normally, the arbitral tribunal will be entitled to proceed to determine its own jurisdiction, even if a foreign national court does not stay its proceedings. But there may be exceptional circumstances justifying a stay of the arbitral proceedings, pending a determination of arbitral jurisdiction by the court.

(4) *Limited scope for consolidation.* The very fact that the jurisdiction of an arbitral tribunal depends upon a contractual choice of jurisdiction itself creates a risk of parallel or closely related arbitral proceedings arising out of the same dispute. At present, one of the limitations of international arbitration is that it offers few avenues for consolidation. But where the arbitral proceedings are parallel, and not merely related, the arbitral tribunal ought to stay its proceedings in order to enable an earlier constituted arbitral tribunal to decide on its jurisdiction.

(5) *Role of Anti-suit injunctions.* The supervisory role of the courts of the seat to control arbitration cannot be excluded. However, injunctions which are granted as an abuse of State power and with a view to denial of justice are illegitimate. Injunctions granted by the courts of the seat to restrain court proceedings brought in breach of an arbitration agreement may

however (*pace* the European Court in *The Front Comor*), be justifiable. The court in such a situation is merely acting in aid of the arbitral process by enforcing the parties' contractual agreement. This is a power which arbitral tribunals also possess, but (as in the case of many provisional measures) the intervention of the court is likely to be required to make such an injunction effective.

## Investment treaty arbitration

Investment treaty arbitration is even more inherently fragmented as a forum for dispute resolution. This is a product of the sources of the rights being found in various separate bilateral treaties, and the concurrence of national law and international remedies relating to the same state measure. Many problems of the interaction between such remedies may, however, be resolved by a separation of the respective planes of national and international law, of contract and treaty, and of the adjudicatory competence of each.

(6) *Breach of treaty and breach of contract.* Claims of breach of rights which were created by treaty are to be distinguished from breach of contract claims. Treaty claims exist on the plane of international law. Their scope of application falls to be determined on their own terms, and in accordance with the principles of international law. Contract claims, on the other hand, flow from the parties' express agreement. They fall to be determined in accordance with the law applicable to the contract, which, even in the case of a concession contract with a State, will often be national law. In each case, it is necessary to ascertain the fundamental basis of the claim. The distinction between treaty and contract claims has the consequences that:

(*a*) The pursuit of a claim for breach of contract does not of itself preclude a claim of breach of treaty, since the legal basis for each claim is different. This conclusion is unaffected even if the investment is founded on an investment contract with the host State, since the question of law is still fundamentally different: namely, whether the actions of the host State constitute a breach of the treaty. Contract rights, on the other hand, will respond according to the terms of the contract to breaches of many different kinds arising in the course of the contract's performance. There must be something more than a mere breach of contract to constitute a breach of treaty. Of their nature, treaty rights will only respond where there has been an exercise of sovereign authority by the host State affecting the investment.

*(b)* The existence of an exclusive jurisdiction or arbitration clause in a contract between host State and investor will be valid and enforceable as regards contract claims, and should be upheld by investment tribunals. But it will not affect claims based upon breach of treaty.

(7) *Prior pursuit of local remedies.* Unless the treaty parties have expressly provided to the contrary, the effect of the prior pursuit of remedies before a national court in respect of a measure taken by the host state affecting the investment upon a subsequent treaty claim is as follows:

(a) *No exhaustion.* Local remedies need not be exhausted as a condition precedent to investment treaty arbitration. This is because one of the purposes of investment arbitration is to provide a neutral forum for resolution of investor-state disputes, which does not carry the strict prerequisites of the diplomatic espousal of claims by home States.

(b) *No estoppel.* The pursuit of local remedies will not

preclude or estop the investor from subsequent invocation of a treaty claim, assuming that the breach of treaty was not thereby cured. Treaty rights such as fair and equitable treatment are concerned with an assessment of systemic failures in the due process accorded to the investor by the administrative and judicial decision-makers of the host State. Such rights can only be invoked by reference to the experience of the investor in resorting to local remedies.

(8) *Election and waiver*. However, this principle may be affected by express treaty provisions as to election and waiver:

(a) *"Fork in the road"*. Where the parties to an investment treaty insert a "fork-in-the-road" clause, the operation of the clause will be affected by whether the claims asserted are in substance parallel or different. Thus, if a contract claim has already been submitted to a national court or other arbitral tribunal, the investor will be precluded from subsequently re-litigating that dispute before an investment tribunal. Similarly, where the investor chooses to bring in substance a treaty cause of action before a host State's courts, he may forfeit the right to challenge the same State measure before an investment tribunal. If, however, the host State court claim is brought in contract, the existence of a fork-in-the-road clause will have no effect upon the subsequent invocation of a treaty claim before an investment tribunal.

(b) *Waiver*. Where the investment treaty requires the waiver of all claims with respect to the measure of the host State which is alleged to be a breach of treaty, as a condition for the valid invocation of treaty arbitration (as, for example, does NAFTA Article 1121), such a waiver will operate as at the

date of filing the investment arbitration (but not
before) to preclude the pursuit of all other claims
arising out of the act of the host State which is
complained of, even if such claims are founded
upon municipal law.

(9) *Impact of an umbrella clause.* An international
tribunal constituted to hear investment disputes by
treaty may nevertheless have jurisdiction over investment contract claims between investor and host State
by one of three routes: (i) express choice of the parties
by contract; (ii) standing consent given by the host
State by treaty to submit to arbitration all disputes
relating to investments, or specifically disputes relating
to investment agreements; or (iii) an umbrella clause in
the treaty, pursuant to which the host State agrees to
observe any undertakings which it has entered into
with regard to investments. In such cases, the tribunal
will apply the law applicable to the contract to the contract dispute.

Where, however, the parties to an investment contract have specifically chosen another court or tribunal
to resolve their *contractual* dispute, that choice will
take priority over the general jurisdiction of an investment treaty tribunal under an umbrella clause. In such
cases, the investment tribunal should stay the exercise
of its own jurisdiction over such claims on grounds of
admissibility.

Exceptionally, a subsequent change in municipal
law by the host State in the exercise of its sovereign
authority, which fundamentally affects the nature of the
contractual bargain, may constitute a free-standing
breach of an umbrella clause, enforceable as a breach
of treaty irrespective of a contractual jurisdiction
clause.

(10) *Parallel treaty arbitrations.* Where the same
underlying dispute gives rise to claims under two dif-

ferent investment treaties, each tribunal is faced with a potential problem of parallel proceedings within the same legal order. To date tribunals have taken a narrow view in determining whether there is sufficient identity of parties and cause of action, upholding separate corporate personality and finding that each treaty creates separate causes of action. It is submitted that in principle a wider approach ought to be adopted in which sufficient identity of parties would be established where the claimants were in privity of interest with each other (as in the case of the shareholders in an investment company) and the identity of the cause of action is assessed substantively by reference to the nature of the right asserted, and not its source. If sufficient identity is thus established either tribunal is entitled, in the exercise of its discretion, to stay its proceedings if it satisfied that it would be in the interests of justice to do so.

CHAPTER IV

PUBLIC INTERNATIONAL LITIGATION

A. *The Judicialization of Public International Law*

*1. The rise of public international adjudication*

The third arena in which the issue of parallel proceedings needs to be considered is that of public international litigation, namely disputes involving sovereign
States. The field of investment treaty arbitration provides a mixed example of this, since the respondent in
such cases is always a State, and the arbitration takes
place by virtue of an agreement between States governed by international law. But other parts of Public
International Law have also experienced problems of
conflicting jurisdiction — both as between international tribunals and between international tribunals and
national courts.

These problems are of recent vintage. They are a
by-product of two inter-related phenomena: the proliferation of international courts and tribunals; and the
increasingly porous nature of the boundary between
national and international adjudication. If the world
had only one international court, and if the roles of
national and international courts were kept in hermeti-
cally-sealed compartments, these problems would not
arise. But to all but the most unrealistic purist, the
developments in international adjudication which have
spawned problems of parallel jurisdiction will be wel-
comed rather than deplored. The growth in the number
and activity of international tribunals is a sign of the
vitality of international law, and of the preparedness of
States to submit their disputes to pacific settlement. The
increased inter-penetration of the national and interna-

tional spheres also marks the increasing influence of
international law upon domestic legal systems. As
Crawford has reminded us, "there is only one world,
however we may divide it conceptually: there is no
such *place* as the 'international plane'" [743].

In order, however, to appreciate the particular significance of the problems of parallel proceedings in
this field, it is necessary first to expose to view in a
little more detail the hallmarks of modern international
litigation. Accordingly, this chapter will first examine
the judicialization of Public International Law. It will
then be possible in Section B to study the way in which
problems of parallel proceedings have actually arisen
in practice, and some of the express techniques
employed to address it, in the context of human rights
disputes and the law of the sea. Then, Section B, subsection 2, will seek to answer the broader question,
outside the framework of express treaty provision,
whether *lis pendens* is a general principle of law applicable to international tribunals. Finally, Section C will
consider the treatment of related proceedings between
national and international courts, looking in particular
at the way in which pending international litigation has
impacted upon national adjudication. The case-study
for this purpose will be the effect of international processes upon criminal prisoners on Death Row.

It is important to sound a note of caution at the outset of this chapter. Consideration of the issues arising
from parallel litigation in the crucible of the litigation
process is in its infancy in Public International Law.
It could not be otherwise in view of the novelty
of the proliferation of international tribunals. In this
respect, however, the jurisprudence inherently stands in

---

[743] Crawford, "Treaty and Contract in Investment
Arbitration: The 22nd Freshfields Lecture on International
Arbitration", 29 November 2007, 2. Available online at
http://www.lcil.cam.ac.uk.

stark contrast with the developed case-law in both Private International Law and International Arbitration. The methodological implication of this fact for the present study is that, while it is necessary to proceed by way of case-studies, experience suggests that the cases which have arisen so far are likely to represent only a fraction of the possible fact patterns which may arise in the future. Moreover, the reactions of tribunals to these novel problems as matters of first impression may not always offer the best guide to future decision. It is hoped that a critical analysis of them may assist the work of tribunals in the future.

The idea that one of the primary functions of Public International Law is the pacific settlement of disputes is perhaps as old as the idea of Public International Law itself. The first word in Hugo Grotius's *De Jure Belli ac Pacis* (1625) is *Controversiae* — disputes [744]. Yet, as every student of Public International Law knows, that objective has ever been but imperfectly achieved. For much of the post-Westphalian period, the only peaceful method of third party determination according to law which was open to States to settle their disputes was *ad hoc* arbitration [745]. It was not until the First Hague Peace Conference of 1899 that even a Permanent Court of Arbitration was created [746]. The Permanent Court of International Justice, the world's

---

[744] Grotius, *De Jure Belli ac Pacis* (1625, 1707 ed.) 1; a point made by Kingsbury, "The International Legal Order", in Cane and Tushnet (eds.), *Oxford Handbook of Legal Studies* (2003) 271.

[745] Darby, *International Tribunals: A Collection of Various Schemes Which Have Been Propounded and of Instances since 1815* (1899), lists 158 different international arbitral tribunals during the course of the nineteenth-century; see also Stuyt, *Survey of International Arbitrations 1794-1938* (1939).

[746] Convention for the Pacific Settlement of International Disputes (signed 29 July 1899), 187 *CTS* 410.

first permanent international tribunal of general jurisdiction, was not to come until 1920.

But today, despite the fact that the United Nations
Charter describes the International Court of Justice
(ICJ) as "the principal judicial organ of the United
Nations" to which "legal disputes should as a general
rule be referred" [747], the World Court shares its function
in the adjudication of international law disputes with a
host of other courts and tribunals [748]. None of these,
save the ICJ, have general jurisdiction *and* global
reach. On the contrary, they are exercises in specializa-
tion, whether for particular subjects of international
law or for regions.

The most important new tribunals of global reach
but limited subject-matter jurisdiction are the *World
Trade Organization Dispute Settlement Body* and
*Appellate Body* (established in 1994) [749]; the
*International Tribunal for the Law of the Sea* (ITLOS)
(established in 1996) [750]; and the *International
Criminal Court* (established in 1998) [751]. Prior to the

---

[747] Charter of the United Nations (signed 26 June 1945,
entered into force 24 October 1945), 59 Stat. 1031, 145
*UKTS* 805.

[748] Romano, "The Proliferation of International Judicial
Bodies: The Pieces of the Puzzle", (1999) 31 *NYUJILP* 709;
Charney, "Is International Law Threatened by Multiple
International Tribunals?", (1998) 271 *Recueil des cours*
101. Statute of the International Court of Justice (26 June
1945), 59 Stat. 1055.

[749] Dispute Settlement Understanding, 1869 *UNTS* 401,
Annex 2 to Marrakesh Agreement establishing the World
Trade Organization (signed 15 April 1994), 1868 *UNTS* 186.

[750] Statute of the International Tribunal for the Law of
the Sea: United Nations Convention on the Law of the Sea
("UNCLOS") (signed 10 December 1982, entered into
force 16 November 1994), 1833 *UNTS* 3, Annex VI.

[751] Rome Statute of the International Criminal Court
(signed 1 July 1998, entered into force 1 July 2002), 2187
*UNTS* 3.

establishment of the ICC, the UN Security Council created two specialist criminal tribunals in the exercise of its powers under Chapter VII of the UN Charter to "restore international peace and security". These are the *International Criminal Tribunal for the Former Yugoslavia* (ICTY)[752] ; and the *International Criminal Tribunal for Rwanda*[753].

In the field of human rights, there are three important regional courts: the *European Court of Human Rights* (established in 1959, with a right of individual petition added in 1990)[754] ; the *Inter-American Commission* and *Court of Human Rights* (established in 1969)[755] ; and the nascent *African Court on Human and Peoples' Rights* (established by protocol in 1998, which entered into force in 2004)[756]. Further, many of the multilateral treaties in the human rights field (or protocols concluded thereunder) make provision for the appointment of Committees to which complaints against States parties may be made. Although only

---

[752] Established by United Nations Security Council resolution 827 (25 May 1993).

[753] Established by United Nations Security Council resolution 955 (8 November 1994).

[754] European Convention for the Protection of Human Rights and Fundamental Freedoms (signed 4 November 1950, entered into force 3 September 1953), 213 *UNTS* 221, as modified by Protocol No. 11 (signed 11 May 1994, entered into force 1 November 1998), *ETS* No. 155.

[755] American Convention on Human Rights (signed 22 November 1969, entered into force 18 July 1978), 1144 *UNTS* 123 ; Statute of the Inter-American Court of Human Rights (OAS Res. 448).

[756] African Charter on Human and Peoples' Rights (signed 27 June 1981, entered into force 21 October 1986) 1520 *UNTS* 217 ; Protocol to the African Charter on Human And Peoples' Rights on the Establishment of an African Court on Human and Peoples' Rights (signed 10 June 1998, entered into force 25 January 2004), now replaced by Protocol on the Statute of the African Court of Justice and Human Rights (signed 1 July 2008).

quasi-judicial in nature, these Committees nevertheless provide an important forum in which individual complaints of human rights abuse may be heard.

Courts are a significant feature of some regional economic integration agreements, notably the *European Court of Justice*; a range of sub-regional courts in Latin America, and the nascent *African Court of Justice*[757].

Finally, there are bodies established to provide compensation for a specific set of international delicts, notably the *Iran-United States Claims Tribunal*, established under the Algiers Accords to adjudicate claims for the loss of American property following the Iranian Revolution[758], and the *UN Compensation Commission,* which provides a mass claims solution for losses arising out of the Iraqi invasion of Kuwait.

Taken together, the new tribunals represent a significant development in international adjudication generally. Pacific settlement of disputes under international law has moved from an exceptional matter to a pervasive aspect of the modern international legal system. Although their jurisdictional reach is far from complete, the new international tribunals present many more opportunities for Public International Litigation than ever before. Secondly, the new tribunals signal a shift from arbitration to litigation as the dominant mode of international dispute settlement. Arbitration is not excluded altogether. It has an important continuing role in investment law, in the Law of the Sea[759], and where States agree on an *ad hoc* basis. But it has been

---

[757] Protocol of the Court of Justice of the African Union (signed 11 July 2003), now replaced by Protocol on the Statute of the African Court of Justice and Human Rights, *ibid*.

[758] Algiers Accords (signed and entered into force 19 January 1981), 20 *ILM* 230.

[759] Art. 287 and Annex VII, UNCLOS, *supra* footnote 750.

overtaken by the trend towards judicialization. Nowhere is this more strongly demonstrated than in the Dispute Settlement Understanding of the World Trade Organization. Further, while State consent remains the basis for jurisdiction, it is now much more common for that consent to be given on a standing basis, rather than *ad hoc*. Such consent may not be given readily for general jurisdiction (as under the Optional Protocol to the Statute of the International Court), but it is a common feature of the specific subject-matter jurisdiction of many multilateral treaties. In this respect, multilateralism has led to the emergence of a *compulsory* paradigm for international dispute settlement [760]. Finally, even where they acted globally rather than regionally, states have chosen to create new courts and tribunals, rather than to develop a single hierarchical system of courts under the International Court of Justice. The resulting "system" of international adjudication is horizontal, not vertical, with no obvious means of co-ordinating overlapping exercises of jurisdiction.

## 2. *Rationales for the proliferation of international tribunals*

What reasons may be advanced for the numerous new standing tribunals in international law? Examination of this question may in turn shed some light on the basis for their interaction. At least five rationales may be identified: *(a)* some tribunals have been created as a response to a particular international crisis or event, which requires the availability of an adjudicated solution; *(b)* others are the result of a perceived need

---

[760] Oxman, "Complementary Agreements and Compulsory Jurisdiction", (2001) 95 *AJIL* 277; Romano, "The Shift from the Consensual to the Compulsory Paradigm in International Adjudication: Elements for a Theory of Consent", (2007) 39 *NYUJ Int'l L. & Pol.* 791.

for a new international organization to have a judicial organ; or *(c)* they form part of a more general scheme for regional economic integration; *(d)* some of the new tribunals are a concomitant of the particular adjudicatory needs of a specialized field of international law, which could not be catered for by existing tribunals; and finally *(e)* the proliferation of new tribunals has been fostered by a "peace dividend" following the end of the Cold War, which facilitated the achievement of Rule of Law objectives in international law.

A number of the tribunals are in the nature of *ad hoc* responses to specific and localized crises, which required an adjudicated solution. In the case of the International Criminal Tribunals for the former Yugoslavia and Rwanda, the UN Security Council responded to the atrocities committed in two major conflicts with an extension of its Chapter VII powers to create a means of bringing the perpetrators to justice. The Iran-United States Claims Tribunal was established as a result of the Algiers Accords to decide claims arising from the Iranian Revolution; and the UN Compensation Commission was established to provide compensation for losses caused by Iraq as a result of its invasion of Kuwait.

In other cases, however, the new tribunal is intended to add a permanent judicial organ to a newly formed international organization that has been formed by multilateral treaty[761]. The most striking example of this is the new Dispute Settlement Body of the World Trade Organization. One of the prime achievements of the Uruguay Round, successfully concluded in Marrakesh in 1994, was to create a new international organization for the administration of international trade, which facilitated the *judicial* settlement of trade disputes.

---

[761] See generally, Blokker and Schermers, (eds.), *Proliferation of International Organizations* (2001).

Thus, the establishment of the Dispute Settlement Body, as the supervisory body for dispute panels, and the Appellate Body, came to be seen as an integral part of the new Organization[762]. The Dispute Settlement Understanding is thus itself one of the Covered Agreements to which member States must adhere. The consequence of this is that the panels and the Appellate Body possess compulsory jurisdiction over member States in relation to disputes which fall within their competence *ratione materiae*. In this way, all member States enjoy a level playing field for the binding resolution of trade disputes. However, as Thirlway has aptly put it, "an international organisation is not *per se* a society in need of a judiciary"[763]. There are many modern international organizations which have been brought into being without their own standing judicial organ. States have preferred instead to leave any subsequent disputes between them either to existing tribunals; or to arbitration; or negotiation[764]. Further, in the environmental field in particular, States have often

---

[762] A consensus on the need for such a co-ordinated judicial system did not emerge until relatively late in the negotiation process. Thus the idea of an appeal mechanism in the dispute settlement system "to correct exceptional errors in the legal reasoning of panel decisions and to help ensure swift implementation of recommendations or rulings" did not emerge in the formal *travaux* of the Negotiating Group on Dispute Settlement until a proposal of Mexico after the mid-term review in 1990: WTO Negotiating Group on Dispute Settlement: Proposal by Mexico (12 July 1990), MTN.GNG/NG13/W/42; Report by the Chairman (18 July 1990), MTN.GNG/NG13/W/43; Draft Text on Dispute Settlement (21 September 1990) MTN.GNG/NG13/W/45.

[763] Thirlway, "The Proliferation of International Judicial Organs: Institutional and Substantive Questions", in Blokker and Schermers, *supra* footnote 761, 251, 253.

[764] See *infra*, Section B 1 *(b)* for a discussion of the impact of this in the *Southern Bluefin Tuna* litigation.

experimented with different types of bodies to secure compliance with treaty obligations[765].

One arena in which new courts have proliferated has been in the context of regional economic integration agreements. The European Communities had from the outset their own judicial organ, which was seen as an essential element in the achievement of the goals of the community in terms of closer economic integration. The European Court of Justice has repeatedly emphasized the importance of this goal in the exercise of its functions to achieve a consistent application of Community legal texts. The tendency for regional economic integration agreements to include provision for a new court has not been confined to Europe. There are examples of such courts also in Africa, Latin America and the Arab world. One reason for this may include the need for all members to ensure compliance with the obligations in the agreement. The traditional remedies of Public International Law (counter-measures and withdrawal) may prove quite inadequate for as a protection in particular for smaller or weaker States in the union[766]. In any event, the shared project of economic integration may itself propel legal convergence, and the need for consistency in its application. States which have already found the requisite degree of common purpose to achieve regional economic integration may find it easier to accept a common adjudicatory body. That said, there are a number of economic integration agreements which do not create an international judicial tribunal[767]. Prominent amongst these are the North American Free

---

[765] Sands *International Environmental Law* (2nd ed., 2003), Chap. 5.

[766] Romano, *supra* footnote 748, 735-738.

[767] For example, there is no standing tribunal under the Closer Economic Relations Trade Agreement between Australia and New Zealand (signed 28 March 1983, entered into force 1 March 1983), 1329 *UNTS* 175.

Trade Agreement (NAFTA)[768]. Many new model Free Trade Agreements make provision for arbitration of disputes (both between member States and between States and private parties), but do not create standing tribunals.

A third reason for the establishment of new tribunals has been the growing density and specificity of international law[769]. Thus, ITLOS does not form part of an international organization. But the establishment of the Tribunal was a key part of the package of mandatory dispute settlement constituted by the UN Law of the Sea Convention[770]. The Tribunal's functions include the establishment of a Chamber to decide seabed disputes. In that context, the Tribunal is linked to the International Seabed Authority established under Part XI of the Convention. But the Court's remit is much wider than such disputes, extending to "all disputes and applications submitted to it in accordance with this Convention and all matters specifically provided for in any other agreement which confers jurisdiction on the Tribunal"[771].

---

[768] North American Free Trade Agreement (signed 17 December 1992, entered into force 1 January 1994), 107 *Stat.* 2057, (1993) 32 *ILM* 289. The MERCOSUR Agreement also adopts an arbitration model, although the awards of *ad hoc* arbitral tribunals may, since 2004, be reviewed by a Permanent Review Court of Arbitrators: Olivos Protocol for the Solution of Controversies in the Mercosur (signed 18 February 2002, entered into force 1 January 2004), 2251 *UNTS* 288.

[769] Higgins, "A Babel of Judicial Voices? Ruminations from the Bench", (2006) 55 *ICLQ* 791, 799; Shany, *The Competing Jurisdictions of International Courts and Tribunals* (2003) 3.

[770] On the mandatory character of the dispute settlement provisions of UNCLOS see Keith J (dissenting) in *Southern Bluefin Tuna, infra,* footnote 782, [24]-[29], citing from the *travaux préparatoires.*

[771] Art. 21, Statute of the International Tribunal for the Law of the Sea, *supra* footnote 750; Thirlway, *supra* footnote 763, 254-255.

In some other cases, it is the nature of the *parties* to the dispute, which have impelled the creation of a tribunal, or the expansion of its jurisdiction — as in the case of individual rights of petition to human rights tribunals[772]. Indeed, inter-State complaints are a relatively rare feature of international human rights jurisprudence. The Inter-American Court of Human Rights even permits an NGO legally recognized in an OAS country to lodge a petition before it[773]. Nevertheless, this factor on its own does not explain the great proliferation of different human rights tribunals and quasi-tribunals.

For this, the answer must be found partly in the attempts to secure more effective protection of human rights on a regional basis; and partly in the way in which the broad principles of the Universal Declaration of Human Rights 1948 have been elaborated in a succession of separate treaties, each with their own Committee to handle complaints of breaches of the relevant convention. The work of these committees is loosely co-ordinated by the High Commissioner for Human Rights in Geneva, who also compiles their general comments with a view to promoting consistency of approach. But each Committee carries a separate responsibility for the treaty under which it was created.

Finally, most of the new tribunals have been created in that last 15 years, since the end of the Cold War[774]. The reversal of superpower intransigence removed the practical impediments to agreement on new international tribunals, making it possible, for example, for

---

[772] See Pinto, "Fragmentation or Unification among International Institutions: Human Rights Tribunals", (1999) 31 *NYUJILP* 833.

[773] American Convention on Human Rights, *supra* footnote 755, Art. 44; and see Pinto, *ibid.*, 837.

[774] Romano, *supra* footnote 748, 729-735.

the UN Security Council to agree on resolutions to create the Yugoslav and Rwandan tribunals. The high-water-mark of this development came at the end of the decade with the creation of the International Criminal Court.

The negotiation of the Rome Statute represented an extraordinary degree of consensus amongst States [775] and civil society as to the need for a new international court to try international crimes. The International Law Commission had considered proposals for a draft code of crimes against the peace and security of mankind in the 1950s, but its work had garnered no acceptance by States in the Cold War era. Then, in 1981, the General Assembly revived its mandate [776] ; and, in 1989 specifically extended it to consideration of the establishment of an international criminal court [777]. The Commission's Working Group on this issue, reporting in 1992 [778], said pithily:

> "The case for some international jurisdictional mechanism starts from the fact that since 1945 there have been notorious cases of crimes against humanity that have gone unpunished. It has proved extremely difficult to bring the offenders to justice, and the lack of any alternative forum at the international level has exacerbated these difficulties ... In some of these cases, there is no effective prospect of trial in any national court." [779]

Yet, from its earliest conception by the Commission,

---

[775] With the notable exception of the United States.

[776] UNGA, A/Res/36/106 of 10 December 1981.

[777] UNGA, A/Res/44/39 of 4 December 1989.

[778] International Law Commission, "Report of the Working Group on the Question of an International Criminal Jurisdiction", in *Yearbook of the International Law Commission* (1992, Vol. II (2)), Annex 58.

[779] *Ibid.*, 62.

the Court was seen as complementary to, and not as pre-empting, the work of national courts[780].

## 3. Polycentric nature of modern disputes

This brief account of the creation of the new tribunals indicates that there are now manifold contexts in which parallel Public International Litigation can arise. As the ICTY Appeals Chamber observed:

> "International law, because it lacks a centralized structure, does not provide for an integrated judicial system operating in an orderly division of labour among a number of tribunals, where certain aspects of components of jurisdiction as a power could be centralized or vested in one of them but not the others."[781]

This means in turn that "[t]here is frequently a parallelism of treaties, both in their substantive content and in their provisions for settlement of disputes arising thereunder"[782]. Only on relatively rare occasions will such parallelism arise between two tribunals exercising general jurisdiction, which is, after all, the norm in Private International Litigation. Even the few international courts of general jurisdiction (most notably the International Court itself) mostly entertain cases as a

---

[780] International Law Commission, Working Group on a Draft Statute for an International Criminal Court, "Report of the Working Group" (19 July 1994), UN doc. A/CN.4/L.491/Rev.2/Add.1, 2.

[781] *Prosecutor* v. *Tadić* (ICTY, Appeals Chamber, Decision on Jurisdiction of 2 October 1995), 105 *ILR* 419, 458 (emphasis added).

[782] *Southern Bluefin Tuna (Australia and New Zealand v. Japan)* (Award on Jurisdiction of 4 August 2000), 119 *ILR* 508 (UNCLOS, Annex VII, Tribunal, Schwebel P, Feliciano, Tresselt, Yamada; Keith dissenting but not on this point) [52].

result of specific agreement of the parties, whether by treaty or *compromis,* which is limited as to subject-matter[783]. The jurisdiction of most international tribunals is limited as to subject-matter by the treaty conferring jurisdiction. This raises directly the question whether the subject-matter of one treaty can ever be treated as the same as that of another, even if the two claims arise out of the same factual matrix — a point which arose in acute form in both of the Law of the Sea cases to be discussed below[784], and on which the tribunals took no consistent view. It will be argued below that the separate treaty source of both the parties' substantive obligations and of the power of the tribunal itself does *not* carry with it any inevitable consequence that related proceedings may, or ought to be, ignored.

So, too, it will be clear from the above account that many instances of closely related proceedings in Public International Litigation will not arise between the same parties. The great expansion in both individual redress and individual responsibility before international tribunals opens the possibility of concurrent proceedings in one international tribunal relating to the position of the individual as well as in another in respect of the state, both of which arise out of the same factual matrix. A narrow conception of the present topic might exclude these cases altogether on the grounds of lack of identity of parties. But this would be to exclude an examination of the effect of such close overlap of cases arising out of the same facts upon the exercise of each tribunal's jurisdiction. The point made in Chapter I was that this is to confuse the *situation* of parallel proceed-

---

[783] Collier and Lowe, *The Settlement of Disputes in International Law*: *Institutions and Procedures* (2000) 132-155.

[784] *Infra* Section B 1 (B).

ings (whether or not precisely identical) with the particular solution offered by a strict *lis pendens* rule.

In the case of both subject-matter and parties, it is only by examining the range of different contexts in which parallel proceedings arising out of the same facts may arise that it will be possible to separate the different problems, and to design solutions for them. In this task, the traditional tools of identity of parties and cause offer some useful guidance but do not complete the picture. These points may be made good by contrasting the *Serbian Genocide* Cases in the ICTY and the ICJ on (respectively) individual and State responsibility for genocide in Bosnia *(a)*; and the *Softwood Lumber* anti-dumping and subsidies dispute between Canada and the United States, which has been played out between the WTO DSU, the dispute settlement procedures of NAFTA (as they apply to both the States and to private litigants) and the national courts of the relevant States *(b)*.

(a) *Concurrent individual and State responsibility for international crimes*

On 20 March 1993, Bosnia brought a claim against Serbia in the International Court alleging violations of the Convention on the Prevention and Punishment of the Crime of Genocide 1948[785]. Bosnia alleged that Serbia had committed genocide of Bosnian Muslims in numerous ways during the course of the armed conflict in Bosnia during the period 1992-1995, culminating in the massacre at Srebrenica in 1995. The case in the ICJ had an extremely convoluted history[786], as a result of

---

[785] Case concerning the *Application of the Convention on the Prevention and Punishment of the Crime of Genocide (Bosnia and Herzegovina* v. *Serbia and Montenegro)* (26 February 2007), General List No 91 ("the *Serbian Genocide* case").

[786] *Ibid.*, [1]-[63].

which the hearings on the merits phase did not take place until 2006. In the interim, the ICTY had been established in pursuant to UN Security Council resolution 827 of 25 May 1993. The Prosecutor issued the first indictment under the auspices of the Tribunal in 1994[787]. Since then, the Tribunal has indicted 161 persons. The Tribunal and the Appeals Chamber have delivered numerous judgments determining individual criminal responsibility. One of those, *Krstić*, involved conviction on a finding of genocide[788]. In so doing the Tribunal heard evidence and made many findings of both law and fact as to the events in Bosnia in the period which was also the subject of Bosnia's ICJ proceedings alleging Serbia's responsibility as a State[789].

The question for the ICJ was what use it ought to make of all of this material. The Court held that the fact-finding processes of the ICTY could be treated as " 'evidence obtained by examination of persons directly involved', tested by cross-examination, the credibility of which has not been challenged subsequently"[790]. The Court went on to identify the decisions made within the ICTY at the various stages of the criminal process. It held

"that it should in principle accept as highly per-

---

[787] *Prosecutor* v. *Tadić*, Case No. IT-94-1-I (ICTY, Indictment), http://www.un.org/icty/indictment/english/tad-ii950213e.htm.

[788] *Prosecutor* v. *Krstić*, Case No. IT-98-33-A (ICTY, Appeals Chamber, Judgment of 19 April 2004).

[789] See Fourteenth Annual Report of the International Tribunal for the Prosecution of Persons Responsible for Serious Violations of International Humanitarian Law Committed in the Territory of the Former Yugoslavia since 1991 (1 August 2007), UN doc. A/62/172-S/2007/469.

[790] *Supra* footnote 785, [214], applying the formulation in its judgment in *Armed Activities on the Territory of the Congo (Democratic Republic of the Congo* v. *Uganda)*, *ICJ Rep. 2005* 168, [61].

suasive relevant findings of fact made by the Tribunal at trial, unless of course they have been upset on appeal. For the same reasons, any evaluation by the Tribunal based on the facts as so found for instance about the existence of the required intent, is also entitled to due weight."[791]

Thus far, the Court's use of the ICTY material appears not merely unobjectionable, but also sensible and appropriate. The unusual course of events in that case did not in fact require the Court to issue a stay of proceedings pending the work of the ICTY. But the vicissitudes of the litigation produced that result in any event, delivering a considerable corpus of judicial findings to which reference could be made. But what position ought the Court to have taken if the proceedings before it had not been delayed? In view of the creation of the ICTY with a specific mandate to investigate and try international crimes committed in the former Yugoslavia, there would have been a strong case for the Court to stay its proceedings as a matter of case management.

But two major caveats must be entered to this approach: one as to the necessary implications of the fact that the ICJ had to render a decision while the work of the ICTY was still proceeding; and the second as to the essential difference in the task entrusted to each tribunal. In a critical passage in the judgment, the Court drew support for its decision to limit any finding in relation to genocide to the events at Srebrenica from a number of decisions of the Tribunal and the Prosecutor on other matters[792]. This included cases, such as that of *Milosević* himself, where the accused had died in the course of proceedings; as well as others where

---

[791] *Ibid.*, [223].
[792] *Ibid.*, [374].

the indictment was still pending. As Goldstone (the first Chief Prosecutor of the ICTY) comments:

> "In doing so, the Court implies that had Milosević, for example, survived trial and been convicted of the crimes for which he was indicted, or had Karadzić and Mladić been arrested and brought to trial, then the Court might have reached a different outcome." [793]

The function of the ICJ was not, after all, to determine whether particular individuals whom it had been possible to bring to trial in The Hague could be found individually guilty of committing genocide. Rather it was to decide whether Serbia, as a State, was responsible for genocide. An approach, therefore, which offers undue deference to the work of another tribunal may risk undermining the mandate of the court in question.

(b) *Concurrent regional and international trade law proceedings*

In contrast to the deferential approach taken the International Court to the jurisprudence of the ICTY, the myriad of tribunals involved in the Canadian Softwood Lumber trade dispute frequently proceeded along parallel lines, without regard to the larger systemic implications arising from the multiplication of endeavour[794]. The cases all involve the same under-

---

[793] Goldstone and Hamilton, "*Bosnia* v. *Serbia*: Lesson from the Encounter of the International Court of Justice with the International Criminal Tribunal for the Former Yugoslavia", (2008) 21 *Leiden JIL* 95, 105-106.

[794] On this very complex litigation see: Carmody, (2006) 100 *AJIL* 664; Pauwelyn, (2006) 9 *JIEL* 197; Bjorklund, (2007) 59 *Hastings LJ* 241, 274-285; Sandford, [2005] *Can. Ybk IL* 297; Mota and Rao, (2007) 1 *World Arb. & Med. Rev.* 539. For an additional example in the trade field, see Lavranos, "Competing Jurisdictions between MERCOSUR and WTO", (2008) 7 *LPICT* 205.

lying factual matrix, namely the exceptionally long-running dispute between Canada and the United States (and their respective timber producers). In essence, this concerns whether the conditions under which timber is milled in Canada amounts to a subsidy by the Canadian Government; and, in turn, whether, and to what extent, the United States is entitled to impose anti-dumping or countervailing duties in response. Earlier disputes between the two States were settled by an agreement in 1996, which expired on 31 March 2001. Two days later, a coalition of American timber producers filed new petitions against Canadian timber imports, thus provoking a round of disputes, known collectively as *Softwood Lumber IV*.

These disputes were litigated at three levels simultaneously: nationally in the United States Court of International Trade; regionally under NAFTA (by both Canada as a State and by Canadian timber producers); and internationally under the WTO DSU. Most, but not quite all, of the litigation has now been settled by agreement between the two States[795]. Scholars of General International Law may perhaps be relieved to know that the complex substantive issues litigated in these proceedings relating to subsidisation and anti-dumping are not germane to the present enquiry. Rather, the question is simply how the respective tribunals dealt with the existence of parallel proceedings.

The framers of NAFTA anticipated the potential for overlap in dispute settlement between their regional

---

[795] WTO, *United States — Final Countervailing Duty Determination with Respect to Certain Softwood Lumber from Canada*, Notification of Mutually Agreed Solution (16 November 2006), WT/DS257/26, G/L/539/Add.1, G/SCM/D45/2. But see the subsequent arbitration pursuant to Art. XIV (6) of the Settlement Agreement: *USA* v. *Canada* (Award on Liability), LCIA Case No. 7941 (2008, Böckstiegel P, Hanotiau and Veeder).

agreement and the WTO. Article 2005 (1) of NAFTA permits the complainant State to choose between either forum for its dispute. Article 2005 (6) then stipulates that such a choice operates as an election, to the exclusion of the alternative remedy[796]. However, the general dispute settlement provisions of Chapter 20 (in which Article 2005 appears) do not apply to anti-dumping cases, which are dealt with in Chapter 19[797]. Chapter 19 establishes its own unique regime of bi-national panels to determine such cases, which may be brought by States or affected parties and which are mandated to apply the national law of the importing State to their review[798]. The parties may elect as to whether they utilize the bi-national panel procedure, or the national courts of the requesting State.

The WTO Appellate Body, however, has taken the view that the rights of member States to invoke the dispute settlement procedures of the Dispute Settlement Understanding are not subject to qualification by reason of the existence of alternative fora under NAFTA. In *Mexico — Tax Measures on Soft Drinks and Other Beverages*[799], Mexico had contended that Panel ought to have declined to exercise its jurisdiction to determine the dispute before it, since it was inextricably linked to a wider dispute with the United States as to access for Mexican cane sugar, which could only be litigated within NAFTA, and where the United States had wrongfully refused to nominate panelists to a NAFTA Panel, thus blocking determination of that wider dispute. The Appellate Body rejected this argument. It held that:

---

[796] Save in cases relating to the protection of the environment and health, which are the subject of specific provision under Art. 2005 (3) and (4): *supra* footnote 768.

[797] *Ibid.*, Art. 2004.

[798] *Ibid.*, Art. 1904.

[799] WTO Appellate Body (6 March 2006), WT/DS308/AB/R, DSR 2006: 1, 3.

"A decision by a panel to decline to exercise validly established jurisdiction would seem to 'diminish' the right of a complaining Member to 'seek the redress of a violation of obligations' within the meaning of Article 23 of the DSU, and to bring a dispute pursuant to Article 3.3 of the DSU. This would not seem to be consistent with a panel's obligations under Articles 3.2 and 19.2 of the DSU. We see no reason, therefore, to disagree with the Panel's statement that a WTO panel 'would seem . . . not to be in a position to choose freely whether or not to exercise its jurisdiction'." [800]

It did, however, go on to make clear that it was not expressing a view on whether a closer identity of subject-matter and claim as between the two matters might make a difference. The Appellate Body observed that:

"Nevertheless, Mexico does not take issue with the Panel's finding that 'neither the subject matter nor the respective positions of the parties are identical in the dispute under the NAFTA . . . and the dispute before us'. Mexico also stated that it could not identify a legal basis that would allow it to raise, in a WTO dispute settlement proceeding, the market access claims it is pursuing under the NAFTA. It is furthermore undisputed that no NAFTA Panel as yet has decided the 'broader dispute' to which Mexico has alluded. Finally, we note that Mexico has expressly stated that the so-called 'exclusion clause' of Article 2005.6 of the NAFTA has not been 'exercised'. We do not express any view on whether a legal impediment to the exercise of a panel's jurisdiction would exist in the event that features such as those mentioned above were present." [801]

---

[800] *Ibid.*, [53] (references omitted).
[801] *Ibid.*, [54] (references omitted).

In *Softwood Lumber IV,* the fact that the claim under Chapter 19 of NAFTA was a claim under United States law, as an alternative to litigation before the United States Court of International Trade, whereas the WTO claim was brought under the WTO Covered Agreements as a matter of international law, was sufficient to mask any direct consideration of *lis pendens,* despite the close parallelism between the two sets of proceedings on the facts.

Some rationalization was achieved in arbitral proceedings brought by the Canadian producers themselves under the investment arbitration provisions of Chapter XI of NAFTA.

Detailed provisions for consolidation are to be found in NAFTA Article 1126. In *Canfor,* a Consolidation Tribunal established under the express provisions of that article decided to consolidate and hear a series of cases on antidumping duty in the softwood lumber industry against the United States[802]. The Order in *Canfor* represents a particularly elaborate consideration of the requirements of Article 1126. The Tribunal found the overriding object and purpose of the procedure to be that of "procedural economy"[803]. It treated this as an objective test, to be judged against the position which would obtain were no consolidation to be ordered. The Tribunal identified three factors which would bear on that question: (i) time, (ii) costs, and (iii) the avoidance of conflicting decisions[804].

---

[802] *Canfor Corp.* v. *United States of America, Tembec et al.* v. *United States of America, Terminal Forest Products Ltd.* v. *United States of America* (Order of the Consolidation Tribunal) (NAFTA, 2005, van den Berg P, de Mestral and Robinson).

[803] *Ibid.,* [73]; accord: Alvarez, "Arbitration under the North American Free Trade Agreement", (2000) 16 *Arb. Int'l* 393, 414.

[804] *Ibid.,* [126].

Deprecating the result in the *Lauder/CME* v. *Czech Republic* cases [805], it observed:

> "The desirability of avoiding conflicting results is not limited to cases where the parties are the same. Cases with different parties may present the same legal issues arising out of the same event or related to the same measure. Conflicting results then may take place if the findings with respect to those issues differ in two or more cases." [806]

The Arbitral Tribunal hearing the consolidated claims then decided that the specific provisions of Chapter 19 barred the pursuit of the Chapter 11 arbitration [807], save in respect of a specific provision of US law, which had only been introduced since NAFTA [808].

The US Court of International Trade has also had to consider the interrelation of its proceedings with those under NAFTA. In *Ontario Forest Industries Assoc* v. *United States* [809], the two States parties were already far advanced in settlement negotiations for the dispute as a whole. The Court was nevertheless pressed with an argument by Canadian producers that it should intervene to force the United States to appoint its members to an Extraordinary Challenge Committee to hear a pending appeal from the decision of a NAFTA bi-

---

[805] Chapter III, Section C 5.

[806] *Ibid.*, [133].

[807] *Canfor Corp.* v. *United States of America, Terminal Forest Products Ltd.* v. *United States of America* (Decision on Preliminary Question) (NAFTA, 2006, van den Berg P, de Mestral and Robinson).

[808] The Continued Dumping and Subsidy Offset Act 2000, inserting a new Section 754 into the Tariff Act 1930 (repealed 8 February 2006).

[809] 444 F. Supp. 2d 1309 (CIT, 2006); see also *Tembec Inc.* v. *United States*, 441 F. Supp. 2d 1302 (CIT, 2006), Appendix A, where the history of the proceedings under the WTO and NAFTA is set out.

national panel. The Court found that it had jurisdiction, but held that:

> "Although courts have a 'virtually unflagging obligation' to exercise jurisdiction which is conferred by Congress[810] . . . federal courts do have the power to dismiss or remand a case based on abstention principles where the relief being sought is equitable or discretionary . . ."[811]

Finding that the relief sought here was equitable or discretionary, the Court continued:

> "Typically, 'courts . . . grapple with the issue of abstention in the context of parallel state court proceedings . . . Nevertheless, in the interest of *international comity,* [courts] apply the same general principles with respect to parallel proceedings in a foreign court'[812] . . . If international comity warrants abstention, the court may dismiss the case."[813]

The Court then held that the bi-national panel system under NAFTA should be treated as equivalent to a foreign court for the purpose of the application of the principle of comity, and cited Ginsburg J in *Medellin I* in the Supreme Court as authority for the proposition that the same principle should also apply to international courts[814]. The Court found the principle of comity applicable here to require abstention, since

---

[810] Citing *Colorado River Water Conservation Dist.* v. *United States*, 424 US 800, 821, 96 S. Ct. 1236 (1976), discussed *supra* Chapter II, Section A 3.

[811] *Supra* footnote 809, 1326, citing *Quackenbush* v. *Allstate Ins. Co.* 517 US 706, 730, 116 S. Ct. 1712 (1996).

[812] Citing *Finova Capital Corp* v. *Ryan Helicopters USA, Inc.*, 180 F. 3d 896, 898 (7th Cir., 1999).

[813] *Supra* footnote 809, 1326.

[814] *Ibid.*, 1327, citing *Medellin* v. *Dretke*, 544 US 660, 670, 125 S. Ct. 2088 (2005) (Ginsburg J concurring), discussed *infra*, Section C 2 *(a)*.

NAFTA had made explicit provision for a remedy in the event of the failure to constitute a panel, but no like provision for an Extraordinary Committee. The statutory requirement on the US courts to provide assistance was limited to cases where it had been requested by a panel or committee, and there was a strong judicial interest in securing the settlement of the litigation, which was currently in progress [815].

Once, therefore, the labyrinthine complexities of the *Softwood Lumber IV* dispute are cleared away, it may be seen that international economic law is as much rich territory for parallel litigation as other fields of law. In the particular context of North America, the position is complicated by two facts. First, all three States are parties to both NAFTA and the WTO. The WTO Covered Agreements contain no explicit rules which require a panel to decline jurisdiction in the light of parallel or related litigations. The rule of election in NAFTA does not apply to all possibly overlapping disputes, nor does it apply in the case of anti-dumping litigation. Second, NAFTA's own dispute settlement procedures in this field are highly decentralised. In anti-dumping cases, they permit a party to choose either the bi-national panel system or a domestic court. In either event, the applicable law is national law not international law. There are provisions for consolidation of Chapter 11 tribunals, but not otherwise.

The response of individual tribunals to the issue of parallel proceedings reflected the spectrum of possible solutions. The WTO Appellate Body had previously asserted, in effect, its version of the "virtually unflagging obligation" doctrine referred to in the American cases, which requires panels to assume jurisdiction irrespective of concurrent litigation. It left open, however, the possibility that a different rule might apply in

---

[815] *Ibid.*, 1328-1329.

cases where there was complete identity of claims in the competing tribunals. In the *Softwood Lumber IV* cases themselves, no such identity could arise, since the claims made before the Bi-national Panels simply sought the application of US law, and involved both Canada as a State and Canadian exporters as parties. The WTO claims, by contrast, were concerned only with the obligations of Canada and the United States, judged according to international law. The Chapter 11 tribunals had an available mechanism to achieve consolidation under NAFTA and showed readiness to adopt an expansive approach to the avoidance of conflicting results, which included cases raising the same legal issues, even if they were not between the same parties. The US Court of International Trade exercised its discretion not to intervene in the NAFTA procedure on grounds of international comity, but applied it to deny relief in a way which could, had the cases not been settled, have led to a denial of justice. In many of the cases, one sees the courts reaching for principles by way of analogy from other contexts in which parallel proceedings may arise in view of the fact that the problems could not, by their nature, be solved merely by internal consideration of the relevant treaty or national legislation.

In view of the resulting complexity, it is perhaps unsurprising that, when the States settled their differences in 2006, they included a new provision in the Settlement Agreement which provided for disputes under it to be settled by inter-State arbitration under the Rules of the London Court of International Arbitration. The provision went on:

> "Except as provided for in this Article, for the duration of the [Settlement Agreement], neither Party shall initiate any litigation or dispute settlement proceedings with respect to any matter arising

under the [Settlement Agreement], including pro-
ceedings pursuant to the Marrakesh Agreement
Establishing the World Trade Organization or
Chapter Twenty of the NAFTA."[816]

This solution is reminiscent of that to which litigants were driven in medieval times in choosing arbitration in the face of a multiplicity of courts with overlapping jurisdictions[817]. The critical question, then, is
the extent to which rules or principles may be found
within international law which may serve to mediate
the inevitable conflicts of jurisdiction between tribunals. It is to a consideration of the sources for such
guidance, both in express treaty language and in the
application of general principles of law, that this
lecture must now turn.

## B. *Relationships between International Tribunals*

### 1. *Express provision*

In searching for solutions to the overlapping jurisdictions of international tribunals, it is necessary to distinguish between cases in which the treaty establishing
the tribunal makes express provision for its inter-rela-
tionship with the jurisdictions of other courts and tribunals, and cases where there is no express provision. In
practice, it is much more common for there to be no
express provision. In that event, the effect of any parallel proceedings can only be considered on the basis of
any relevant general principles of law applicable to
international tribunals. The question whether *lis pendens* is such a principle, and the possible consequences
of that, are considered in Section B, subsection 2, below.
There are, however, some notable examples in treaty

---

[816] Art. XIV (2) *supra* footnote 795.
[817] Chapter III, Section A 1.

practice in which an express regime of interaction has been provided. It is proposed here to discuss first briefly the election mechanism adopted in human rights treaties *(a)*. Then the complex provisions of the UN Convention on the Law of the Sea will be discussed *(b)*. These have given rise to two important, and troubling, cases on parallel proceedings: *Southern Bluefin Tuna* and *MOX Plant*. Both cases illustrate a more general limitation of express treaty provision for conflict of jurisdiction. Such rules, by the nature, are unilateral, and not multilateral, conflicts rules. They regulate the exercise of the tribunal endowed with jurisdiction under the treaty in question. But all cases of conflict of jurisdiction involve two tribunals under two different treaty regimes. As will be seen, it is quite possible for each such regime to take a different approach to the priority of proceedings. In this event, it will be necessary to look beyond *lex specialis* to the general law to resolve the conflict.

### (a) *Human rights*

The field of international human rights protection provides some of the most fertile sources of parallel litigation, since the right of individual petition applies simultaneously to substantially the same rights in many different international and regional conventions. In most cases, the potential overlap of proceedings has been dealt with by express rules of precedence in the relevant treaty arrangements[818].

The International Covenant on Civil and Political Rights 1966 provided generally that its provisions shall apply without prejudice to other UN procedures and shall not prevent the States parties from having

---

[818] Shany, *supra* footnote 769, 59-66 and 197-199 contains detailed citation to the jurisprudence of the human rights bodies on these rules.

recourse to other dispute settlement mechanisms in force between them[819]. However, the right of individual petition to the Human Rights Committee under the Optional Protocol permits the Committee to deal with individual communications only insofar as there is no actual *lis pendens* before another international procedure. Article 5 (2) provides:

> "The Committee shall not consider any communication from an individual unless it has ascertained that:
>
> *(a)* The same matter is not being examined under another procedure of international investigation or settlement."[820]

A number of States have gone further and entered a reservation upon becoming party to the Protocol to the effect that

> "the Human Rights Committee shall not have competence to consider a communication from an individual if the same matter is being examined *or has already been considered* under another procedure of international investigation or settlement"[821].

This provision, which requires the individual to elect his form of international complaint procedure, resulted principally from a recommendation to the Council of Europe in order to avoid the possibility of decisions of

---

[819] Art. 44, International Covenant on Civil and Political Rights (signed 16 December 1966, entered into force 23 March 1976), 999 *UNTS* 171.

[820] Optional Protocol to the International Covenant on Civil and Political Rights (signed 16 December 1966, entered into force 23 March 1976), 999 *UNTS* 302, Art. 5 (2).

[821] http://www.unhchr.ch/html/menu3/b/treaty6_asp. htm (emphasis added).

the Committee conflicting with those of the European Commission and Court[822].

The European Convention on Human Rights 1950 already contained a mirror provision precluding proceedings before the European Court once the case has been submitted to another international procedure:

> "The Court shall not deal with any application submitted under Article 34 [the provision for individual petitions] that ... *(b)* is substantially the same as a matter that has already been examined by the Court or has already been submitted to another procedure of international investigation or settlement and contains no new relevant information."[823]

### (b) *The Law of the Sea*

The United Nations Convention on the Law of the Sea 1982 (UNCLOS)[824] establishes, in Part XV, a system of arbitration of disputes under the Convention, or litigation before ITLOS. But the framers of the Convention sought to respect (perhaps to a fault) the freedom of States to choose their own methods of dispute settlement — judicial or otherwise. There are two key provisions of the Convention, which have already given rise to difficulty in practice. These are Articles 281 and 282, which provide as follows:

---

[822] Report of the Committee of Experts to the Committee of Ministers of the Council of Europe (29 February 1968), Doc. No. CM (68) 39.

[823] Originally Art. 27 (1) *(b)* of the European Convention for the Protection of Human Rights and Fundamental Freedoms, *supra* footnote 754, renumbered Art. 35 (2) *(b)* by Protocol No. 11 to the European Convention for the Protection of Human Rights and Fundamental Freedoms, *supra* footnote 754, Art. 1.

[824] *Supra* footnote 750.

*"Article 281*

*Procedure where no settlement has been reached
by the parties*

1. If the States Parties which are parties to a dispute concerning the interpretation or application of this Convention have agreed to seek settlement of the dispute by a peaceful means of their own choice, the procedures provided for in this Part apply only where no settlement has been reached by recourse to such means and the agreement between the parties does not exclude any further procedure.

. . . . . . . . . . . . . . . . . . . . . . . . . . . .

*Article 282*

*Obligations under general, regional or bilateral
agreements*

If the States Parties which are parties to a dispute concerning the interpretation or application of this Convention have agreed, through a general, regional or bilateral agreement or otherwise, that such dispute shall, at the request of any party to the dispute, be submitted to a procedure that entails a binding decision, that procedure shall apply in lieu of the procedures provided for in this Part, unless the parties to the dispute otherwise agree."

The meaning and scope of each of these rules of election — which permit parties to choose other forms of dispute settlement than those prescribed by the Law of the Sea Convention itself were tested in two key disputes: *Southern Bluefin Tuna*[825], which was concerned

_____

[825] *Ibid.*; Oxman, *supra* footnote 760; Mansfield, "Compulsory Dispute Settlement after the Southern Bluefin Tuna Award", in Elferink and Rothwell (eds.), *Oceans Management in the 21st Century: Institutional Frameworks and Responses* (2004) 255; Stephens, *International Courts and Environmental Protection* (2009), Chap. 9.

with Article 281; and *MOX Plant*[826], which was concerned with Article 282.

In *Southern Bluefin Tuna,* Australia, New Zealand and Japan had entered into a treaty, the Convention for the Conservation of Southern Bluefin Tuna 1993 (CCSBT), the purpose of which was to seek to provide a basis for an agreed management of the fishing stocks of this highly-migratory species of tuna — which had declined precipitously since commercial fishing of the stocks had begun in the 1960s. The CCSBT had been prepared in the light of UNCLOS, but before UNCLOS had come into force in the three States[827]. Article 16 of the CCSBT provided:

> "1. If any dispute arises between two or more of the Parties concerning the interpretation or implementation of this Convention, those Parties shall consult among themselves with a view to having the dispute resolved by negotiation, inquiry, mediation, conciliation, arbitration, judicial settlement or other peaceful means of their own choice.
>
> 2. Any dispute of this character not so resolved shall, with the consent in each case of all parties to the dispute, be referred for settlement to the International Court of Justice or to arbitration; but failure to reach agreement on reference to the International Court of Justice or to arbitration shall not absolve parties to the dispute from the responsibility of continuing to seek to resolve it by any of the various peaceful means referred to in paragraph 1 above."[828]

When the parties were unable to reach agreement as to the quotas of fish stocks applicable to each of them,

---

[826] For references see *infra*, footnotes 838-841.

[827] *Supra* footnote 782, [29].

[828] Convention for the Conservation of Southern Bluefin Tuna (signed 10 May 1993, entered into force 20 May 1994), 1819 *UNTS* 360, Art. 16.

and as to Japan's claim to be able to undertake an experimental fishing programme in addition to commercial fishing, Australia and New Zealand instituted proceedings under Part XV, Section 2, of UNCLOS, seeking first provisional measures from ITLOS[829], and then the constitution of an arbitral tribunal under Annex VII of UNCLOS. They claimed that Japan had failed to conserve, and to co-operate in the conservation of, this highly migratory species in breach of UNCLOS Articles 64 and 116-119. Japan contended that the dispute between the parties was solely concerned with the CCSBT; in any event, Article 16 was a peaceful means of the parties' choice, which excluded any further procedure, and thus that the Annex Tribunal had no jurisdiction.

ITLOS found that an Annex VII Tribunal would have prima facie jurisdiction, considering that the existence of the CCSBT did not exclude a party's right to invoke UNCLOS; and that a party was not obliged to pursue settlement procedures when it concluded that the possibilities of settlement had been exhausted[830]. However, this did not preclude the Arbitral Tribunal from deciding upon its competence for itself. The Tribunal rejected Japan's contention that the dispute fell solely under the CCSBT, and not UNCLOS. It found:

"The current range of international legal obligations benefits from a process of accretion and cumulation; in the practice of States, the conclusion of an implementing convention does not necessarily vacate the obligations imposed by the framework

---

[829] *Supra*, under UNCLOS, *supra* footnote 750, Art. 290 (5).

[830] *Southern Bluefin Tuna (Australia* v. *Japan, New Zealand* v. *Japan)* (ITLOS, Provisional Measures, Order of 27 August 1999), 117 *ILR* 148, [51] and [55].

convention upon the parties to the implementing convention."[831]

Nevertheless, that did not dispose of Japan's jurisdictional challenge. It left the question of the construction of Article 16 in the light of Article 281 of UNCLOS. Central to the Tribunal's approach to this question was it finding that, even though the dispute arose under both treaties, it was *"a single dispute arising under both Conventions"*[832]. Any other construction would be "artificial"[833]. Since Article 16 (2) of the CCSBT required the parties' further consent to litigation or arbitration, it "exclude[d] the application to a specific dispute of any procedure of dispute resolution that is not accepted by all parties to the dispute", including the procedures in Section 2 of Part XV of UNCLOS[834]. As a result, the Tribunal was, by the operation of Article 281, deprived of jurisdiction.

Sir Kenneth Keith dissented on this critical point. He emphasized the key intention of the framers of UNCLOS to create a mandatory system of dispute settlement[835]. He pointed out that the two sets of procedures under UNCLOS and the CCSBT were parallel, but not fully coincident[836]. There could be disputes which arose solely under the CCSBT (as, for example, an application to set the total catch limits in the event of a failure to agree upon these in the Commission). But the language of Article 16 was not specific enough to exclude the parties' right to resort to mandatory arbitration under UNCLOS in relation to the obligations created by that Convention. He considered that

---

[831] *Supra* footnote 782, [52].
[832] *Ibid.*, [54] (emphasis added).
[833] *Ibid.*
[834] *Ibid.*, [57].
[835] *Ibid.*, Dissenting Opinion of Keith, [24]-[29].
[836] *Ibid.*, [11].

"strong and particular wording would appear to be required, *given the presumption of the parallel and overlapping existence of procedures for the peaceful settlement of disputes appearing in international judicial practice*"[837].

If Article 281 played a determinative role in the *Southern Bluefin Tuna Case,* Article 282 came to assume decisive importance in litigation brought by Ireland in various fora against the United Kingdom concerning the operation of the MOX nuclear reprocessing plant at Sellafield. The dispute has produced four relevant decisions: (i) a judgment of ITLOS on a request for provisional measures[838]; (ii) an arbitration award under the OSPAR Convention in proceedings for access to certain information concerning the operation of the MOX plant[839]; (iii) an order in an Annex VII arbitration under the provisions of the 1982 UNCLOS[840]; and (iv) a judgment of the European Court of Justice in a claim brought by the European Commission against Ireland alleging that the other proceedings were a breach of Ireland's European law obligations[841].

---

[837] *Ibid.,* [18] (emphasis added).

[838] *MOX Plant Case (Ireland* v. *United Kingdom)* (ITLOS, Provisional Measures, Order of 3 December 2001) (2002), 126 *ILR* 334.

[839] The Convention for the Protection of the Marine Environment of the North-East Atlantic (signed 22 September 1992, entered into force 25 March 1998), 32 *ILM* 1069; *MOX Plant Case: Dispute concerning Access to Information under Article 9 of the OSPAR Convention (Ireland* v. *United Kingdom)* (Permanent Court of Arbitration, Final Award of 2 July 2003), 126 *ILR* 334, 42 *ILM* 1118.

[840] *MOX Plant Case (Ireland* v. *United Kingdom)* (UNCLOS, Annex VII, Tribunal, Order No. 3 of 24 June 2003), 126 *ILR* 310, 42 *ILM* 1187 (Mensah P, Crawford, Fortier, Hafner and Watts).

[841] *European Commission* v. *Ireland*, Case C-459/03, [2006] *ECR* I-4635.

*ITLOS* emphasized the separate and distinct nature of each of the treaty regimes referred to. It held:

"[T]he dispute settlement procedures under the OSPAR Convention, the EC Treaty and the Euratom Treaty deal with disputes concerning the interpretation or application of those agreements, and not with disputes arising under the [UNCLOS] Convention;

[E]ven if the [other treaties] contain rights or obligations similar to or identical with the rights or obligations set out in the Convention, the rights or obligations under those agreements have a separate existence from those under the Convention;

[S]ince the dispute before the Annex VII arbitral tribunal concerns the interpretation or application of the Convention, and no other agreement, only the dispute settlement procedures under the Convention are relevant to that dispute;

[F]or the purpose of determining whether the Annex VII arbitral tribunal would have *prima facie* jurisdiction, article 282 of the Convention is not applicable to the dispute submitted to the Annex VII arbitral tribunal." [842]

As a result of this decision, the Tribunal held that it had jurisdictional competence to order provisional measures and that Ireland was entitled to constitute an arbitral tribunal under UNCLOS, which could proceed concurrently with other proceedings brought by Ireland under other treaties.

The *OSPAR* Proceedings were brought by Ireland pursuant to a specific arbitration clause in the OSPAR Convention [843]. Objecting to jurisdiction the United

---

[842] *MOX Plant Case* (Provisional Measures Order), *supra* footnote 838, [49], [50], [52].

[843] Art. 32, *supra* footnote 839.

Kingdom submitted that Ireland's only cause of action, was before the European Court of Justice, in the light of a European Directive which limited a complainant to domestic remedies. The United Kingdom argued that the domestic implementation of this Directive fulfilled exhaustively its responsibilities under Article 9 of the Convention, and this excluded the jurisdiction of the OSPAR Tribunal. The Tribunal rejected this argument[844]. It held:

> "Each of the OSPAR Convention and Directive 90/313 is an independent legal source that establishes a distinct legal regime and provides for different legal remedies . . . The similar language of the two legal instruments . . . does not limit a Contracting Party's choice of a legal forum to only one of the two available, i.e. either the ECJ or an OSPAR Tribunal. Nor, contrary to the United Kingdom's contention, does it suggest that the only cause of action available to Ireland is confined exclusively to those provided for by Directive 90/313 and implementing legislation. The primary purpose of employing similar language is to create uniform and consistent legal standards in the field of the protection of the marine environment, and not to create precedence of one set of legal remedies over the other."[845]

When the substantive claim came before an *UNCLOS Annex VII Tribunal*, one of the objections raised by the United Kingdom to the jurisdiction of the Tribunal was that competence in relation to the relevant obligations under UNCLOS had been transferred by European Union States to the European Commission.

---

[844] By a majority (Mustill and Griffith, Reisman C dissenting).
[845] *Supra* footnote 838, [142]-[143].

The Tribunal decided that the real risk of European competence over the dispute justified a stay of proceedings, pending the hearing by the European Court of a threatened action by the European Commission against Ireland alleging that the arbitral proceedings were themselves a breach of Ireland's obligation under European law to submit any such dispute to the European Court. The Tribunal reasoned:

> "[T]here is a real possibility that the European Court of Justice may be seized of the question whether the provisions of the Convention on which Ireland relies are matters in relation to which competence has been transferred to the European Community and, indeed, whether the exclusive jurisdiction of the European Court of Justice, with regard to Ireland and the United Kingdom as Member States of the European Community, extends to the interpretation and application of the Convention as such and in its entirety . . . [I]f this view were to be sustained, it would preclude the jurisdiction of the present Tribunal entirely, by virtue of article 282 of the Convention.
>
> [W]hatever the Parties may agree in these proceedings as to the scope and effects of European Community law applicable in the present dispute, the question is ultimately not for them to decide but is rather to be decided within the institutions of the European Communities, and particularly by the European Court of Justice.
>
> In these circumstances, and bearing in mind considerations of mutual respect and comity which should prevail between judicial institutions both of which may be called upon to determine rights and obligations as between two States, the Tribunal considers that it would be inappropriate for it to proceed further with hearing the Parties on the merits

of the dispute in the absence of a resolution of the problems referred to. Moreover, a procedure that might result in two conflicting decisions on the same issue would not be helpful to the resolution of the dispute between the Parties." [846]

The European Court finally determined that Ireland was not entitled to bring the arbitration proceedings at all, in view of the exclusive competence of the European Court to determine such a dispute, under Article 292 of the Treaty of Rome [847]. The Court dealt with the potential conflict with the Law of the Sea Convention in the following way:

"[A]n international agreement cannot affect the allocation of responsibilities defined in the Treaties and, consequently, the autonomy of the Community legal system, compliance with which the Court ensures under Article 220 EC. That exclusive competence is confirmed by Article 292 EC . . .

It should be stated at the outset that [UNCLOS] precisely makes it possible to avoid such a breach of the Court's exclusive jurisdiction in such a way as to preserve the autonomy of the Community legal system.

It follows from Article 282 of [UNCLOS] that, as it provides for procedures resulting in binding decisions in respect of the resolution of disputes between Member States, the system for the resolution of disputes set out in the EC Treaty must in principle take precedence over that contained in Part XV of the Convention.

It has been established that the provisions of the Convention in issue in the dispute concerning the

---

[846] *MOX Plant Case (Ireland* v. *United Kingdom)* (UNCLOS, Annex VII, Tribunal, Order of 14 November 2003), 126 *ILR* 310, [21], [22], [26], [28].

[847] *Supra* footnote 841, [123]-[127].

MOX plant come within the scope of Community competence which the Community exercised by acceding to the Convention, with the result that those provisions form an integral part of the Community legal order.

Consequently, the dispute in this case is indeed a dispute concerning the interpretation of application of the EC Treaty, within the terms of Article 292 EC [under which member States undertake not to submit such a dispute to any method of settlement other than that provided under the EC Treaty]."

The Court further emphasized that it was for the European Court alone to determine whether a particular dispute did, or did not, fall within exclusive European competence [848] ; and that the general duty of loyalty imposed upon Member States as a matter of European law required them to inform and consult with the European institutions before instituting legal proceedings between themselves before any other dispute settlement body [849]. Ireland subsequently withdrew its claim before the UNCLOS tribunal [850].

A contrasting decision to those in the *MOX Plant* débâcle is the decision of an *ad hoc* arbitral tribunal in the *Iron Rhine Case* in 2005 [851]. In that case, Belgium submitted its claim against the Netherlands for a rail transit corridor to Germany under an *ad hoc* arbitration agreement entered into between the two States in 2003.

---

[848]  *Ibid.* [135].

[849]  *Ibid.* [179].

[850]  (Order No. 6 of 6 June 2008, Termination of Proceedings).

[851]  *Iron Rhine Railway Case (Belgium v. Netherlands)* (Award of 24 May 2005) (PCA, Higgins P, Schrans, Simma, Soons and Tomka) ; Warbrick, in Macmahon (ed.), *The Iron Rhine (Ijzeren Rijn) Arbitration (Belgium-Netherlands) Award of 2005* (2007) 1, and Lavranos, *infra* footnote 860.

The claim was brought under a series of nineteenth-century treaties, commencing with the 1839 Treaty of Separation between Belgium and the Netherlands[852]. Both parties were at pains to avoid the fate of the *MOX Plant* arbitration. Accordingly, they wrote a joint letter to the Secretary-General of the European Commission confirming that their dispute was limited to the interpretation and application of the 1839 Treaty, and that, in the event that issues of European law should arise, they committed themselves to respecting Article 292 of the EC Treaty[853]. The Tribunal was thus requested by the parties in their *compromis* "to render its decision on the basis of international law, *including European law if necessary, while taking into account the Parties' obligations under article 292 of the EC Treaty*"[854]. The Tribunal took its own decision in the knowledge of the pending proceedings (though not the result) in the case brought by the European Commission against Ireland in *MOX*[855]. The Tribunal decided that it could deal with any issues of European law in an analogous way to that of a domestic court with the European Union — so that, if the European law were clear, it could simply apply it. Only if the law was unclear, and a decision on it was necessary to its decision, would the obligation to refer the matter to the European Court arise[856]. Examining the respects in which European law was relied upon by the parties, the Tribunal concluded that

---

[852] Treaty between Belgium and the Netherlands relative to the Separation of their Respective Territories (1838-1839), 88 *CTS* 427; see also the Iron Rhine Treaty itself (1872-1873), 145 *CTS* 447.

[853] *Supra* footnote 851, [15].

[854] *Ibid.*, [97] (emphasis in original).

[855] *Ibid.*, [101].

[856] *Ibid.*, [103]. The Tribunal noted that, in the context of an arbitration, this would have to be done by means of a special agreement to refer under Art. 239 EC Treaty, rather than by way of direct reference under Art. 234.

these constituted "no more than a background" to the interpretation of the 1839 Treaty[857]. Its decision would be the same without reference to the European law provisions[858].

The reaction of scholars to these cases of interaction between dispute settlement under Public International Law and that provided under European law seems to depend upon whether one takes a European or an international perspective. Lavranos argues that, within the internal logic of European law, the approach of the European Court in *MOX Plant* is compelling, if expansive[859]. By contrast, he contends the attempts of the arbitral tribunals in both the *OSPAR* proceeding and subsequently in *Iron Rhine* to avoid the application of this logic are contestable[860]. Thus, as a matter of European law, international law is "communitarized" — it is part of the Community legal order. This was the major premise which enabled the European Court in *MOX Plant* to decide that the dispute between the parties necessarily involved Community law[861], and thus had to be determined by the European Court. Lavranos proceeds from this premise, and from the proposition

---

[857] *Ibid.*, [117].

[858] *Ibid.*, [137].

[859] Lavranos, "Protecting Its Exclusive Jurisdiction: The *MOX Plant* Judgment of the ECJ", (2006) 5 *LPICT* 479.

[860] Lavranos, "The *MOX Plant* and *IJzeren Rijn* Disputes: Which Court Is the Supreme Arbiter?, (2006) 19 *Leiden JIL* 223.

[861] *Supra* footnote 841, [126], as set out above; and see also the more recent decision of a Grand Chamber of the Court in *R ex parte International Association of Independent Tanker Owners (Intertanko)* v. *Secretary of State for Transport*, Case C-308/06, [2008] 3 *CMLR* 9, [2008] 2 Lloyd's Rep. 260, in which the Court decided that, although UNCLOS formed part of the Community legal order, and could therefore potentially invalidate inconsistent secondary legislation, this would only be so where the Convention established rules of direct application.

that European law represents a form of *lex specialis,* a *sui generis* form of supra-national law, to the much broader conclusion that:

> "[t]herefore the international legal order cannot superimpose itself on the Community legal order, but rather has to accept the supremacy of Community law over international law that is applied within the EC and its member states" [862].

To the international lawyer, this form of reasoning is wholly unconvincing. It led Koskenniemi for example, to compare the attitude of the European Court in *MOX Plant* to "the hermetic absolutism of the Soviet order", in "imagining the European Union as a sovereign whose laws override any other legal structure" [863]. The European Court's approach is not unique. As will be seen later in this chapter, the supreme courts of other federations also have a strong imperative to treat their own Constitutions as internally superior to international law, even when the latter has a place within the federation's Constitutional order [864]. But the approach of the European Court is particularly inverted. International law has effect within the Community legal order *and therefore* is to be treated as part of Community law, with the consequence that, as between Member States, only the European Court can adjudicate upon it. This is a *non sequitur,* with potentially grave consequences. The obligations of States under international law may perfectly well be recognized within European law without the imperial attempt to

---

[862] *Supra* footnote 860, 233.

[863] Koskenniemi, "International Law: Between Fragmentation and Constitutionalism" (unpublished lecture, Canberra, 27 November 2006) available at www.helsinki. fi/eci/Publications/Talks_Papers_MK.htm, [3].

[864] Compare the Consular Convention cases in the US Supreme Court, discussed *infra*, Section C 2 *(a)*.

convert the international obligation into a European one. Such an attempt seeks to arrogate to the European Court decision-making responsibility to construe the obligations under international treaties, to which many other non-European States are party, and where all States have specifically agreed to a particular form of dispute resolution.

To be sure, in the case of UNCLOS, the Convention itself adopts a highly decentralized approach to regional forms of dispute settlement under Article 282 — a point which the European Court in *MOX* hastened to make as a way of avoiding an outright conflict of jurisdictions. At least as interpreted by the Tribunals in *Southern Bluefin Tuna* and *MOX*, the attempt of the drafters of UNCLOS to establish a general framework for the resolution of Law of the Sea disputes which permits a wide variety of party choice appears deferential to a fault. The effect of the construction placed upon Articles 281 and 282 in these cases respectively was not that the parties' UNCLOS dispute had to be determined by another tribunal. It was that the parties' dispute was not determined by any tribunal at all. There is a substantial argument for saying that this achieves the very opposite to that which the framers intended [865] : namely the increase in the possibilities for the pacific settlement of maritime disputes, not the negation of such possibilities. But perhaps the seeds of this difficulty lie in the way in which Articles 281 and 282 serve to divert the power of decision away from bodies with a specific remit to protect the operation of the rights and duties of states under UNCLOS. The consequences of these decisions for the effective enforcement of the fundamental obligations of states under this major multilateral treaty are bleak indeed.

These cases also graphically illustrate the extent to

---

[865] Oxman, *supra* footnote 760.

which a field such as international environmental law
has today become a kaleidoscope of overlapping treaty
obligations, each with their own dispute settlement
mechanisms. In this new reality, the *laissez-faire*
approach of ITLOS — treating each obligation as distinct — would serve not merely to permit, but actually
to require, a multiplicity of parallel proceedings, each
tribunal dealing with separate obligations relating to
the same dispute. Now, of course, to some extent, this
necessarily reflects reality. Each international tribunal
has only so much jurisdictional competence as the
States parties have vouchsafed to it under the relevant
treaty. Absent the agreement of the parties, it cannot
simply arrogate to itself the competence to apply rights
and obligations arising under other instruments. But on
the other hand, nor is such a tribunal prevented from
considering the legal effect of "other relevant rules of
international law applicable in the relations between
the parties" in construing the treaty before it [866].

Despite the proliferation of international tribunals, it
certainly cannot be said that the resulting "system"
achieves perfect coverage. On the contrary, as the
experience of these cases shows, there is still the real
possibility of a denial of justice by reason of decisions
by tribunals to decline jurisdiction. From a practical
perspective, the most serious aspect of the decision of
the European Court in *MOX Plant* is the Court's insistence that it, and only it, is competent to decide on dis-

---

[866] Art. 31 (3) *(c)*, Vienna Convention on the Law of Treaties (signed 23 May 1969, entered into force 27 January
1980), 1155 *UNTS* 331; McLachlan, "The Principle of
Systemic Integration and Article 31 (3) *(c)* of the Vienna
Convention", (2005) 54 *ICLQ* 279; International Law
Commission Report of the Study Group on the Fragmentation of International Law, UN doc. A/CN.4/L.682,
13 April 2006; Conclusions, UN doc. A/CN.4/L.702,
18 July 2006.

puted questions of its own jurisdictional competence, as, for example, in the case of UNCLOS, where responsibility for the Convention is split between the Community and its Member States. Of course the Court has competence to determine its own jurisdiction *when seised of a dispute*. But the implication of the decision is to deny the competence of another tribunal, such as an UNCLOS Annex VII Tribunal or indeed ITLOS itself, to decide on its own jurisdictional competence. Such an approach runs counter to the basic notion of *Kompetenz-Kompetenz* — that each Tribunal may decide for itself on its own jurisdiction. As Warbrick comments perceptively, this is "a crucial point which will inevitably complicate attempts to resolve jurisdictional conflicts"[867]. In this regard, the approach of the UNCLOS Annex VII Tribunal is itself overly deferential. It was the Tribunal first seised with the dispute. There were no other proceedings pending at the time when it decided to stay its proceedings — merely an indication that the European Commission was considering bringing a claim against Ireland in the European Court. The desire of the Tribunal to avoid a head-on collision with the European Court is understandable. But the result of the stay was not to transfer Ireland's claim against the United Kingdom to the European Court. It was that Ireland was left with no proceedings against the United Kingdom at all.

Considering the implications of the European Court's decision, Lavranos concedes that the Court's "massive protection of its exclusive jurisdiction" may be unduly restrictive of the right of Member States to choose their preferred form of dispute resolution[868]. He suggests that the Court "should show some more respect and comity towards the jurisdiction of the other

---

[867] *Supra* footnote 851, 12.
[868] *Supra* footnote 859, 493.

international courts and tribunals"[869]. However, as
these lectures have abundantly shown[870], absent the
imposition of a hierarchical solution — a remote
prospect in international law — international courts
and tribunals can only mediate jurisdictional conflicts
between themselves through the application of general
principles of international law outside the framework
of their own legal order. It is therefore to a consideration of the extent to which *lis pendens* and other relevant principles for resolving jurisdictional conflicts
may properly be said to be part of general international
law that this chapter must now turn.

## 2. *Is* lis pendens *a general principle of law appli-cable to international tribunals*?

The question which remains, then, is what principles may or ought to be applied, in the absence of
express provision by treaty, when a court or tribunal is
faced with parallel or overlapping litigation between
the same parties arising out of the same facts in
another international court or tribunal. As was seen at
the outset of these lectures[871], the question whether
the doctrine of litispendence was a general principle of
law was left undecided by the Permanent Court of
International Justice.

In *Certain German Interests in Polish Upper
Silesia*[872], the Court was concerned with a claim by
Germany against Poland for a declaration of rights,
relating to the alleged expropriation of a factory owned
by a German company at Chorzów in Poland. It had to
consider the effect of a pending claim brought by the

---

[869] *Ibid.*, 491.
[870] *Supra* Chapter I, Section B 2, and Chapter IV, Section A 3.
[871] Chapter I, Section A.
[872] (1925) *PCIJ Rep., Ser. A, No. 6.*

owners of the factory against Poland before a Mixed Arbitral Tribunal. The Court held that it need not decide whether *lis pendens* was a general principle of law because "the essential elements which constitute *litispendance* are not present"[873]. There was no identity of parties; the Mixed Arbitral Tribunal and the Permanent Court were not courts of the same character; and the remedy sought in each case was different (restitution to the private company in the Mixed Arbitral Tribunal and a declaration as to the rights of the State under an international treaty in the other).

The Permanent Court was asked to revert to this question in relation to another aspect of the same dispute in *Factory at Chorzów (Jurisdiction)*[874]. In that case, there was a greater possibility of overlap between the proceedings before the Court on the claim brought by Germany on behalf of its national, and the claim lodged and still pending before the Mixed Arbitral Tribunal, brought by the national company itself, since both claims sought compensation for the expropriation of assets[875]. But the Court held, on analysis, that the jurisdictional scheme of the Geneva Convention allocated distinct competences for different disputes. It observed that in any event the Court

"cannot allow its own competency to give way unless confronted with a clause which it considers sufficiently clear to prevent the possibility of a negative conflict of jurisdiction involving the danger of a denial of justice"[876].

Thus, the only indication that the Permanent Court might have been disposed to stay its proceedings to

---

[873] *Ibid.*, 20.
[874] (1927) *PCIJ Rep., Ser. A, No. 9.*
[875] *Ibid.*, 27.
[876] *Ibid.*, 30.

take account of related proceedings in another court, comes from *Prince von Pless Administration*[877]. Little, however, may be gleaned from that decision, since the Court merely decided that it would arrange its proceedings so as to be able to consider the decision of the Supreme Polish Administrative Tribunal before arriving at its own[878]. Since that case was concerned with the interrelationship between an international court and a national court, and with the application of the exhaustion of local remedies rule, little can be taken from it for present purposes[879].

Nor did the adoption of the United Nations Charter resolve the issue. Article 95 merely provides:

> "Nothing in the present Charter shall prevent Members of the United Nations from entrusting the solution of their differences to other tribunals by virtue of agreements already in existence or which may be concluded in the future."[880]

This provision neither subordinates the jurisdiction of the International Court of Justice to the competence of other courts or tribunals, nor does it establish a presumption that resort to the ICJ is considered to be the member States' preferred method of dispute resolution[881]. No case has yet arisen where the International Court has been called upon to decide its own approach to parallel proceedings. The question

---

[877] (Preliminary Objection), (1933) *PCIJ Rep. Ser. A/B, No. 52.*

[878] *Ibid.*, 16.

[879] The claim was subsequently withdrawn before a decision on the merits: (Order) (1933) *PCIJ Rep., Ser. A/B, No. 59.*

[880] *Supra* footnote 747.

[881] Gaja, "Relationship of the ICJ with Other International Courts and Tribunals", in Zimmermann/Tomuschat/Oellers-Frahm, *The Statute of the International Court of Justice: A Commentary* (2006) 533, 535.

must therefore be considered as a matter of general principle.

One possible approach to the proliferation of new international courts and tribunals would be to treat the jurisdiction of each tribunal as "*a self-contained system*", as the ICTY Appeals Chamber observed in *Tadić*[882]. The context in which that statement was made was simply to establish the inherent power of the ICTY to rule upon its own jurisdiction under the principle of *Kompetenz-Kompetenz*. But, as has been seen, the WTO Appellate Body in *Mexico Soft Drinks* went further and concluded that a WTO panel was not entitled under the Dispute Settlement Understanding to "choose freely whether or not to exercise its jurisdiction"[883]. May such an "unflagging obligation" to exercise jurisdiction give way when another court is seised with the *same* dispute? That question was expressly left open by the WTO Appellate Body in 2006[884], as it had been by the Permanent Court of Justice some 80 years before.

In the first place, regardless of the fact that international tribunals do not form part of a single judicial hierarchy, they nevertheless do form part of a single legal system — namely Public International Law. This was the conclusion reached by the International Law Commission in its compelling analysis of self-contained regimes in the course of its study of the fragmentation of substantive international law[885]. The Study Group's Report observed:

> "[T]he term 'self-contained regime' is a misnomer. No legal regime is isolated from general

---

[882] *Supra* footnote 781, 458 (emphasis added).
[883] *Supra* footnote 799, [53].
[884] *Ibid.*, [54].
[885] *Supra* footnote 866 (Report), [14] (1).

international law . . . [which] contains principles of hierarchy that control the operation of the special regime above all in determining the peremptory norms of international law but also in providing resources for determining in case of conflict what regime should be given priority or, at least, what consequences follow from the breach of the requirements of one regime by deferring to another . . ." [886]

If this analysis holds good for interactions between substantive sources of law in international law, it is submitted that it may also assist in the analysis of the development of solutions to jurisdictional interactions. Since the jurisdiction of all international tribunals ultimately flows from a treaty between States, the tribunal is obliged to take into account other rules of international law in interpretation of the treaty [887], or, to adopt the dictum of Verzijl,

"[e]very international convention must be deemed tacitly to refer to general principles of international law for all questions which it does not itself resolve in express terms and in a different way" [888].

The requirement to consider other rules of general international law includes all of the sources indicated in Article 38 (1) of the Statute of the International Court, including "general principles of law common to

---

[886] *Ibid.* (Report), [193]-[194].

[887] Vienna Convention on the Law of Treaties, *supra* footnote 866, Art. 31 (3) *(c)*, as to which see McLachlan "The Principle of Systemic Integration and Article 31 (3) *(c)* of the Vienna Convention", (2005) 54 *ICLQ* 279.

[888] *Georges Pinson (France)* v. *United Mexican States* (French-Mexican Claims Commission, Verzijl P), (1928) 5 *RIAA* 327 (Original French text), (1927-1928) AD Case No. 292 (English Note).

civilised nations"[889]. Where the source of such principles is sought in municipal law[890], it is important to be clear about the nature of the exercise. As Lord McNair put it:

> "The way in which international law borrows from this source is not by means of the importing of private law institutions 'lock, stock and barrel', ready-made and fully equipped with a set of rules. It would be difficult to reconcile such a process with the application of 'general principles of law' . . . [T]he duty of international tribunals in this matter is to regard any features or terminology which are reminiscent of the rules and institutions of private law as an indication of policy and principles rather than as directly importing these rules and institutions."[891]

Mosler elaborates this function, in explaining that the function of the international judge in this regard:

> "Starting from a common denominator, he has the creative task of maintaining the essential features of the general principle while at the same time finding the appropriate solution for the international legal relation upon which he has to pass judgment."[892]

This does not require a finding that the principle is observed by all States in the world. Rather, there must

---

[889] *Supra* footnote 748, Art. 38 (1) *(c)*, *Golder* v. *United Kingdom* (21 February 1975), *ECHR, Ser. A, No. 18*, 57 *ILR* 200, 213; Huber, *Annuaire* (1952-I) 200-208.

[890] See the classification adopted by Mosler in "General Principles of Law", in Bernhardt (ed.), *Encyclopedia of Public International Law* (Vol. I, 1992) 511.

[891] *International Status of South-West Africa* (Advisory Opinion) *ICJ Rep. 1950* 128, 146, 148 (Separate Opinion of McNair J).

[892] *Supra* footnote 890, 517.

be evidence that it is observed by a representative majority, which includes "the main forms of civilisation and of the principal legal systems of the world"[893].

The focus of many general principles referred to by international tribunals is procedural. This is because, as Schlesinger explains:

> "Many questions of procedure and evidence ... which necessarily arise in treaty and non-treaty cases alike, are not regulated by specific provisions of treaty or charter; in filling the gap, an international court will expressly or silently resort to procedural and evidentiary principles which are felt to be inherent in all civilized legal systems."[894]

Is *lis pendens* such a principle? Evidence of its adoption by international courts and tribunals is thus far limited to the stay orders issued by the UNCLOS Tribunal in *MOX Plant,* and the developing practice of investment arbitral tribunals[895]. The principle does not even merit a mention in Cheng's classic 1953 study[896], or in Sir Hersch Lauterpacht's earlier work on private law sources[897]. But this in itself should occasion little surprise, since, as Verzijl observed, as Presiding Commissioner in the *Caire* case in 1929, the incidence of litispendence between international tribunals:

> "n'a pas eu beaucoup d'occasions de se présenter

---

[893] ICJ Statute, *supra* footnote 748, Art. 9 cited in Mosler, *ibid.*

[894] Schlesinger, "Research on General Principles of Law Recognized by Civilized Nations", (1957) 51 *AJIL* 734, 736.

[895] Chapter III, Section C 2 *(b).*

[896] Cheng, *General Principles of Law as Applied by International Courts and Tribunals* (1953).

[897] Lauterpacht, *Private Law Sources and Analogies of International Law (with Special Reference to International Arbitration)* (1927).

dans le passé, pour la simple raison qu'il n'existait pas beaucoup de tribunaux ou autres organes internationaux dont l'activité simultanée pût donner lieu à des décisions divergentes ou contradictoires . . ."[898]

Thus, it has only been the development of numerous new international tribunals in modern times which has raised the issue.

In an early path-finding article, Lowe suggested that *lis alibi pendens* was a doctrine which

"relates to the good order of judicial proceedings . . . is common to all the major legal systems, and may properly be applied by a tribunal in any legal system, including the international legal system, in the exercise of the tribunal's competence to regulate its own proceedings"[899].

However, Shany, in his 2003 study, concluded in a more qualified fashion that:

"In sum, it looks as if existing case-law on the question of *lis alibi pendens* is also too scarce and non-definitive to establish the existence of such a general rule or principle in international law, in the relations between international courts and tribunals. Nonetheless . . . one can make a plausible case that *lis alibi pendens* may qualify as a general principle of law, recognized by most legal systems, at least with respect to intra-systematic jurisdictional competition."[900]

---

[898] *Caire Case (France* v. *Mexico)*, (1929) 5 *RIAA* 516, 523.

[899] Lowe, "Overlapping Jurisdiction in International Tribunals", (1999) 20 *Aust. YIL* 191, 203; Gaja, *supra* footnote 881, 541, notes of this statement that "[t]he author's premise that [the] doctrine is 'common to all the major legal systems' would require some further analysis".

[900] *Supra* footnote 769, 244.

The detailed analysis in these lectures has shown, in the first place, that there is widespread acceptance that duplicative litigation *within the same legal system* is not permitted, as being contrary to due process and the Rule of Law. Further, and importantly, in the 80 years since the Permanent Court of Justice decided *Certain German Interests*, the principle that courts should also take account of litispendence when it occurs *between different legal systems* has gained widespread acceptance in Private International Law, even if the methods for dealing with it differ as between Civil Law and Common Law legal systems.

The proposition that the avoidance of duplicative litigation is a general principle of law gains further powerful support from the 2004 Resolution of the Institut de droit international which held:

> "Parallel litigation in more than one country between the same, or related, parties in relation to the same, or related, issues may lead to injustice, delay, increased expense, and inconsistent decisions [and] should be discouraged." [901]

Similarly, the ALI/UNIDROIT Principles of Transnational Civil Procedure 2004 provide that:

> "The Court should decline jurisdiction or suspend the proceeding, when the dispute is previously pending in another court competent to exercise jurisdiction, unless it appears that the dispute will not be fairly, effectively, and expeditiously resolved in that forum." [902]

The member States of UNIDROIT are drawn from all of the world's major legal systems, as were the

---

[901] *Annuaire* (2004) 70-II, recital *(d)* and [4].

[902] American Law Institute/UNIDROIT, *Principles of Transnational Civil Procedure* (adopted 2004) (2006) [2.6].

international advisers and consultants on the Principles[903].

Furthermore, the application of a general principle of the avoidance of duplicative litigation gains force from its close connection, since the inception of the doctrine in the writings of the early modern Dutch jurists, with the doctrine of *res judicata*[904]. Since the very introduction of "general principles of law common to civilised nations" into the Statute of the (then) Permanent Court of International Justice in 1920, the principle of *res judicata* has been cited as an example of such a principle[905]. The Court has proceeded to interpret Article 59 of its own Statute (which provides that "[t]he decision of the Court has no binding force except between the parties and in respect of the particular case") by conscious reference to the general principles of *res judicata*. This was what Judge Anzilotti did in his classic dictum in *Chorzów Factory* in expressing the view that Article 59 encapsulates the three traditional elements of identification for the purpose of *res judicata* (*persona, petitum* and *causa petendi*) as being "derived from the very conception of *res judicata*"[906]. Most recently, the International Court has returned to the doctrine of *res judicata* as a general principle of law in the *Serbian Genocide* case[907], where it held that the doctrine met both the general purpose

---

[903] *Ibid.*, vii, xiv, xxi-xxii.

[904] *Supra* Chapter I, Section C 1.

[905] Permanent Court of International Justice, Advisory Committee of Jurists, *Procès-verbaux of the Proceedings of the Committee, June 16-June 24, 1920* (1920) 335; Cheng, *supra* footnote 896, 336-372; Scobbie, "*Res Judicata*, Precedent and the International Court: A Preliminary Sketch", (1999) 20 *Aust. YIL* 299.

[906] *Factory at Chorzów: Interpretation Case (Germany* v. *Poland)* (1927) *PCIJ, Ser. A, No. 13*, Anzilotti (Dissenting Opinion) [26].

[907] *Supra* footnote 785, [114]-[120].

of the stability of legal relations, and the specific purpose of not depriving the litigant of a judgment which it has already obtained, which was one of the "principles governing the legal settlement of disputes"[908].

The principle of *res judicata* had been held to apply, not merely as regards prior judgments of the same tribunal, but also, providing the requisite conditions are met, to prior judgments of other international courts and tribunals[909]. In consequence, as Reinisch argues:

> "The existence of an international *lis pendens* rule also follows from the applicability of *res judicata*. As a matter of legal logic it would be inconsistent to permit parallel proceedings between the same parties in the same dispute before different dispute settlement organs up to the point where one of them has decided the case and then prevent the other ('slower') one from proceeding as a result of *res judicata*."[910]

It has been seen in examining the solutions adopted to the problem of parallel proceedings in Private International Litigation that this link is not necessarily essential[911]. But nevertheless, the avoidance of the risk of inconsistent judgments is one of the reasons commonly advanced for *both* the doctrine of *res judicata* and the doctrine of *lis pendens*. Once it is accepted that

---

[908] *Ibid.*, [116].

[909] *Trail Smelter Case (USA v. Canada)* (1941) 3 *RIAA* 1938, 1950-1953; case concerning the *Arbitral Award Made by the King of Spain on 23 December 1906 (Honduras v. Nicaragua), ICJ Rep. 1960* 192, 214-216; Shany, *supra* footnote 769, 253.

[910] Reinisch, "The Use and Limits of *Res Judicata* and *Lis Pendens* as Procedural Tools to Avoid Conflicting Dispute Settlement Outcomes", (2004) 3 *LPICT* 37, 50.

[911] Chapter I, Section D 1, citing *Laker Airways Ltd. v. Sabena, Belgian World Airlines*, 731 F. 2d 909, 926-927 (DC Cir., 1984).

*res judicata* may apply to the prior decisions of other international tribunals, it is difficult to see on what basis *lis pendens* in principle should be excluded.

However, this conclusion does not, of itself, deal with two issues of critical importance to the actual application of the doctrine in international cases: the consequences of the establishment of litispendence; and the determination of identity of cause in the context of tribunals of limited jurisdiction. In the first place, as has been seen, it does not follow from the fact that a tribunal should avoid duplicative litigation that it must automatically stay its proceedings, deferring to the tribunal first seised of the dispute. The analysis in Chapter II showed that, in the absence of a treaty obligation, both Civil Law and Common Law States commonly treat the grant of a stay on grounds of *lis pendens* in international cases as a matter of *discretion*, not obligation. This is the approach which was adopted, both by the UNCLOS arbitral tribunal in *MOX Plant*, and by an ICSID Tribunal, presided over by Jiménez de Aréchaga, in *SPP* v. *Egypt,* referring to a discretion exercised "in the interest of international judicial order . . . and as a matter of comity"[912].

Even then, the application of the doctrine as between public international tribunals adds a particular dimension, which is not found in either private international litigation or in international commercial arbitration[913]. National courts typically exercise plenary jurisdiction in civil matters. This means that there will always be, in any national legal system, a court capable of deciding any civil dispute which may be submitted

---

[912] *Southern Pacific Properties (Middle East) Ltd. [SPP]* v. *Arab Republic of Egypt* (First Jurisdiction), 3 *ICSID Rep.* 101, 129 (ICSID, 1985, Jiménez de Aréchaga P, El Mahdi and Pietrowski), discussed *supra*, Chapter III, Section C 5.

[913] Lowe, *supra* footnote 899, 199-200.

to it under the law of the State in question. This basic premise greatly facilitates the transfer of cases from one national legal system to another. Each national court may usually make the assumption that the plaintiff will not lose his cause of action if it relinquishes its jurisdiction in favour of another court. Indeed, the system of Private International Law facilitates this transferability by making provision for the application of foreign law to the substance of the dispute, where the relevant choice of law rules so permit. So, too, in international commercial arbitration, a change in arbitral tribunal will not necessarily change the applicable law, which the parties may determine by contract.

By contrast, the jurisdiction of most public international tribunals is not plenary. It is limited to disputes arising under its constitutive treaty, which will, applying the reasoning of the tribunal in the *Channel Tunnel* case, constitute the "source of the Parties' respective rights and obligations", furnishing the cause of action which gives rise to the treaty claim, and delimiting the scope of the arbitrators' powers[914]. The reasoning of ITLOS in *MOX Plant* was that this, of its nature, produced separate causes of action, an approach which was also expressly adopted by the *CME* Tribunal in the field of investment arbitration[915]. Now, there may well be instances where, even though the dispute is between the same States parties, and arises out of the same facts, the cause of action is quite different. An example of this is the OSPAR proceedings in the *MOX* dispute, which were concerned with the provision of environ-

---

[914] *Channel Tunnel Group Ltd.* v. *United Kingdom and France* (Partial Award), 132 *ILR* 1 (2007, Crawford P, Fortier, Guillaume, Millett and Paulsson), [98].
[915] *CME Czech Republic BV (The Netherlands)* v. *Czech Republic* (Final Award), 9 *ICSID* 264 (UNCITRAL, 2003, Kühn C, Schwebel and Brownlie) (*CME II*) 355, discussed *supra*, Chapter III, Section C 5.

mental information under a distinct treaty regime
developed for this purpose, and not with Ireland's
underlying substantive claim to prevent the re-commissioning of the nuclear reprocessing plant. Thus, *lis pendens* will not, of its nature, catch all cases of overlap
between proceedings, and it is neither necessary nor
desirable that it should.

However, the fact that a particular tribunal has jurisdiction does not mean that it is bound to exercise it.
The existence of a situation of litispendence does not
deprive an international tribunal of its jurisdiction, it
merely gives rise to a question where it should stay its
exercise of that jurisdiction[916]. The analysis of the
operation of the doctrine in private international litigation has already shown that the determination of identity of cause of action does not depend upon the *source*
of the legal obligation, but rather upon its identity in
*substance*[917]. It is submitted that there is no reason to
adopt a different approach in public international litigation. Indeed, this is what the Tribunal in *Southern
Bluefin Tuna* did when it concluded that the parties
before it were "grappling not with two separate disputes but with what in fact is a single dispute arising
under both Conventions"[918]. It held that, to split this
into two separate disputes, one under each Convention,
"would be artificial"[919].

Seen in this light, the question may perhaps be
better formulated as one of the inherent power of an
international tribunal to manage its proceedings[920].

---

[916] *SPP* v. *Egypt, supra* footnote 912.
[917] Accord Reinisch *supra* footnote 910, 71-72.
[918] *Supra* footnote 782, [54].
[919] *Ibid.*
[920] Brown, "The Inherent Powers of International
Courts and Tribunals", (2005) 76 *BYIL* 195; Brown, *A
Common Law of International Adjudication* (2007) 55-82,
250-255.

The International Court described the concept of inherent powers in the following terms in the *Nuclear Tests* case:

> "[I]t should be emphasized that the Court possesses an inherent jurisdiction enabling it to take such action as may be required, on the one hand, to ensure that the exercise of its jurisdiction over the merits, if and when established, shall not be frustrated, and on the other, to provide for the orderly settlement of all matters in dispute, to ensure the observance of the 'inherent limitations on the exercise of the judicial function' of the Court, and to 'maintain its judicial character' ... Such inherent jurisdiction, on the basis of which the Court is fully empowered to make whatever findings may be necessary for the purposes just indicated, derives from the mere existence of the Court as a judicial organ established by the consent of States, and is conferred upon it in order that its basic judicial functions may be safeguarded." [921]

The inherent power to safeguard proceedings before an international tribunal may require the issue of an interim order requesting one party not to proceed with parallel proceedings. Thus, in *E-Systems Inc.* v. *Iran* [922], after the institution of the claim before the Iran-United States Claims Tribunal, the Government of Iran had filed a claim against E-Systems in the Iranian courts. E-Systems argued that it was properly a counter-claim, and that Iran was obliged to bring it in the Tribunal, and not before its own courts. The Tribunal rejected the

---

[921] *Nuclear Tests (Australia* v. *France), ICJ Rep. 1974* 253, 259-260.
[922] (1983) 2 *Iran-US CTR* 51, followed in *Component Builders Inc.* v. *Iran*, (1985) 8 *Iran-US CTR* 216; *USA (Tadjer-Cohen Assoc. Inc.)* v. *Iran*, (1985) 9 *Iran-US CTR* 302.

argument that there was any such obligation. But it then continued:

> "But it does not follow from what has been said that the requests should be entirely dismissed. This Tribunal has an *inherent power* to issue such orders as may be necessary to conserve the respective rights of the Parties and to ensure that this Tribunal's jurisdiction are made fully effective." [923]

For this reason, the Tribunal requested Iran to move for a stay of the Iranian court proceedings until the Tribunal had completed its case.

But it may also require the tribunal to suspend its own proceedings. As the International Court put it in *Northern Cameroons*:

> "[E]ven if, when seised of an Application, the Court finds that it has jurisdiction, it is not obliged to exercise it in all cases. If the Court is satisfied, whatever the nature of the relief claimed, that to adjudicate on the merits of the Application would be inconsistent with its judicial function, it should refuse to do so." [924]

Gaja argues that it follows from this proposition that, even though its jurisdiction is unaffected, the International Court (or the other tribunal) "may consider whether, in order to avoid the exercise of overlapping jurisdictions, judicial propriety should not require the Court to refrain from examining the merits of the dispute" [925]. It is just such an approach which the tribunals in *SPP* and in *MOX Plant* adopted.

As a means of mediating conflicts of jurisdiction, the notion of a stay or suspension, rather than a finding

---

[923] *Ibid.*, 57 (emphasis added).
[924] *Northern Cameroons (Cameroon* v. *United Kingdom)* (Preliminary Objections), *ICJ Rep. 1963* 15, 37.
[925] Gaja, *supra* footnote 881, 540.

that the court lacked jurisdiction, or should decline it, has much to commend it. As Oxman puts it:

> "[A] tribunal could retain jurisdiction while declining to adjudicate the merits for the time being in the light of the agreement of the parties regarding alternative procedures. Among other things, this means that the standards for provisional measures would not be affected; . . . prima facie jurisdiction would persist."[926]

Given the incomplete jurisdictional coverage of international tribunals, a court seised of a case which has determined that it has jurisdiction, must be cautious about relinquishing it, lest it cause a denial of justice by rendering the plaintiff's claim incapable of adjudication before any tribunal. This was the very concern expressed by the Permanent Court in *Factory at Chorzów*[927]. This, in essence, is the reservation which one must enter to the — overly deferential — approach of the two UNCLOS Tribunals in *Southern Bluefin Tuna* and *MOX Plant* respectively.

## C. Relationship between National and International Litigation

### 1. Rules of separation of international from national proceedings

If one turns to the separate question of the relations between international tribunals and *national courts*, it must immediately be observed that the fact that the national courts and international courts sit within different legal systems which are not in a horizontal relationship with each other fundamentally alters the

---

[926] Oxman, *supra* footnote 760, 311.
[927] *Supra* footnote 906.

nature of the interaction between them[928]. Indeed, the fundamental postulate of international law is that the two systems are jurisdictionally separate. Thus, as has been seen, in principle the jurisdiction of an international tribunal is not affected by the fact that the same question is before a national court[929]. This flows from the more general principle of international law that the characterization of an act as lawful under internal law does not affect its characterization as wrongful under international law[930]. It follows also that litispendence cannot arise in such a situation, since, as the Permanent Court of Justice observed in *Certain German Interests,* an international court and a national court are not courts of the same character[931]. The international remedy is independent of the national court relief[932]. Moreover, the international tribunal is entitled, as has been seen, to ensure that its jurisdiction if made fully effective, where the actions of a State before its own courts may otherwise prejudice the ability of the tribunal to preserve the rights of the parties[933].

The customary international law of diplomatic protection reinforces this separation of the respective spheres of national and international adjudication

---

[928] See generally Shany, *Regulating Jurisdictional Relations between National and International Courts* (2007).

[929] *Selwyn Case (British-Venezuelan Claims Commission)* (Interlocutory), (1903) 9 *RIAA* 380, 381 (Plumley), cited *supra* Chapter III, Section C 2 *(a)*.

[930] Vienna Convention on the Law of Treaties, *supra* footnote 866, Art. 27 and Art. 3 of the ILC Draft Articles on Responsibilities of States for Internationally Wrongful Acts (2001) Supp. No. 10, UN doc. A/56/10, 26, [76].

[931] *Supra* footnote 872, accord *Caire Case, supra* footnote 898, 525.

[932] *Camouco Case (Panama* v. *France)* (ITLOS, 7 February 2000), 125 *ILR* 164, [55]-[58].

[933] *Supra* Section B 2 citing *E-Systems Inc.* v. *Iran, supra* footnote 922, 57.

through the requirement of the exhaustion of local remedies[934]. This rule has been repeatedly recognized by the International Court of Justice as an important element of customary international law[935]. The rule ensures that "the State where the violation occurred should have an opportunity to redress it by its own means, within the framework of its own domestic system"[936]. The requirement of exhaustion is not unqualified. It only applies where the claim is brought preponderantly on the basis of injury to a national, rather than on the basis of direct injury to the claimant State[937]. Nor does it apply where there is no reasonable possibility of local redress[938].

For present purposes, it is sufficient, however, to note that the *effect* of the local remedies rule is to radically reduce the possibility of parallel national and international proceedings. It will be injuries to aliens which will most likely give rise to the possibility of claims at each level. But the local remedies rule, which is a prerequisite to the presentation of an international claim, ensures that all national court proceedings must be completed before the international claim can commence.

The exhaustion of local remedies rule now also plays a very important function as a jurisdictional limitation upon individual petitions to international human

---

[934] International Law Commission Draft Articles on Diplomatic Protection (2006) Supp. No. 10, UN doc. A/61/10, Art. 14, 70-71.

[935] *Interhandel Case (Switzerland* v. *United States of America)* (Preliminary Objections), *ICJ Rep. 1959* 6, 27; *Elletronica Sicula SpA (ELSI) (United States of America* v. *Italy*), *ICJ Rep. 1989* 15, 42, [50].

[936] *Interhandel, ibid.*

[937] ILC Draft Articles, Art. 14 (3), *supra* footnote 934, 71; for the importance of this distinction see the decision of the ICJ in *Avena, infra*, Section C 2 *(a)*.

[938] *Ibid.*, Art. 15, 76-77.

rights courts. Thus, Article 35 (1) of the European Convention provides (in relevant part):

> "The Court may only deal with the matter after all domestic remedies have been exhausted, according to the generally recognised rules of international law . . ."[939]

Another rule of priority can be found in the principle of complementarity in modern international criminal law. Article 1 of the Rome Statute provides that the jurisdiction of the International Criminal Court is "complementary to national criminal jurisdictions". Article 17 goes on to provide for the consequence of this requirement in terms of admissibility of claims before the ICC:

> "*Article 17*
> *Issues of Admissibility*
>
> 1. Having regard to paragraph 10 of the Preamble and article 1, the Court shall determine that a case is inadmissible where:
>
> *(a)* The case is being investigated or prosecuted by a State which has jurisdiction over it, unless the State is unwilling or unable genuinely to carry out the investigation or prosecution;
> *(b)* The case has been investigated by a State which has jurisdiction over it and the State has decided not to prosecute the person concerned, unless the decision resulted from the unwillingness or inability of the State genuinely to prosecute;

---

[939] *Supra* footnote 754; and see American Convention, *supra* footnote 755, Art. 62 (3); African Charter, *supra* footnote 756, Art. 50; Optional Protocol to the International Covenant on Civil and Political Rights, Art. 5 (2) *(b)*, *supra* footnote 820.

*(c)* The person concerned has already been tried for conduct which is the subject of the complaint, and a trial by the Court is not permitted under article 20, paragraph 3;

*(d)* The case is not of sufficient gravity to justify further action by the Court.

2. In order to determine unwillingness in a particular case, the Court shall consider, *having regard to the principles of due process recognized by international law*, whether one or more of the following exist, as applicable:

*(a)* The proceedings were or are being undertaken or the national decision was made for the purpose of shielding the person concerned from criminal responsibility for crimes within the jurisdiction of the Court referred to in article 5;

*(b)* There has been an unjustified delay in the proceedings which in the circumstances is inconsistent with an intent to bring the person concerned to justice;

*(c)* The proceedings were not or are not being conducted independently or impartially, and they were or are being conducted in a manner which, in the circumstances, is inconsistent with an intent to bring the person concerned to justice.

3. In order to determine inability in a particular case, the Court shall consider whether, due to a total or substantial collapse or unavailability of its national judicial system, the State is unable to obtain the accused or the necessary evidence and testimony or otherwise unable to carry out its proceedings." [940]

---

[940] *Supra* footnote 751 (emphasis added).

This rule preserves the priority of national adjudication in a more absolute way[941]. The Court is required, in determining unwillingness to prosecute domestically, to have regard to "the principles of due process recognized by international law". This requires the application of an objective procedural standard for a fair trial derived from general principles of law common to civilized nations and enshrined in international human rights law[942].

Neither exhaustion nor complementarity requires that the applicable law in the municipal court be the same as in the international court. Indeed the assumption is the reverse: that each tribunal will judge the legality of the impugned acts according to the norms of its own legal system.

The necessary identity of action is found in the injury allegedly caused by the state which is said to be a breach of international law, in the first situation, or in the conduct which gives rise to the case against the accused person in the second[943].

## 2. *Effect of pending international proceedings before national courts*

What, then, of the reverse situation, where it is the national court which must consider the effect of the

---

[941] Simpson, *Law, War and Crime: War Crimes Trials and the Reinvention of International Law* (2008) 38.

[942] Williams and Schabas, "Article 17", in Triffterer, *Commentary on the Rome Statute of the International Criminal Court* (2nd ed., 2008) [29]; Razesberger, *The International Criminal Court; The Principle of Complementarity* (2006) 41-42.

[943] Accord Williams and Schabas, *ibid.*, [23]; but, for an early indication of the Pre-Trial Chamber taking a narrower view, requiring exact equivalence of claims, see *Prosecutor* v. *Lubanga*, Case No. ICC-01/04-01/06-8 (Decision on Prosecutor's Application for a Warrant of Arrest of 10 February 2006).

pendency of parallel proceedings before an international tribunal?[944] The most frequent context in which the issue of directly overlapping claims has arisen in practice has already been discussed in Chapter III, namely parallel proceedings in national courts and before international arbitral tribunals in State contract and investment treaty arbitration cases[945]. In these cases, as has been seen, it may well be that there is substantial equivalence between the parties and the underlying factual matrix, since they concern a direct claim by the investor against the State. In the State contract cases, the existence of the arbitration agreement provides a rule of priority based upon party autonomy, although the extent of permissible intervention left to the courts of the seat remains controversial[946]. In the investment treaty cases, the only ground of distinction between the proceedings has been the difference in the rights to be vindicated — being contractual or other private law rights in the claim brought by the investor before national courts and public international rights in the treaty arbitration claim[947].

But modern international law has brought national

---

[944] Shany, *supra* footnote 769, Chap. 4; Schreuer, *Decisions of International Institutions before Domestic Courts* (1981), Chap. XIV "Concurrent Jurisdiction of Domestic Courts and International Organs".

[945] See Schreuer, *ibid.*, 330-332 for a discussion of the related earlier (inconsistent) practice of national courts vis-à-vis mixed claims commissions, citing *inter alia Landwirtschaftlicher Zentralverband in Polen* v. *Liquidating Committee in Poznam* (Poland) 17 November 1927, (1927-1928) 4 *AD* 476; *S. A. Belge HAV* v. *Belgium* (Belgium), 14 July 1930 (1929-1930) 5 *AD* 447; *Compagnie des Wagons-Réservoirs* v. *Ministry of Industry and Commerce and Italian Railways* (France), 7 October 1950 (1951) 18 *ILR* 394.

[946] *Supra*, Chapter III, Section B 3 *(c)*.

[947] *Supra*, Chapter III, Section C 2 *(a)*.

and international processes into much closer engagement in other contexts as well. Sometimes these situations may not involve the international court in determination of the whole of the claim in the national court. Rather, States may, by treaty, have conferred upon an international tribunal the power to decide on particular international rights which may in turn affect the outcome of national proceedings. The right of individual petition to international human rights tribunals presents an obvious example, where the individual may be seeking redress from the very State which is subjecting him to criminal process. Where the accused person is a foreign national, his home State may also have rights of recourse before an international tribunal.

Two sets of cases decided over the last decade on the rights of condemned prisoners on Death Row in the Americas involve issues of this kind. The responses of the final courts of appeal at national level in both the United States and in the Caribbean have exposed deep divisions of view amongst the judiciary as to the role to be accorded to pending international proceedings.

The first set of cases concerned the rights of condemned prisoners of foreign nationality to be informed of their rights to seek consular assistance under Article 36 (1) *(b)* of the Vienna Convention on Consular Relations 1963[948]. By an Optional Protocol to that treaty, member States could agree to submit disputes between them as to the interpretation or application of the treaty to the International Court of Justice[949]. The

---

[948] Vienna Convention on Consular Relations 1963 (signed 24 April 1963, entered into force 19 March 1967), 596 *UNTS* 261.

[949] Optional Protocol to the Vienna Convention on Consular Relations concerning the Compulsory Settlement of Disputes (signed 24 April 1963, entered into force 19 March 1967), 596 *UNTS* 487.

United States gave such agreement, upon its ratification of the treaty in 1969, until withdrawing from the Protocol in 2005. The Court heard three cases brought by other member States of the Convention, whose nationals had been convicted and condemned to death in the United States. The first of these, *Breard*[950], began dramatically with the issue by the International Court of a provisional measures order to stay execution of the prisoner pending its decision, but did not proceed beyond the provisional measures stage. The second two, *LaGrand* and *Avena*, led to final judgments on the merits[951]. Before the commencement of any of these cases, Mexico had petitioned the Inter-American Court of Justice for an Advisory Opinion on "The Right to Information on Consular Assistance in the Framework of the Guarantees of the Due Process of Law", and Court delivered its Opinion on 1 October 1999[952]. The question of the effect of the proceedings before the ICJ has provoked in turn four decisions of the United States Supreme Court, *Breard, Medellin I, Sanchez-Llamas* and *Medellin II*[953]. In all of them, a majority of the Court ultimately denied effect to the International Court's decisions. There were in each

---

[950] *Vienna Convention on Consular Relations (Paraguay* v. *United States of America)* (Provisional Measures, Order of 9 April 1998), *ICJ Rep. 1998* 248.

[951] *LaGrand (Germany* v. *United States of America)*, *ICJ Rep. 2001* 466, 134 *ILR* 1; *Avena and Other Mexican Nationals (Mexico* v. *United States of America), ICJ Rep. 2004* 12, 134 *ILR* 95.

[952] *The Right to Information on Consular Assistance in the Framework of the Guarantees of the Due Process of Law*, Advisory Opinion, OC-16/99 (1 October 1999), Inter-American Court of Human Rights.

[953] *Breard* v. *Greene*, 523 US 371, 118 S. Ct. 1352 (1998); *Medellin* v. *Dretke*, 544 US 660 (2005) *(Medellin I)*; *Sanchez-Llamas* v. *Oregon*, 548 US 331, 126 S. Ct. 2669, 134 *ILR* 719 (2006); *Medellin* v. *Texas*, 128 S. Ct. 1346 (2008) *(Medellin II)*.

case vigorous dissenting judgments. Finally, as these lectures were being delivered in The Hague, the International Court of Justice issued a further provisional measures order in relation to Medellin (one of about 50 nationals cited in *Avena*) pending a further case filed by Mexico requesting an interpretation of the Court's earlier *Avena* judgments[954]. Efforts to forestall Medellin's execution by this means ultimately failed. The US Supreme Court, by a vote of 5:4 refused further review[955]. Medellin was executed by the State of Texas in August 2008[956].

The second set of cases concerns the effect of a condemned prisoner's rights to pursue an individual petition to a regional or international human rights body under the due process protections of the constitutions of Caribbean island States. In these cases, after conviction and sentence, the prisoners pursued complaints under the Inter-American Human Rights system, and then sought to place reliance on the pendency of these complaints to forestall execution of the death sentence. The Inter-American Court ordered provisional measures to preserve the lives of the prisoners in a series of cases in Trinidad in 1998[957]. The Privy Council then considered the effect of the Inter-American proceedings in four cases: two from Trinidad, *Thomas*[958] and

---

[954] *Request for Interpretation of the Judgment of 31 March 2004 in the Case concerning Avena and Other Mexican Nationals (Mexico* v. *United States of America)* (Provisional Measures, Order of 16 July 2008), ICJ General List No. 139.

[955] *Medellin* v. *Texas*, 129 S. Ct. 360 (2008).

[956] Crook, "Contemporary Practise of the United States Relating to International Law", (2008) 102 *AJIL* 860.

[957] *Hilaire* v. *Trinidad and Tobago*, Inter-American Commission on Human Rights, Report No. 43/98 (25 September 1998).

[958] *Thomas* v. *Baptiste*, [2000] 2 AC 1 (PC (Trinidad and Tobago), Browne-Wilkinson, Steyn and Millett; Goff and Hobhouse dissenting).

*Briggs* [959]; one from the Bahamas, *Higgs* [960]; and one from Jamaica, *Lewis* [961]. The results of these cases are not easily reconcilable, and may have at least as much to do with the composition of the particular panel than real distinctions between the cases themselves.

Considered together, these cases offer a unique insight into the kinds of interaction which may now be expected between international tribunals and national courts. The new elements which have prompted this include:

(a) *Rights of individual petition.* Many human rights conventions have made provision for the right of an individual to petition an international tribunal against his own State. For present purposes, this can have the consequence that the same litigants may be before the court, both at the national and the international level.

(b) *Standing jurisdiction of international tribunals.* Even where this identity of parties is not present, as in the case of proceedings before the ICJ, the existence of the Optional Protocol to the Consular Convention creates a standing submission to the jurisdiction of an international tribunal. Although the claimant in such a case is a State, the breach of the Convention consists in the failure of another State party to accord rights which the Convention accords to nationals of other Convention States. The International Court made the point in *LaGrand*

---

[959] *Briggs* v. *Baptiste*, [2000] 2 AC 40 (PC (Trinidad and Tobago), Millett, Hoffmann, Clyde and Russell; Nicholls dissenting).

[960] *Higgs* v. *Minister of National Security*, [2000] 2 AC 228 (PC (Bahamas) Hoffmann, Hobhouse and Henry; Steyn and Cooke dissenting).

[961] *Lewis* v. *Attorney-General of Jamaica*, [2001] 2 AC 50 (PC (Jamaica), Slynn, Nicholls, Steyn and Hutton; Hoffmann dissenting).

in the following way: "Article 36, paragraph 1, creates individual rights, which, by virtue of Article I of the Optional Protocol may be invoked in this Court by the national State of the detained person." [962]

(c) *Reduced impact of exhaustion of local remedies rule.* The fact that these cases all arose shortly before the execution of a sentence of death meant that there was no real question of applying the exhaustion of local remedies rule to preclude consideration of the case by the international tribunal. In any event, the International Court held in *Avena* [963] that the duty to exhaust local remedies did not apply to Article 36 (1), since it created interdependent rights for both the affected individual and his sending State.

(d) *Compulsory advisory opinion jurisdiction.* The jurisdiction of some international tribunals has been further enlarged by their ability to render advisory opinions. In the case of the Inter-American Court, this is especially wide, as the contracting States to the American Convention on Human Rights chose to confer upon the Court the jurisdiction to render advisory opinions on both the Convention itself and "other treaties concerning the protection of human rights in the American states". [964]

(e) *Constitutional basis for domestic reception of international decisions.* Finally, consideration of these issues was also facilitated by particular characteristics of the constitutional arrangements in

---

[962] *Supra* footnote 951, [77].

[963] *Ibid.*, [40].

[964] Art. 64 (1) American Convention on Human Rights. On the use of the advisory opinion jurisdiction as a form of compulsory jurisdiction see Romano, *supra* footnote 760.

the affected States. Thus the framers of the US
Constitution, in a conscious break with British
practice, provided that "all Treaties . . . shall be the
supreme Law of the Land"[965]. This departure from
a strictly dualistic approach raised the prospect that
proceedings brought in the International Court pursuant to such a treaty might themselves have effect
within the law of the United States. Whether it
would do so depended upon the Court's determination of whether the treaties concerned were "self-
executing"[966]. Further, each of the Caribbean States
from which the Privy Council heard appeals had
adopted upon independence written Constitutions,
containing a Bill of Rights. The texts of these Bills
of Rights closely followed, although did not completely replicate, the international obligations of
the State under international and regional human
rights treaties[967]. Although these Constitutions
were silent as to the application of treaty rights, the
written Constitution nevertheless provided a framework within which such individual rights of petition could be considered.

---

[965] United States Constitution, Art. VI, cl. 2; and see
Breyer J (dissenting) in *Medellin II*, *supra* footnote 953,
1375-1380 for an account of the legislative history of the
provision.

[966] Vázquez, "The Four Doctrines of Self-executing
Treaties", (1995) 89 *AJIL* 695; Vázquez, "Treaties as Law
of the Land: The Supremacy Clause and the Judicial
Enforcement of Treaties", (2008) 122 *Harvard LR* 599.

[967] But see *Matthew* v. *Trinidad and Tobago*, [2005] 1
AC 433, 134 *ILR* 687 (PC (Trinidad and Tobago)) and
*Boyce* v. *The Queen*, [2005] 1 AC 400, 134 *ILR* 439 (PC
(Barbados)), where a 5:4 majority of an enlarged Board of
the Privy Council, in a speech delivered by Lord
Hoffmann (Lords Bingham, Nicholls, Steyn and Walker
dissenting), held, contrary to the position taken in international human rights tribunals, that the mandatory death
sentence was not contrary to the Constitution.

(a) *The Consular Convention cases — ICJ and US Supreme Court*

The judicial dialogue between the International Court and the US Supreme Court on the effect of the Vienna Consular Convention on American Death Row prisoners began in a dramatic way. Paraguay commenced its action against the United States in the ICJ with an application for provisional measures in an attempt to prevent the execution of Mr. Breard, a Paraguayan national in Virginia. The case was filed in the ICJ on 3 April 1998, just 11 days before Breard's scheduled execution on 14 April.

The Court issued an order for provisional measures on 9 April, on the basis of irreparable harm. The order directed the United States to "take all measures at its disposal" to ensure that Mr. Breard was not executed before the Court's final decision on Paraguay's claim [968].

Breard then petitioned the US Supreme Court by writ of *habeas corpus* seeking enforcement of the International Court's order [969]. The Court, by majority, denied the relief on the day scheduled for Breard's execution [970]. It held that the point about the failure to advise Breard of his consular rights should have been taken, if at all, at trial. Member States of the Vienna Convention were only obliged to give effect to rights under Article 36 (2) "in conformity with the law and regulations of the receiving State". In the case of the United States, this included the procedural default rule, precluding the later raising of defences in a federal action which ought to have been raised in the course of

---

[968] *Supra* footnote 950, 258, [41].
[969] *Supra* footnote 953.
[970] Rehnquist CJ, O'Connor, Scalia, Kennedy and Thomas JJ; Souter (Separate Opinion), Stevens, Ginsburg and Breyer JJ, dissenting.

a state criminal trial. Congress had subsequently legislated to give effect to this rule in priority to treaty obligations. Thus, the Court concluded that, while it
"should give respectful consideration to the interpretation of an international treaty rendered by an international court with jurisdiction to interpret such"[971], it
had no power as a matter of existing US law to order
the relief sought. Intervention by the US State Department with the Governor of Virginia was equally unsuc-
cessful, and Breard was eventually executed on
14 April, following which Paraguay discontinued its
ICJ proceedings[972].

However, this early set-back did not in the event
prevent a full consideration of the matter by both the
ICJ and the US Supreme Court. In *LaGrand*, the convicted prisoners were German nationals, Karl and
Walter LaGrand. After the execution of Karl LaGrand,
but immediately before the execution of Walter
LaGrand, the ICJ issued an order for provisional measures in the same terms as in *Breard*[973]. The United
States Supreme Court again denied relief, and Walter
LaGrand was executed on the same day. But, on this
occasion, Germany decided nevertheless to pursue its
claim against the United States on the merits in the
ICJ, challenging the failure of the United States to
comply with the Court's order.

While the case was still pending in the International
Court, on 1 October 1999 the Inter-American Court of
Human Rights delivered its Advisory Opinion in
response to Mexico's request. One of the objections to
the competence of the Court which had been raised by
the United States was the pendency of the contentious

---

[971]   *Supra* footnote 953, 375.

[972]   (Order of 10 November 1998), *ICJ Rep. 1998* 426.

[973]   *LaGrand (Germany* v. *United States)* (Order of
3 March 1999), *ICJ Rep. 1999* 9.

ICJ proceedings. One of the earliest cases rendered by
the Court on the scope of its advisory jurisdiction
had decided that the possibility the different international courts would reach different conclusions on the
interpretation of the same treaty provisions "is a
phenomenon common to all those legal systems that
have certain courts which are not hierarchically
integrated"[974]. It was not a reason for the Court to
decline to exercise its advisory jurisdiction. But the
question raised in *Consular Assistance* was different, in
that the other cases which were pending against the
United States (an OAS member) were contentious in
nature.

The Court resolved the issue by emphasizing its
independence as an "autonomous judicial institution"[975]. It pointed out the different character of the advisory jurisdiction, as permissive rather than mandatory, and insisted that member States should not be
denied its guidance on the interpretation of their obligations for this reason. The Court concluded that, in
death penalty cases, if there were a failure to observe
Article 36 (1) *(b)*, then imposition of the death penalty
would amount to a violation of the right not to be
arbitrarily deprived of one's life, engaging the responsibility of the State[976].

The ICJ delivered its judgment in the *LaGrand* case
on the merits on 27 June 2001. Two arguments raised
by the parties relate directly to the question of parallel
proceedings. First, the United States argued that
Germany's submissions sought to transform the International Court into an "ultimate court of appeal in

---

[974] *"Other Treaties" Subject to the Advisory Jurisdiction of the Court*, Advisory Opinion, OC-1/82 (24 September 1982), *Series A, No. 1*, [50].

[975] Statute of the Inter-American Court of Human
Rights, *supra* footnote 755, Art. 1.

[976] *Supra* footnote 952, [137] and *dispositif* [7].

national criminal proceedings"[977]. The Court rejected this argument. It held:

> "Although Germany deals extensively with the practice of American courts as it bears on the application of the Convention, all three submissions seek to require the Court to do no more than apply the relevant rules of international law to the issues in dispute between the Parties to this case. The exercise of this function, expressly mandated by Article 38 of its Statute, does not convert this Court in a court of appeal of national criminal proceedings."[978]

Secondly, Germany had submitted that the United States had breached of Court's provisional measures order, which sought to prevent Walter LaGrand's execution pending the Court's final decision. This in turn raised for the decision of the Court for the first time the controversial question whether its provisional measures orders were binding. The Court acknowledged that the text was ambiguous, particularly comparing the equally authoritative English and French versions. It held, however, that the object and purpose of provisional measures, which were based on the necessity of avoiding prejudice to the rights of the parties pending the final decision of the Court, suggested that such measures had to be binding. Having examined the *travaux*, it pointed out that the framers of Article 41 of its Statute had chosen reticent language because the Court lacked the means of execution of its orders, not because they were not binding[979]. The Court found the United States in breach of its order.

On the substantive questions, the Court found that the use of the "procedural default" rule to deny review and reconsideration of a sentence pronounced after a

---

[977] *Supra* footnote 951, [50].
[978] *Ibid.*, [52].
[979] *Ibid.*, [107].

failure to accord a foreign national consular assistance was a breach of Article 36 (2). Should in the future German nationals be sentenced to severe penalties in cases where the accused had not been informed of his right to consular assistance, the United States must, by means of its own choosing, allow review and reconsideration of the sentences.

Then, on 9 January 2003, Mexico began its own contentious proceedings in the International Court alleging breaches of Article 36 of the Consular Convention in relation to some 52 Mexican nationals on Death Row. On this occasion, the Court's provisional measures order elicited a confirmation from the United States that none of the named individuals had been executed[980], and this remained the position when the Court gave judgment on the merits. Moreover, none of the proceedings in the United States had reached the point where there was no further opportunity for review or reconsideration. Thus, the question of the nature of such review became the central issue in *Avena*. The International Court gave its final judgment on the merits on 31 March 2004. The Court concluded that the "procedural default" rule breached the Convention, since it barred the defendant from raising the issue of his rights under Article 36[981]. The review and reconsideration process had to guarantee that the violation and the possible prejudice caused by that violation be fully examined[982]. The Court concluded that it was for the United States to find an appropriate remedy of review and reconsideration in the case of the particular Mexican nationals on Death Row[983].

This put the ball firmly in the court of the United

---

[980] *Supra* footnote 951, [3] (*Avena* judgment).
[981] *Ibid.*, [134].
[982] *Ibid.*, [139].
[983] *Ibid.*, [152].

States. The Executive responded in two ways. First, President Bush issued a memorandum on 28 February 2005 determining that the United States "will discharge its international obligations" under the *Avena* judgment "by having State courts give effect to the decision in accordance with general principles of comity in cases filed by the Mexican nationals addressed in that decision"[984]. Then, a week later, the Secretary of State gave notice of the United States' withdrawal from the Optional Protocol to the Vienna Convention[985].

The decision of the United States Supreme Court in the light of these new circumstances, in *Medellin I* (decided on 23 May 2005), was to remit the questions of the effect of both the *Avena* judgment and President Bush's executive order to the state courts for determination[986]. Then, on 28 June 2006, the Court decided a case brought by a Mexican national who had not been named in the *Avena* judgment, together with a case of Honduran national: *Sanchez-Llamas* v. *Oregon, Bustillo* v. *Johnson*[987]. One of the arguments raised by Bustillo was that the Court's earlier holding in *Breard*, which upheld the validity of State procedural default rules, could no longer stand in the light of the ICJ's subsequent judgments in *LaGrand* and *Avena*.

The Court began its response to that submission by emphasizing that the Constitution endowed it with the authority to interpret such treaties as are given effect as a matter of federal law:

> "Under our Constitution, '[t]he judicial Power of the United States' is 'vested in one supreme Court, and in such inferior Courts as the Congress may from

---

[984] Memorandum for the Attorney-General (28 February 2005), 44 *ILM* 964.
[985] *Medellin II*, *supra* footnote 953, 1354.
[986] *Medellin I*, *supra* footnote 953.
[987] *Supra* footnote 953.

time to time ordain and establish'. Art. III, s 1. That
'judicial Power . . . extend[s] to . . . Treaties', *Id.* s 2.
And, as Chief Justice Marshall famously explained,
that judicial power includes the duty "to say what
the law is' [988] . . . If treaties are to be given effect as
federal law under our legal system, determining
their meaning as a matter of federal law 'is empha-
tically the province and duty of the judicial department', headed by the 'one supreme Court' established by the Constitution." [989]

It held, by contrast, that:

> "Nothing in the structure or purpose of the ICJ
> suggests that its interpretations were     intended to
> be conclusive in our courts. The ICJ's decisions
> have '*no binding force* except between the parties
> and in respect of that particular case' [990] . . . Any
> interpretation of law the ICJ renders in the course of
> resolving particular disputes is thus not binding
> precedent *even as to the ICJ itself*; there is accord-
> ingly little reason to think that such interpretations
> were intended to be controlling on our courts. The
> ICJ's principal purpose is to arbitrate particular dis-
> putes between national governments . . . While each
> member of the United Nations has agreed to comply
> with decisions of the ICJ 'in any case to which it is
> a party', . . . the Charter's procedures for noncom-
> pliance — referral to the Security Council by the
> aggrieved state — contemplates quintessentially
> *international* remedies . . ." [991]

---

[988] Citing *Marbury* v. *Madison*, 1 Cranch 137, 177
(1803).
[989] *Supra* footnote 953, 334.
[990] Citing ICJ Statute, *supra* footnote 748, Art. 59.
[991] *Supra* footnote 953, 334 (references omitted,
emphasis in original).

The Court held that the President's direction did not amount to a statement "that the ICJ's interpretation of Article 36 is binding on our courts"[992], particularly where the United States had subsequently withdrawn from the Optional Protocol. The Court then excoriated the ICJ's decision as "inconsistent with the basic framework of an adversary system" where "the responsibility for failing to raise an issue generally rests with the parties themselves"[993]. It held that Article 36 rights could be given no higher status than other procedural rights within the US criminal justice system, and that the procedural default rule applied to them.

The majority judgment[994] was the subject of a vigorous dissent filed by Breyer J[995]. He pointed out that the majority had not in fact decided whether the Convention created rights on which a defendant could rely directly in ordinary criminal proceedings. He concluded that it did[996]. It was common ground in that case that the Convention was "self-executing", in the sense that it "operates of itself without the aid of any legislative provision"[997]. The Convention provisions by their terms were intended to set forth standards which were judicially enforceable, speaking directly to the rights of foreign nationals[998]. The International Court's judgment should be given particular weight, both because of the importance of uniform treaty interpreta-

---

[992] *Ibid.*, 335.

[993] *Ibid.*, 357.

[994] Roberts CJ, Scalia, Kennedy, Thomas and Alito JJ, Ginsburg J concurring.

[995] In which Stevens and Souter JJ joined, and in which Ginsburg J joined as to Part II.

[996] In Part II of the judgment, in which Ginsburg J also concurred.

[997] *Supra* footnote 953, 372, citing *Foster* v. *Neilson*, 2 Pet. 253, 314, 7 L. Ed. 415 (1829).

[998] *Ibid.*, 375, citing *Head Money Cases*, 112 US 580, 5 S. Ct. 247 (1884).

tion, and because of that Court's particular experience in matters of international law. Breyer J pointed out that the conflict between the majority's judgment and that of the ICJ was "unprecedented"[999]. He concluded that the majority's approach:

"leaves States free to deny effective relief for Convention violations, despite America's promise to provide just such relief. That approach risks weakening respect abroad for the rights of foreign nationals, a respect that America, in 1969, sought to make effective throughout the world. And it increases the difficulties faced by the United States and other nations who would, though binding treaties, strengthen the role that law can play in assuring all citizens, including American citizens, fair treatment throughout the world." [1000]

Finally, on 25 March 2008 in *Medellin II*[1001], the majority of the Supreme Court took the opportunity to deliver the *coup de grâce* to the International Court's judgment in *Avena*. The Supreme Court accepted *certiorari* after the Texas Court of Criminal Appeals had denied Medellin's *habeas corpus* writ on procedural default grounds. Since Medellin was one of the Mexican nationals specifically named in *Avena,* the Supreme Court took the case specifically in order to decide whether the ICJ's judgment was directly enforceable as domestic law in a state court in the United States. The Court answered that question by addressing the further question whether the Optional Protocol to the Vienna Consular Convention, together with the UN Charter and the ICJ Statute supplied a relevant obligation which was "self-executing".

---

[999] *Ibid.*, 386.
[1000] *Ibid.*, 398.
[1001] *Supra* footnote 953.

The Court found the Optional Protocol itself to be "a bare grant of jurisdiction" [1002], saying nothing itself about the enforceability of any judgment of the ICJ which might result. That obligation would have to come, if at all, from Article 94 of the United Nations Charter, pursuant to which each member State "undertakes to comply with the decision of the [ICJ] in any case to which it is a party" [1003]. But the Court accepted the submission of the United States Government that Article 94 is not "an acknowledgement that an ICJ decision will have immediate legal effect in the courts of UN members", but rather "a *commitment* on the part of UN Members to take *future* action through their political branches to comply with an ICJ decision" [1004]. Enforcement ultimately depended upon the Security Council, where the United States would have a power of veto [1005]. The result was that this treaty was not self-executing in the terms of American Constitutional law, and therefore the ICJ judgment was not directly enforceable within the several states of the United States.

The Court then went on to find that the President's Memorandum was likewise unenforceable. Only congressional legislation could give domestic effect to this treaty [1006].

On this occasion, Breyer J was joined by Souter and Ginsburg JJ in dissenting. They held that this question could not be answered simply by interpretation of the treaty in question, simply because so few treaties contained express language that might meet the majority's strictures [1007]. It would be surprising if they did,

---

[1002] *Ibid.*, 1349.
[1003] Citing ICJ Statute, *supra* footnote 748, Art. 94.
[1004] *Supra* footnote 953, 1358, citing US Brief as *amicus curiae* in *Medellin I* (emphasis in original).
[1005] *Ibid.*, 1359.
[1006] *Ibid.*, 1369.
[1007] *Ibid.*, 1380-1381.

since national practice as to incorporation of treaties is so diverse. Citing early precedents of the Supreme Court[1008], they argued that the adoption of the US Constitution had represented a decisive shift in the approach of the common law towards the direct self-executing effect of treaties, which was expressly designed to limit the power of the states. Determination of whether a treaty was self-executing had to be a context-specific enquiry into the nature of the treaty's subject-matter and the rights protected, as well as the character of the treaty's own provisions.

Applying those considerations here, the terms of the UN Charter and the ICJ Statute were perfectly clear in requiring each State to give binding effect to the judgments of the ICJ, where that State had submitted to its compulsory jurisdiction. They did not prescribe how that was to be done. They could not do so, given the diverse position in the national laws of the different member States. But in the United States, that was sufficient to render ICJ judgments enforceable in domestic courts at least sometimes[1009]. The terms of the Optional Protocol concerned an individual's rights; they were precise; and they set forth judicially manageable standards. Logic suggested that, if the treaty itself were self-executing, so too should a judgment given in pursuance of the treaty. The implications of the majority's judgment to the contrary were considerable. Breyer J pointed to some 70 treaties in which the United States had submitted to ICJ jurisdiction. If the Optional Protocol to the Consular Convention was insufficient to create self-executing obligations to give effect to ICJ judgments, it was difficult to see how such an effect could be given in these many other cases[1010].

---

[1008] *Ibid.*, 1377-1379, citing *Ware* v. *Hylton*, 3 Dall. 199; *Foster*, 2 Pet. 253; *US* v. *Percheman*, 7 Pet. 51 (1833).

[1009] *Ibid.*, 1383-1386.

[1010] *Ibid.*, 1389.

He concluded that the majority's holdings "weaken that *rule of law* for which our Constitution stands" [1011].

Mexico's renewed application to the ICJ for provisional measures had more than a whiff of desperation about it. By this time, the United States had withdrawn from the Optional Protocol, and therefore the only basis upon which Mexico could invoke the jurisdiction of the Court was by claiming that there was a dispute between the parties as to the interpretation of the Court's prior judgment. In its provisional measures order, a majority of the Court held that there was such a dispute, since, although both parties agreed that the obligation imposed by the Court's judgment was an obligation of result,

> "the Parties nonetheless apparently hold different views as to the meaning and scope of that obligation of result, namely, whether that understanding is shared by all United States federal and state authorities and whether that obligation falls upon those authorities" [1012].

Finding that the rights of the parties would be irreparably prejudiced if no provisional measures order were granted, the Court ordered by seven votes to five that the United States take all necessary measures to prevent the execution of the condemned men pending its hearing on the merits. The US Supreme Court, in a brief Opinion, saw no reason to change its earlier decision [1013], and Medellin was executed.

---

[1011] *Ibid.*, 1391 (emphasis added).

[1012] *Supra* footnote 954, [55] (Order of 16 July 2008, Buergenthal, Owada, Tomka, Keith, Skotnikov JJ dissenting).

[1013] *Supra* footnote 953, Stevens, Souter, Ginsburg and Breyer dissenting on the grounds that the views of the Solicitor-General should be sought on the steps being taken by the United States to comply with the ICJ's judgment.

The present study is not the place to enter upon the American Constitutional law debate as to the meaning of the clause establishing treaties as "the supreme Law of the Land" [1014] ; or the effect of these recent decisions on the dramatic revival of the exception to that requirement for treaties which are not "self-executing" [1015]. These are matters of high moment in the United States, which must now engage the close attention of Constitutional law scholars, as well as State Department officials and lower courts, as they seek to determine the impact of the rulings for the application of the supremacy clause in the context of the numerous other treaties to which the United States is party [1016]. If a scholar from outside the United States finds himself in agreement with the analysis of Breyer, Souter and Ginsburg JJ — that the Supremacy clause was originally intended to represent a decisive break with the prior law, which must be given a real scope of operation, and that the recent judgments eviscerate such meaning — that is likely to be of little moment in such a debate.

Rather, these cases are considered in these lectures for what they have to say about the relationship between international and national exercises of adjudicatory power over what was in substance the same dispute. Now, of course, on a conventional analysis, the Consular Convention cases would fail the test for identity of action. The cases in the International Court were inter-State cases, as they had to be. By contrast, the cases in the US Supreme Court were brought by the condemned prisoners against the relevant state officials, as they had to be. But, for all that, it would be impossible to imagine a closer interrelationship of

---

[1014] *Supra* footnote 965.
[1015] *Foster* v. *Neilson*, 27 US (2 Pet.) 253 (1829).
[1016] See for example Vázquez, *supra* footnote 966.

actions short of complete identity. Article 36 (1) of the
Consular Convention creates a right to seek consular
assistance which was specifically addressed to the
nationals of sending Contracting States[1017]. This is
reinforced in Article 36 (2) by the obligation on the
competent authorities of the receiving State to inform
such a person of this right, if he is taken into custody.
The International Court proceedings were brought
specifically in respect of the effect of the actions of the
United States against named foreign nationals, and
the interim and final orders of that Court addressed
the position of those individuals. The United States
appeared, and was represented, in both the International Court and the US Supreme Court.

On one view, the issues raised by the effect of the
International Court's judgments more properly raise
questions of recognition and enforcement — of *res
judicata* rather than *lis pendens*. By the time of
*Sanchez-Llamas* and *Medellin II,* the International
Court had already delivered final judgments in
*LaGrand* and *Avena.* It happened in *Sanchez-Llamas*
that the individual prisoner was not one of those
specifically named in the *Avena* proceedings. But
*Medellin* was so named, which is why his case raised
squarely the binding effect of the ICJ judgment itself
— rather than merely its effect as an authoritative
interpretation of the Convention.

But in substance the Consular Convention cases
contain many instances of overlapping pending proceedings. They began in this way with the provisional
measures application to the International Court on
behalf of Breard, and the *habeas corpus* application to
the US Supreme Court for a stay of execution pending
the International Court's full consideration of the matter. They ended in a similar fashion, with the renewed

---

[1017]  *Supra* footnote 948.

application to the International Court for provisional measures to forestall the execution of Medellin, and the rejection of its enforcement by the US Supreme Court.

All of the cases over the decade in which they were litigated were also linked in terms of the substantive issue raised: the effect of the obligation of consular assistance enshrined in Article 36 (2) upon the rights of a prisoner who had already been tried and condemned to death, not having either been advised of his rights under the Convention, or taken the point as to the effect of this default at trial. The issue was one which, of its nature, involved both international law (which created the right) and national law (where the right had to be given effect). Because of the serial, and cumulative, nature of the cases, this was no mere question of the enforcement of an isolated judgment. It was a conversation between the two courts, in which each step served to develop the jurisprudence. It is regrettable that this conversation in the end drove the courts into conflict rather than co-operation.

It is submitted that this conflict was not grounded simply, or even predominantly, in a debate about the proper construction of the international law obligation, or even in questions of the reception of international law obligations generally within the national legal system of the United States. Rather, it turned upon a conflict in the exercise of adjudicatory power. Nowhere is this more clearly demonstrated than in the passage from *Sanchez-Llamas* already cited [1018]. The Supreme Court opens its reasoning by emphasizing that the exercise of judicial power of the United States is "vested in one supreme Court", and that this power includes the power to determine the meaning of treaties as a matter of federal law. By contrast, the work of the International Court is described as merely to "arbitrate partic-

---

[1018] *Supra* footnote 989.

ular disputes between national governments"[1019]. The reasoning is substantially the same as that adopted by the European Court in *MOX Plant*[1020]. The very act of giving effect to international law obligations is held to transform those obligations into federal ones for the purpose of the exercise of the power of adjudication, a purpose treated by both courts as superior to an agreement by the States to refer the matter to international arbitration.

Now, the characterization of the International Court as an arbitration tribunal does considerable violence to the function of the Court under the United Nations Charter as "the principal judicial organ of the United Nations"[1021], a point which the Court belatedly had to confront in *Medellin II*. It also ignores the original intentions of those who first created the World Court. It was Elihu Root (one of the founding fathers of this Academy), who, as US Secretary of State, issued the following instructions to the United States delegation to the Second Hague Peace Conference in 1907. Root dismissed inter-State arbitration as little more than diplomatic negotiation and wrote:

> "It should be your effort to bring about in the Second Conference a development of the Hague tribunal[1022] into a permanent tribunal composed of judges who . . . will devote their entire time to the trial and decision of international causes by judicial methods . . . The court should be made of such dignity, consideration, and rank that the best and ablest jurists will accept appointment to it, and that the

---

[1019] *Supra* footnote 991.

[1020] *Supra* footnote 841.

[1021] Charter of the United Nations, *supra* footnote 747, Art. 92.

[1022] A reference to the Permanent Court of Arbitration, established at the First Hague Peace Conference in 1899, *supra* footnote 746.

whole world will have confidence in its judgments." [1023]

The resulting creation in 1920 of a Permanent Court of International Justice was thus a decisive shift from arbitration to the judicial settlement of international disputes. But then, as now, it left the jurisdiction of the Court to individual exercises in State consent [1024].

States, therefore, are under no compulsion to accept the adjudicatory competence of the International Court. But, where they voluntarily do so, then, with respect, it adds nothing, and excludes much, to characterize such consent as "a bare grant of jurisdiction" [1025]. The decision to invest the Court with adjudicatory competence is an exercise of party autonomy which must carry with it consequences for the Court's process and its outcome. This is not to be reduced to a question of the ultimate sanctions between States for breach under Article 94 (2) of the Charter. The direct obligation of each State to recognize the Court's process and judgment exists independently from this [1026]. It flows from the very fact of the parties' original agreement. Nor, however, can the fact that a breach of such obligation entails international responsibility carry with it the negative consequence that it thereby cannot have direct effect within the municipal legal system, where the relevant State's Constitution so permits. It would be a mistake to look for indicia of direct effect within the

---

[1023] Scott (ed.), *Instructions to the American Delegates to the Hague Peace Conferences and Their Official Reports* (1916) 79-80.

[1024] Art. 36, Statute of the International Court of Justice, *supra* footnote 748.

[1025] *Medellin II*, *supra* footnote 953, 1349.

[1026] Art. 12, International Law Commission Draft Articles on the Responsibilities of States for Internationally Wrongful Acts (2001), Supp. No. 10, UN doc. A/56/10, 43, and Commentary, *ibid.*, 59, 124-126.

text of treaties themselves, since, as the minority in *Medellin II* point out, treaties must take effect within many different States, with different practices in relation to treaty incorporation.

The real question here thus tended to be obscured, rather than illuminated, by the focus on self-execution of treaties. Rather, it is properly viewed as a question of the extent to which the national constitution admits a specific and agreed right to international adjudication within its own concept of what is required of due process. The Supreme Court decided in *Sanchez-Llamas,* that due process in the US legal system was exhausted by the procedural default rule; and in *Medellin II* that the International Court's decision could not be given effect within that system. But a closer examination of what due process might require where a State has voluntarily accepted international judicial process was made in a series of judgments of the Privy Council rendered concurrently with those of the US Supreme Court.

(b) *The Caribbean cases: the Privy Council and the Inter-American Human Rights system*

The jurisprudence of the US Supreme Court may be compared with that of the Judicial Committee of the Privy Council, hearing appeals from convicted prisoners on Death Row in the Caribbean. At issue in all of these cases was the question whether the pendency of individual petitions within the Inter-American Human Rights system entitled the prisoners to delay their execution. Earlier jurisprudence of the Privy Council had sought to deal with this issue by specifying an overall period within which all avenues of redress must be exhausted lest the prisoner's continued incarceration awaiting execution itself become inhuman or degrading treatment, prohibited under the Constitution and requiring the prisoners' release[1027]. In so doing, it had taken into account indications from the relevant States as to their compliance with the Inter-American procedures. But the Judicial Committee had stopped short of finding that a failure to await the decision of the Inter-American Commission or Court could itself constitute inhuman or degrading treatment[1028].

The Judicial Committee took the next step in *Thomas* v. *Baptiste*[1029], relying on the different provisions of the Constitution of Trinidad and Tobago, which contained a right not to be deprived of life "except by due process of law"[1030]. The two appellants, Darren Thomas and Hanif Hilaire, had been convicted of murder, receiving the mandatory sentence of death. By 1997 a significant number of persons who had been convicted of murder and sentenced to death in Trinidad and Tobago were petitioning the Inter-American Commission complaining of violations of their rights under the American Convention of Human Rights. The Government of Trinidad became concerned that, even if the petitions were dismissed, they would not be dealt with in time to allow the sentences to be carried out within the time limits required by previous Privy Council jurisprudence. On 13 October 1997, the Government had therefore published time-limits for each stage of prisoners' appeals to the Inter-American Commission of Human Rights.

The appellants' petitions had been held admissible by the Commission[1031]. But, once the Government's

---

[1027] *Pratt* v. *Attorney-General for Jamaica*, [1994] 2 AC 1 (PC (Jamaica)).

[1028] *Fisher* v. *Minister of Public Safety and Immigration (No. 2)*, [2000] 1 AC 434 (PC (The Bahamas), Lords Slynn and Hope dissenting).

[1029] *Supra* footnote 958.

[1030] Section 4 *(a)*.

[1031] *Supra*.

prescribed time-limits had expired, and before the
Commission had reached a decision on the merits, execution warrants were read to the Thomas and Hilaire.
They then applied to the courts in Trinidad and Tobago
for declarations that execution would violate their
Constitutional rights not to be deprived of life except
by due process of law (Section 4 *(a)*) and to be free
from cruel and unusual punishment. The first instance
decisions varied, but on appeal the Court of Appeal
refused to vacate their death sentence. On 29 August
1999, the Inter-American Court (to whom the cases
had been referred by the Commission) issued provisional measures orders to preserve the lives of the
appellants[1032]. On 17 March 1999, the Judicial Committee of the Privy Council held that the time-limits
were unlawful and the executions ought to be stayed
until the Commission and the Inter-American Court of
Human Rights had rendered their decisions and these
had been considered by the relevant Trinidad and
Tobago authorities.

Lord Millett, delivering the opinion for the majority
of the Board, held that the Instructions were unlawful
as a disproportionate measure under the law of
Trinidad and Tobago[1033] which infringed the Constitutional protection of the due process of law. In a seminal passage, he explained the meaning of this concept:

"In their Lordships' view 'due process of law' is
a compendious expression in which the word 'law'
does not refer to any particular law and is not a
synonym for common law or statute. Rather it
invokes the concept of the rule of law itself

---

[1032] Provisional Measures, Orders of 29 August 1999,
noted in *Hilaire* v. *Trinidad and Tobago* (Inter-American
Court of Human Rights, Judgment of 21 June 2002) 134
*ILR* 293, [28].
[1033] *Supra* footnote 958, 20.

and the universally accepted standards of justice observed by civilised nations which observe the rule of law . . ." [1034]

He then addressed the key element of the State's defence, namely that the effect of the judgment would be to infringe the principle that international obligations are not binding as a matter of domestic law, until given effect by statute:

"The right for which [the petitioners] contend is not the particular right to petition the commission or even to complete the particular process which they initiated when they lodged their petitions. It is the general right accorded to all litigants not to have the outcome of any pending appellate or other legal process pre-empted by executive action. This general right is not created by the Convention; it is accorded by the common law and affirmed by section 4 *(a)* of the Constitution. The applicants are not seeking to enforce the terms of an unincorporated treaty, but a provision of the domestic law of Trinidad and Tobago contained in the Constitution. By ratifying a treaty which provides for individual access to an international body, the government made that process for the time being part of the domestic criminal justice system and thereby temporarily at least extended the scope of the due process clause in the Constitution." [1035]

He held that the fact that the proceedings before the Commission could at best result in a recommendation to the Trinidad Government was irrelevant, since the Commission had power to refer the matter to the Inter-American Court, whose rulings would be binding. "For the government to carry out the sentences of death

---

[1034] *Ibid.*, 22.
[1035] *Ibid.*, 23.

before the petitions have been heard would deny the applicants their constitutional right to due process." [1036]

Lord Goff and Lord Hobhouse dissented, finding that the only rights upon which the appellants could rely were those vouchsafed to them by Trinidadian law, and this could not include the terms of unincorporated treaties [1037]. Their Lordships said this about the concept of "due process of law":

> "The phrase 'due process of law' has a long history, being first found in English legislation some six and a half centuries ago. It is derived from the use of the words in Chapter 39 of the Magna Carta: 'except by the lawful judgment of his peers or by the law of the land'. The expression 'due process of law' came to be used as a synonym for the expression 'law of the land'. Thus 'due process of law' was used instead in later legislation and Coke in his *Institutes* (1628) Pt II, vol 1, treated the two expressions as interchangeable. (25 Edw 1, c 29) . . . It is the law of the land which gives the concept of due process its broader meaning . . . The due process of law provision fulfills the basic function of preventing the arbitrary exercise of executive power and places the exercise of that power under the control of the judicature. It also limits the power of the Legislature to legislate so as to derogate from that requirement: . . . *Lassalle* v. *Attorney-General* 18 WIR 379. In this last case, Phillips JA, at p 391, summarised the requirement as being '(i) reasonableness and certainty in the definition of criminal offences; (ii) trial by an independent and impartial tribunal; [and] (iii) observance of the rules of natural justice'. The authorities show that the requirement is that rights and liabilities, criminal and civil,

---

[1036] *Ibid.*, 24.
[1037] *Ibid.*, 31.

be determined in accordance with the law of the land as a matter of both substance and procedure. The laws of the Republic apply this principle. The understanding that the law referred to is the municipal law is confirmed to be correct: indeed, no authority has been cited to contradict this . . .

The widest possible adoption of humane standards is undoubtedly to be aspired to. But it is not properly to be achieved by subverting the Constitutions of states nor by a clear misuse of legal concepts and terminology; indeed, the furthering of human rights depends upon confirming and upholding the rule of law. Suppose that an international treaty declares certain conduct to be criminal wherever committed (and such examples exist), unless and until the legislature of a state party to the treaty has passed a law making such conduct criminal under its municipal law, it would be contrary to due process (and in the Republic, contrary to section 4 of the Constitution) for the executive of the state to deprive any individual of his life, liberty or property on the basis of the international treaty. It would be a clear breach of that individual's constitutional rights. An unincorporated treaty cannot make something due process: nor can such a treaty make something not due process unless some separate principle of municipal law makes it so." [1038]

The dissent concluded by pointing out that the applicants' position was logically inconsistent. The Board had already considered and denied their previous appeals against conviction. That decision was conclusive as a matter of the Constitution of Trinidad. If they sought to rely before the Inter-American Court upon a right which was not open to them as a matter of

---

[1038] *Ibid.*, 32-33.

Trinidadian law, then by definition it could not provide a legal basis for setting aside the convictions. Thus, their Lordships concluded: "The claimed assertion of a constitutional right turns out to be a contradiction of the constitutional right." [1039]

On 21 June 2002, the Inter-American Court finally delivered judgment on the merits, finding the Trinidad and Tobago had committed multiple breaches of the Convention, and declaring that it should abstain from executing the appellants [1040].

The scope of the principle opened by the majority judgment of the Privy Council in *Thomas* was almost immediately tested by another case on appeal from Trinidad, *Briggs* v. *Baptiste* [1041]. Mr. Briggs had also petitioned the Inter-American system following his conviction for murder. The Commission had found that, although he had not been denied the right to a fair trial, the period for which he was detained before trial was a denial of his right to liberty. Its report, recommending that he be considered for early release or commutation of his sentence, was considered by the Advisory Committee on the Power of Pardon. The Committee recommended that the sentence of death should be carried out. The Court of Appeal then upheld the rejection of a constitutional motion by Briggs, holding that carrying out the sentence would not infringe his rights because his petition to the Commission had been finally disposed of and the resulting report considered by the appropriate authorities.

However, the Inter-American *Court* refused to discharge an earlier order granting provisional measures to halt Briggs's execution until the *Court* (as opposed to the Commission) had considered his position. After

---

[1039] *Ibid.*, 34.
[1040] *Supra* footnote 1032.
[1041] *Supra* footnote 959.

a further execution warrant was read to him, Briggs filed another constitutional motion. The Privy Council dismissed the appeal, holding that since the Advisory Committee had considered the Commission's decision and no disputed facts remained to be determined that could be relevant to the Advisory Committee's decision, execution would not violate the appellant's right not to be deprived of life. Thus, although the interlocutory order of the Inter-American Court was still in force, there was in fact no issue left outstanding for decision by the Court. In these circumstances, the Privy Council concluded that "[t]here is no longer any lis" [1042]. It offered the following explanation of what *Thomas* did and did not decide:

> "It did not overturn the constitutional principle that international conventions do not alter domestic law except to the extent that they are incorporated into domestic law by legislation. It did not decide that the recommendations of the commission (which are not binding even in international law) or the orders of the Inter-American Court are directly enforceable in domestic law. It mediated the proceedings before the Inter-American system through the due process clause in the Constitution. It confirmed the principle that the consideration of a reprieve is not a legal process and is not subject to the constitutional requirement of due process, and that the advisory committee is not bound to consider, let alone adopt, the recommendations of the commission." [1043]

The next case was *Higgs* [1044]. This appeal came from the Bahamas, which was a member of the Organization of American States, but not a party to the American

---

[1042] *Ibid.*, 53 (Lord Nicholls dissenting).
[1043] *Ibid.*, 54.
[1044] *Supra* footnote 960.

Convention. The consequence of this was that it was possible for Bahamian nationals to make communications to the Inter-American Commission, which could make non-binding recommendations. But there was no right of petition, either to the Commission or to the Inter-American Court. Concerned at the impact of delay, the Bahamas Government had announced that the Commission would be given 18 months to render a decision. When no decision was forthcoming within that time, warrants of execution were read to the appellants, who then applied for an order, *inter alia*, that execution would breach Article 16 (1) of the Constitution, which prohibited deprivation of a person's life except where he had been sentenced to death.

Lord Hoffmann, speaking for a majority of the Board (Lords Steyn and Cooke dissenting) rejected the appeal, holding that the announcement of an 18 month time-limit precluded any claim to reasonable expectation that execution would be stayed until the Commission rendered a decision. Importing "due process" requirements into Article 16 (1) could not have the effect of making wholly international remedies part of the domestic legal process and, therefore, execution before the Commission had rendered a decision was not a violation of Article 16 (1). His point of departure was that rights acquired by treaty (as an exercise of the prerogative powers of the Crown) could not be construed by a domestic court, and could have no effect on the rights of citizens [1045]. He continued:

> "The rule that treaties cannot alter the law of the land is but one facet of the more general principle that the Crown cannot change the law by the exercise of its powers under the prerogative. This was the great principle which was settled by the Civil

---

[1045] *Ibid.*, 241.

War and the Glorious Revolution in the 17th century. And on no point were the claims of the prerogative more resented in those times than in relation to
the establishment of courts having jurisdiction in
domestic law. There have been no prerogative courts
in England since the abolition of Star Chamber and
High Commission. But the objection to a prerogative court must be equally strong whether it is created by the Crown alone or as an international court
by the Crown in conjunction with other sovereign
states. In neither case is there power to give it any
jurisdiction in domestic law." [1046]

*Thomas*'s case was distinguished on the basis that
the Constitution of the Bahamas, unlike that of
Trinidad, contained no express protection of due process. It was on the basis of that express Constitutional
protection (and not on the broader Common Law doctrine) that the Judicial Committee had rested its decision in *Thomas* [1047]. Lords Steyn and Cooke dissented
on other grounds, and did not therefore deal with the
effect of the pending Inter-American proceedings.

The next case in this sequence is *Lewis* v. *Attorney
General of Jamaica* [1048]. Jamaica was party to the
American Convention, and had accepted the right of
individual petition to the Commission. But it had not
accepted the jurisdiction of the Inter-American Court.
The Government had issued an Instruction giving the
Inter-American Commission only six months to render
a decision on a communication. Once this period
elapsed the Jamaican Privy Council was to advise the
Governor General whether or not to exercise the prerogative of mercy. The Governor General did not exercise the prerogative in the case of the applicants. After

---

[1046]  *Ibid.*, 241-242.
[1047]  *Ibid.*, 246.
[1048]  *Supra* footnote 961.

execution warrants were read, the applicants commenced actions claiming, *inter alia*, that the instructions were unlawful and that their right under Section 13 *(a)* of the Constitution to "the protection of the law" had been infringed by the issue of death warrants while petitions to the Commission were outstanding.

The Privy Council allowed the appeal. Lord Slynn, for the majority, decided that there was no material distinction to be made between "the protection of the law" in the Jamaican Constitution and "due process of law" in that of Jamaica. Accordingly, *Thomas*'s case was applicable [1049]. Lord Hoffmann dissented, stating:

> "On the Inter-American Commission issue, the majority have found in the ancient concept of due process of law a philosopher's stone undetected by generations of judges which can convert the base metal of executive action into the gold of legislative power . . . In particular, there is no explanation of how, in the domestic law of Jamaica, the proceedings before the commission constitute a legal process (as opposed to the proceedings of any other non-governmental body) which must be duly completed." [1050]

Finally, the application of the doctrine developed by the Judicial Committee of the Privy Council in *Thomas* and *Lewis* was tested by the Caribbean Court of Justice, sitting in its Appellate Jurisdiction on appeal from Barbados in *Attorney-General* v. *Joseph and Boyce* [1051]. In a lengthy and nuanced judgment, the Court reviewed all of the prior jurisprudence. The Court rejected the approach in *Thomas* and *Lewis,* finding that:

---

[1049]  *Ibid.*, 85.

[1050]  *Ibid.*, 88.

[1051]  [2006] CCJ 3 (AJ), 69 WIR 104, [2007] 4 LRC 199, 134 *ILR* 469.

"the effect which the majority gave to the treaty, ie expansion of the domestic criminal justice system so as to include the proceedings before the Commission, was inconsistent with their protestations of support for the strict dualist doctrine of the unincorporated treaty. Nor did the judgments explain how, if ratification has that effect, the appropriate domestic authorities can be entitled to impose even reasonable time-limits for the disposal of the case in the absence of any such limitation on the state's obligation in the treaty itself." [1052]

Nevertheless, the Court considered that the advent of international human rights treaties which provided for rights of direct individual petition required some recognition within the domestic legal system [1053]. The Court preferred to achieve this through the doctrine of legitimate expectation, finding that ratification of the treaty gave the condemned men a legitimate expectation that they would be allowed a reasonable time within which to pursue their petitions before the international tribunal [1054]. This was subject to an overriding public interest which would justify the State in proceeding with the execution if the international body did not complete its review within a reasonable time [1055].

The debate about the conception of due process of law developed by a majority in *Thomas* and *Lewis* and that preferred by its dissenters is of first importance to the subject of these lectures. The lengthy passage from the dissent of Lords Goff and Hobhouse in *Thomas* is cited above for the reason that it states with great erudition the constitutional case for treating due process as limited to the procedures available within the

---

[1052] *Ibid.*, [76] (de la Bastide and Saunders JJ).
[1053] *Ibid.*, [105].
[1054] *Ibid.*, [125].
[1055] *Ibid.*, [126].

domestic legal system, and for excluding any reference to international legal process within that term. Their Lordships' conception of due process is that it underpins the Rule of Law by ensuring that decisions of the Executive cannot affect the rights of the citizen to adjudication by the ordinary courts in accordance with the law, as promulgated by Parliament and as enforced by the courts themselves. Seen in this light, an Executive decision to admit reference to an international tribunal is as objectionable as the imposition of trial by Executive Star Chamber.

But, in the present author's view, this line of reasoning fails to take account of two fundamental points. The first flows from the very evolution of the system of international adjudication. For Coke and Blackstone, there could be no judicial bulwark against the power of the Executive other than that provided by national courts, since (self-evidently) there were no international courts to which the citizen could have recourse. Thus, only resort to the ordinary courts of the land could protect the citizen from the arbitrary exercise of public power. But this is no longer the case. States have chosen to create international tribunals as an additional supra-national protection against abuses of public power, and have voluntarily agreed to open such tribunals to complaints about their conduct from their own citizens. The concept of due process is not a static one. On the contrary, it must be capable of evolution to take account of changes in the way in which State power is established and controlled. The courts will surely not find difficulty in distinguishing judicial processes designed for the further protection of the citizen from those established by the Executive for the citizen's persecution.

The second point is one about the source of the doctrine of due process. The fact that its origins in the Common Law system may be traced back to the

Magna Carta (and are not therefore *derived* from international law) should not obscure the function of the doctrine. Indeed, unless stated in more general terms, the doctrine loses much of its force and effect, since it could otherwise become a licence for the narrow legalism of Parliamentary autocracy, and not a protection against it. Thus, the short statement by Lords Goff and Hobhouse of the essential features of the doctrine as a means of controlling the power of the legislature (reasonableness and certainty in the definition of criminal offences; trial by an independent tribunal; and natural justice) is surely not intended to be limited in its application merely to those States with a written Constitution enshrining "due process". On the contrary, these are basic precepts of any legal system governed by the Rule of Law. As such, the concept States a general principle of law common to civilized nations, as applicable to international law as to civilized municipal legal systems, and therefore capable of embracing both.

## D. *Interim Conclusions*

In the result, then, the analysis of parallel proceedings in Public International litigation permits the following five conclusions:

(1) *Jurisdiction and* lex specialis. In many cases, the separate mandate of specialist tribunals under their constituent treaty will permit, or even require, the establishment of jurisdiction, even if there are related proceedings elsewhere. That will be especially so where the parties are different (such as where one case concerns claims involving individuals, and another involves States). The treaty may itself contain its own rules of priority, which must take precedence as *lex specialis* over the general law.

(2) *The unity of international law.* Nevertheless, Public International Law is a single legal system. The fact that different tribunals may be enforcing obligations under different treaties does not change the fact that the source of the rights in both cases is simply international law. For this reason, the highly fragmented approach to parallel litigation championed by ITLOS in *MOX Plant* is not tenable. On the contrary, an international tribunal ought, at least, to consider the relationship between its proceedings and related proceedings brought before another international tribunal.

(3) *Scope for a general principle of* lis pendens. The question whether the doctrine of *lis pendens* is a general principle of law common to civilized nations has still not been authoritatively answered by an international tribunal. However, the research presented in these lectures strongly suggests the existence of such a principle. Further weight is given to this proposition by the widely recognized connection between *lis pendens* and *res judicata,* and the accepted status of the latter as a general principle of law. As a general principle, litispendence requires both courts to take account of the parallel proceedings. It does not import a strict "first seised" requirement. In the exercise of this discretion, international courts possess inherent powers both to protect the exercise of their jurisdiction in appropriate cases, and to suspend the exercise of their jurisdiction in the light of pending proceedings elsewhere. However, this is subject to two conditions. First, each Tribunal retains jurisdiction to determine its own jurisdiction and should normally exercise the power to make that determination. The problem of litispendence only arises once a tribunal has already determined that its jurisdiction overlaps with that of another tri-

bunal. Second, there must be a prior pending proceeding actually on foot before another tribunal. Otherwise, the grant of a stay may perpetrate a denial of justice.

(4) *Rules of separation of international from national proceedings*. In most cases, the traditional doctrines of international law will serve to keep the jurisdictions of national and international courts apart, and situations of exact equivalence are unlikely to arise. Such rules operate both to require initial deference to national courts (the exhaustion of local remedies, and complementarity in international criminal law); and to ensure that the jurisdiction of an international tribunal is not precluded by the prior consideration of the matter by a national court.

(5) *Effect of pending international proceedings before national courts*. To the extent that a State voluntarily agrees to accept the jurisdiction of an international tribunal to rule upon a matter which could impact upon pending proceedings before a national court, due process as a constituent element of the Rule of Law requires the municipal court to take account of, and give effect to, the proceedings before the international court.

CHAPTER V

CONCLUSION

*A. The Exercise of Adjudicatory Authority*
*in a Plural World*

*1. The fact of decisional fragmentation*

These lectures began with the proposition that the enquiry into the problems posed by parallel proceedings was not simply a matter of "fine-tuning" [1056] rules of jurisdiction. Rather it was symptomatic of a larger issue of decisional fragmentation in the international legal system — public and private.

Of course, the Private International lawyer is accustomed to taking such a notion as the status quo. In Private International Law one starts with a miscellany of national legal systems, and then seeks solutions to deal with their interaction. Yet, as the discussion in Chapter II showed, the solutions to the problems of parallel proceedings in Private International Law, though shaped by national legal tradition, are not pre-ordained by it. On the contrary, national legal systems (whether Common or Civil Law) had to make a policy choice about their treatment of foreign parallel proceedings. It was possible to ignore them, insisting on the local court's duty to exercise a jurisdiction entrusted to it, and leaving problems of overlap to be dealt with as issues of judgment enforcement. Alternatively,

---

[1056] The expression used by von Mehren, "Theory and Practice of Adjudicatory Authority in Private International Law: A Comparative Study of the Doctrine, Policies and Practices of Common- and Civil-Law Systems", (2002) 295 *Recueil des cours* 9, 306.

the court could seek to restrain the parties from pursuing parallel litigation abroad. Finally, it could choose to defer to the foreign court.

Either of the latter choices necessarily requires the national court to take account of other systems of adjudicatory authority outside its own, in the private interests of the litigants, and in the public interest of decisional order. Unless the court is prepared to look beyond its own national legal system, it will find neither a parallel claim, nor a reason to defer. The equivalence of the claims has to be judged by a standard which is not purely domestic.

Equally, the international arbitral process, analysed in Chapter III, cannot be seen as hermetically sealed. The principal purpose of the development of international arbitration was to provide a means of dispute settlement which stood outside national systems of adjudication, offering a single agreed forum in place of a multiplicity of competing national fora. Yet the very exercise of party autonomy creates a fragmented form of dispute resolution, in which the jurisdiction of each arbitral tribunal is limited by the extent of the parties' arbitration agreement. By its very nature, arbitration is an atomized form of dispute resolution. It presupposes that there will be other closely related disputes which will be have to be decided by other courts or tribunals. The very exercise of party autonomy may require a preliminary determination, whether by a national court or the tribunal, as to the validity and scope of the arbitration agreement.

Investment treaty arbitration necessarily takes place within a matrix of other fora in which aspects of the same dispute between investor and host State may fall for determination. If there is a contract between State and investor, that contract will create its own justiciable rights and duties, the breach of which may give rise either to litigation before host State courts or to arbitration before a tribunal to whose jurisdiction the parties have submitted. Even if there is no such contract, the underlying property rights of the investor, which form the subject-matter of the investment, may be the subject of adjudication by the host State courts. Further, the investor may seek vindication of its rights in the host State courts. In any one of these situations, the very nature of investment arbitration gives rise to the possibility of parallel proceedings, or of determinations in another forum which may be said to affect the issue to be determined by the investment tribunal. Moreover, it is possible that more than one investment tribunal, each constituted by a different investment treaty, may be asked to rule upon the same underlying factual dispute.

Nor can it be said that Public International Law has avoided the phenomenon of fragmentation. On the contrary, as the enquiry in Chapter IV showed, States deliberately chosen to create a multitude of different courts and tribunals to handle international claims. Sometimes, as in the case of the criminal and human rights tribunals, this has been necessarily so, since the nature of the parties would take the work of the tribunals well outside the established framework of inter-State disputes. In other cases, such as trade and the law of the sea, it has been as a result of a conscious choice in institutional design to create a specialist adjudicatory body.

At the same time, the much more pervasive reach of international tribunals has necessarily brought their work into closer contact with national courts — posing, with some urgency, the question of how national courts are best to mediate the increasingly porous border between national and international law. Here, too, a choice has to be made between isolation and cosmopolitanism, as the contrasting case-law of the US Supreme Court and the Privy Council on the fate of prisoners on Death Row demonstrates.

## 2. A constitutional or administrative law model?

In the light of these considerations, it is tempting to suggest, as some have done in both Public [1057] and Private International Law [1058], that international law may be reconceived as a set of constitutional norms which control and direct the exercise of power in human society. Of course, this does not have to operate in an inevitably centripetal way. Indeed, a core function of constitutions within federations — and nascent federations such as the European Union — is to hold the ring of power between the centre and the participating States.

Within European law, the need to create a centrifugal impulse to serve as a counter-measure to the power of Brussels has led to the development of a legal principle of subsidiarity [1059]. In the present field, the very architecture of the Brussels I Regulation respects this notion. The civil procedure of member States has not become the subject of Community Law (sometimes at a considerable price in terms of the practical impact of the Regulation's rules). Instead, the Regulation's rules operate to allocate competence between the national courts of member States. Within such a system, a rule of *lis pendens* becomes imperative. Without it, the

---

[1057] de Wet, "The International Constitutional Order", (2006) 55 *ICLQ* 51.

[1058] Mills, *The Confluence of Public and Private International Law: Justice, Pluralism and Subsidiarity in the International Constitutional Ordering of Private Law* (2009).

[1059] Treaty of Maastricht (29 July 1992), OJ C 191 (signed 7 January 1992, entered into force 1 November 1993) Art. A; Treaty of Nice (10 March 2001) OJ C 80 (signed 26 January 2001, entered into force 1 February 2003), inserting revised text of Art. 5 (2) into the Treaty establishing the European Union; Mills, "Subsidiarity in EU and US Private International Law", *Journal of Private International Law Conference*, New York, 2009.

courts of member States would be driven into conflict in a way which would be inconsistent with the objectives of the Regulation, and (more largely) with those of the Union itself.

An approach analogous to that of subsidiarity may be also be seen at work within the Statute of the International Criminal Court, and in particular through its concept of "complementarity" to national jurisdictions under Article 17. As Simpson puts it:

"it is only in cases of national paralysis that the International Criminal Court fills the jurisdictional lacuna . . . In this way, international criminal law is the exception, the place where the law goes when it is annihilated or undermined by local politics."[1060]

But envisioning the problems created by decisional fragmentation as having constitutional solutions, while providing some valuable insights, is also fraught with possibility of both danger and overstatement. The major examples of constitutional thinking we have examined in earlier lectures have often proved dangerously anti-cosmopolitan in their application to parallel proceedings outside their respective empires.

Thus, the application of the *anti-suit injunction* to the control of foreign litigation was a function of British nineteenth-century imperial expansionism — extending the controls of the Court of Chancery first to Scottish and Irish proceedings; then to those in the colonies; and finally to foreign proceedings. All of this was done just at the time when the integration of Law and Equity at home rendered the use of the injunction all but redundant in its original purpose — to assert the supremacy of Equity over the Common Law courts.

The rules of the *Brussels I Regulation* were created

---

[1060] Simpson, *Law, War and Crime: War Crimes and the Reinvention of International Law* (2007) 38.

for the benefit of the member States, and not for third States. The use of a general discretion to decline jurisdiction in favour of the courts of a third State has been ruled out by the European Court. So, too, has the power of the court at the seat of an arbitration to control litigation brought elsewhere in breach of an arbitration agreement. Nor has the Court been prepared to cede decisional power to the dispute settlement mechanisms of the UN Law of the Sea Convention, despite the claims to universality which can be made on the latter's behalf. It remains to be seen what the Court will make of the continued application of the principle of *lis pendens* vis-à-vis litigation pending in third States. The auguries are not good. There is a worrying trend to seek to re-envision international law in the image of the European Union — a conception which all-too-easily admits of no logic beyond the internal logic of the common market[1061].

In a like vein, the jurisprudence of *United States courts* has displayed only limited willingness to defer to foreign pending proceedings, often preferring "the virtually unflagging obligation of the federal courts to exercise the jurisdiction given them"[1062]. Nor was deference any more in evidence in the series of cases in which the US Supreme Court deconstructed the applicability of the judgments of the International Court in its parallel series of cases as to the rights of prisoners on Death Row to consular assistance.

It was in no small measure intransigence between these two great federations, and reluctance on the part of either to relinquish their existing constitutional

---

[1061] See, for example, Wouters, Nollkaemper and de Wet (eds.), *The Europeanisation of Public International Law: The Status of Public International Law in the EU and Its Member States* (2008).

[1062] *Colorado River Water Conservation District* v. *United States*, 424 US 800, 817, 96 S. Ct. 1236 (1976).

arrangements, which led to the failure of the negotiations at the Hague Conference on Private International Law for a global jurisdiction and enforcement of judgments convention[1063] — a convention that would have included a *lis pendens* rule of general application[1064].

In Public International Litigation, perhaps the nearest to a constitutional regime which has been achieved is that of the *World Trade Organization*[1065]. Yet, here again, the initial jurisprudence of the Appellate Body suggests a reluctance to accept deference to proceedings outside the WTO system[1066].

If these existing precedents for Constitutional thinking in relation to parallel proceedings appear on examination to be anti-cosmopolitan in their application to those outside the Constitutional framework, there is also a real danger in seeking to extrapolate from them principles of general application internationally. The world is not made in the image of the United States, nor of the European Union. Rules governing the interaction between courts within a federation, where some degree of reciprocity can be expected, will not neces-

---

[1063] Brand and Herrup, *The 2005 Hague Convention on Choice of Court Agreements Commentary and Documents* (2008) 8-9.

[1064] Art. 21, Preliminary Draft Convention on Jurisdiction and Foreign Judgments in Civil and Commercial Matters (adopted by the Special Commission) in Hague Conference on Private International Law, Enforcement of Judgments, Prel. Doc. No. 11 (2000); Nygh "Declining Jurisdiction under the Brussels I Regulation 2001 and the Preliminary Draft Hague Judgments Convention: A Comparison", in Fawcett (ed.), *Reform and Development in Private International Law: Essays in Honour of Sir Peter North* (2002) 303.

[1065] Cass, *The Constitutionalization of the World Trade Organization* (2005).

[1066] *Mexico — Tax Measures on Soft Drinks and Other Beverages* (6 March 2006), WTO Appellate Body, WT/DS308/AB/R, DSR 2006: 1, 3.

sarily provide a good guide to decision-making outside that context. The demise of the Hague Judgments Convention suggests that truly global constitutional solutions to the problems of parallel proceedings may be as far away as ever.

Moreover, the particular solution to litispendence adopted by the European Union in Article 27 of the Brussels I Regulation embodies a rigid approach which, as the discussion in Chapter II has shown, is capable of wreaking injustice and encouraging forum shopping rather than inhibiting it. It is difficult to resist the conclusion that a more nuanced approach may be needed to deal with the many different interrelationships between courts and tribunals which have been the subject of this study.

Nor can it be said that the solutions in this area can be solely technocratic — a "global administrative law" [1067] for decisional harmony. As Koskenniemi put it:

"Thinking of international law in apolitical and technical terms opened the door for expert rule and managerialism, not in competition with politics as in the domestic realm, but as a *substitute* for it . . .

[I]t is no surprise that international relations experts — particularly strong at US universities — have suggested replacing international law's archaic mores by a political science inspired language of governance, regulation, compliance and legitimacy." [1068]

The problem is that the utilitarian language of efficiency does not of itself suggest a solution to problems

---

[1067] Kingsbury *et al.* (eds.), "Foreword: Global Governance as Administration — National and Transnational Approaches to Global Administrative Law", (2005) 68 (3-4) *Law & Cont. Prob.* 1.

[1068] Koskenniemi, "The Fate of Public International Law: Between Technique and Politics", (2007) 70 *MLR* 1, 29 (emphasis in original).

of parallel proceedings, especially when they do not
arise within the same legal system (or sub-system).
Some larger principle is required. It is necessary, then,
to conceive of each court or tribunal dealing with a
case which overlaps with those pending before other
courts or tribunals as concerned with a larger enterprise
of justice within an international community. This is
*not* to say that technical solutions are unnecessary. On
the contrary, as the next section will attempt to show,
functional innovations in the techniques available to
courts to deal with parallel litigation may address many
of the problems which are currently encountered. But
the point is that functional innovations must be guided
by common principles as to the objective to be secured.
Without a conception of the fundamental purposes of
the litigation process — private and public — which
requires and justifies taking account of other exercises
of adjudicatory competence, there can be no effective
functional accommodations.

## 3. *General principles in the resolution of the conflict of litigation*

The Supreme Court of Canada observed in 1990 that:

> "[W]hat must underlie a modern system of pri-
> vate international law are principles of order and
> fairness, principles that ensure security of transac-
> tions with justice.
>
> [T]he business community operates in a world
> economy and we correctly speak of a 'world com-
> munity' even in the face of decentralized political
> and legal power. Accommodating the flow of
> wealth, skills and people across state lines has now
> become imperative." [1069]

---

[1069] *Morguard Investments Ltd.* v. *De Savoye*, [1990] 3
SCR 1077, 1097-1098.

The question for the would-be architect of solutions to the problems of parallel proceedings, however, is how those twin, but sometimes contradictory, notions of order and fairness may be balanced in order to achieve both security of transactions and justice.

At the very outset of these lectures[1070], it was suggested that it is no longer possible or necessary (if indeed it ever was) to solve all of the problems of litispendence by the application of a single rule or principle. Rather, what is needed is a new science of the conflict of litigation, in which detailed sets of rules and processes would be developed, which may differ depending upon the nature of the issue and the relationship between the respective courts or tribunals. As will be seen in the next section, there are signs that exactly this process of elaboration is already beginning to take place. But before the reader's attention is turned to functional solutions, it is first necessary to summarize the evidence for the emergence of general principles of law applicable to the problems of parallel proceedings.

*International litispendence.* In the first place, as has been seen[1071], there is now much more substantial evidence in both the practice of States, and in the opinions of the most highly qualified scholars, that the avoidance of international litispendence is a general principle of law. The State practice discussed in Chapter II showed a widespread increase over the last quarter century of judicial acceptance of a discretion to defer to foreign pending proceedings, irrespective of treaty provision. In Civil Law countries, that was achieved through the judicial extension to international cases of the domestic doctrine of *lis pendens.* In Common Law countries, it has been achieved through the judicial

---

[1070] Chapter I, Section A.
[1071] Chapter IV, Section B 2.

adoption from Scots law of the doctrine of *forum non conveniens*. To be sure — there are major differences between these two models. But both rules provide a route by which the effect of foreign pending proceedings may be taken into account.

The most authoritative recent scholarly statements on international litispendence are found in the work of the Institut de droit international and in the joint work of the American Law Institute and UNIDROIT on Transnational Rules of Civil Procedure. In 2004, the Institut, considering the issues of *forum non conveniens* and anti-suit injunctions, resolved that parallel litigation between the same or related parties "should be discourged"[1072], since it "may lead to injustice, delay, increased expense, and inconsistent decisions"[1073]. The UNIDROIT/ALI Principles adopted in the same year resolve that a court should generally decline in the face of previously pending parallel litigation "unless it appears that the dispute will not be fairly, effectively, and expeditiously resolved in that forum"[1074]. In each case, these resolutions gain particular significance from the international reach of the sponsoring institutions and the scholars consulted.

The well-conceived American Law Institute Proposed Federal Statute on the Recognition and Enforcement of Foreign Judgments 2005 also contains a *lis*

---

[1072] The Principles for Determining When the Use of the Doctrine of *Forum Non Conveniens* and Anti-Suit Injunctions Is Appropriate (Resolution of 28 August 2003) in (2004) 70-II *Annuaire* 252, [4] (Sir Lawrence Collins and Georges Droz (Rapporteurs)).

[1073] *Ibid.*, Recital *(d)*.

[1074] American Law Institute/UNIDROIT, *Principles of Transnational Civil Procedure* (adopted 2004) (2006) [2.6]; for an account of the process of exposition of these Principles see *ibid.*, "Introduction", 1-15.

*pendens* rule[1075]. Section 11 would oblige an American court to stay or dismiss an action before it where "a proceeding concerning the same subject matter and including the same or related parties" is already pending in another court, provided that the foreign court is not exercising jurisdiction on a basis which would render its judgment unenforceable in the United States, and its judgment is likely to be rendered on a timely basis. The Section is subject to an exception to the first-in-time rule in cases of abuse of process[1076]. Although this proposal cannot be said to encapsulate an international consensus, it is of great significance for another reason. It represents a decisive endorsement of the principle of international litispendence, as a principle of the general law (and not on the basis of reciprocity under treaty) in a State where (as has been seen[1077]) authority has been divided.

The inclusion of Section 11 in the Proposed Federal Statute is of all the more interest since the Statute does not otherwise contain rules of primary jurisdiction, nor does it make general provision for the declining of jurisdiction on grounds of *forum non conveniens*. The formulation of the rule does leave the court with a discretion, in which the question whether the United States is the more appropriate forum remains a relevant factor[1078]. Nevertheless the Statute treats *lis pendens* as an independent ground upon which an otherwise valid jurisdiction should be declined, isolating it alone for treatment within a text otherwise devoted to enforcement of foreign judgments.

---

[1075] Section 11, American Law Institute, *Recognition and Enforcement of Foreign Judgments*: *Analysis and Proposed Federal Statute* (adopted 2005, Lowenfeld and Silberman, Reporters) (2006) 131-139.

[1076] S. 11 *(b)*.

[1077] Chapter II, Section A 3.

[1078] S. 11 *(b)* (i).

So, too, the International Law Association Committee on International Commercial Arbitration concluded
its Report on "Lis Pendens and Arbitration" with the
recommendation that where parallel proceedings "are
pending before another arbitral tribunal, the arbitral tribunal should decline jurisdiction or stay the Current
Arbitration, in whole or in part, and on such conditions
as it sees fit" provided that the other tribunal has jurisdiction to resolve the issues in the current arbitration,
and there is no material prejudice to the opposing
party [1079]. The Report adds a further discretion for the
arbitral tribunal to stay its proceedings temporarily in
the face of other material related proceedings, whether
or not they raise the same issues "as a matter of sound
case management, or to avoid conflicting decisions, to
prevent costly duplication of proceedings or to protect
a party from oppressive tactics" [1080].

But the increasing recognition of international
litispendence itself is not the only general principle
which may be relevant to determination of issues involving parallel proceedings. Five other core principles
have emerged from consideration of the different contexts in which *lis pendens* issues arise: comity; party
autonomy; consolidation; denial of justice; and abuse
of rights *(abus de droit)*. It is necessary to say a word
about each, since not only have such principles already
been applied in the practice of courts and tribunals,
they will also have an impact on the design of solutions
for the future. Further, such principles are inextricably
linked, such that the 2007 draft model Norwegian
bilateral investment treaty is able to provide elegantly
and compendiously:

---

[1079] International Law Association Committee on
International Commercial Arbitration, "Final Report on Lis
Pendens and Arbitration", in (2006) 72 *ILA Rep. Conf.*
146, 184-185 [5.13], Principle 5.
[1080] *Ibid.*, 185, [5.13], Principle 6.

"The Tribunal shall, as appropriate, take into account the principles of *res judicata* and *lis pendens*, in accordance with international law, to hinder abuse of rights under this agreement, as well as otherwise exercising sound judicial economy. If all parties to the dispute so agree, the Tribunal may consolidate claims."[1081]

*Comity*. In Chapter I, it was submitted that a *positive* conception of comity might provide a justification for the recognition of the effects of foreign pending proceedings, just as it has long been seen as a justification for the application of foreign law[1082]. But comity also has a *negative* function. It serves as a short-hand expression for the rules of jurisdiction in Public International Law, that limit the extent to which one State may permissibly intervene in the affairs of another. It has been in this sense that Common Law courts have consistently used the concept as a factor limiting the grant of anti-suit injunctions[1083].

*Party Autonomy*. The principle of party autonomy — the selection by *both* parties to a dispute of the forum for its resolution — has had a particular impact on the relationship between parallel arbitration and judicial proceedings. As was seen in Chapter III[1084], respect for party autonomy, as enshrined in Article II of the New York Convention, carries with it the notion of *Kompetenz-Kompetenz* — that an arbitral tribunal is

---

[1081] Agreement between the Kingdom of Norway and [ ] (Draft 191207), available at www.regjeringen.no/upload/NHD/Vedlegg/hoeringer/Utkast%20til%20modellavtale2.doc.

[1082] Chapter I, Section E.

[1083] Chapter II, Section [D 3]; Collins, "Comity in Modern Private International Law", in Fawcett (ed.), *Reform and Development of Private International Law* (2002) 89, 95-104; Institut Resolution, *supra* footnote 1072, [5].

[1084] Chapter III, Section B 1.

entitled to determine its own jurisdiction (irrespective of whether that issue is also pending before a national court)[1085]. But it has also been submitted that the best way of resolving the overlap between parallel judicial and arbitral determinations of arbitral jurisdiction will normally be to give *Kompetenz-Kompetenz* a negative application, requiring a court faced with a prima facie valid arbitration agreement to suspend its own proceedings in order to enable the arbitral tribunal to determine its own jurisdiction first (subject of course to subsequent review in the courts of the seat).

A general priority for arbitration was endorsed by the ILA International Commercial Arbitration Committee in its Final Report on *Lis Pendens* and Arbitration[1086]. The Committee adopted as its point of departure the notion that the principle of *Kompetenz-Kompetenz* required an arbitral tribunal to proceed with the arbitration and determine its own jurisdiction "regardless of any other proceedings pending before a domestic court"[1087]. In considering exceptions to this principle, the Committee drew a distinction between parallel proceedings in the courts of the seat, and parallel proceedings in other courts. Where the judicial proceedings were taking place outside the seat, the Committee considered that the arbitral tribunal should generally continue "unless the party initiating the arbitration has effectively waived its rights under the arbitration agreement or save in other exceptional circumstances"[1088]. However, the Committee considered that it would be presumptuous of it to adopt a negative

---

[1085] As the Swiss legislature expressly recognized when it added Art. 186 1*bis* to the Swiss Code on Private International Law in 2006, see *supra* Chapter III, Section B 1 *(b)*.

[1086] *Supra* footnote 1079.

[1087] *Ibid.*, Principle 1.

[1088] *Ibid.*, Principle 4.

*Kompetenz-Kompetenz* rule vis-à-vis the courts of the seat. It recommended a more cautious approach, accepting the legitimate supervisory role of the *lex arbitri* "particularly having regard to the possibility of annulment of the award in the event of conflict between the award and the decision of the court" [1089].

Party autonomy may also apply to choice of court agreements. The Institut resolved that "[i]t is universally recognized that (subject to special rules based on the policy of the protection of the interests of the weaker party) effect should be given to choice of court agreements in international transactions" [1090]. Of course, the European Court has held that a choice of court does not itself take priority over the first-in-time rule [1091]. The Institut took the opposite view, considering that the normal priority of the court first seised should be ceded "when the parties have conferred exclusive jurisdiction on the courts of another country" [1092].

This is also the solution adopted in the 2005 Hague Convention on Choice of Court Agreements [1093]. Articles 5 (1) and (2) of the Convention provide that:

"1. The court or courts of a Contracting State designated in an exclusive choice of court agreement shall have jurisdiction to decide a dispute to which the agreement applies, unless the agreement is null and void under the law of that State.

2. A court that has jurisdiction under paragraph 1 shall not decline to exercise jurisdiction on the

---

[1089] *Ibid.*, Principle 3.

[1090] *Supra* footnote 1072, recital *(e)*.

[1091] *Erich Gasser GmbH* v. *MISAT Srl*, Case C-116/02, [2003] *ECR* I-14693, discussed *supra* Chapter II, Section B 3 *(a)*.

[1092] *Supra* footnote 1072, [4].

[1093] Available at www.hcch.net, and see Brand and Herrup, *supra* footnote 1063.

ground that the dispute should be decided in a court of another State."

This imposes a positive obligation upon the chosen court to proceed to hear the case, irrespective of whether proceedings have already been commenced in the courts of another State. Article 5 (2) is specifically designed to eliminate the possibility of a plea of *lis pendens* as well as of *forum non conveniens* before the parties' chosen court in cases of exclusive jurisdiction agreements, giving priority to the parties' common choice of forum[1094]. The Convention achieves this result by tolerating some risk of parallel proceedings. Thus, Article 6 requires a court not chosen to suspend or dismiss proceedings to which an exclusive jurisdiction clause applies. But that Article is subject to six exceptions, including the nullity of the agreement. It is inherent in the structure of Article 6 that the court not chosen is to make the determination as to whether there is an exclusive choice of court agreement, and, if there is, whether one of the exceptions applies[1095] (although the option to suspend rather than to dismiss proceedings would permit that court to defer to the chosen court, if there is a pending motion to dismiss in the chosen court as well). Furthermore, the chosen court may proceed to hear the action irrespective of the decision of another court under Article 6. Thus, the Hague Convention achieves a priority for jurisdiction agreements, without completely eliminating the possibility of parallel proceedings[1096].

This Convention seems destined to have consider-

---

[1094] Hartley and Dougachi, "Convention of 30 June 2005 on Choice of Court Agreements Explanatory Report" (2007) [133].

[1095] *Ibid.*, [144].

[1096] Accord: Brand and Herrup, *supra* footnote 1063, 88-89.

able impact in practice. It was ratified by Mexico in 2007, and, in 2009, both the United States and the European Community signed it — thus signifying their intention to ratify in due course [1097]. When ratified, the Hague Convention would thus become the first treaty between these two great trading federations on civil jurisdiction, providing a platform for the accession of a wider group of States.

The Convention's rules would not directly supplant the operation of the Brussels I Regulation between the member States *inter se* [1098]. However, the current law in Europe may change as a result of the recommendations in the highly influential Heidelberg Report, which reviewed the operation of the Brussels I Regulation at the request of the European Commission in 2007, and which now seems highly likely to provide the basis for its revision. The Report found a substantial degree of disquiet amongst a number of member States at the absence of any exceptions to Article 27, and the potential in particular for the abusive flouting of jurisdiction clauses [1099]. The authors recommend an exception to Article 27 in cases of exclusive jurisdiction clauses, so as to permit the chosen court to continue to hear the case, even if there had been a prior reference to another court [1100]. But they considered that it would be going

---

[1097] See http://www.hcch.net/index_en.php?act=conventions.status&cid=98.

[1098] Art. 26 (6).

[1099] Hess/Pfeiffer/Schlosser, *The Brussels I Regulation 44/2001* (2008), [369]-[375] ("The Heidelberg Report"), citing in particular the attempt at forum shopping by the debtor on a corporate loan in *J. P. Morgan Europe Ltd.* v. *Primacom AG*, [2005] EWHC 508, [2005] 2 Lloyd's Rep. 665; L. G. Mainz, 13 September 2005, WM 2005, 2319; and see the Commission's Report and Green Paper thereon: COM (2009) 174 (21 April 2009), 5-6; COM (2009) 175 (21 April 2009), 5-6.

[1100] *Ibid.*, [437].

too far to require any other court always to defer to the court so designated to determine jurisdiction, particularly where there might be an issue over the validity of the jurisdiction clause[1101].

Thus, in the context of choice of court agreements, as well as that of arbitration agreements, the preferred approach is to recognize a principle of positive *Kompetenz-Kompetenz*, which permits the chosen court to proceed irrespective of parallel proceedings in another court (irrespective of whether another court is first seised); but not to impose a blanket rule of negative *Kompetenz-Kompetenz* requiring the court first seised (and not chosen) always to defer.

*Consolidation.* Where the proceedings are related, but not identical, the guiding principle is one of consolidation. Indeed, the principle of consolidation is of considerably greater antiquity than that of litispendence. The Roman Law concept of the *litis contestatio* carried with it a clear rule requiring connected cases to be tried before the same judge[1102]. This is reflected in the broad provisions in Civil Codes permitting the court to decline jurisdiction in order to enable related cases to be tried together[1103]. In the scheme of the Brussels I Regulation, the operation of Article 28 on related claims is itself closely related to Article 6, the provision permitting a court to consolidate related claims before it. Although their scope and operation is not the same, "an identical, functional, definition of the required connection between claims appears in both contexts"[1104].

The desire to achieve consolidation in types of litigation which have traditionally been highly fragmented

---

[1101]  *Ibid.*, [438].
[1102]  *Code* III, 9, 1.
[1103]  Chapter II, Section A 2.
[1104]  Magnus/Mankowski/Muir Watt, *Brussels I Regulation* (2007), Art. 6, note [8].

may also be seen in the recent proposals of the American Law Institute in the field of intellectual property litigation[1105]. Sections 221-222 of the draft Principles make elaborate provision for the co-ordination authority of the court first seised over other "actions involving the same transaction, occurrence, or series of transactions or occurrences"[1106]. Their objective is to achieve either consolidation of those actions, or co-operation between the parties and the courts, or a combination of the two.

In arbitration, the consolidation of related claims cannot usually be achieved without the consent of all the parties[1107]. Nevertheless, particularly in the field of investment treaty arbitration, there is a growing readiness of States to provide for consolidation in advance as a condition of their own consent to investor-State arbitration. Some existing investment treaties already establish a specific mechanism, permitting a Consolidation Tribunal to decide to consolidate several claims that have a question of law or fact in common[1108]. Recent reviews of trends in investment treaty rule-making have suggested that the concerns of States over the risk of inconsistent decisions and waste of judicial resources have driven the inclusion in new model investment treaties of consolidation provisions[1109].

---

[1105] American Law Institute, *Intellectual Property Principles Governing Jurisdiction, Choice of Law, and Judgments in Transnational Disputes* (Dreyfuss, Ginsburg and Dessemontet, Reporters) (2008).

[1106] *Ibid.*, §§ 221-222.

[1107] Chapter III, Section B 3.

[1108] For example Art. 1126 (2) of NAFTA discussed *supra* Chapter I, Section D 3.

[1109] OECD, "Improving the System of Investor-State Dispute Settlement; An Overview", Working Papers on International Investment No. 2006/1, [83]-[92]; UNCTAD, *Investor-State Dispute Settlement and Impact on Investment Rule-making*, (2007) UNCTAD/ITE/IIA/2007/3, 83-84; and see IISD Model Agreement on Investment for Sustainable Development, Art. 12, available at www.iisd.org.

If, however, many cases of parallel litigation in fact arise out of deliberate attempts to frustrate the just determination of the dispute in the most appropriate forum, what general principles may apply to correct or control such abuses? In Chapter II, it was seen that parties have abused the provisions of the Brussels I Regulation by commencing a prior claim for a negative declaration in the courts of a member State, such as Italy, where it is not possible to obtain a prompt early jurisdictional determination[1110]. The European Court has refused to treat *general* considerations of this kind as sufficient to outweigh the requirements of mutual trust underlying the *lis pendens* rule in the Regulation[1111]. But what might be the effect of *specific* evidence in a particular case of abusive conduct? There are two principles, each recognized as having general application to legal proceedings, which may be pertinent: denial of justice and abuse of rights.

*Denial of justice.* The concept of denial of justice in Public International Law has always included not merely a refusal or failure to adjudicate a claim, but also unreasonable delays in rendering a judgment[1112]. In more recent times, this concept has found expression in the human right to a fair trial "within a reasonable time"[1113]. This concept is applicable in prin-

---

[1110] Chapter II, Section B 3 *(a)*.

[1111] *Gasser, supra* footnote 1091, [70]-[72].

[1112] *Antoine Fabiani Case (France* v. *Venezuela)* (1905) 10 *RIAA* 83, 117 (Lachenal U); Freeman *The International Responsibility of States for Denial of Justice* (1938), Chap. X; Paulsson, *Denial of Justice in International Law* (2005), Chap. 7.

[1113] European Convention for the Protection of Human Rights and Fundamental Freedoms (signed 4 November 1950, entered into force 3 September 1953), 213 *UNTS* 222, Art. 6 (1); American Convention on Human Rights (signed 22 November 1969, entered into force 18 July 1978), 1144 *UNTS* 123, Art. 8 (1).

ciple as much to jurisdictional determinations as to other exercises of judicial power[1114].

In *Gasser,* although the Court rejected an argument based upon Article 6 of the European Convention on Human Rights where there were *in general* excessive delays within the legal system of a member State, it did not accede to the European Commission's submission that Article 6 could never be applied by the ECJ in the construction of the Brussels jurisdiction and judgments regime. On the contrary, the ECJ has expressly held that the right to a fair trial does so apply[1115]. Thus, the requirement of a fair trial does apply where in a particular case there is excessive delay in reaching a jurisdictional determination The authors of the Heidelberg Report on the Brussels I Regulation have recommended that "[i]t might strengthen the acceptance of the principle of mutual trust rather than provoke the danger of its collapse" if this be said expressly[1116].

*Abuse of rights.* An equally fundamental general principle of law is that of abuse of rights as an application of the overarching principle of good faith. In his classic study, Cheng suggested, on the authorities, that a right could not be exercised maliciously; fictitiously — where the form of the law is misused for acts which are really aimed at its evasion; or in unreasonable dis-

---

[1114] Schlosser, "Jurisdiction in International Litigation: The Issue of Human Rights in Relation to National Law and the Brussels Convention", (1991) 74 *Rivista di diritto internazionale* 5.

[1115] *Krombach* v. *Bamberski*, Case C-7/98, [2000] *ECR* I-1935, [43], citing *Debaecker and Plouvier* v. *Bouwman*, Case C-49/84, [1985] *ECR* 1799, [10]; Nuyts, "The Enforcement of Jurisdiction Agreements further to *Gasser* and the Community Principle of Abuse of Right", in de Vareilles-Sommières (ed.), *Forum Shopping in the European Judicial Area* (2007) 55, 61.

[1116] *Supra* footnote 1099, [385].

regard of the rights of others[1117]. The concept that proceedings may be dismissed when they are an abuse of process (well known in national legal systems) has also received recognition in the procedure of international tribunals[1118].

This principle has particular relevance to the resolution of issues of parallel proceedings. Thus, for example, the Institut recognized an exception to the first-seised rule in cases of litispendence "when the first seised court is seised in proceedings which are designed (e.g. by an action for a negative declaration) to frustrate proceedings in a second forum which is clearly more appropriate"[1119]. In the European Union context, Nuyts has illuminatingly shown that *abus de droit* has now been recognized by the European Court as an autonomous principle of Community law[1120], and applied in the context of the Brussels I Regulation. He argues that, despite the decision of the European Court in *Gasser*[1121], there is still scope for the application of this principle by a national court to deny a litigant the benefit of provisions of Community law which he is seeking to abuse.

The concept of *abus de droit* may be very closely related to the original concept of vexation and oppression enunciated in the Common Law cases as part of the test

---

[1117] Cheng, *General Principles of Law as Applied by International Courts and Tribunals* (1953), Chap. 4.

[1118] For example, United Nations Convention on the Law of the Sea (signed 10 December 1982, entered into force 16 November 1994), 1833 *UNTS* 3, Arts. 294 and 300; *United States — Import Prohibition of Certain Shrimp and Shrimp Products* (WTO Appellate Body), WT/DS58/AB/R (8 October 1998), DSR 1998: VII, 2755 (1999), [158]; Shany *The Competing Jurisdictions of International Courts and Tribunals* (2003) 255-260.

[1119] *Supra* footnote 1072, [4 *(b)*].

[1120] *Supra* footnote 1115; accord Bureau and Muir Watt, *Droit international privé* (2007) [223].

[1121] *Supra* footnote 1091, [53].

for the grant of an anti-suit injunction[1122]. As Bowen LJ put it in *Peruvian Guano Co.* v. *Bockwoldt* in 1883 :

"Of course that rule does not mean that a plaintiff, under the pretence of asking for justice, is to do that which is oppressive and vexatious, and the Courts have always … interfered to prevent a plaintiff under colour of asking for justice from harassing others. Therefore, when that which he is asking for is frivolous, or sometimes when he is asking for it in a way which necessarily involves injustice, the Courts have interfered."[1123]

Now it will be readily appreciated that these general principles do not themselves necessarily indicate a specific solution to a particular problem of parallel proceedings. Indeed, as the many controversial cases discussed in earlier lectures show, particular cases may well throw up fact patterns which drive these principles into apparent conflict with each other — the outcome being dependent on the relative weight to be given to each. This is true, for example, of the relative weight to be given to part autonomy and litispendence seen in *Fomento* and the Swiss legislature's reaction to it[1124] ; it is also true of the balance to be struck between comity and *abus de droit* in the grant of anti-suit injunctions.

Rather, the purpose of isolating the relevant principles at stake is to help to shape the application and direction of the law by identifying the rationale which particular rules should seek to serve, in order to accom-

---

[1122] Chapter II, Section D 1 ; *Société Nationale Aerospatiale* v. *Lee Kui Jak*, [1987] 1 AC 871 (PC (Brunei)); Raphael, *The Anti-suit Injunction* (2008) [4.28]-[4.31].

[1123] (1883) LR 23 Ch. D. 225, 233, cited with approval in *Aerospatiale*, *ibid.*, 894 ; and see Institut Resolution *supra* footnote 1072, [5 *(b)*].

[1124] Chapter III, Section B 1 *(b)*.

modate conflicting rights and interests which it is the very "function of jurisprudence" [1125] to resolve. As the Study Group of the International Law Commission on the Fragmentation of International Law put it:

> "[I]f legal reasoning is understood as a *purposive* activity, then it follows that it should be seen not merely as a mechanic[al] application of apparently random rules, decisions or behavioural patterns but as the operation of a whole that is directed towards some human objective." [1126]

It is to the search for functional solutions to the human objectives behind the regulation of parallel litigation that we must now turn. In order to do so, it is necessary to return, however briefly, to the beginning.

## B. The Search for New Solutions

### 1. From a Westphalian to a cosmopolitan paradigm

These lectures began by tracing the emergence of the doctrine of *lis pendens* to seventeenth-century Holland. Its emergence then was no accident. The Netherlands had struggled in the sixteenth century under the yoke of Hapsburg imperial tyranny and religious oppression [1127]. Thirty years before Johannes

---

[1125] *Eastern Extension, Australasia and China Telegraph Co. Ltd. Case* (British-United States Claims Arbitral Tribunal), (1923) 6 *RIAA* 112, 114.

[1126] International Law Commission Report of the Study Group on the Fragmentation of International Law, "Fragmentation of International Law: Difficulties Arising from the Diversification and Expansion of International Law", UN doc. A/CN.4/L.682 (Koskenniemi C), [34].

[1127] See, for example, *A Request Presented to the King of Spayn and the Lordes of the Counsel of the State by the Inhabitantes of the Louue Countreyes* (1578) (St. John's College Library, Cambridge).

Zangerus had published the first-known proto-study of *lis pendens*[1128], Pieter Brueghel had painted his famous image *The Tower of Babel*[1129] depicting the account from *Genesis* in which humanity sets out to build a tower to rival the Almighty[1130]. God's response is to destroy the tower and to scatter humanity across the face of all the earth. Brueghel's painting may be seen in part as a deeply political comment on the delusions of empire — in particular that of the Hapsburgs.

It took until 1648 for the Treaty of Westphalia to end 80 years of war between Spain and the Seven Provinces of the Netherlands and to achieve Dutch independence. The resulting peace produced the template for the modern system of Public International Law (already envisaged by Hugo Grotius in 1625[1131]) *and* the modern system of Private International Law[1132]. Both were based upon the same premise — the sovereign independence of States, and thus the need to respect the separate territorial scope of each State's jurisdiction in order to avoid conflicts between States. But the new science of Private International Law also recognized the essential need for the peaceful interaction of private persons between States, and, for this purpose, the requirement to recognize and give effect to the laws and the judicial acts of other States, where these properly applied to the situation in question. Finally, the seventeenth century saw the reworking of Roman Law into a modern system of private law, taking account of the increasing diversity of local legislation (itself a spur to Private International Law) *and* a new fragmentation in judicial decision-making amongst different courts — requiring a doctrine of *lis*

---

[1128] Chapter I, Section C 1.
[1129] Kunsthistorisches Museum, Vienna (1563).
[1130] Genesis XI, 1-9.
[1131] Grotius *De Jure Bellis ac Pacis* (1625).
[1132] Chapter I, Section E.

*pendens.* In all of this the world was to be decidedly plural — just as the account of humanity's destiny in *Genesis* suggests.

The great Dutch jurists of the seventeenth century — in particular Voet and Huber — never suggested that the doctrine of *lis pendens* could apply to pending proceedings in foreign countries. Perhaps this was because the application of the doctrine in this way already requires a strong version of Cosmopolitanism. The recognition of foreign law and judgments recognizes the consequences of the sovereign independence of other States, and the practical and commercial needs of private persons acting across national borders. But it does so only on the receiving State's terms. The doctrine of *lis pendens*, on the other hand, and whether or not it is applied as an automatic rule of deference to the court first-seised or as part of a discretion, inevitably involves the relinquishment of an aspect of State power — the right to adjudicate the dispute. Moreover, it has a consequence for the litigants beyond the rules applicable to the merits — requiring them to resort to the courts of another country.

Current debates on the appropriate solutions for rules of jurisdiction frequently founder on the very different paradigms applied in Civil and Common Law systems to solve problems which at a functional level are apparently the same [1133]. Yet it has been a central purpose of these lectures to demonstrate that neither of these paradigms — at least as they relate to parallel proceedings — is hard-wired into the respective systems of Private International Law. On the contrary, in both cases, the rules were borrowed from *internal* rules of civil procedure. In both cases, their translation on to the international plane has had a series of unintended

---

[1133] Michaels, "Two Paradigms of Jurisdiction", (2005-2006) *Mich. JIL* 1003.

consequences which could not have arisen within a single legal system. These have already been discussed in earlier lectures and may now be summarized as follows.

*Civil Law*. The Civil Law's simple court first-seised rule has unassailable logic *within* a single legal system — since no other factors enter the equation other than avoidance of multiplicity of litigation. A tie-break rule is therefore all that is required. Moreover, the deferring court can be sure that court first seised will exercise jurisdiction. In international cases, the rule promotes legal certainty (itself a goal of the Rule of Law) in cases in which both courts have a claim to jurisdiction. However, great differences between procedures (and recoveries) in different legal systems motivate forum choice, even within an area with common jurisdiction rules, such as Europe. In this context, a strict court first-seised rule can actually promote forum shopping by encouraging a race to commence proceedings, especially where a claim for a negative declaration is used as forum shopping device. The international effect of the rule may be further distorted in contexts where there are no common rules of jurisdiction. Here the court first seised may be in a forum with a very limited connection with the defendant or the subject-matter of the action. Finally, the rule leads to excessive formalism in the determination of identity of claims — essential for the preclusive effect of *res judicata* but not necessary in the case of parallel proceedings.

*Common Law*. The Common Law's classic remedy to deal with cases of parallel litigation has been the anti-suit injunction. Here, however, the cure may be worse than the malady. Equity's desire to prevent harassment may end up producing harassment of its own. Indeed, intensive experience with the application of the anti-suit injunction to international cases has produced some very serious conflicts between courts.

The remedy offers no ready solution in the face of two courts each equally determined not to cede jurisdiction[1134]. Thus, concerns about the *negative* aspect of comity — the avoidance of trespass upon the sovereign jurisdiction of foreign courts — has led in recent times to significant retrenchment in the remedy — at least to cases where there is a sufficient connection with the forum[1135]. A requirement of sufficient connection may well justify the exercise of international jurisdiction to grant the anti-suit injunction[1136]. But it does *not* mean that remedy is suitable one to resolve international conflicts of jurisdiction. Indeed peremptory intervention of this kind is difficult to justify, save where it is essential to protect the court or tribunal's ability to hold a fair trial[1137] ; to enforce its judgments[1138] ; or (*pace West Tankers*) to hold parties to their common choice of an exclusive forum.

The Common Law's far more recent embrace of the doctrine of *forum non conveniens* offers the considerable advantage of flexible deference to foreign proceedings. The objection to it cannot rest simply on the ground that it involves an exercise of discretion. After all, the exercise of discretion in cases of *related* litigation *(connexité)* is widely accepted in Civil Law countries as well. The principal problems with the operation of the doctrine are not in cases of litispendence, but

---

[1134] As in the example of the *Laker* litigation discussed *supra* Chapter II, Section D 3 *(a)*.

[1135] Chapter II, Section D 3.

[1136] Accord Mann, "The Doctrine of Jurisdiction in International Law", (1964) 111 *Recueil des cours* 1, reprinted in Mann, *Studies in International Law* (1973) 131-132.

[1137] A factor which has also led arbitral tribunals to make similar orders : *supra* Chapter III, Section B 3 *(a)*.

[1138] The principal application of the anti-suit injunction when it was first extended to international cases : *Masri* v. *Consolidated Contractors International Co. SAL* [2008] EWCA Civ. 625, [2008] 1 CLC 887, [84].

rather where the plaintiff's choice of forum is overridden in favour of a forum which has not been invoked at all. But nevertheless, the exercise of discretion tends to promote heavy satellite litigation about where to litigate in many cases, which could be solved by standing rules of jurisdiction. The risk of re-invention of the wheel case-by-case is particularly acute in those States where the forum question has become in effect the only controlling test for the assumption of jurisdiction[1139], rather than being seen as a residual corrective against possible excesses of jurisdiction. Moreover, the doctrine of *forum non conveniens* may give too little weight to the fact of parallel litigation. Rather than deferring to the foreign court's determination of its own jurisdiction, it instead requires the court to second-guess the forum determination. The doctrine assumes that every case has a natural forum — a proposition which litigation experience suggests is often highly debatable. Since a situation of litispendence only arises where two courts are seised with the case, the doctrine does not resolve the question of which court decides whether to exercise jurisdiction.

Quite apart from these criticisms which may be levelled at each of the existing paradigms, there is a more fundamental observation which may be made about both of them. Each mechanism is predicated upon the separate character of each of the judicial systems, with each court deciding for itself, and without reference to the other court, whether to retain or to decline jurisdiction. Thus the most that can be done in any case is for the court to stay or dismiss the action before it in deference to the foreign proceeding. Both solutions are

---

[1139] For example, United States: *International Shoe Co.* v. *Washington*, 326 US 310 (1945); Canada: *Morguard Investments Ltd.* v. *De Savoye, supra* footnote 1069; *Tolofson* v. *Jensen*, [1994] 3 SCR 1022, 120 DLR (4th) 289; New Zealand: HCR 6.28 (as added in 2009).

essentially *Westphalian* in the sense that they assume the sovereign independent character of each State and its judicial system, and offer merely the declining of the exercise of jurisdiction by one State in favour of its exercise by another. This is true even of the system of litispendence developed within the European Union under the Brussels I Regulation.

Is this really the best that can be done in the face of the imperatives of globalization, observed by the Supreme Court of Canada as the new driving force behind the reform of the rules of Private International Law?[1140] Michaels concludes a recent insightful piece on the paradigms of jurisdiction with this observation on the common limitations of the Westphalian conception of State sovereignty which underlies both systems of jurisdiction:

> "If this traditional image of sovereignty is inadequate under conditions of globalization, as is frequently claimed, then both paradigms are inadequate as well, and both sides must come together to create a new, third paradigm of jurisdiction."[1141]

The notion that scientific communities can only survive for so long working within a particular paradigm in the face of mounting contrary evidence has been with us at least since Kuhn wrote his ground-breaking *The Structure of Scientific Revolutions* in 1962[1142]. Can the huge pressures of globalization provide the impetus for a revolution in jurisdictional thought?

It is the burden of this chapter to suggest that the contours of a new solution may already be upon us, developed in part as a result of co-operative law reform

---

[1140] *Supra* footnote 1069.

[1141] Michaels, *supra* footnote 1133, 1069.

[1142] Kuhn, *The Structure of Scientific Revolutions* (1962).

in the past decade, and partly as a result of *ad hoc* developments driven by the very practical imperatives of globalization. The key elements of the new system do indeed involve a synthesis of the Civilian and Common Law solutions. But they are fundamentally transformed in the service of a new model of litispendence, which conceives both courts as involved in a common enterprise. Seen in this light, what was once declining jurisdiction now becomes the *referral* of a case between courts; facilitated by direct communication between them. It is necessary to take each of these elements in turn, and to trace a little of the recent intellectual history of the development of these ideas, as they come off the drawing-board and leap into real life.

## 2. *Declining and referring jurisdiction — new model* lis pendens

At the Millennium, the International Law Association adopted by Resolution the *Leuven/London Principles on Declining and Referring Jurisdiction in Civil and Commercial Litigation*[1143].

The Principles had been developed as a result of research by the Association's International Civil and Commercial Litigation Committee from 1997-1999 — the essential points of which were agreed at Leuven in 1998[1144].

It is necessary to set out the Principles in full text, so that the interrelated nature of their provisions can be appreciated.

---

[1143] Res. 1/2000, (2000) 69 *ILA Rep. Conf.* 13; Report (2000), 69 *ILA Rep. Conf.* 137.

[1144] Report, *ibid.*, [37]. The Committee consisted of 31 eminent experts from both Civil and Common Law jurisdictions: Report, *ibid.*, 137. Its Chairman was the late Dr. Peter Nygh. The author was Rapporteur.

## "The Leuven/London Principles on Declining and Referring Jurisdiction in Civil and Commercial Litigation

[THE INTERNATIONAL LAW ASSOCIATION:]

RECOGNISING that all systems of civil and commercial jurisdiction afford the parties some choice of forum in many cases

DESIRING to promote the proper allocation of cases between courts; to discourage improper forum shopping; and to reduce the unnecessary incidence of concurrent jurisdiction and the risk of irreconcilable judgments

ENCOURAGING the adoption of a system of resolving questions of jurisdiction and forum which promotes international civil justice

MINDFUL of the fundamental right of all persons to access to a fair hearing before an impartial tribunal without undue delay and without discrimination on grounds of nationality

CONSIDERING that, irrespective of whether there exists an international convention governing civil and commercial jurisdiction between relevant states, circumstances may arise in which it will be desirable for a national court to decline jurisdiction in favour of the court of another state, and that the above objectives may be assisted by elucidation of the principles upon which a court shall decline jurisdiction

BELIEVING that, when a court declines jurisdiction, the fairest and most efficient means of resolving the matter shall be to refer it to an alternative available forum

URGING enhanced co-operation between courts for the more efficient referral of cases

*HEREBY DECIDES TO ADOPT the following Principles:*

## Scope and Purpose

1.1. These Principles determine the extent to which a court otherwise having original jurisdiction shall decline to exercise such jurisdiction, whether by suspension or termination, and refer the matter to a court of competent jurisdiction in another state in the exceptional circumstances set out below.

1.2. These Principles do not determine the rules of original jurisdiction in civil and commercial matters. Such rules are a matter of national law subject to international law, including any applicable international conventions.

## Preliminary Matters

2.1. It shall be for a party to make and substantiate an application to an originating court. The originating court shall not act of its own motion.

2.2. An application shall be made at the outset of the proceedings. It shall be finally determined by the originating court on summary proceedings by separate order at the earliest opportunity and in any event before the defendant is required to plead on the merits.

2.3. If either party wishes to pursue such rights of appeal as are allowed under national law from such an order, it must do so expeditiously.

## Jurisdiction Clauses

3.1. If the parties have chosen the originating court as the exclusive forum for resolution of the matter, then that court shall exercise jurisdiction and shall not decline it under Principle 4.

3.2. If the parties have chosen an alternative court as the exclusive forum for the resolution of the

matter, then the originating court shall either terminate its proceedings on the ground that it has no
jurisdiction over the matter or as the case may be
decline jurisdiction.

3.3. If the parties' choice of forum is not exclusive, the court may hear an applicant pursuant to
Principle 4.

### Declining Jurisdiction

4. The originating court shall decline jurisdiction
in the following exceptional circumstances:

### Lis pendens

4.1. Where proceedings involving the same parties and the same subject-matter are brought in the
courts of more than one state, any court other than
the court first seized shall suspend its proceedings
until such time as the jurisdiction of the court first
seized is established, and not declined under this
Principle, and thereafter it shall terminate its proceedings. The court first seized shall apply Principle 4.3. Should that court refer the matter to a
court subsequently seized in accordance with
Principle 4.3, the latter court will not be obliged to
terminate its proceedings.

### Related actions

4.2. Where related actions are pending in the
courts of more than one state either court may
suspend or terminate its proceedings and refer the
matter to the alternative court in accordance with
procedures in Principle 5, provided that the actions
can be consolidated in the alternative court.

### Other grounds for referral

4.3. An originating court shall decline jurisdiction and refer the matter to an alternative court

where it is satisfied that the alternative court is the manifestly more appropriate forum for the determination of the merits of the matter, taking into account the interests of all the parties, without discrimination on grounds of nationality. In making this decision, the court shall have regard in particular to the following factors:

(*a*) the location and language of the parties, witnesses and evidence;

(*b*) the balance of advantages of each party afforded by the law, procedure and practice of the respective jurisdictions;

(*c*) the law applicable to the merits;

(*d*) in cases under Principle 4.1, the desirability of avoiding multiplicity of proceedings or conflicting judgments having regard to the manner of resort to the respective court's jurisdiction and the substantive progress of the respective actions;

(*e*) the enforceability of any resulting judgment;

(*f*) the efficient operation of the judicial system of the respective jurisdictions;

(*g*) any terms of referral under Principle 5.3.

### *Referral*

*Procedure in the originating court*

5.1. On the hearing of an application under Principle 4.3, and subject to any terms of referral under Principle 5.3, the applicant shall satisfy the originating court that the alternative court:

(*a*) has and will exercise jurisdiction over the matter; and

(*b*) is likely to render its judgment on the merits within a reasonable time.

5.2. The originating court may communicate

directly with the alternative court on any application for referral in order to obtain information relevant to its determination under Principle 4, where such communication is permitted by the respective states. States are encouraged to permit their courts to make, and respond to, such communications.

Any such communication shall be either on the application of one of the parties or on its own motion. Where the court acts on its own motion it shall give reasonable notice to the parties of its intention to do so, and hear the parties on the information to be sought.

The originating court shall either communicate in writing or otherwise on the record. It shall communicate in a language acceptable to the alternative court.

5.3. The parties and the originating court are encouraged to consider appropriate terms of referral. These may deal in particular with:

*(a)* the applicant's submission to the jurisdiction of the alternative court;
*(b)* the terms on which the applicant may assert a defence of limitation or prescription of action in the alternative court.

5.4. Save where international convention provides otherwise, the originating court, if satisfied of the matters in paragraph 5.1, shall on an order to decline jurisdiction either suspend further proceedings at least until the jurisdiction of the alternative court has been established, or, where national law provides, terminate its proceedings.

*Procedure in the alternative court*

5.5. The alternative court shall decide any question as to its own jurisdiction at the outset of the proceedings before it and in any event before the defendant is required to plead on the merits.

5.6. The applicant shall transmit the order for referral, together with the originating court's reasons for judgment, if any, to the alternative court which shall be entitled to take it, and the terms of referral, into account whether in deciding its own jurisdiction or as otherwise relevant to the issues before it.

5.7. The applicant shall promptly inform the originating court when the alternative court has assumed jurisdiction over the matter and shall cooperate in the making of any further order which the originating court may wish to make, including an order to terminate its proceedings.

5.8. In the event that the alternative court were not for any reason to assume jurisdiction, then the originating court may lift any suspension of its own proceedings and shall be entitled to resume jurisdiction over the merits.

### Consequences of Referral

6.1. Without prejudice to any other grounds upon which the courts of the state originally applied to may be entitled to decline to recognise or enforce any resulting judgment of the alternative court, once the originating court has, pursuant to Principle 3 or 4, declined jurisdiction in favour of the alternative court, the courts of its state shall not be entitled to review the jurisdiction of the alternative court on an application for the recognition or enforcement of a judgment of that court.

### Injunctions in Relation to Foreign Proceedings

7.1. Where the respective states are parties to an international convention providing common rules for the exercise of original jurisdiction, no court of either state shall be entitled to restrain by injunction any party from proceeding in the court of the other state.

It shall be for the court in which the proceedings on the merits are instituted to determine its own jurisdiction and any application pursuant to these Principles.

7.2. Where there is no such applicable international convention, a court to which a request for such an injunction is made shall not grant an injunction where it is satisfied that these Principles will be applied by the court in which proceedings have been instituted.

7.3. This Principle is without prejudice to the power of a court to grant redress where an exclusive jurisdiction clause has been manifestly breached according to the law applicable in the courts of both states."

What do these Principles tell us about a new model for litispendence? It will immediately be appreciated that, while the Principle 4.1 preserves a strict rule requiring deference to the court first seised, the operation of the rule departs in the result radically from the automatic priority on the merits vouchsafed to the court first seised under the Brussels I Regulation [1145]. That is because Principle 4.1 simply requires courts subsequently seised to suspend their proceedings until the court first seised has established its jurisdiction, and not declined it under the Principles. The court first seised has a positive obligation to consider the application of the other grounds of referral in Principle 4.3. If the court first seised then decides to refer the matter to the court subsequently seised, the latter court may lift its suspension and continue with the proceedings.

---

[1145] This section draws upon the Committee's Report, written by the author, *ibid.*, at [60]-[62].

Thus, all that Principle 4.1 does is to give priority to the court first seised in the determination of the appropriate court for adjudication of the merits of the matter.

In this way, the Committee considered that the potential for the abuse of a *lis pendens* system by a race to the courthouse could be curbed, whilst a specific regime for the determination of priorities between competing actions was still preserved. This was seen as a more effective mechanism than one which sought to proscribe the use of actions for negative declarations, which Committee members observed had been the means by which prospective defendants had sought to ensure litigation in the forum of their choice. As Principle 4.3 *(d)* makes clear, one of the factors which the originating court must consider is the desirability of avoiding multiplicity of proceedings or conflicting judgments *having regard to the manner of resort to the respective court's jurisdiction and the substantive progress of the respective actions*. The Committee considered that this provision would enable the court first seised to distinguish between cases in which its jurisdiction had been invoked for purely forum shopping purposes from cases where there was a much more substantial link to the forum. It would also enable the court first seised to consider how far advanced the action in its own courts was, so as to avoid a purely mechanistic application of the *lis pendens* rule, when the two courts were seised of the action within days, or even hours, of each other.

By contrast, the Principles take a restrictive approach to anti-suit injunctions. Subject to the exception in Principle 7.3, Principle 7.1 accepts that there is no place for such a remedy where both states are parties to an international convention specifying common rules for the exercise of original jurisdiction. Nor indeed should such a remedy be ordered where the court is satisfied that the other court will apply the

Principles (Principle 7.2). In this way, the Committee sought to build upon the idea that ordinarily deference should be given to the court seised of the substantive proceedings, at least where that court has rules permitting it to decline jurisdiction in certain cases [1146]. However, importantly Principle 7.3 qualifies both of the previous paragraphs by permitting an exception in the case of a manifest breach of an exclusive jurisdiction clause under the law of both States. This Principle was agreed by consensus following a strong sentiment by Committee members from different legal families that the possibility of such a remedy should not be wholly excluded in such situations.

The Leuven/London Principles represent the first agreed statement of common principles as to declining jurisdiction agreed by scholars and practitioners from across different legal traditions. But the scheme of the Principles also involves important procedural mechanisms in cases of parallel litigation, which may be as significant as the substantive principles. Indeed, the Report comments that: "The research and experience of the Committee has shown that these practical matters may offer the key to an improved system for the allocation of international jurisdiction." [1147]

Two aspects should be highlighted:

(a) *Referral.* The Principles employ the technique of the *referral* of a matter to another court [1148]. This ensures that, in all cases where a court is permitted

---

[1146] *Amchem* v. *Workers' Compensation Board*, [1993] 1 SCR 897; Committee Report, *ibid.*, [81].

[1147] *Ibid.*, [71].

[1148] The Committee drew its inspiration in particular from the Canadian Uniform Jurisdiction and Proceedings Transfer Act 1994; the Australian Jurisdiction of Courts (Cross-Vesting) Act 1987; and Arts. 8 and 9 of the Hague Convention on the Protection of Children 1996: see Report, *ibid.*, [31]-[34].

to decline jurisdiction, it shall refer the matter to an alternative court, and provides a mechanism to ensure that such referral is effective. In the case of litispendence, where, by definition, two courts are seised of the same matter, this process ensures that the chosen court "will exercise jurisdiction over the matter"[1149]. Once the case has been referred, the referring court may not review the jurisdiction of the chosen court on a subsequent application for enforcement of its judgment[1150].

(b) *Inter-court communication.* The Principles also encourage direct court-to-court communication on an application for referral[1151]. In this way, the Principles seek to break down the barriers between adjudicators who are each asked to determine the same issue in their respective jurisdictions. As will be seen in the next section, this is process which is already being applied in some contexts. Principle 5.2 seeks to encourage it as a specific means of reaching decisions as to which court will exercise its jurisdiction on the merits. It also adds important due process provisions, in order to safeguard the right to a fair trial on jurisdictional allocation.

The Principles were in general well received by scholars[1152]. But have they had any impact in practice?

---

[1149] *Ibid.*, Principle 5.1 *(a)*.
[1150] *Ibid.*, Principle 6.
[1151] *Ibid.*, Principle 5.2.
[1152] For example von Mehren, *supra* footnote 1056, 401, fn. 1298, "thoughtful and innovative"; Walker "Parallel Proceedings — Converging Views", [2000] *Canadian Yearbook of International Law* 155, 168-173; Schlosser, "Jurisdiction and International Judicial and Administrative Cooperation", (2000) 284 *Recueil des cours* 9, 418, "courageous"; Nuyts, *L'exception de forum non conveniens* (2003) [616], "très grand intérêt théorique et pratique".

They had an immediate impact on the formulation of the *lis pendens* provisions of the Preliminary Draft Hague Convention on Jurisdiction and Foreign Judgments in Civil and Commercial Matters[1153]. As the late Peter Nygh (who was chairman of the ILA Committee and co-reporter of the Special Commission of the Hague Conference) acknowledged, the formulations of the ILA Committee greatly influenced Articles 21 and 22 of the draft Hague Convention[1154]. In particular, the Hague Draft adopted the relationship between litispendence and the residual grounds for declining jurisdiction pioneered in the Principles, such that the court first seised should itself defer if the residual grounds for establishing that another court "is clearly more appropriate" apply[1155]. The Hague Draft also provides that the court which wishes to relinquish jurisdiction shall in the first instance simply suspend its proceedings, until it is clear that the other court will decide to exercise jurisdiction[1156]. Nevertheless, the two drafts are not identical. Article 21 of the Hague Draft goes further by actually reversing the court first-seised rule in the case of actions for negative declarations[1157]. However, it does not contain the more innovative procedural provisions of the Principles regarding referral and co-operation.

Of course, regrettably the Hague Preliminary Draft Convention has not (at least yet) been adopted. Efforts to secure consensus failed in 2001, and subsequent diplomatic efforts were limited to drafting the Choice of Court Convention 2005, which has a much narrower focus. But Articles 21 and 22 of the Hague Draft are

---

[1153] *Supra* footnote 1064.
[1154] Nygh, *supra* footnote 1064, 330 fn. 129.
[1155] *Supra* footnote 1064, Art. 21 (7) and Art. 22 (1).
[1156] *Ibid.*, Art. 21 (1) and Art. 22 (5).
[1157] *Ibid.*, Art. 21 (6).

nevertheless highly significant for the present study, since they represent one of the (relatively few) areas where real agreement was reached between all parties negotiating at The Hague [1158]. This is remarkable in itself, when one considers the diversity of solutions adopted in existing national and supra-national law on the subject; the degree of commitment which Civilians and Common lawyers each felt to their own solutions; and the existence of a very different solution in the Brussels I Regulation.

The Principles are also expressly acknowledged as having influenced the formulation of Section 11 of the subsequent ALI Draft Federal Statute on Enforcement of Judgments [1159].

But perhaps the most notable legacy of this "new model *lis pendens*" is to be found in a binding European text: the Brussels II*bis* Regulation on Jurisdiction and Enforcement in Matrimonial and Parental Responsibility Matters [1160]. Article 19 (2) contains a standard *lis pendens* rule, requiring the court second seised to decline jurisdiction in favour of the court first seised in matters of parental responsibility. But Article 15 then also provides:

---

[1158] Hague Conference on Private International Law, "Enforcement of Judgments, Preliminary Draft Convention on Jurisdiction and Foreign Judgments in Civil and Commercial Matters" (Nygh and Pocar, Rapporteurs), Prel. Doc. No. 11, 2000, 89; Brand and Jablonski, *Forum Non Conveniens: History, Global Practice, and Future under the Hague Convention on Choice of Court Agreements* (2007) Chap. 8; von Mehren, *supra* footnote 1075, 413-417.

[1159] *Supra* footnote 1056, 135.

[1160] Council Regulation (EC) No. 2201/2003 of 27 November 2003 concerning jurisdiction and the recognition and enforcement of judgments in matrimonial matters and the matters of parental responsibility, OJ L 338/1.

*"Article 15*

*Transfer to a Court Better Placed to Hear the Case*

1. By way of exception, the courts of a Member State having jurisdiction as to the substance of the matter may, if they consider that a court of another Member State, with which the child has a particular connection, would be better placed to hear the case, or a specific part thereof, and where this is in the best interests of the child:

*(a)* stay the case or the part thereof in question and invite the parties to introduce a request before the court of that other Member State in accordance with paragraph 4; or

*(b)* request a court of another Member State to assume jurisdiction in accordance with paragraph 5.

2. Paragraph 1 shall apply:

*(a)* upon application from a party; or

*(b)* of the court's own motion; or

*(c)* upon application from a court of another Member State with which the child has a particular connection, in accordance with paragraph 3.

A transfer made of the court's own motion or by application of a court of another Member State must be accepted by at least one of the parties.

3. The child shall be considered to have a particular connection to a Member State as mentioned in paragraph 1, if that Member State:

*(a)* has become the habitual residence of the child after the court referred to in paragraph 1 was seised; or

*(b)* is the former habitual residence of the child; or

*(c)* is the place of the child's nationality; or

*(d)* is the habitual residence of a holder of parental responsibility; or

*(e)* is the place where property of the child is located and the case concerns measures for the protection of the child relating to the administration, conservation or disposal of this property.

4. The court of the Member State having jurisdiction as to the substance of the matter shall set a time limit by which the courts of that other Member State shall be seised in accordance with paragraph 1.

If the courts are not seised by that time, the court which has been seised shall continue to exercise jurisdiction in accordance with Articles 8 to 14.

5. The courts of that other Member State may, where due to the specific circumstances of the case, this is in the best interests of the child, accept jurisdiction within six weeks of their seisure in accordance with paragraph 1 *(a)* or 1 *(b)*. In this case, the court first seised shall decline jurisdiction. Otherwise, the court first seised shall continue to exercise jurisdiction in accordance with Articles 8 to 14.

6. The courts shall cooperate for the purposes of this Article, either directly or through the central authorities designated pursuant to Article 53."

Given the conservatism shown in relation to the structure of the Brussels I Regulation, it is submitted that Brussels II*bis* is an extraordinarily radical document to have entered the canon of the current European codification of Private International Law[1161]. It invests the court first seised with a discretion to stay the proceedings where the courts of another member State would be "better placed to hear the case or a specific

---

[1161] Compare the earlier adoption of a similar scheme in Arts. 8 and 9 of the Hague Convention on the Protection of Children 1996, as to which see Lagarde, "Explanatory Report", in Hague Conference on Private International Law, *Proceedings of the Eighteenth Session* II, 534, [53]-[60].

part thereof". Moreover, it treats the issue as one of
*transfer* of the case, based upon a request to the other
court to assume jurisdiction. This technique of referral,
found in the Principles, is still apparently regarded as
too radical for inclusion in the Brussels I Regulation[1162]. Article 15 (6) goes on to *require* the courts to
co-operate for the purposes of this Article, and includes
the possibility of direct co-operation. Finally, the provision deals expressly with the problem of delay, by
ensuring that the court second seised must make a
decision within a specified time as to whether it will
accept jurisdiction. Essentially, then, all the elements
of new model *lis pendens* have now been put into operation in this new Regulation. It remains now only to
consider finally the developing concepts of judicial
communication and co-operation.

### 3. *Judicial co-operation and communication*

Deciding an anti-suit injunction case, Lord Denning
once observed with his customary foresight: "In the
interests of comity, one [court] or other must give way.
I wish that we could sit together to discuss it."[1163]

The idea of direct judicial interaction in cases of
parallel proceedings may, even as recently as 1983,
have seemed a remote possibility. But the pace of globalization has, since then, begun to transform Lord
Denning's wish into a reality. Direct judicial co-operation has developed most swiftly in two types of civil
disputes: insolvency and the protection of children[1164].
This is in itself remarkable. After all, insolvency and
family law have traditionally been areas in which States

---

[1162] Heidelberg Report, *supra* footnote 1099, [434]-[435].

[1163] *Smith Kline & French Laboratories Ltd.* v. *Bloch*,
[1983] 1 WLR 730, 735 (CA).

[1164] Schlosser, *supra* footnote 1152, Part II; Schlosser,
"Direct Interaction of Courts of Different Nations" in *Studi*

have struggled to find common ground. In the case of insolvency, this reflects the very different policies pursued in national insolvency legislation (as to the degree to which the law favours the debtor or his creditors). In the case of family law, the constraints have rather been in the form of entrenched social and cultural differences between peoples. Yet in both of these fields, globalization and the increased mobility of people and property have frequently produced concurrent litigation in different States about the same issue. In turn, courts have been driven out of necessity into closer engagement in order to manage the disputes before them.

*Insolvency*. In the case of insolvency, the defining moment was the collapse of the Maxwell publishing empire in 1991 after the sudden and suspicious death of its founder, Robert Maxwell. This corporate empire had spanned the globe. The top holding company was Maxwell Communication Corporation (MCC), which was incorporated in England. MCC had some 400 subsidiaries around the world. But there was a particularly high concentration of business activity in the United States, where some 75 per cent of MCC's assets were concentrated. This made it inevitable that there would have to be concurrent bankruptcy proceedings in both the United Kingdom and the United States. MCC thus filed for reorganization in the United States on 16 December 1991, and, on the following day, sought administration in England.

This could have led to considerable conflict between courts, as the diverging pressures of the creditors in each jurisdiction exacerbated differences between the respective insolvency codes. But instead conflict was

---

*di Diritto Processuale Civile in onore di Giuseppe Tarzia* (2005), I, 589; Westbrook, "International Judicial Negotiation", (2003) 38 *Texas ILJ* 567.

averted by direct judicial co-operation [1165]. Judge Broz-
nan of the US Bankruptcy Court for the Southern
District of New York and Hoffmann J in the English
High Court approved a Protocol agreed between the
English Administrators and the US Examiner, which
made detailed provision for the co-operative administration of MCC's insolvency.

This piece of inspired judicial initiative has subsequently been replicated in other large global insolvencies [1166]. The practice-driven revolution has in turn led
to a number of international instruments seeking to
formalize and develop what had been informal and
*ad hoc*. This began with a Cross-Border Insolvency
Concordat adopted by the International Bar Association in 1995 [1167]. Work initiated in UNCITRAL [1168]
resulted in the adoption in 1997 of the most significant
international instrument in this field: the UNCITRAL
Model Law on Cross-Border Insolvency [1169]. Then, in
2001, the American Law Institute in collaboration with

---

[1165] *In re Maxwell Communications Corp.* v. *Société Générale*, 93 F. 3d 1036 (2d Cir., 1996), and see also Hoffmann J's refusal (upheld by the Court of Appeal) to grant an anti-suit injunction restraining related US proceedings in *Barclays Bank* v. *Homan* [1992] BCC 757; Westbrook, "The Lessons of Maxwell Communication", (1996) 64 *Fordham LR* 2531.

[1166] For example, *Re Bank of Credit and Commerce International SA (No. 1)*, [1992] BCLC 570, *(No. 3)* [1993] BCLC 106, *(No. 11)* [1997] Ch 213. On the Canadian-US practice see Brenner, "Cross Border Court Communications", (2009) 83 *ALJ* 90.

[1167] Available at www.ibanet.org.

[1168] In collaboration with INSOL, the International Association of Insolvency Professionals.

[1169] United Nations, "Report of the United Nations Commission on International Trade Law on the work of its thirtieth session, 12-30 May 1997", UN doc. A/52/17, Annex 1; Fletcher, *Insolvency in Private International Law* (2nd ed., 2005, Supp. 2007).

the International Insolvency Institute agreed, as part of a wide-ranging project dealing with insolvency amongst the NAFTA countries, detailed "Guidelines Applicable to Court-to-Court Communications in Cross-Border Cases" [1170].

The UNCITRAL Model Law has begun to receive significant legislative adoption, including in the United States [1171], Australia [1172], New Zealand [1173] and the United Kingdom [1174], as well as in Mexico, Japan and Poland amongst other countries [1175].

Chapter IV of the Model Law provides for direct co-operation and communication between courts in matters within the Law's scope. One form which this may take is in the "[c]oordination of concurrent proceedings regarding the same debtor" [1176]. Chapter V then deals with the co-ordination of concurrent insolvency proceedings. The Model Law requires the proceeding in the place "where the debtor has the centre of its main interests" [1177] to be recognized as the main proceeding. Where this is in a foreign State, the recognizing court must defer by ensuring that its relief is consistent with the main proceeding [1178]. In this way, the Model Law's provisions for judicial co-operation and communication are employed in the service of a clear rule of *priority* as between concurrent proceedings.

---

[1170] Available at www.ali.org/doc/Guidelines.pdf.

[1171] Chap. 15, Bankruptcy Code (US) (entered into force 17 October 2005).

[1172] Cross-Border Insolvency Act 2008 (Cth).

[1173] Insolvency (Cross-Border) Act 2006 (NZ).

[1174] Cross-Border Insolvency Regulations 2006, SI2006/1030 (UK).

[1175] See http://www.uncitral.org/uncitral/en/uncitral_texts/insolvency/1997Model_status.html.

[1176] *Supra* footnote 1169, Art. 27 *(e)*.

[1177] *Ibid.*, Art. 2 *(b)* and Art. 17 (2) *(a)*.

[1178] *Ibid.*, Art. 29.

The concept of judicial communication is developed still further in the ALI/III Guidelines. These are designed for specific adoption by insolvency courts in particular cases. They are intended to provide for rapid co-operation, while ensuring due process for the parties. The Guidelines make provision for direct communication between courts, and even for joint hearings. Guideline 15 provides that communication may be undertaken

> "for purposes of coordinating and harmonizing proceedings before it with proceedings in the other jurisdiction . . . whenever there is commonality among the issues and/or the parties in the proceedings" [1179].

As between Common Law countries (and notably between Canada and the United States) this degree of judicial co-operation in insolvency cases has already taken place [1180]. To date, despite the adoption of the UNCITRAL Model Law in some Civil Law countries, and some Common Law judicial encouragement [1181], there is little to be found in the way of reported experience within the Civilian legal family [1182].

*Children.* The other context in which direct judicial communication has begun to take hold is that of the rights of children. The most significant step forward in this regard was the inclusion in The Hague Convention on the Protection of Children 1996 of specific provisions dealing with the transfer of cases between courts,

---

[1179] *Supra* footnote 1170, Guideline 15.

[1180] Brenner, *supra* footnote 1166; Justice Jack D. Ground, "Direct Cooperation between Courts of Different Nations", unpublished paper delivered at IBA Conference "Plotting Litigation in the Global Context", Chicago, 19-20 June 2003.

[1181] *Stonington Partners Inc.* v. *Lernout & Hauspie Speech Products NV*, 310 F. 3d 118, 133 (3rd Cir., 2002).

[1182] Schlosser, *supra* footnote 1164.

and communication between them in order to facilitate this[1183]. Article 8 provides that the court which otherwise has jurisdiction may, by way of exception, request the court of another country which has one of a number of specified connections with the child to assume jurisdiction. Under Article 9 the courts of that other country may themselves initiate a request that they be authorized to accept jurisdiction if they consider that it is in the best interests of the child. In either case "[t]he authorities concerned may proceed to an exchange of views"[1184].

There are more elaborate provisions in the new Brussels II*bis* Regulation which has just been discussed in the previous section, including a requirement for judicial co-operation[1185].

The practice of judicial communication in matters concerning children is growing apace[1186]. In January 2009 judges from more than 50 countries met in Brussels under the joint auspices of the European Commission and the Hague Conference to discuss direct judicial communications on family law matters. The Conference endorsed and encouraged the ongoing work of the Hague Conference to draft General Principles on Direct Judicial Communications[1187]. At the

---

[1183] Arts. 8 and 9, Convention on Jurisdiction, Applicable Law, Recognition, Enforcement and Co-operation in Respect of Parental Responsibility and Measures for the Protection of Children (19 October 1996), The Hague, www.hcch.net.

[1184] *Ibid.*, Arts. 8 (3) and 9 (2).

[1185] Art. 15 (6): see text, *supra* footnote 1160.

[1186] See the detailed empirical information gathered from member States by the Hague Conference, in Lortie, "Report on Judicial Communications in International Child Protection", Hague Conference on Private International Law, International Child Abduction, Prel. Doc. No. 8 (2006).

[1187] Recommendation 16, available at http://www.hcch. net/upload/judcomm_concl2009e.pdf.

time of writing, this work has not yet come to final
fruition. Yet it appears that this area, too, is heading pro-
gressively towards a more formalized system of inter-
court communication, developing the notion of due
process as it might apply in this cross-border context.

To what extent may these remarkable developments
presage a larger revolution in international judicial
practice? It must be accepted that the barriers to international judicial co-operation, particularly across different legal traditions and languages, are considerable.
But Schlosser speculates that, if conceived as an aspect
of court-centred case management of related cases (as
opposed to a joint trial), there might be little objection
in principle in Civil Law countries[1188]. The practical
work of the Hague Conference in particular in building
networks of judges may ultimately achieve more than
treaties alone ever could.

But in the end, while judicial communication may
greatly facilitate the resolution of problems of parallel
proceedings, it is not a universal panacea. As La Forest
J of the Supreme Court of Canada wisely put it: "[i]n
dealing with legal issues having an impact in more than
one legal jurisdiction . . . [w]e are engaged in a struc-
tural problem"[1189]. The innovative provisions for inter-
court communication and co-operation in the insolvency
and family law fields work because they are harnessed in
the service of specific rules and procedures governing the
relationship and priority between identical or related proceedings. They are not a substitute for such rules.

## C. Final Conclusions

Looking back over the terrain mapped in these
lectures, the following insights may be advanced by
way of conclusion:

---

[1188]  Schlosser, *supra* footnote 1164, 589-592.
[1189]  *Tolofson* v. *Jensen*, *supra* footnote 1139, 302.

(1) *Parallel proceedings are endemic in international litigation.* The concept of *lis pendens* does not denote a legal rule. Rather, it describes a factual situation of parallel proceedings relating to the same subject-matter proceeding concurrently in more than one court or tribunal. Such a situation is not necessarily an aberration. On the contrary, the phenomenon of parallel litigation may be seen as characteristic of modern international litigation. The process of globalization has not been centripetal. The plurality of legal systems at national level has been matched by a similar diversity in the creation of international tribunals. Parallel litigation is the simple consequence of the availability of multiple fora, and the natural desire of litigants (whether individuals, corporations or States) to take advantage of the opportunities which such fora may offer. Thus issues of parallel proceedings may arise between all levels of international litigation: as between national courts; between national courts and arbitral tribunals; between international tribunals; and as between international tribunals and national courts. The different character of these institutional relationships may indicate a different solution to the problems of litispendence. But the issues of principle, and the range of potential solutions, are comparable.

In some cases, the pendency of related proceedings in different tribunals may be both positive and necessary. This is certainly the case where a court is asked to provide judicial assistance in the provision of interim measures or evidence in aid of proceedings in another tribunal. But there are also cases where closely related parallel substantive cases may be better tried in different courts. Insolvency and fraud litigation are both fields, for example, where it is often essential to be able to determine aspects of a larger dispute, as they apply to particular persons or property, where the person or property may be found. Further, material differences between the parties, applicable law or relief may require parallel related litigation. These circumstances do not, however, necessarily preclude positive interactions between courts. In these cases, the issue becomes one of co-ordination, rather than an all-or-nothing choice between jurisdictions.

(2) *Identification of a conflict of litigation*. Where, however, there is the potential for the operations of parallel courts to conflict, the principle of litispendence may require a decision as to which of two competing tribunals should take precedence. It is important in this context to determine whether there is a true conflict of litigation. Many apparent problems of overlapping jurisdiction may be solved by a careful application of international law rules of jurisdiction. Thus, for example:

(a) Rules of international law may allocate priority to a particular forum. This is the case, for example, where the parties have chosen to subject their dispute to arbitration by virtue of Article II of the New York Convention. Where the parties have chosen the exclusive forum for their dispute, such a choice should normally be respected by other courts and tribunals. This general principle applies to arbitration agreements and choice of court clauses. It extends, in the case of arbitration, to the choice of the control of the courts at the seat of the arbitration. It also applies to cases where, under the applicable rules, the choice of a particular forum operates as an election of one forum and a waiver of the right to pursue other avenues of redress.

(b) The vertical relationship between International Law and national legal systems will also, in many instances indicate which disputes should properly be submitted to which tribunal. This is not always a matter of conceding preference to the international tribunal. The rules regarding exhaustion of local remedies and complementarity in Public International Law, and the distinction drawn in investment arbitration between breach of contract and breach of treaty, also achieve this objective of allocation of responsibility as between potentially competing jurisdictions.

*(c)* In many cases in Private International Law, apparent problems of litispendence may be solved by application of the rules of original jurisdiction, with one of the two courts seised finding that it does not have jurisdiction to determine the dispute.

(3) *Declining jurisdiction in cases of overlapping jurisdictional competence.* However, the allocation of jurisdictional competence will not, of itself, solve all problems of parallel litigation. Many international disputes are, of their nature, properly amenable to the jurisdiction of more than one tribunal. In such a situation, it is no answer for the tribunal to claim either *(a)* a priority derived from its own jurisdictional competence; or *(b)* a difference in the source of the applicable law.

(a) *Jurisdictional priority.* Courts frequently maintain that they have an "unflagging obligation" to hear the dispute before it, regardless of the existence of other litigation on the same subject-matter. The question of *lis pendens* by definition requires the tribunal to consider declining or staying the exercise of a jurisdiction which it undoubtedly enjoys, in favour of another tribunal which is similarly endowed.

(b) *Difference in source of applicable law.* Nor is it necessarily any answer for a tribunal to claim that the case before it cannot overlap with that of another tribunal, since each is applying a different applicable law. In Private International Law, rules of *lis alibi pendens* were created by the courts to apply across borders irrespective of the fact that each court seised would be applying its own law to resolve the dispute. Thus, even a strict approach derived by analogy from the rule of *res judicata* applies an objective test to determine whether the cause of action and the claim are the same. It does not matter, for this purpose, that the law applicable may be French law in one case, and English law in the other, or that the substantive outcome may be different as a result of material differences in the content of the applicable law.

(4) *General principles of litispendence.* Systems of adjudication do not exist for their own sake. They exist in order to further a human objective — to facilitate, for private and public purposes, the just resolution of disputes. In the context of international disputes, therefore, rules of litispendence are not simply about pre-emptive enforcement of judgments or judicial efficiency. They give effect to a central function of the Rule of Law as applied to exercises of adjudicatory authority. Approaching problems of litispendence with this insight has at least the consequences that: *(a)* a simple rule of priority will be inadequate to resolve all issues of conflict of jurisdiction; and *(b)* rules of litispendence must be designed to secure, so far as possible, a wider set of principles, including to avert a denial of justice and to prevent abuse of rights:

(a) *No simple rule of priority.* The simplest rule for dealing with litispendence automatically vests jurisdiction in the court first seised, requiring all other courts to cede jurisdiction automatically. Such a rule gives absolute priority to order over fairness, since it does not provide for cases of abusive forum shopping, where the court is first seised by a party intent on achieving an illegitimate advantage. The vice inherent in such a system may be reduced if the court first seised promptly decides upon its own jurisdiction, so that the question of jurisdiction is not merely pre-empted by a race to begin proceedings; and has the discretion itself to stay or dismiss the case before it in favour of another court of competent jurisdiction.

(b) *Denial of justice and abuse of rights.* No tribunal should decline its own jurisdiction unless it is satisfied that there is another court of competent jurisdiction which will determine the dispute. Where, however, a party by his conduct engages in abusive parallel litigation, the court or tribunal of primary jurisdiction should be able to control such abuses in order to prevent a denial of justice. Examples include: invoking the jurisdiction of a court in breach of an arbitration clause; engaging in parallel litigation designed to disrupt the fair disposal of the matter; and cases of a State's intervention through its own courts in an attempt to disrupt the disposal of the matter by a tribunal to which it had submitted.

(5) *Transfer, consolidation and co-ordination.* The interests of reducing parallel related litigation also justify the application of techniques of transfer of cases, and of consolidation and co-ordination, even where the extent of overlap between the proceedings does not reach complete identity. The emerging practice of direct judicial communication, if regulated in order to secure due process for the parties, may reduce the risk of conflict between courts, and greatly facilitate their interaction in solving problems of litispendence.

If the foregoing analysis of the practice of courts and tribunals across the private/public divide in international law helps us to understand anything better, it may be because it exposes to view the essential dependence of the system upon a set of norms which are not fully explained within any *lex specialis* — whether a particular treaty or national legal system. The apparently divergent solutions to the problems of litispendence adopted in different systems have proved on examination to have been developed to meet internal rather than international needs. It is both possible and necessary to recast the science of the conflict of international litigation in the service of general principles of law which are common to civilised nations and their courts in their relations with one another. As the Privy Council put it in *Thomas* v. *Baptiste*:

> " 'due process of law' is a compendious expression in which the word 'law' does not refer to any particular law and is not a synonym for common law or statute. Rather it invokes the concept of the rule of law itself and the universally accepted standards of justice observed by civilized nations which observe the rule of law." [1190]

In the foyer of the magnificent new Hague Academy building there is a bas relief which used to be mounted above the rostrum in the old lecture hall, called "Leçon de droit". It is a copy of a famous relief from Bologna carved in 1397, and shows a group of law students learning from a professor who is expounding the law. The law, like other parts of human learning, is vitally transmitted in this way. It has been an essential premise of these lectures that it is only by understanding the insights, and the errors, of the past that it is possible to develop new and better solutions to the problems which the world faces today.

But there is another, and even older, tradition of

[1190] [2000] 2 AC 1 (PC (Trinidad and Tobago) [22].

learning the law in human society. In Book III of Plato's *Republic*, Socrates asks:

> "doth it not appear to be base, and a great sign of want of education, to be obliged to observe justice pronounced upon us by others, as our masters and judges, and to have no sense of it in ourselves?" [1191]

In this field, unless our solutions are motivated by a common sense of what justice requires in the interaction between diverse systems of adjudicatory authority, they will avail us naught.

---

[1191] Plato, *The Republic*, trans. H. Spens (1763), Book III, 143.

# SELECT BIBLIOGRAPHY

*Books*

Barnett, P., *Res Judicata, Estoppel and Foreign Judgments*, Oxford, Oxford University Press, 2001.

Bell, A. S., *Forum Shopping and Venue in Transnational Litigation*, Oxford, Oxford University Press, 2003.

Blokker, N. M., and H. G. Schermers (eds.), *Proliferation of International Organizations*, The Hague, Kluwer Law International, 2001.

Born, G. B., *International Commercial Arbitration*, Austin, Wolters Kluwer Law & Business, 2009.

Born, G. B., and P. B. Rutledge, *International Civil Litigation in United States Courts,* 4th ed., New York, Aspen Publishers, 2007.

Brand, R. A., and P. M. Herrup, *The 2005 Hague Convention on Choice of Court Agreements Commentary and Documents*, Cambridge, Cambridge University Press, 2008.

Brand, R.A., and S. R. Jablonski, *Forum Non Conveniens: History, Global Practice, and Future under the Hague Convention on Choice of Court Agreements*, New York, Oxford University Press, 2007.

Brown, C., *A Common Law of International Adjudication*, Oxford, Oxford University Press, 2007.

Bureau, D., and H. Muir Watt, *Droit international privé*, Paris, Presses universitaires de France, 2007.

Cheng, B., *General Principles of Law as Applied by International Courts and Tribunals*, London, Stevens, 1953.

Collier, J. G., and V. Lowe, *The Settlement of Disputes in International Law: Institutions and Procedures*, Oxford, Oxford University Press, 2000.

Collins, L. A., A. Briggs, J. Harris, C. McLachlan, J. D. McLean and C. G. J. Morse (eds.), *Dicey, Morris & Collins on the Conflict of Laws*, 14th ed., London, Sweet & Maxwell, 2006.

Craig, W. L., W. W. Park and J. Paulsson, *International Chamber of Commerce Arbitration,* 3rd ed., Dobbs Ferry, N.Y., Oceana Publications, 1998.

Cremades, B. M., and J. D. M. Lew (eds.), *Parallel State and Arbitral Procedures in International Arbitration*, Paris, ICC Publishing, 2005.

Dalloz, V. A. D., *Répertoire méthodique et alphabétique de législation de doctrine et de jurisprudence,* Vol. 23, Paris, Bureau de la jurisprudence générale, 1852.

Dicey, A. V., *A Digest of the Law of England with Reference to the Conflict of Laws*, London, Stevens, 1896.

Droz, G., *Compétence judiciaire et effets des jugements dans le Marché commun*, Paris, Librairie Dalloz, 1972.

Fawcett, J. (ed.), *Declining Jurisdiction in Private International Law: Reports to the XIVth Congress of the International Academy of Comparative Law Athens, August 1994*, Oxford, Oxford University Press, 1995.

Fletcher, I. F., *Insolvency in Private International Law*, 2nd ed., Oxford, Oxford University Press, 2005, Supp. 2007.

Fœlix, J. J. G., *Traité de droit international privé, ou du conflit des lois de différentes nations en matières de droit privé*, Paris, Joubert, 1843.

Freeman, A. V., *The International Responsibility of States for Denial of Justice*, London, Longmans, Green & Co., 1938.

Gaillard, E. (ed.), *Anti-suit Injunctions in International Arbitration*, Huntingdon, N.Y., Juris Publishing, 2005.

—, *Aspects philosophiques du droit de l'arbitrage international*, Leiden, Martinus Nijhoff, 2007.

Gaillard, E., and J. Savage, *Fouchard, Gaillard, Goldman on International Commercial Arbitration*, The Hague, Kluwer Law International, 1999.

Handley, K. R. (ed.), *The Doctrine of Res Judicata: The Original Text by George Spencer Bower,* 3rd ed., London, Butterworths, 1996.

Hanotiau, B., *Complex Arbitrations: Multiparty, Multi-contract, Multi-issue and Class Actions*, The Hague, Kluwer Law International, 2005.

Hess, B., T. Pfeiffer and P. Schlosser, *The Brussels I Regulation 44/2001*, Munich, C. H. Beck, 2008.

Huber, U., *Heedensdaegse Rechtsgeleertheyt (The Jurisprudence of My Time)*, 1686; trans. P. Gane, Durban, Butterworth, 1939.

Karrer, P. A. (ed.), *Arbitral Tribunals or State Courts: Who Must Defer to Whom?*, ASA Swiss Arbitration Association IBA International Bar Association Conference in Zurich of January 28, 2000, Basel, ASA Special Series No. 15, 2001.

Kerr, W. W., *Treatise on the Law and Practice of Injunctions in Equity,* 1st ed., London, W. Maxwell & Son, 1867; J. M. Paterson, 6th ed., London, Sweet & Maxwell, 1927.

Lauterpacht, H., *Private Law Sources and Analogies of International Law (with Special Reference to International Arbitration)*, London, Longmans, Green and Co. Ltd., 1927.

Lew, J. D. M., L. A. Mistelis and S. M. Kröll, *Comparative International Commercial Arbitration*, The Hague, Kluwer Law International, 2003.

Magnus, U., and P. Mankowski (eds.), *Brussels I Regulation*, Munich, Sellier, 2007.

Mann, F. A., *Foreign Affairs in English Courts*, Oxford, Clarendon Press, 1986.

McLachlan, C. A., L. Shore and M. Weiniger, *International Investment Arbitration: Substantive Principles,* Oxford, Oxford University Press, 2007.

Mills, A., *The Confluence of Public and Private International Law: Justice, Pluralism and Subsidiarity in the International Constitutional Ordering of Private Law*, Cambridge, Cambridge University Press, 2009.

Mistelis, L. A., and J. D. M. Lew (eds.), *Pervasive Problems in International Arbitration*, The Hague, Kluwer Law International, 2006.

Moissinac Massénat, V., *Les conflits de procédures et de décisions en droit international privé*, Paris, Librairie générale de droit et de jurisprudence, E.J.A., 2007.

Nadelmann, K. H., *Conflict of Laws: International and Interstate: Selected Essays*, The Hague, Martinus Nijhoff, 1972.

Nuyts, A., *L'exception de* forum non conveniens, Brussels, Bruylant, 2003.

Paulsson, J., *Denial of Justice in International Law*, Cambridge, Cambridge University Press, 2005.

Petrochilos, G., *Procedural Law in International Arbitration,* Oxford, Oxford University Press, 2004.

Raphael, T., *The Anti-suit Injunction*, Oxford, Oxford University Press, 2008.

Razesberger, F., *The International Criminal Court; the Principle of Complementarity,* Frankfurt am Main, Lang, 2006.

Sands, P., *Principles of International Environmental Law*, 2nd ed., Cambridge, Cambridge University Press, 2003.

Savigny, F. C. von, *System des Heutigen Römischen Rechts*, Berlin, Veit, 1840-1849; trans. W. Guthrie (1880), N. J. Clark, The Law Book Exchange, 2003.

Schreuer, C. C., *Decisions of International Institutions before Domestic Courts*, London, Oceana Publications, 1981.

Shany, Y., *The Competing Jurisdictions of International Courts and Tribunals*, Oxford, Oxford University Press, 2003.

—, *Regulating Jurisdictional Relations between National and International Courts*, Oxford, Oxford University Press, 2007.

Shaw, M., *International Law*, 5th ed., Cambridge, Cambridge University Press, 2003.

Stephens, T., *International Courts and Environmental Protection*, Cambridge, Cambridge University Press, 2009.

Story, J., *Commentaries on the Conflict of Laws*, 5th ed., Boston, Little, Brown and Company, 1857.

Voet, J., *Commentarius ad Pandectas,* Hagæ-Comitum, apud Abrahamum de Hondt, 1698; trans. P. Gane, Durban, Butterworth, 1957.

Watson, A., *Joseph Story and the Comity of Errors: A Case Study in Conflict of Laws*, Athens, University of Georgia Press, 1992.

Wenger, L. (trans. O. H. Fisk.), *Institutes of the Roman Law of Civil Procedure*, New York, Veritas Press, 1940.

Westlake, J., *A Treatise on Private International Law*, 1st ed., London, Maxwell & Son, 1858; N. de M. Bentwich, 7th ed., London, Sweet & Maxwell, 1925.

Zangerus, J., *Tractatus de Exceptionibus,* Witebergae, 1593; post. edition within *Tractatus Duo,* 1675.

## Reports

American Law Institute, *Recognition and Enforcement of Foreign Judgments: Proposed Federal Statute* (adopted 2005, Lowenfeld and Silberman, Rapporteurs), Philadelphia, American Law Institute, 2006.

—, "Intellectual Property: Principles Governing Jurisdiction, Choice of Law, and Judgments in Transnational Disputes" (Dreyfuss, Ginsburg and Dessemontet, Rapporteurs), 2007.

American Law Institute/UNIDROIT, *Principles of Transnational Civil Procedure* (adopted 2004), New York, Cambridge University Press, 2006.

European Communities, "Explanatory Report on the Brussels Convention 1968" (Jenard, Rapporteur) (5 March 1979) OJ C59.

—, "Study on Residual Jurisdiction" (General Report) (Nuyts, Rapporteur), 3 September 2007.

—, "Report on the Application of Regulation Brussels I in the Member States" (Hess, Pfeiffer, Schlosser, Rapporteurs), September 2007.

Hague Conference on Private International Law, "Convention on the Protection of Children 1996 Explanatory Report" (Lagarde, Rapporteur) in (1996) *Proceedings of the Eighteenth Session* II, 534.

—, "Enforcement of Judgments, Preliminary Draft Convention on Jurisdiction and Foreign Judgments in Civil and Commercial Matters" (Nygh and Pocar, Rapporteurs) Prel. Doc. No. 11, 2000.

—, "Report on Judicial Communications in International Child Protection" (Lortie, Rapporteur), Prel. Doc. No. 8, 2006.

—, "Convention of 30 June 2005 on Choice of Court Agreements Explanatory Report" (Hartley and Dougachi, Rapporteurs), 2007.

Institut de droit international, "Report of the Second Commission: Principles for Determining When the Use of the Doctrine of *Forum non Conveniens* and Anti-suit Injunctions Is Appropriate" (Collins and Droz, Rapporteurs) (2002-2003) 70-I *Annuaire* 14; Resolution of 28 August 2003 (2004) 70-II *Annuaire* 252.

International Law Association, Committee on International Civil and Commercial Litigation, "Declining and Referring Jurisdiction in International Litigation" (McLachlan, Rapporteur) (2000) 69 *ILA Rep. Conf.* 137.

—, International Commercial Arbitration Committee, "*Lis Pendens* and Arbitration" (Sheppard, Rapporteur) (2006) 72 *ILA Rep. Conf.* 146.

International Law Commission, "Responsibility of the States for Injuries Caused in Its Territory to the Person or Property of Aliens" (García Amador, Rapporteur) UN doc. A/CN.4/SER.A/1959/Add.1, *Yearbook of the International Law Commission 1959,* Vol. II, New York, United Nations, 1960, 1.

—, "Report of the Working Group on the Question of an International Criminal Jurisdiction", in *Yearbook of the International Law Commission 1992,* Vol. II (2), Annex, New York, United Nations, 1994, 58.

—, "Risks Ensuing from Fragmentation of International Law" (Hafner), *Official Records of the General Assembly, Fifty-fifth Session, Supp. No. 10*, Annex, UN doc. A/55/10, 144.

— Study Group on the Fragmentation of International Law, "Fragmentation of International Law: Difficulties Arising from the Diversification and Expansion of International Law, Report of the Study Group of the International Law Commission" (Koskenniemi, Chairman) UN doc. A/CN.4/L.682, 13 April 2006 (Report); UN doc. A/CN.4/L.702, 18 July 2006 (Conclusions).

—, "Draft Articles on Diplomatic Protection with Commentaries" (Dugard, Special Rapporteur), in *Report of the*

*International Law Commission on its Fifty-eighth Session (1 May-9 June, 3 July-11 August 2006), Official Records of the General Assembly, Sixty-first Session, Supplement No. 10*, UN doc. A/61/10, 22-100.

Organization for Economic Co-operation and Development, *Draft Convention on the Protection of Foreign Property and Resolution of the Council of the OECD on the Draft Convention*, Paris, OECD, 1967

—, "Improving the System of Investor-State Dispute Settlement; an Overview", *Working Papers on International Investment No 2006/1.*

United Nations Commission on Trade and Development, *Investor-State Dispute Settlement and Impact on Investment Rule-making*, UNCTAD/ITE/IIA/2007/3, 2007.

*Articles*

Abs, H., and H. Shawcross, "The Proposed Convention to Protect Private Foreign Investment", (1960) 9 *J. Public Law* 115.

Alvarez, H., "Arbitration under the North American Free Trade Agreement", (2000) 16 *Arbitration International* 393.

Anton, A. E., "The Introduction into English Practice of Continental Theories on the Conflict of Laws", (1956) 5 *International & Comparative Law Quarterly* 534.

Baumgartner, S. P., "Related Actions", (1998) 3 *Zeitschrift für Zivilprozeß International* 203.

Bell, A. S., "Negative Declarations in Transnational Litigation", (1995) 111 *Law Quarterly Review* 674.

Bjorklund, A. K., "Private Rights and Public International Law: Why Competition among International Economic Law Tribunals Is Not Working", (2007) 59 *Hastings LJ* 241.

Brenner, D., "Cross Border Court Communications", (2009) 83 *Australian LJ* 90.

Briggs, A., "Anti-suit Injunctions and Utopian Ideals", (2004) 120 *Law Quarterly Review* 529.

—, "Anti-suit Injunctions in a Complex World", in F. D. Rose (ed.), *Lex Mercatoria: Essays on International Commercial Law in Honour of Francis Reynolds*, London, Lloyds of London Press, 2000, 219.

Brown, C., "The Inherent Powers of International Courts and Tribunals", (2005) 76 *British Year Book of International Law* 195.

Bucher, A., "L'examen de la compétence internationale par le juge suisse", 2007 II No. 5 *La Semaine judiciaire* 153.

Burbank, S. B., "Jurisdictional Equilibration, the Proposed Hague Convention and Progress in National Law", (2001) 49 *American Journal of Comparative Law* 203.

Cappalli, R. B., "Locke as the Key: A Unifed and Coherent Theory of *In Personam* Jurisdiction", (1992-1993) 43 *Case Western Reserve LR* 97.

Carmody, C., "Softwood Lumber Dispute (2001-2006)", (2006) 100 *American Journal of International Law* 664.

Charney, J. I., "Is International Law Threatened by Multiple International Tribunals?", (1998) 271 *Recueil des cours* 101.

Collins, L. A., "*Forum Non Conveniens* and the Brussels Convention", (1990) 106 *Law Quarterly Review* 535.

—, "Provisional and Protective Measures in International Litigation", (1992) 234 *Recueil des cours* 9.

—, "Comity in Modern Private International Law", in J. Fawcett (ed.), *Reform and Development of Private International Law*, Oxford, Oxford University Press, 2002, 89.

Crawford, J., "Treaty and Contract in Investment Arbitration: The 22nd Freshfields Lecture on International Arbitration", 29 November 2007, www.lcil.cam.ac.uk.

Crook, J. R., "Contemporary Practise of the United States Relating to International Law", (2008) 102 *American Journal of International Law* 860.

De Wet, E., "The International Constitutional Order", (2006) 55 *International & Comparative Law Quarterly* 51.

Donnedieu de Vabres, H., "L'action publique et l'action civile dans les rapports de droit pénal international", (1929) 26 *Recueil des cours* 207.

Douglas, Z., "The Hybrid Foundations of Investment Treaty Arbitration", (2003) 74 *British Year Book of International Law* 151.

Fawcett, J., "General Report", in J. Fawcett (ed.), *Declining Jurisdiction in Private International Law: Reports to the XIVth Congress of the International Academy of Comparative Law Athens, August 1994*, Oxford, Oxford University Press, 1995, 1.

Fitzmaurice, G., "The Law and Procedure of the International Court of Justice: Treaty Interpretation and Certain Other Treaty Points", (1951) 28 *British Year Book of International Law* 1.

—, "The Law and Procedure of the International Court of Justice 1951-4: Treaty Interpretation and Other Treaty Points", (1957) 33 *British Year Book of International Law* 203.

Gaillard, E., "Anti-suit Injunctions Issued by Arbitrators", (2007) *ICCA Congress Series No. 13*, 235.

—, "Aspects philosophiques du droit de l'arbitrage international", (2007) 329 *Recueil des cours* 61.

Gaja, G., "Relationship of the ICJ with Other International Courts and Tribunals", in A. Zimmermann, C. Tomuschat and K. Oellers-Frahm (eds.), *The Statute of the International Court of Justice: A Commentary*, Oxford, Oxford University Press, 2006, 533.

Gardella, A., and L. G. Radicati di Brozolo, "Civil Law, Common Law and Market Integration: The EC Approach to Conflicts of Jurisdiction", (2003) 51 *American Journal of Comparative Law* 611.

Garnett, R., "Stay of Proceedings in Australia: A 'Clearly Inappropriate' Test?", (1999) 23 *Melbourne University LR* 30.

Gaudemet-Tallon, H., "La Litispendence internationale dans la jurisprudence française", in P. Jestaz (ed.), *Mélanges dédiés à Dominique Holleaux*, Paris, Litec, 1990, 121.

Gebauer, M., "*Lis Pendens,* Negative Declaratory-Judgment Actions and the First-in-Time Principle", in E. Gottshalk (ed.), *Conflict of Laws in a Globalized World*, New York, Cambridge University Press, 2007, 89.

Geisinger, E., and L. Lévy, "*Lis Alibi Pendens* in International Commercial Arbitration", [2003] *ICC Bulletin (Special Supp.)* 53.

George, J. P., "Parallel Litigation", (1999) 51 *Baylor LR* 769.

Goldstone, R. J., and R. J. Hamilton "*Bosnia v Serbia:* Lessons from the Encounter of the International Court of Justice with the International Criminal Tribunal for the Former Yugoslavia", (2008) 21 *Leiden Journal of International Law* 95.

Guillaume, G., "Address to the UNGA" (26 October 2000), available at www.icj-cij.org.

Hare, C., "Forum Non Conveniens in Europe: Game Over or Time for Reflexion?", [2006] *Journal of Business Law* 157.

Higgins, R., "A Babel of Judicial Voices? Ruminations from the Bench", (2006) 55 *International & Comparative Law Quarterly* 791.

Holleaux, D., "La litispendence", [1971-1973] *Travaux du Comité français de droit international privé* 203.

Huet, A., "Compétence des tribunaux français à l'égard des litiges internationaux", (2004) *Juris-Classeur*, Fasc., 581-543.

Jiménez de Aréchaga, E., "International Law in the Past Third of a Century", (1978) 159 *Recueil des cours* 9.

Kawharu, A., "Arbitral Jurisdiction", (2008) 23 *New Zealand Universities Law Review* 238.

Kessedjian, C., "Judicial Regulation of Improper Forum Selections", in J. L. Goldsmith (ed.), *International Dispute*

*Regulation: The Regulation of Forum Selection*, New York, Transnational Publishers, 1997, 273

Kingsbury, B., *et al.*, "The Proliferation of International Tribunals: Piecing together the Puzzle", Special Symposium Issue (1999) 31 (4) *New York University Journal of International Law and Politics* 679.

Kingsbury, B. "The International Legal Order", in P. Cane and M. Tushnet (eds.), *Oxford Handbook of Legal Studies*, Oxford, Oxford University Press, 2003, 271.

Kingsbury, B., *et al.* (eds.), "Foreword: Global Governance as Administration — National and Transnational Approaches to Global Administrative Law", (2005) 68 (3-4) *Law & Contemporary Problems* 1.

Koskenniemi, M., "International Law: Between Fragmentation and Constitutionalism" (unpublished lecture, Canberra, 27 November 2006) available at www.helsinki.fi/eci/Publications/Talks_Papers_MK.htm.

—, "The Fate of Public International Law: Between Technique and Politics", (2007) 70 *Modern Law Review* 1.

Lagarde, P., "Le principe de proximité dans le droit international privé contemporain", (1986) 196 *Recueil des cours* 9.

Lavranos, N., "Protecting its Exclusive Jurisdiction: The *MOX Plant* Judgment of the ECJ", (2006) 5 *Law & Practice of International Courts & Tribunals* 479.

—, "The *MOX Plant* and *IJzeren Rijn* Disputes: Which Court Is the Supreme Arbiter?", (2006) 19 *Leiden Journal of International Law* 223.

—, "Competing Jurisdictions between MERCOSUR and WTO", (2008) 7 *Law & Practice of International Courts & Tribunals* 205.

Lévy, L., "Anti-suit Injunctions Issued by Arbitrators", in Gaillard, *op. cit.*, 115.

Lorenzen, E. G., "Huber's De Conflictu Legum", in A. Kocowrek (ed.), Wigmore, *Celebration Legal Essays*, Chicago, Northwestern University Press, 1919.

Lowe, V., "Overlapping Jurisdiction in International Tribunals", (1999) 20 *Australian Yearbook of International Law* 191.

Mann, F. A., "The Doctrine of Jurisdiction in International Law", (1964) 111 *Recueil des cours* 1, reprinted in F. A. Mann, *Studies in International Law*, Oxford, Clarendon Press, 1973, 1.

—, "The Protection of Shareholders' Interests in the Light of the *Barcelona Traction* Case", (1973) 67 *AJIL* 259, reprinted in F. A. Mann, *Further Studies in International Law*, Oxford, Clarendon Press, 1990, 217.

Mansfield, W. "Compulsory Dispute Settlement after the Southern Bluefin Tuna Award", in A. G. O. Elferink and D. Rothwell (eds.), *Oceans Management in the 21st Century*, Leiden, Martinus Nijhoff, 2004, 255.

Mayer, P., "Le phénomène de la coordination des ordres juridiques", (2007) 327 *Recueil des cours* 13.

McClean, D., "Jurisdiction and Judicial Discretion", (1969) 18 *International & Comparative Law Quarterly* 931.

McLachlan, C., "International Litigation and the Reworking of the Conflict of Laws", (2004) 120 *Law Quarterly Review* 580.

—, "The Principle of Systemic Integration and Article 31 (3) *(c)* of the Vienna Convention", (2005) 54 *International & Comparative Law Quarterly* 279.

—, "Investment Treaty Arbitration: The Legal Framework", [2008] *ICCA Congress Series No. 15* (in press).

Meron, T., "Repudiation of *Ultra Vires* State Contracts and the International Responsibility of States", (1957) 6 *International & Comparative Law Quarterly* 273.

Michaels, R., "Two Paradigms of Jurisdiction", (2005-2006) 27 *Michigan Journal of International Law* 1003.

Mosler, H., "General Principles of Law", in R. Bernhardt (ed.), *Encyclopedia of Public International Law*, Vol. I, Amsterdam, North-Holland, 1992, 511.

Mota, S. A., and D. Rao, "The WTO and NAFTA — A Comparation of Dispute Resolution Systems and Outcomes Involving the United States, Mexico and Canada", (2007) 1 *World Arbitration & Mediation Review* 539.

Muir Watt, H., "Harcèlement sur harcèlement ne vaut", *Justices*, 1999, 747.

Niboyet-Hoegy, M., "Les conflits de procédures", [1995-1998] *Travaux du Comité français de droit international privé* 71.

Nuyts, A., "The Enforcement of Jurisdiction Agreements further to *Gasser* and the Community Principle of Abuse of Right", in P. de Vareilles-Sommières (ed.), *Forum Shopping in the European Judicial Area*, Oxford, Hart Publishing, 2007, 55.

Nygh, P., "The Common Law Approach", in C. McLachlan and P. Nygh (eds.), *Transnational Tort Litigation: Jurisdictional Principles*, Oxford, Clarendon Press, 1996.

—, "Declining Jurisdiction under the Brussels I Regulation 2001 and the Preliminary Draft Hague Judgments Convention: A Comparison", in J. Fawcett (ed.), *Reform and Development of Private International Law*, Oxford, Oxford University Press, 2002, 303.

Oxman, B. H., "Complementary Agreements and Compulsory

Jurisdiction", (2001) 95 *American Journal of International Law* 277.

Pålsson, L., "The Institute of *Lis Pendens* in International Civil Procedure", (1970) 14 *Scandinavian Studies in Law* 59.

Park, W. W., "The Arbitrator's Jurisdiction to Determine Jurisdiction", (2007) *ICCA Congress Series No. 13*, 55.

Paulsson, J., "Arbitration without Privity", (1995) 10 *ICSID Review — Foreign Investment Law Journal* 232.

Pauwelyn, J., "Adding Sweeteners to Softwood Lumber: The WTO–NAFTA 'Spaghetti Bowl' Is Cooking", (2006) 9 *Journal of International Economic Law* 197.

Pinto, M., "Fragmentation or Unification among International Institutions: Human Rights Tribunals", (1999) 31 *New York University Journal of International Law & Politics* 833.

Raack, D. W., "A History of Injunctions in England before 1700", (1985-1986) 61 *Indiana LJ* 539.

Reinisch, A., "The Use and Limits of *Res Judicata* and *Lis Pendens* as Procedural Tools to Avoid Conflicting Dispute Settlement Outcomes", (2004) 3 *Law & Practice of International Courts & Tribunals* 37.

Romano, C., "The Proliferation of International Judicial Bodies: The Pieces of the Puzzle", (1999) 31 *New York University Journal of International Law & Politics* 709.

—, "The Shift from the Consensual to the Compulsory Paradigm in International Adjudication: Elements for a Theory of Consent", (2007) 39 *New York University Journal of International Law & Politics* 791.

Sandford, I., "Determining the Existence of Countervailable Subsidies in the Context of the Canada-United States Softwood Lumber Dispute: 1982-2005", [2005] *Canadian Yearbook of International Law* 297.

Schlesinger, R., "Research on General Principles of Law Recognized by Civilized Nations", (1957) 51 *American Journal of International Law* 734.

Schlosser, P., "Jurisdiction in International Litigation: The Issue of Human Rights in Relation to National Law and the Brussels Convention", [1991] *Rivista di diritto internazionale* 5.

—, "Jurisdiction and International Judicial and Administrative Co-operation", (2000) 284 *Recueil des cours* 9.

—, "Direct Interaction of Courts of Different Nations", in *Studi di diritto processuale civile in onore di Giuseppe Tarzia* (2005) I, 589.

—, "Anti-suit injunctions zur Unterstützung von internationalen Schiedsverfahren", (2006) *Recht der Internationalen Wirtschaft* 486.

Schreuer, C., "Travelling the BIT Route: Of Waiting Periods, Umbrella Clauses and Forks in the Road", (2004) 5 *J. World Investment and Trade* 231.

Schweizer, P., and O. Guillod, "L'exception de litispendance et l'arbitrage international", in F. Knoepfler (ed.), *Le juriste suisse face au droit et aux jugements étrangers: ouverture ou repli?*, Fribourg, Editions universitaires de Fribourg, 1988, 71.

Scobbie, I., *"Res Judicata,* Precedent and the International Court: A Preliminary Sketch", (1999) 20 *Australian Yearbook of International Law* 299.

Seidl-Hohenveldern, I., "The Abs-Shawcross Draft Convention to Protect Private Foreign Investment: Comments on the Round-table", (1961) *10 J. Public Law* 100.

Sinclair, A. C., "The Origins of the Umbrella Clause in the International Law of Investment Protection", (2004) 20 *Arbitration International* 411.

Slaughter, A., "A Global Community of Courts", (2003) 44 *Harvard International LJ* 191.

Thirlway, H., "The Proliferation of International Judicial Organs: Institutional and Substantive Questions", in N. M. Blokker and H. G. Schermers (eds.), *Proliferation of International Organizations*, The Hague, Kluwer Law International, 2001, 251.

Treviño de Coale, M., "Stay, Dismiss, Enjoin, or Abstain?: A Survey of Foreign Parallel Litigation in the Federal Courts of the United States", (1999) 17 *Boston University International LJ* 79.

Vázquez, C., "The Four Doctrines of Self-executing Treaties", (1995) 89 *American Journal of International Law* 695

—, "Treaties as Law of the Land: The Supremacy Clause and the Judicial Enforcement of Treaties", (2008) 122 *Harvard LR* 599.

Veeder, V. V., "The *Lena Goldfields* Arbitration: The Historical Roots of Three Ideas", (1998) 47 *International & Comparative Law Quarterly* 747.

Vollmer, A., "US Federal Court Use of the Antisuit Injunction to Control International Forum Selection", in J. L. Goldsmith (ed.), *International Dispute Regulation: The Regulation of Forum Selection*, New York, Transnational Publishers, 1997, 237.

Von Mehren, A. T., "Theory and Practice of Adjudicatory Authority in Private International Law: A Comparative Study of the Doctrine, Policies and Practices of Common- and Civil-Law Systems", (2002) 295 *Recueil des cours* 9.

Wälde, T., "The 'Umbrella' (or Sanctity of Contract/Pacta Sunt

Servanda) Clause in Investment Arbitration: A Comment on Original Intentions and Recent Cases", (2004) 1 (4) *Transnational Dispute Management* 1.

Wälde, T., and A. Kolo, "Environmental Regulation, Investment Protection and 'Regulatory Taking' in International Law", (2001) 50 *International & Comparative Law Quarterly* 811.

Waldron, J., "The Concept and the Rule of Law", NYU Public Law & Legal Theory Research Paper Series Working Paper No. 08-50, (2008) 43 *Georgia LR* 1.

Walker, J., "Parallel Proceedings — Converging Views", [2000] *Canadian Yearbook of International Law* 155.

Walter, G., "*Lis Alibi Pendens* and *Forum Non Conveniens;* from Confrontation via Co-ordination to Collaboration", (2002) 4 *European Journal of Law Reform* 69.

Westbrook, J. L., "The Lessons of *Maxwell Communications*", (1996) 64 *Fordham LR* 2531.

—, "International Judicial Negotiation", (2003) 38 *Texas International LJ* 567.

Williams, S. A., and W. A. Schabas, "Article 17", in O. Triffterer (ed.), *Commentary on the Rome Statute of the International Criminal Court*, 2nd ed., Munich, Beck, 2008.

# ABOUT THE AUTHOR

## BIOGRAPHICAL NOTE

*Campbell McLachlan QC,* born Christchurch, New Zealand in 1960.

Professor of Law, Victoria University of Wellington Law School, New Zealand; Barrister (Bankside Chambers, Auckland; Essex Court Chambers, London).

Junior Scholarship, Christchurch Boys' High School (1977); LL.B. (Hons, 1st class), Senior Scholarship, Chapman Tripp Centenary Award, Commonwealth Scholarship, Victoria University of Wellington (1983); Diploma *cum laude,* Hague Academy of International Law (1985); Ph.D., University of London (1988).

Junior Lecturer, Victoria University of Wellington (1983-1984); Commonwealth Secretariat, Legal Division (1985); Herbert Smith, Solicitors, London (Assistant Solicitor (1988-1991), Partner (1992-2003), Member, Partnership Council (1998-2001), Head of Public International Law Practice Group (2001-2003)); Professor of Law, Victoria University of Wellington (since 2003), Deputy Dean of Law (2003-2005).

President, Australian & New Zealand Society of International Law (2006-2009); Rapporteur, International Law Association, Committee on International Civil & Commercial Litigation (1992-2002); Secretary, International Law Association (British Branch) (1997-2002); Co-Chair, International Law Association, Study Group on the Practice & Procedure of International Courts & Tribunals (since 2003); Director of Studies, Private International Law, Hague Academy of International Law (1996); Visiting Fellow, Lauterpacht Research Centre for International Law, University of Cambridge (2007); Member, Editorial Advisory Board, *International & Comparative Law Quarterly;* Member, American Law Institute (elected 2005); awarded Legal Research Foundation J. F. Northey Book Prize (2008).

Panel of Arbitrators, International Centre for the Settlement of Investment Disputes (since 2007) (appointed as President or Member of a number of *ad hoc* annulment committees); New Zealand Alternate Member, International Chamber of Commerce Court of Arbitration (2004-2009);

Chairman, International Bar Association, International Litigation Committee (2002-2004).

Barrister, New Zealand (call 1984, Queen's Counsel, 2007); Solicitor, England and Wales (admission 1992; Solicitor-Advocate (Civil) 2001). Counsel in numerous litigations and arbitrations, involving sovereign States and corporations, in English and New Zealand courts and before international tribunals, as well as supervising litigation globally.

## PRINCIPAL PUBLICATIONS

### Books

*International Investment Arbitration: Substantive Principles* (with L. Shore and M. Weiniger), Oxford, Oxford University Press, 2007, paperback edition, 2008.

*Dicey, Morris and Collins on the Conflict of Laws* (specialist editor, with L. Collins (General Editor), A. Briggs, J. Harris, J. D. McLean and C. G. J. Morse), 14th ed., London, Sweet & Maxwell, 2006, 1st Supp., 2007, 2nd Supp, 2008.

*International Law and Democratic Theory* (ed.) (2007) 38, No. 2, *Victoria University of Wellington Law Review*, Special Symposium Issue.

*Transnational Tort Litigation: Jurisdictional Principles* (ed., with P. Nygh), Oxford, Oxford University Press, 1996.

### Selected Articles and Book Chapters

"Investment Treaties and General International Law" (2008) 57 *International & Comparative Law Quarterly* 361.

"From Savigny to Cyberspace: Does the Internet Sound the Death-Knell for the Conflict of Laws?" (2006) 11 *Media & Arts Law Review* 418.

"The Principle of Systemic Integration and Article 31 (3) *(c)* of the Vienna Convention" (2005) 54 *International & Comparative Law Quarterly* 279-320.

"The Continuing Controversy over Provisional Measures in International Disputes" (2005) 7 *International Law FORUM du droit international* 5.

"International Litigation and the Reworking of the Conflict of Laws" (2004) 120 *Law Quarterly Review* 580-616.

"After Baghdad: Conflict or Coherence in International Law?" (2003) 1 *New Zealand Journal of Public & International Law* 25-53.

"Reflections from the Practice of International Litigation", in M. Evans (ed.), *International Law* (Oxford, Oxford University Press, 2003) 15.

"Introduction: Papers Presented at the Villa La Pietra Symposium on the Independence and Accountability of the International Judge" (with P. Sands and C. Romano) (2003) 2 *Law and Practice of International Courts and Tribunals* 3.

"*Pinochet* Revisited" (2002) 51 *International & Comparative Law Quarterly* 959.

"The Jurisdictional Limits of Disclosure Orders in Transnational Fraud Litigation" (1998) 47 *International & Comparative Law Quarterly* 3.

"Obtaining Evidence in England in Aid of a US Proceeding: A Concise Practical Guide for US Lawyers", in J. Fellas (ed.), *International Commercial Litigation* (New York, Practising Law Institute, 1998) 183.

"Provisional Measures in Aid of Foreign Proceedings: Has the English Response Been Adequate?", in J. Goldsmith (ed.), *International Dispute Resolution: The Regulation of Forum Selection* (Irvington, New York, Transnational Publishers, 1997) 169.

"An Overview", in C. McLachlan and P. Nygh (eds.), *Transnational Tort Litigation: Jurisdictional Principles* (Oxford, Oxford University Press, 1996).

"Restitution", in C. McLachlan and P. Nygh (eds.), *Transnational Tort Litigation: Jurisdictional Principles* (Oxford, Oxford University Press, 1996).

"Transnational Interlocutory Measures for the Preservation of Assets", in Lye Lin Heng (ed.), *Current Legal Issues in the Internationalization of Business Enterprises* (Butterworths, Singapore, 1996).

"Extraterritorial Orders Affecting Bank Deposits", in K. Meessen (ed.), *Extraterritorial Jurisdiction in Theory and Practice* (Kluwer, 1996).

"The Impact of International Law on Civil Jurisdiction", [1993] *Hague Yearbook of International Law* 125.

"Export Control: United Kingdom Report" (with L. Collins), in K. Meessen (ed.) *The International Law of Export Control* (1992) 147.

"Splitting the Proper Law in Private International Law", (1990) 61 *British Year Book of International Law* 311.

"Remedies Affecting Bank Deposits", in R. Cranston (ed.), *Legal Issues of Cross-Border Banking* (1989) 23.

"Legal Practitioner Mobility in the Commonwealth", in W. Twining and R. Dhavan (eds.), *Access to Legal Education and the Legal Profession* (1989) 258.

"The Recognition of Aboriginal Customary Law: Pluralism beyond the Colonial Paradigm: A Review Article", (1988) 37 *International & Comparative Law Quarterly* 368.

"Transnational Applications of Mareva Injunctions and Anton Piller Orders", (1987) 36 *International & Comparative Law Quarterly* 669.

"The Fiji Constitutional Crisis of May 1987: A Legal Assessment", [1987] *New Zealand Law Journal* 175.

"The New Hague Sales Convention and the Limits of the Choice of Law Process" (1986) 102 *Law Quarterly Review* 591.

"Matrimonial Property and the Conflict of Laws", (1986) 12 *New Zealand Universities Law Review* 66.

"ANZUS: The Treaty Reappraised", [1985] *New Zealand Law Journal* 271.

"Reforming New Zealand's Conflicts Process: The Case for Internationalisation", (1984) 14 *Victoria University of Wellington Law Review* 443.

## *Reports*

*International Law Commission, Study Group on Fragmentation of International Law*

"The Interpretation of Treaties in the Light of Any Relevant Rules of International Law Applicable in the Relations between the Parties" (with W. Mansfield) (2004) UN doc. ILC(LVI)/SG/FIL/CRD.3/Rev.1.

*International Law Association Committee on International Civil and Commercial Litigation*

"Jurisdiction in Transnational Torts", in (1994) 66 *International Law Association Report of Conference* 600.

"Provisional and Protective Measures in International Litigation", in (1996) 67 *International Law Association Report of Conference* 185.

"Declining and Referring Jurisdiction in International Litigation", in (2000) 69 *International Law Association Report of Conference* 137.

*International Law Association, Study Group on the Practice & Procedure of International Courts and Tribunals*

"The Burgh House Principles on the Independence of the International Judiciary" (with P. Sands and R. Mackenzie), (2005) 4 *Law and Practice of International Courts and Tribunals* 247.

*International Council for Commercial Arbitration*

"Investment Treaty Arbitration: The Legal Framework" (General Report for Dublin Congress 2008), in Van den Berg (ed.) (2008) ICCA Congress Series No. 13.

*Commonwealth Secretariat*

*The Hague Convention on the Taking of Evidence Abroad: Explanatory Documentation prepared for Commonwealth Jurisdictions* (with D. McClean) (1985).

*Admission of Commonwealth Lawyers: A Technical Survey for Commonwealth Law Ministers and the Commonwealth Lawyers Association* (1985).

"Legal Practitioner Mobility in the Commonwealth" (Memorandum, Meeting of Commonwealth Law Ministers, 1986, Commonwealth Secretariat) 483.

"Transnational Litigation for Commonwealth Governments" (Memorandum for Meeting of Commonwealth Law Ministers, 1990).

**PUBLICATIONS
OF THE HAGUE ACADEMY
OF INTERNATIONAL LAW**

## COLLECTED COURSES

Since 1923 the top names in international law have taught at the Hague Academy of International Law. All the volumes of the *Collected Courses* which have been published since 1923 are available, as, since the very first volume, they are reprinted regularly in their original format. There is a complete and detailed catalogue.

Since 2008, certain courses have been the subject of a pocketbook edition (see below).

In addition, the total collection now exists in electronic form. All works already published have been put "on line" and can be consulted under one of the proposed subscription methods, which offer a range of tariffs and possibilities.

## WORKSHOPS

The Academy publishes the discussions from the Workshops which it organizes. The latest title of the Workshops already published is as follows: *Topicality of the 1907 Hague Conference, the Second Peace Conference* (2007).

## CENTRE FOR STUDIES AND RESEARCH

The scientific works of the Centre for Studies and Research in International Law and International Relations of the Hague Academy of International Law, the subjects of which are chosen by the Curatorium of the Academy, have been published, since the Centre's 1985 session, in a publication in which the Directors of Studies report on the state of research of the Centre under their direction. The titles of the latest booklets published are as follows: *The Cultural Heritage of Mankind* (2005); *Terrorism and International Law* (2006); *Rules and Institutions of International Humanitarian Law Put to the Test of Recent Armed Conflicts* (2007). In addition, when the work of the Centre has been of particular interest and originality, the reports of the Directors of Studies together with the articles by the researchers form the subject of a collection published in the series The Law Books of the Academy. (See below.)

**Requests for information, catalogues and orders for publications must be addressed to**

MARTINUS NIJHOFF PUBLISHERS

P.O. Box 9000, 2300 PA Leiden — The Netherlands

**(http://www.brill.nl)**

## THE LAW BOOKS OF THE ACADEMY

*(By chronological order of publication)*

Dupuy, R.-J. (dir. publ./ed.) : Manuel sur les organisations internationales/A Handbook on International Organizations. (1988, 714 pages.)

(ISBN 978-90-247-3658-4)

Dupuy, R.-J., and D. Vignes (eds.) : A Handbook on the New Law of the Sea. (2 volumes)
Volume 1 : 1991, 900 pages.  (ISBN 978-0-7923-0924-3)
Volume 2 : 1991, 882 pages.  (ISBN 978-0-7923-1063-1)

Bardonnet, D. (dir. publ./ed.) : Le règlement pacifique des différends internationaux en Europe : perspectives d'avenir/ The Peaceful Settlement of International Disputes in Europe : Future Prospects. (1992, 704 pages.) (Broché/PB.)

(ISBN 978-0-7923-1573-5)

Carreau, D., et/and M. N. Shaw (dir. publ./eds.) : La dette extérieure/The External Debt. (1995, 818 pages.)

(ISBN 978-90-411-0083-2)

Dupuy, R.-J. (dir. publ./ed.) : Manuel sur les organisations internationales/A Handbook on International Organizations. (2e éd./2nd ed., 1998, 1008 pages.)

(ISBN 978-90-411-1119-7)

Eisemann, P. M., et/and M. Koskenniemi (dir. publ./eds.) : La succession d'Etats : la codification à l'épreuve des faits/State Succession : Codification Tested against the Facts. (2000, 1058 pages.)

(ISBN 978-90-411-1392-4)

Caron, D. D., et/and Ch. Leben (dir. publ./eds.) : Les aspects internationaux des catastrophes naturelles et industrielles/ The International Aspects of Natural and Industrial Catastrophes. (2001, 912 pages.)

(ISBN 978-90-411-1485-3)

Bothe, M., et/and P. H. Sands (dir. publ./eds.) : La politique de l'environnement. De la réglementation aux instruments économiques/Environmental Policy. From Regulation to Economic Instruments. (2002, 958 pages.)

(ISBN 978-90-411-1604-8)

Forlati Picchio, L., et/and L.-A. Sicilianos (dir. publ./eds.):
Les sanctions économiques en droit international/Eco-
nomic Sanctions in International Law. (2004, 912 pages.)
(ISBN 978-90-04-13701-1)

Boisson de Chazournes, L. et/and S. M. A. Salman (dir.
publ./eds.): Les ressources en eau et le droit interna-
tional/Water Resources and International Law. (2005,
848 pages.)
(ISBN 978-90-04-13702-8)

Mahiou, A., et/and F. Snyder (dir. publ.): La sécurité alimen-
taire/Food Security and Food Safety. (2006, 992 pages.)
(ISBN 978-90-04-14543-6)

Kahn, Ph., et T. W. Wälde (dir. publ./eds.): Les aspects
nouveaux du droit des investissements internationaux/
New Aspects of International Investment Law. (2007,
1072 pages.)
(ISBN 978-90-04-15372-1)

Glennon, M. J., et/and S. Sur (dir. publ./eds.): Terrorisme
et droit international/Terrorism and International Law.
(2008, 864 pages.)
(ISBN 978-90-04-16107-8)

Nafziger, J. A. R., et/and T. Scovazzi (dir. publ./eds.): Le
patrimoine culturel de l'humanité/The Cultural Heritage
of Mankind. (2008, 1168 pages.)
(ISBN 978-90-04-16106-1)

Daudet, Y. (dir. publ./ed.): Actualité de la Conférence de La
Haye de 1907, Deuxième Conférence de la Paix/Topi-
cality of the 1907 Hague Conference, the Second Peace
Conference. (2008, 528 pages.) (Broché/PB.)
(ISBN 978-90-04-17422-1)


*Forthcoming*

Momtaz, D., et M. J. Matheson (dir. publ./eds.): Les règles
et institutions du droit international humanitaire à
l'épreuve des conflits armés récents/Rules and Institutions of International Humanitarian Law Put to the Test
of Recent Armed Conflicts. (2009)
(ISBN 978-90-04-17283-8)

## POCKETBOOKS OF THE ACADEMY

*(By chronological order of publication)*

Gaillard, E. : Aspects philosophiques du droit de l'arbitrage international, 2008, 252 pages.

(ISBN 978-90-04-17148-0)

Schrijver, N. : The Evolution of Sustainable Development in International Law : Inception, Meaning and Status, 2008, 276 pages.

(ISBN 978-90-04-17407-8)

Moura Vicente, D. : La propriété intellectuelle en droit international privé, 2009, 516 pages.

(ISBN 978-90-04-17907-3)

Decaux, E. : Les formes contemporaines de l'esclavage, 2009, 264 pages.

(ISBN 978-90-04-17908-0)

McLachlan, C. : *Lis Pendens* in International Litigation, 2009, 492 pages.

(ISBN 978-90-04-17909-7)

Printed in August 2009
by Triangle Bleu,
01960 Péronnas (France)

Setting: R. Mirland,
59870 Warlaing (France)